Apostles of Reason

Apostles
of
Reason

The Crisis of Authority in American Evangelicalism

Molly Worthen

OXFORD
UNIVERSITY PRESS

OXFORD

UNIVERSITY PRESS

Oxford University Press is a department of the University of Oxford.
It furthers the University's objective of excellence in research, scholarship,
and education by publishing worldwide.

Oxford   New York
Auckland   Cape Town   Dar es Salaam   Hong Kong   Karachi
Kuala Lumpur   Madrid   Melbourne   Mexico City   Nairobi
New Delhi   Shanghai   Taipei   Toronto

With offices in
Argentina   Austria   Brazil   Chile   Czech Republic   France   Greece
Guatemala   Hungary   Italy   Japan   Poland   Portugal   Singapore
South Korea   Switzerland   Thailand   Turkey   Ukraine   Vietnam

Oxford is a registered trademark of Oxford University Press
in the UK and certain other countries.

Published in the United States of America by
Oxford University Press
198 Madison Avenue, New York, NY 10016

Library of Congress Cataloging-in-Publication Data
Worthen, Molly.
Apostles of reason : the crisis of authority in American evangelicalism / Molly Worthen.
pages cm
ISBN 978-0-19-989646-2 (hardback)
1. Evangelicalism—United States.   I. Title.
BR1642.U6W67 2013
262'.80973—dc23 2013012871

1 3 5 7 9 8 6 4 2
Printed in the United States of America
on acid-free paper

For Michael

Contents

Part III
Let Them Have Dominion

APOSTLES OF REASON

Introduction

*For the honest infidel, according to the American Evangelical pulpit,
there is no heaven.... Why should the fatal gift of brain be given to any
human being, if such gift renders him liable to eternal hell? Better be
a lunatic here and an angel there. Better be an idiot in this world, if
you can be a seraph in the next.*[1]

—Robert Ingersoll, 1881

*Americans since 1800 have in effect been given the hard choice between
being intelligent according to the prevailing standards in their intellectual centers or being religious according to the standards prevalent
in the denominations. This really is no secret.*[2]

—Sidney Mead, 1963

*Of all America's religious traditions, evangelical Protestantism, at least
in its twentieth-century conservative forms, has ranked dead last in
intellectual stature.*[3]

—Alan Wolfe, 2012

S ECULAR INTELLECTUALS HAVE NOT BEEN KIND TO THE EVANGELICAL MIND.
They are inclined to see evangelicals as a menace to progress and free
thought. Yet their scorn cannot erase a vexing fact: American evangelicals,
so maligned as anti-intellectual, have a habit of taking certain ideas very
seriously. True conversion is, of course, a matter of the heart. One cannot
cogitate all the way to Jesus. However, if your heart is right with Christ,
your head must be in order too. Evangelicals have always understood the
sins of modern life as both the misadventures of unsaved souls and as the
fruit of intellectual error, even as they have disagreed on the best path to
salvation and enlightenment.

This book examines modern American evangelicals' fraught relationship with secular reason and imagination. It takes up the riddle of
anti-intellectualism in a community that believes ardently in the power
of ideas, and examines its sources and consequences in the past seventy
years of evangelical theology, worship, and culture. Evangelicalism is a
far more thoughtful and diverse world than most critics—and even most
evangelicals themselves—usually realize. Yet it does host a potent strain of
anti-intellectualism, a pattern of hostility and ambivalence toward the standards of tolerance, logic, and evidence by which most secular thinkers in the
West have agreed to abide. Contrary to the insinuations of many who have
chronicled the fortunes of American evangelicals, this anti-intellectualism
is not, primarily, due to "a potent and disturbing set of authoritarian tendencies" in conservative evangelical culture.[4] There is no denying that the
Bible has tremendous power among evangelicals, or that pastors, activists,
and other leaders wield influence over their flocks. However, evangelicals
are less like Jesus and more like Jacob. They constantly wrestle with the
forces that rule them.

The central source of anti-intellectualism in evangelical life is the antith-
esis of "authoritarianism." It is evangelicals' ongoing crisis of authority—
their struggle to reconcile reason with revelation, heart with head, and
private piety with the public square—that best explains their anxiety and
their animosity toward intellectual life. Thinkers in the democratic West
celebrate their freedom of thought but practice a certain kind of unwavering obedience—bowing to the Enlightenment before all other gods—that
allows modern intellectual life to function. Evangelicals, by contrast, are
torn between sovereign powers that each claim supremacy.

To some degree, this is a universal human problem. All of us, at one time
or another, find ourselves tormented by rival pressures and drawn toward
incompatible goods. Evangelicals' theological heritage, however, has aggra-
vated this plight. Their intellectual history is peppered with compromises,
sleights of hand, and defensive maneuvers, a combination of pragmatism
and idealism that has made evangelicalism one of the most dynamic and
powerful phenomena in Christian history, as well as a minefield for independent thought.

This story's most recent chapter began with the assembly of a small
group of evangelical thinkers in the years after World War II. These men
sought to banish the stereotype of evangelicals as unschooled rubes and

to mold disparate believers into a single evangelical mind. Any consensus they achieved was imaginary, but sometimes fiction is nearly as powerful as truth. Their ideas spurred other thinkers across a spectrum of theological traditions to reconsider the essence of what it meant to be "evangelical" in modern America. Even if no single set of doctrines can neatly summarize evangelicalism, its leaders found themselves circling around a common set of questions that had preoccupied their communities for hundreds of years. They grappled with these dilemmas not in secluded cells cordoned off by creed, but in the same whirl of social change and global upheaval through which all Americans trekked toward the end of the twentieth century. Like everyone else, they were looking for firm footing. They craved an intellectual authority that would quiet disagreement and dictate a plan for fixing everything that seemed broken with the world. They did not find it, and are still looking.

The challenges they encountered and the solutions they devised had implications for American politics, but this book is not a chronicle of the Christian Right. Few of the actors in these pages thought of themselves as political activists (though a small number did). We cannot comprehend conservative Protestants, or their place in American culture, solely in terms of "values voting." We have to take seriously the intellectual traditions— both those peculiar to Christian circles, and those circulating in the broader bazaar of ideas—that have influenced the way evangelicals think about the world. American evangelicals are not just followers of an ancient faith. In recent decades, they have proved themselves to be both the challengers and children of the Cold War age of ideology and the fight to save—or scrap— Western civilization.

The term *evangelical* has produced more debate than agreement. The word is so mired in adjectives and qualifiers, contaminated by politicization and stereotype, that many commentators have suggested that it has outlived its usefulness.[5] In America alone, the broad tent of evangelicalism includes a definition-defying array of doctrines, practices, and political persuasions. Perhaps no label is elastic enough to contain a flock that ranges from churchly Virginia Baptists to nondenominational charismatics in Los Angeles. At the same time, the mudslinging of the 1990s culture wars turned many conservative American Protestants away from a label now synonymous in the media with right-wing radicalism and prejudice. Yet we are stuck with it. Believers and atheist scholars, politicians and pundits, all continue to use the word *evangelical*. To observers and insiders alike there still seems to be a "there" there: a nebulous community that shares something, even if it is not always clear what that something is.

A logical place to start is to ask Christians who call themselves evangelical what they believe. The trouble is that evangelicals differ widely in how they interpret and emphasize "fundamental" doctrines.[6] Even the "born again experience," supposedly the quintessence of evangelicalism, is not an ironclad indicator. Some evangelicals have always viewed conversion as an incremental process rather than an instantaneous rebirth (and their numbers may be increasing).

History—rather than theology or politics—is the most useful tool for pinning down today's evangelicals. If evangelicalism encompasses a wide spectrum of believers, they share a common heritage in the revivals and moral crusades of the eighteenth and nineteenth centuries. It is no stretch to trace those roots all the way back to European Pietists' zeal for private Bible study and personal holiness following on the heels of the Protestant Reformation.[7] Evangelical catchphrases like "Bible-believing" and "born again" are modern translations of the Reformers' slogan *sola scriptura* and Pietists' emphasis on internal spiritual transformation.

Evangelicals share this history, and they also share a set of fundamental questions. While they differ from one another on the details of their ideas about God and humankind, three elemental concerns unite them: how to repair the fracture between spiritual and rational knowledge; how to assure salvation and a true relationship with God; and how to resolve the tension between the demands of personal belief and the constraints of a secularized public square. These are problems of intellectual and spiritual authority. None, on its own, is unique to evangelicals. But in combination, under the pressures of Western history, and in the absence of a magisterial arbiter capable of settling uncertainties and disagreements, these concerns have shaped a distinctive spiritual community. This is a historian's definition meant to account for the patterns of history, rather than a believer's self-description that tries to relay evangelicals' internal perspective in language that they might use themselves. American evangelicals have a strong primitivist bent. They often prefer to think their faith indistinguishable from the faith of Christ's apostles, and scoff at history's claims on them. But they are creatures of history like everyone else, whether they like it or not.

This broad vantage point requires grappling not only with the individuals and institutions that typically star in histories of American evangelicalism—Billy Graham and friends—but also the communities on the fringes of evangelicalism's "mainstream" that might contest the term altogether, such as Wesleyans, Anabaptists, and Pentecostals. I have taken core samples in traditions ranging from the diminutive Mennonite Church U.S.A. (roughly 130,000 members as of 2010) to the immense Southern Baptist Convention (16,000,000 members). I have focused on church archives that provide a clearer portrait of evangelicals' varied theological inheritance than one finds in the files of nondenominational ministries, though I also combed the papers of some of evangelicalism's great "parachurch" juggernauts, such as the Billy Graham Evangelistic Association and InterVarsity Christian Fellowship. The records of church-affiliated and nondenominational Christian colleges, seminaries, and fundamentalist Bible schools, as well as a range of conservative Protestant media, helped to map shifting and clashing patterns of intellectual authority in American evangelicalism. The result, I hope, is a portrait of evangelical intellectual life that is broader and more diverse than we have seen before.

A caveat: No single volume can include every faith tradition in the evangelical universe. For every denomination, school, or ministry featured here, the reader will wonder why I chose to exclude another. I particularly regret that I have had to omit African-American Protestants, Latinos, Asian evangelicals, and other new immigrants. While these groups share many beliefs in common with the white evangelicals profiled in this book, their historical trajectories and theological priorities often have been quite different. Many, especially in the African-American community, view evangelicalism as a white word and claim the label rarely, and always cautiously.[8] This book has no pretensions to encyclopedic comprehension, even within the world of conservative white Protestantism. Rather than attempt an impossibly inclusive scope at the expense of depth and detail, I have selected traditions, institutions, and individuals that reflect the range of evangelicalism's most influential theological heritage. Every evangelical community has made its own way through the twentieth century, but most have experienced some recognizable version of the challenges and compromises described here.

A BRIEF HISTORY OF THREE QUESTIONS

Three questions unite evangelicals: how to reconcile faith and reason; how to know Jesus; and how to act publicly on faith after the rupture of Christendom. These questions have a long history.

The word *evangelical* dates to the Reformation. Evangelicalism as we know it today—as a discernible "ism," however amorphous—is a creature of the Puritan and Pietist revivals that followed. In the late seventeenth century, Pietist preachers critiqued the state churches that emerged from the Reformation as overly formal and cerebral. They called on believers to study the Bible and strive for personal holiness. German leaders like Philipp Jakob Spener and English Puritan writers such as John Bunyan taught that heartfelt piety was more important than a head full of theological knowledge. The movement that they helped inspire emphasized the crisis of conversion and the cultivation of an intimate relationship with Christ.[9]

This heyday of "heart religion," however, was also the age of the Enlightenment—a movement that challenged traditional authority in a different way. Tensions between faith and reason were no new thing in Christendom, but the Enlightenment unshackled science and inflamed the problem of squaring the Bible with new conceptions of knowledge and human identity. Theology was no longer "queen of the sciences," commanding one to submit to the authority of religion in order to study it. During these years, the words in which Christians spoke of their faith were slowly changing. Wilfred Cantwell Smith has traced the evolution of "I believe" in popular speech from a declaration of love and fidelity to the divine into an assent to doctrinal propositions newly under threat.[10]

The preoccupations that define evangelicalism emerged here, at the intersection of premodern dogma, personal religious experience, and modern anxieties. The Puritans turned inward to reform the soul and founded godly city-states in the New World after their attempts to "purify" the Church of England failed. Jonathan Edwards, the eighteenth-century preacher known for urging revival and dangling doubters over Satan's maw, spent his free afternoons dancing a minuet with John Locke in the New England wastes, trying to tame Enlightenment ideas about the human brain. In Germany, Count Zinzendorf pushed and pulled against rationalist philosophy while he urged his followers to forgo modern desires and imitate the earliest Christians. These men were among the very first evangelicals, simultaneously troubled and inspired by the new problems in postmedieval political and intellectual life. Since that time a broad swath of Protestant believers have found themselves united, not by specific doctrines (in which they have always varied widely), but by questions borne out of their peculiar relationship to the convulsions of the early modern era.

From the beginning, their concerns were existential and epistemological: They had to do not just with points of belief, but with how Christians accounted for human knowledge, how they lived in the world, and how they claimed to "know" the divine in their minds and hearts. While many ancient Christians assented to the basic doctrines that scholars mark as "evangelical," that assent took on a different character after the seventeenth-century rebirth of reason and the invention of our present-day notions of "religious" and "secular." The sundry believers who share the evangelical label have all lacked an extrabiblical authority powerful enough to guide them through these crises. Roman Catholics obey the Vatican (more or less). Liberal Protestants tend to allow the goddess of reason to rule over the Bible (or to rule, relatively untroubled, in her separate sphere). Evangelicals claim *sola scriptura* as their guide, but it is no secret that the challenge of determining what the Bible actually means finds its ultimate caricature in their schisming and squabbling. They are the children of estranged parents— Pietism and the Enlightenment—but behave like orphans. This confusion over authority is both their greatest affliction and their most potent source of vitality.

The evangelicals who populate the pages to come are, in part, the creatures of historical circumstances unique to twentieth-century America, but they did not first appear crawling out from the primordial muck of the Scopes trial. Their story is part of the American political chronicle and the "culture wars"—but it is inseparable from the larger narrative of Western intellectual history. Their driving questions are the questions that defined the postmedieval age. Evangelicals were, in this sense, among the first moderns. In their attempts to subjugate reason to the rule of faith and personal experience, we will find that, in some ways, they anticipated postmodernity too.

THE PROBLEM OF ANTI-INTELLECTUALISM

Evangelicals have earned a reputation for swaddling one of their abiding questions—how to reconcile faith and reason—in prickly certainty. Many of the conflicts that have marred Protestant history arose not because evangelicals confessed their worries about how scientific discoveries or historical investigation might change the Bible's role in society, but because they declared that the Bible's authority would never change. "Extreme orthodoxy betrays by its very frenzy that the poison of skepticism has entered the soul of the church; for men insist most vehemently upon their certainties when their hold upon them has been shaken," Reinhold Niebuhr wrote. "Frantic orthodoxy is a method for obscuring doubt." H. L. Mencken, Richard Hofstadter, and other observers convinced the American intelligentsia that a mutual antagonism between evangelical religion and critical inquiry fueled the country's "anti-intellectualism": a muddle-minded fear of any threat to the Bible whetted by an enthusiasm for the "common sense" of the ordinary American, a "Jacksonian dislike of specialists and experts." Any hope for sophisticated debate was left pinned in the rubble of evangelicals' limitless church schisms. Separation and condemnation replaced reasoned discussion.[11] In the free marketplace of American religion, where preachers survived by hawking their wares to the greatest number of people, head counts at the baptismal font—not the coherence of doctrine or the mastery of new knowledge—became the test of a church.

Hofstadter and his peers identified a real impulse, a mental posture long present in evangelicalism and energized by the fundamentalist-modernist battles. Yet *anti-intellectual* is an unhelpful term if employed as a vague epithet, one that obscures the fact that even the staunchest fundamentalists, the sort that Mencken mocked for "denouncing the reading of books" and declaring that "education was a snare," have been staunchly committed to ideas. Of course, intellectual life means a great deal more than accumulating ideas as one might collect butterflies, dried and still on a pin. Some of the figures in this book were true intellectuals on Hofstadter's own terms. They combined "piety" with mental "playfulness," challenging and reshaping orthodoxy.[12] They viewed themselves as both trustees of knowledge and agents of change. Others fled, fought, or covered their ears rather than hear any challenge. They esteemed the pretense of wisdom over intellectual engagement: the safekeeping of a body of fixed knowledge, rather than open debate and creative invention. Both intellectuals and dogmatists, however, are worthy subjects in a history of ideas. The intellectual historian's governing assumption is not that all thoughts and thinkers are equally good, but simply that all people think, and that material forces alone cannot explain human experience.

This book traces the past seventy years of American evangelical intellectual life. I have construed "intellectual life" broadly to include self-consciously cerebral pursuits as well as acts of worship and communion that most believers would say require as much of the heart as the mind. Evangelicals have often balanced and blended rational knowledge with the kind of spiritual experience that defies the constraints of reason.

Anti-intellectualism is a useful concept, and a serious charge, if it leads us to ask how a community succeeds or fails at nurturing inquiry and debate. This requires examining that community's regime of intellectual authority: the rules, assumptions, rewards, and punishments that govern the exchange of ideas. The subject of this study, then, is not "paranoia," as Hofstadter might put it, or the "irritable mental gestures" that Lionel Trilling saw in American conservatism, but a discernable family of intellectual traditions—and the institutions through which those traditions have interacted with the wider world, yielding the religious landscape we know today.[13]

The evolution of the evangelical community—and whether, and why, it might be called anti-intellectual—is best traced through the lives of elites: the preachers, teachers, writers, and institution-builders in the business of creating and disseminating ideas. When critics describe evangelicalism as anti-intellectual, usually they are not blaming ordinary laypeople. A casual glance at the latest Amazon.com best-seller list, chock full of celebrity memoirs and pulpy novels, or the amateur talent shows and dating competitions that top the television ratings, demonstrates that when it comes to intellectual shallowness evangelicals have no advantage on the rest of America. When critics condemn the "evangelical mind," they are talking about the people who ought to know better, who bear some responsibility for the Darwin-bashing and history-hashing that pollsters hear when they survey evangelical America. They are comparing evangelical elites with the nonevangelical intelligentsia. They are asking how it can be that college professors believe in creationism, or that educated activists deny evidence of global warming. They are wondering how evangelicals define the purpose of higher education (for which they have long shown great zeal) when they so regularly demean the fruits of critical inquiry, and how they can reconcile their fervor for evangelism with American pluralism.[14]

Much recent scholarship has focused on the political consequences of these contradictions. For more than ten years scholars have been debunking the old claim that evangelicals were politically dormant until the 1970s. The image of conservative Protestants as sleeping bears suddenly roused to political rampage is a myth that observers have long used to hide the fact that they simply weren't paying attention. In 1923, a liberal journalist called that era's fundamentalists—who were then campaigning to ban evolution from public schools—"a revivification of a movement long since supposedly dead and buried."[15] While conservative Protestants' more recent political endeavors are not seamless with the campaigns of their forefathers, scholars have demonstrated that it is absurd to open any history of the Christian Right with Jimmy Carter's election or the organization of the Moral Majority. Any serious effort must now begin no later than the anticommunist campaigns of the 1950s, if not with Prohibition—or, if you've got time on your hands, the Civil War.[16]

Some scholars have suggested that theology has become merely politics in disguise.[17] There is no doubt that theology and politics are inextricable. But the Pew polls and sociological surveys that are a hallmark of "culture war studies" are poor tools for analyzing underlying worldviews. They make no provision for the history and intellectual traditions that inform results. Pollsters often assume that if a respondent does not answer a question in theological or historical terms, then history or theology must not matter. It is foolish to reckon that ideas are present only where they explicitly declare themselves. An individual need not have a conscious knowledge of historical timelines or fluency in doctrinal terminology in order to be counted as a creature and bearer of ideas.[18]

Neither politics nor theology makes sense without consideration of the broader worldview that contains them both, and attention to the intellectual authority that provides the framework, the rules and logic, for that worldview. Intellectual authority is power by appeal to ideas, what Edward Gibbon called "force of persuasion."[19] This power may have psychological or political dimensions, but at its core is a set of assumptions about what is real and true and what is not. By examining the history of intellectual authority among American evangelicals, we can trace the questions that link them with their ancestors and that help explain how evangelicals have navigated the upheavals in modern American culture and global Christianity. Those upheavals have caused plenty of rows and rifts. Yet if American evangelicals do not share a single mind, they do share an imagination: one grounded in a substrate of basic questions about the relationship of faith and experience to human reason, and the direction of the modern world.

Part I

Knights Inerrant

Chapter 1

Errand from the Wilderness

KARL BARTH, THE GREATEST PROTESTANT THINKER OF THE TWENTIETH century, visited the United States only once. At the end of his long 1962 tour, after lectures in Princeton and Chicago, Barth was weary, but he agreed to a luncheon and question-and-answer session at George Washington University in the nation's capital. On a muggy spring afternoon two hundred religious leaders and a phalanx of newspapermen swarmed the room, including a journalist named Carl Henry. Henry worked in Washington as editor in chief of *Christianity Today*, the "magazine of evangelical conviction" that he had helped found six years earlier. His hair grimly pomaded across his skull, Henry stated his credentials and, as soon as he could gain the elderly theologian's attention, called out his challenge:

"The question, Dr. Barth, concerns the historical factuality of the resurrection of Jesus." He gestured to the press table. If these reporters had been covering the news of first-century Judea, he asked, would they write up the resurrection? "Was it news in the sense that the man in the street understands news?"

Barth was seventy-five years old, but his hedgelike eyebrows were still black and forbidding beneath a tussock of white hair. "Did you say Christianity *Today* or Christianity *Yesterday*?" he asked, to roars of laughter.

Henry raised his voice: "*Yesterday, Today,* and *forever.*"

Barth jeered again. "And what of the virgin birth? Would the photographers come and take pictures of it?" His position, he declared, was that Jesus appeared only to believers, not to the wider world. Christ was a matter of personal faith, not historical fact.[1]

Years later, Henry recounted this confrontation gleefully in his memoirs. He had sparred with the great man and held his ground. He had stepped into the world of fashionable modern theology but had not capitulated to it. Yet the encounter must have been as devastating as it was thrilling. Henry and his colleagues founded *Christianity Today* in order to wrangle with the defining thinkers of the age—to earn their respect, not their disdain. His question amused and embarrassed Barth and his admirers because it revealed the essential difference between their worldview and Henry's. For Barth, the modern world's standards of truth and falsehood did not apply neatly to scripture. For Henry, by contrast, there was one kind of truth and one inerrant Word. He believed that the Bible, a fantastical set of documents written thousands of years ago in which burning bushes speak, water turns to wine, and a God-man rises from the grave, was without error in every historical and scientific detail: true in the same way, indeed more true, than the headlines of a Sunday newspaper.

Barth soon outraged Henry and his fellow editors by titling his collected American lectures *Evangelical Theology*, claiming a label they considered their rightful heritage. Barth used the word both in the German sense— *evangelische* had meant "Protestant" since Reformation days—and to stress that his theology was centered on the *evangelion*, the gospel, in contrast to the "man-centered" theology of liberal Protestantism. He despised the modernists who cast Jesus as a great philosopher rather than God incarnate, but he also kept his distance from the self-proclaimed evangelicals of America, the bickering bumpkins who usually misread his books (when they read them at all) and whose literal-minded questions made him cringe.[2]

Despite this antagonism, Henry and his colleagues pursued the same fundamental project that preoccupied Barth: presenting the gospel persuasively to modern man as not just a set of wise and ancient documents, but as the basis for an all-encompassing worldview. Barth published his first book, a commentary on Paul's epistle to the Romans, in 1918. The Great War had razed liberal Christian confidence in Christ as a moral exemplar who made possible the self-perfection of the human race. By contrast, Barth's Christ was not a perfect man, but a wholly alien deity whose grace alone bridged the chasm between the divine and depraved humankind. With this thunderclap over the ivory towers of liberal Protestantism, Barth redirected the course of Christian theology. His influence emerged partly from his biography—he courageously opposed German aggression in both world wars—but stemmed primarily from force of argument. "In the church of Jesus Christ there can and should be no non-theologians," he wrote.[3] Ideas mattered.

This was the sort of intellectual authority that Henry and other evangelical intellectuals craved. They were convinced that they could stem the tide of world war and cultural decay by using their pens to prepare the way for God's transforming grace, by filling their pages with the rational case for Christ. Two generations earlier, liberals intent on modernizing the gospel had driven "orthodox" Christians from the pulpits and seminaries of mainline Protestantism, ridiculed them as superstitious fools, and deprived them of their standing to speak biblical truth to the world. Now a coterie of journalists, evangelists, and educators were determined to rebuild evangelicals' authority by repackaging the doctrine they saw as the core of Protestant orthodoxy—the inerrancy of the Bible—for twentieth-century skeptics.

Fundamentalism begged for a facelift. This network of conservative Protestants, young scholars and preachers who came of age amid the schisms and pulpit wars that troubled many denominations in the two decades prior to World War II, planned to renovate the facade of their tradition, but not its foundation. Most shared roots in the Reformed tradition, the stream of Protestant thought that has its headwaters in the work of John Calvin and the Swiss, English, and Scottish reformers who emphasized the depravity of humankind, the awesome sovereignty of God, and the Christian mandate to transform earthly society according to God's command. They also shared the conviction that belief in the inerrant truth of the Bible was more than a doctrine. It was the clarifying lens necessary to rightly perceive reality, a biblical "world and life view." They retained their forefathers' commitment to soul-winning, but with a difference: Spiritual crusades would melt away without lasting intellectual revival.

These young thinkers were not the only ones calling for a rebirth of the modern Western mind. While their fundamentalist heritage impelled them to condemn the profanities and vanities of twentieth-century culture and separate from all wickedness, they lived their lives embedded in the intellectual currents of wartime and postwar America. They navigated an epoch of contending worldviews, when so many on the Left and Right had an "ism" to offer the world, a plan for modern man's political and spiritual salvation. These would-be saviors of old-time religion knew that reciting their forebears' "fundamentals" and fulminations against Darwin and dancing would no longer suffice.

A RESTLESS FUNDAMENTALIST

Carl Henry grew up on Long Island, the oldest of eight, a chubby and rheumatic child with religiously indifferent parents. They were German immigrants who cared more about the fact of religious faith than its content and settled on the Episcopal Church as a compromise between his father's Lutheranism and his mother's Catholicism. As a boy, Henry himself was "no more regenerate than the Long Island telephone directory." He grew curious about Christianity after a coworker at the local newspaper, where he was a cub reporter, scolded him for taking the Lord's name in vain and took an interest in the state of his soul. In 1933, when Henry was twenty, evangelist Gene Bedford came to town, and "he told me about Christ as we drove around Long Island in my battered old Chevy," Henry said.[4] At an age when his peers were having more worldly revelations in the backseat, he "knelt in the back of that car and dedicated myself to Jesus Christ."

Two years later, Henry enrolled at Wheaton College in Illinois, a limestone and brick bastion of fundamentalism twenty-five miles west of Chicago. He roomed with an overbearing trombonist in the Green Lantern lodging house, worked for a local newspaper, and taught typing and journalism classes to pay his expenses.[5] Bustling with the children of missionaries who served around the world and zealous members of "Lit" societies who met on Fridays to play music, debate, and recite their efforts at poetry, the Wheaton of the 1930s was, in some ways, a cosmopolitan place. Its worldliness was the approved and godly kind, befitting an oasis where parents sent their children to spare them from the hazards of secular culture and fortify their confidence in the Bible.

Henry admired the dual commitment to orthodoxy and learning that he saw in Wheaton's president, J. Oliver Buswell, Jr. Buswell was a fundamentalist separatist when it came to church affairs but a "participationist" in education who shared many of the same goals of his colleagues at secular colleges. He earned Wheaton state accreditation, membership in the Association of American Universities, and built a curriculum that matched those on offer at secular liberal arts schools. However, Buswell involved himself so deeply in the controversy then roiling the northern Presbyterian Church that the college's trustees, weary of his taste for schism, fired him. The battles between fundamentalists who demanded that true believers abandon the mainline churches and those who vowed to stay left a sour taste in Henry's mouth: "Whatever early inclination I then had of possibly seeking Presbyterian ordination and ministry was discouraged by the condemnatory spirit and one-sided propaganda of the 'come-out-ers' and the machine loyalty of the 'stay-in-ers,'" he later wrote. While he and his classmates bemoaned church division with sarcastic ditties—"You split the one next to you,/And I'll split the one next to me;/In no time at all/We'll split them all/So split them, split them, one by one"—in class and at campus worship they learned that when it came to doctrine and the authority of scripture, compromise was anathema.[6]

Separation and schism: This is what the fundamentalist movement meant in the everyday lives of many conservative American Protestants. The movement quickly spread until few American denominations or geographical regions were untouched, but its epicenter lay in Baptist and Presbyterian churches in the urban North. These denominations shared an age-old obsession with doctrine and proximity to two demons of the twentieth century—modern research universities and crowded, toiling, multiethnic cities—which made them specially prone to picking a fight over the Bible's role in modern life. This struggle was about more than whether Darwin ought to triumph over Noah, or whether seminaries ought to teach their students that many different human beings, rather than one God, wrote the sacred texts. This was a crisis of authority in every human institution that these Christians had built to help them interpret and live by the Bible. In the years between the world wars, conservatives found themselves expelled from or silenced in denominational leadership, church seminaries, colleges, and periodicals, not to mention secular academia and media. But if the battles against modernists represented the end of an institutional age for fundamentalists, the survivors believed the wreckage was a price worth paying to defend biblical inerrancy.

THE RUDDER OF "GOD-BREATHED" SCRIPTURE

Inerrancy was not an esoteric doctrine. It was the essential claim that would, in one form or another, dog and divide American evangelicals for the rest of the twentieth century and beyond. So it is worth pausing to examine what inerrancy means and where it came from. The basic idea—that scripture is free from all error—is an ancient one. The earliest Christians had little notion of the scientific method or modern standards of historical inquiry, but they were keen to defend the Bible as the record of God's word and a perfect source of truth. Christians intent on asserting the Bible's authority through logical argument quarreled with mystics and prophets who claimed to know God's will through their own experience, and with doubters who found inconsistencies in the biblical text or preferred apocryphal writings to those that eventually became the canon. Paul's second letter to Timothy asserted that all scripture is "God-breathed," and the second-century church father Clement believed the Bible to be "the true utterances of the Holy Spirit...nothing false is written in them." Irenaeus, Bishop of Lyon, articulated the broad outlines of "verbal inspiration"—the divine authorship of every word of the Bible—to defend a literalistic reading of scripture against Gnostics who concealed their subversive interpretations behind the veil of metaphor.[7]

Orthodoxy finds its mature form under the pressures of controversy. Like the shifting weight of earth that conjures a diamond from a dull carbon vein, local pressures have great influence over doctrine's final shape. Inerrancy meant one thing when Christians' primary concerns were Plato-drunk heretics and pagans, and quite another after the Reformation. John Calvin and Martin Luther had other priorities. They were more concerned with the authority of the Bible as a whole than in parsing every detail. Luther taught that errors in the predictions of Old Testament prophets or the battle statistics in Chronicles did not undermine the Bible's authority in matters of salvation, and Calvin suggested that God "stammers" to accommodate his revelation to human ears.[8] Their followers, however, found themselves attacked on one side by Catholic soldiers of the Counter-Reformation, and on the other by disciples of the Enlightenment's new cult of rationalism. Some reacted to the age's new learning by urging believers to embrace nonrational communion with the divine. They trumpeted revival and a more experiential, inwardly focused Protestantism. But second-generation Calvinists and Lutherans also defended their faith with the tools of reason and learned to write and think in the language of their opponents.

They developed a highly rationalistic method of argumentation based on the technique of the medieval Catholic scholastics. These Protestant thinkers took as their starting point the assumption—which may owe more to Christianity's roots in Greek philosophy than to any explicit teaching in the Bible—that the Supreme Being is wholly perfect and unchanging. It followed that his revelation must be perfect and unchanging too, for a perfect God who errs is a logical fallacy. He chose to reveal himself through fallible human agents, but he must have safeguarded his revelation from even the smallest error—at least in "the original autographs" laid down by the biblical authors themselves. (The Swiss-Italian theologian Francis Turretin believed that an all-powerful God would never permit the corruption of his revelation by copyists, but most defenders of inerrancy make no apologies for the mistakes of scribes, and inerrantists have found a great deal of wiggle room in this caveat.)[9] These theologians transformed the edicts of the church fathers and the doctrines of the Reformers into a complex theological edifice that could, they claimed, stand up to rational inquiry just as well as the new science and philosophy did.

The doctrine of inerrancy blossomed into its most methodical and vibrant form in the mid-nineteenth century, in the hands of theologians at Princeton Theological Seminary. Alarmed by the hubris of modern biblical critics and the atheistic conclusions that some drew from Darwin's theories, repulsed by the glorification of human consciousness in the romantic writings of Samuel Taylor Coleridge and the treatises of Friedrich Schleiermacher, these men defended scripture as a wholly reliable text for modern man. Charles Hodge, the seminary's principal from 1851 until 1878, declared the Bible a God-given "storehouse of facts" that, under the guidance of "those laws of belief which God has impressed upon our nature," the theologian must "arrange and harmonize" into a systematic body of teachings just as a scientist infers the laws of the cosmos by collecting data from the material world. Hodge granted that scripture seemed to contain some trivial discrepancies, but these were apparent rather than real, each like a mere "speck of sandstone" that in no way diminished the flawless marble of the Parthenon.[10]

Hodge and his colleagues toiled in the thrall of the day's dominant philosophy, Common Sense Realism: a strand of the Scottish Enlightenment that combined Francis Bacon's methods of induction and empiricism with a democratic faith in the ability of every human to access metaphysical truths by God-given "common sense." They viewed themselves not as theological innovators, but as loyal spokesmen for the ancient church. At the same time, they were professional scholars open to legitimate biblical criticism—when "carried on with infinite humility and teachableness, and with prayer for the constant guidance of the gracious Spirit."[11] Benjamin Warfield and

Charles Hodge's son, Archibald Alexander Hodge, allowed that Genesis did not preclude some form of theistic evolution. Warfield's lifelong experience collaborating with his father, a cattle breeder in Kentucky, predisposed him to take seriously Darwin's ideas about the transformation of species over time. He worked to reformulate inerrancy to avoid the facile notion that the biblical authors were merely God's dictaphones—although there was often no functional difference between the "dictation theory" that Warfield denounced and his assertion that God used the biblical writers "to proclaim His messages purely as He gives them to them."[12]

Self-described inerrantists could, and did, disagree over biblical claims of scientific or historical fact. The Princeton theologians worried less over the discrete challenges of science or historical discovery than they did over the assumptions that, they feared, lay behind liberal Christians' efforts to reinterpret problematic verses as metaphor, or to dismiss them as mistakes by human authors. These liberals—so it seemed to the conservatives at Princeton—did not merely seek to expand humankind's knowledge of the world. They hoped to strike a fatal blow to the sovereignty of God himself by casting doubt on his "plenary inspiration" of the Bible: the belief that God inspired the entirety of scripture, from the trees of Eden to the trumpets and seals of Revelation. Faithful criticism offered in a humble Christian spirit was one thing, but most of the scholarship emanating from august faculties in Germany and infesting American seminaries outraged conservatives with "naturalistic" presuppositions and impious intentions.[13] These modernist scholars tried to paper over the consequences of their criticism by arguing that they left the fundamentals of Christ's message intact, but Warfield warned that they wielded a sledgehammer rather than a scalpel:

If criticism has made such discoveries as necessitate the abandonment of the doctrine of plenary inspiration, it is not enough to say that we are compelled to abandon only a "particular theory of inspiration," though that is true enough. We must go on to say that that "particular theory of inspiration" is the theory of the apostles and of the Lord, and that in abandoning *it* we are abandoning *them* as our doctrinal teachers and guides, as our "exegetes," in the deep and rich sense of that word.... This real issue is to be kept clearly before us, and faced courageously. Nothing is gained by closing our eyes to the seriousness of the problem which we are confronting.[14]

The Princeton scholars granted that "critical investigation must be made, and we must abide by the result when it is unquestionably reached." If their insistence that biblical critics always presuppose the doctrine of plenary inspiration made their support of the scientific enterprise a bit disingenuous, at least the inerrantists at Princeton read and thoughtfully engaged with their liberal rivals' work. In the late nineteenth century, conservative evangelical scholars were still active participants in the academic societies and journals on the frontier of biblical interpretation. But by the time of the First World War, many scholars had embraced the German universities' model of skeptical innovation and ceased to think of their scholarship as service to the church. Alienated conservatives retreated into an echo chamber of like minds. They wrote and preached to edify faithful students, ministers, and laypeople, rather than to persuade their liberal colleagues. The inerrantist faculty at old Princeton—before moderates gained control of the seminary in the 1920s—published hundreds of articles and books and trained two generations of ministers to defend the Bible's authority. They joined other conservative scholars in writing the pamphlet series *The Fundamentals* (1910–1915) to defend traditional interpretations of the Bible. The diverse roster of contributors demonstrated the range of opinion still permissible in the fundamentalist camp during those years: The authors ranged from revivalists such as R. A. Torrey to the subtle Scottish theologian James Orr, who argued that inerrancy doctrine was disastrous for Christian faith.[15]

These pastors and scholars did, however, share a common scorn for the liberal assertion that biblical criticism could be a "neutral task" that hewed to modern scientific standards of inquiry. To paraphrase Augustine, unwavering faith had to precede understanding. Reading the Bible correctly demanded orthodox presuppositions. Modern scholars' claims that no theological perspective clouded their work seemed to conservative Protestants to be a kind of insidious, idolatrous theology itself. The theory of evolution and modern biblical criticism were not just scientific hypotheses or academic paradigms, but ideologies with political and spiritual consequences that threatened "civilization as well as religion," William Jennings Bryan warned in 1923.[16]

Pastors and laymen who encountered the careful critiques of Warfield or Orr second- and third-hand rarely preserved their prudence and intellectual agility. As conflict against modernists intensified in the 1920s and 1930s, fundamentalists lost interest in nuance. They refashioned a once-subtle doctrine into a shield to protect the Bible from the revisions of blasphemers. Orr and the scholars of old Princeton had understood themselves as explicating centuries of Christian wisdom in modern terms. They held steady at the siren call of *sola scriptura*—that problematic promise that every believer could grasp scripture's plain meaning—by binding themselves to the mast of a venerable theological tradition. Later fundamentalists, however, became polemicists rather than apologists. The difference is subtle but crucial. Winning the war against modernism became more important than illuminating orthodoxy. Inerrancy came to represent not only a set of beliefs about creation or the reality of Jesus's miracles, but the pledge that human reason must always bow to the Bible. As fear of modernist theology and new science began to infect a wide range of Protestant churches, this new variety of fundamentalist deployed inerrancy as a simple shibboleth to separate the sheep from the goats. It was no longer a doctrine with historical roots or an ongoing debate among theologians. Inerrancy was common sense.

Second-generation fundamentalists like Carl Henry were too young to be veterans of those battles, but they worshiped and studied in fundamentalist institutions, imbibing their philosophical rationalism and militant posture toward much of modern life and thought. However, by the time of World War II, some evangelicals—the word was not yet fully distinguished from "fundamentalist"—began to think that their central priority, the spread of the gospel to the widest possible number of human beings, suffered from the inward turn that fundamentalists had taken. They tired of isolation. But as they began to revisit their approach to culture, education, and evangelism, their commitment to inerrancy remained firm. They aspired to the intellectual sophistication of old Princeton, but it was not clear whether nuance was compatible with their crusading sense of mission. Inerrantist intellectuals considered themselves something like Protestant Marines, a warrior corps whose confidence in the authority of scripture—and commitment to taking the principle of God's sovereignty to its logical extreme—anointed them as the Bible's shock troops, favorite sons, and truest defenders.

NEW EVANGELICALS

In his autobiography, Carl Henry admitted the limitations of his Wheaton College education. The pedagogy was often "stuffy," and his Bible professors strayed little beyond the obsessive and esoteric view of the end-times prescribed in the favorite fundamentalist annotated edition of the King James Version, the Scofield Reference Bible. The faculty fixated on old enemies cold in their graves for generations but ignored more pressing threats: They wrung their hands over Schleiermacher but had never read Barth. Nevertheless, Henry applauded the college for "insisting that the Christian world-life view is not only intellectually tenable, but that in fact it also explains reality and life more logically and comprehensively than do modern alternatives."[17]

Henry married Helga Bender, a hazel-eyed daughter of pioneer German Baptist missionaries whom he met in typing class, and enrolled at Northern Baptist Theological Seminary, the fundamentalists' alternative to the University of Chicago Divinity School. He also earned a master's degree in theology at Wheaton and preached at various Baptist and Presbyterian churches in the Chicago area. During World War II, he drove to Detroit to address large gatherings of Youth for Christ, an evangelistic organization that initially aimed at footloose soldiers and sailors but earned a massive following among evangelical youth. Henry had no vocation to preach from a fundamentalist pulpit, but he felt called to spread the gospel. He was still a graduate student when, in 1942, conservative Protestants dissatisfied with the progress of evangelism gathered in St. Louis to organize the National Association of Evangelicals.

The establishment of the NAE signaled that a growing number of conservative Protestants shared Henry's sentiments: a new self-consciousness, and a desire for cooperation after years of infighting and demoralizing losses to modernists. Henry had written his ThD thesis on "successful church publicity" and volunteered to help advertise the NAE's early meetings. At the organization's "constitutional convention" on May 4, 1943, shortly after eleven o'clock in the morning, a dapper Presbyterian minister with wire-rim glasses and deep-set blue eyes took the podium at the LaSalle Hotel in downtown Chicago. Harold Ockenga, the NAE president who would coin the term *neo-evangelical* to name those who echoed his discontent with the state of the church, reminded his audience of the crisis that brought them together. "Neo-evangelical" would come to describe a self-aware intellectual movement of pastors, scholars, and evangelists within the conservative Protestant community roughly (but not entirely) contained within the NAE. Over the following years, while *evangelical* connoted a broad swath of conservative Protestants averse to the old fundamentalist model of feuding separatism but still eager to defend the authenticity of religious experience and the authority of the Bible, *neo-evangelical* became a more precise label, embraced by a small circle of self-appointed leaders.[18]

The churchmen who convened the NAE had down-to-earth problems in mind. They met to talk about how to break the liberal Federal Council of Churches' control of the radio waves; to gain adequate representation among the chaplains serving the armed forces; to shore up Sunday School curricula and counteract humanistic trends in public education; and to cooperate in missions work and challenge the worldwide ecumenical movement, which diluted doctrine and imperiled souls. But the organization's leaders explained their mission in terms of a grander narrative: one that began with "The Great Apostasy" among nineteenth-century European intellectuals who had abandoned traditional interpretations of the Bible.[19] These thinkers dared to dissect scripture as they would any other man-made document. Some suggested that God was merely a mortal invention, a projection of human fears and longings. Others redrafted history as a story of progress and humanity's self-improvement, rather than a divine plan that required sinners to beg for salvation. Even if American liberals were not usually so radical as the Europeans, the difference was one of degree, not kind. American "modernists" had still violated the First Commandment. They worshiped the idol of human intellect, rather than submitting reason to the service of Jehovah. They preached self-reliance rather than surrender to God's will.

Without a firm defense of biblical inerrancy, Ockenga predicted, America would fall to enemies within and without, as had imperial Rome. Western civilization was sick with secularism and socialism, the modern spores that had overrun their hosts in the Soviet Union. "We are standing at the crossroads and there are only two ways that lie open before us," he said. "One is the road of the rescue of western civilization by a re-emphasis on and revival of evangelical Christianity. The other is a return to the Dark Ages of heathendom, which powerful force is emerging in every phase of world life today." The "Kingdom of Hell" was at hand.[20] Ockenga reminded his audience that prior to the advent of modern biblical criticism and the theory of evolution, all Westerners shared a Christian *Weltanschauung*—by which he meant unqualified respect for biblical authority, even if corrupted in some regions by Catholic rule. World War II provided grisly evidence for the disintegration of civilization under way ever since.

The neo-evangelicals were overfond of this word, *Weltanschauung*, and its English synonyms: worldview, world-and-life view. They intoned it like a ghostly incantation whenever they wrote of the decline of Christendom, the decoupling of faith and reason, and the needful pinprick of the gospel in every corner of thought and action. The term originated in the same late eighteenth-century ferment in which German scholars began to treat the Bible as they would any other historical artifact. At that time, Immanuel Kant launched his philosophical revolution in which man and his worldview, his *Weltanschauung*, became the epistemological and moral center of the universe. Most neo-evangelicals did not acquire the word from reading Kant or the other German philosophers who sharpened its meaning. They picked it up from the works of Reformed theologians versed in German theology, such as the Dutch churchman and politician Abraham Kuyper and James Orr (Henry read Orr's *The Christian View of God and the World* in class at Wheaton).[21]

By the time Ockenga used it in 1943, *Weltanschauung* was a familiar term to most educated English speakers for a more regrettable reason: It was a Nazi rallying cry. Newsmen covering Nazi Germany found the word untranslatable. They often printed the German in all its multisyllabic menace. *Weltanschauung* appeared sporadically in English-language newspapers before the 1930s (usually in reviews of German books and in highbrow cultural commentary), but now readers following world affairs could not avoid this ominous term. Upon his election as chancellor in 1933, Adolf Hitler assured Germans that "a new philosophy has impressed itself upon this nation; a new philosophy (Weltanschauung) has saved the nation from lethargy, resignation, and despair...there is no denying that this movement stands for ideas which must be better than the ideas of our opponents."[22]

Americans and readers across the Anglosphere encountered the word in regular reports of the Nazis' subjugation of German churches in favor of their own neo-pagan rituals; the eradication of peoples who were out of step with this worldview of Aryan blood and power; and Nazi wedding ceremonies, Teutonic pastiches of torches, uniforms, peasant costumes, crowns of flowers and greenery in which the officiant pronounced each couple "united in the Nazi weltanschauung."[23] Here was "a Weltanschauung with which we have nothing in common, an ethical system in which force is the highest argument and the destruction of all who do not think as the pagan does is meritorious, not condemnable," the *Washington Post* observed in 1944. The rise of Nazism prodded some Westerners to realize that the conflict required not only manpower and matériel, but a coherent intellectual front as well. Hitler mocked the West's insufficient ideology, contending in his speeches that "democracies like Britain, France and the United States are inherently weak through lack of a Weltanschauung or definite ideological content essential to their firmer consolidation."[24]

The Allies extinguished Nazism in 1945, but the victory inaugurated the West's long war of ideology against the Soviet Union and other communist states. Marxism–Leninism and Maoism proved to be highly sophisticated world-and-life views, each a pseudo-religion complete with its own sacred texts, rituals, plans of salvation, and transcendent meaning. Even Norman Thomas, six-time Socialist Party candidate for president, warned that "today your Communist is not so much a dissenter as an ultra-orthodox member of an opposing political church, subject in every respect to its discipline."[25] By the mid-twentieth century, it was clear that human beings residing in the same civilization—or subject to the same rules of the international state system—no longer proceeded from shared premises. Astute analysts saw that the key to winning the Cold War lay in understanding the assumptions, history, and psychology of the communist worldview. George Kennan, then deputy head of the U.S. mission in Moscow, took up this argument in his 1946 "Long Telegram": "Our first step must be to apprehend, and recognize for what it is, the nature of the movement with which we are dealing," he wrote. A clear-eyed appraisal of how the Kremlin's mindset refracted reality would help Americans muster the "courage and self-confidence to cling to our own methods and conceptions of human society."[26] Now the way to understand one's enemy was to see beyond his rhetoric, decipher his *Weltanschauung*—and defend one's own.

Evangelicals were not the only conservative Christians to grasp the power of this word. After Leo XIII instructed Catholics that the best way to reconcile faith with modern reason was to follow the principles of thirteenth-century theologian Thomas Aquinas, American Catholic colleges devoted their energy to reviving Thomist ideas as a *"Weltanschauung,"* an intellectual fortress that could protect students' faith while arming them against the salvos of the twentieth century.[27] The loose alliance of Catholic traditionalists and libertarians who came together to found the *National Review* in 1955 saw rival worldviews not only among Cold War enemies abroad, but lurking at home. They condemned American liberals' arguments as a "whole *Weltanschauung*...that denies the mysterious ravages of original sin, the relevance of divine redemption, the subordination of matter to spirit."[28] Deciphering an opponent's worldview meant unlocking their unifying theory of everything. It meant refuting the claims of liberal empiricists and pragmatists like John Dewey and William James—who suggested that our knowledge about the world is a changing mass of provable and useful facts—and exposing instead the semiconscious and unverifiable assumptions that shape a person's perception of reality.

These nonevangelical conservatives shared many of neo-evangelicals' concerns about the direction of the modern world. Just four years after Ockenga's address to the NAE, libertarian scholars from across Europe and the United States convened at Mont Pèlerin, Switzerland, to organize their opposition to socialism. The Mont Pelerin Society's "statement of aims" echoed Ockenga in secular terms: "The central values of civilization are in danger. Over large stretches of the earth's surface the essential conditions of human dignity and freedom have already disappeared...these developments have been fostered by the growth of a view of history which denies all absolute moral standards and...the rule of law."[29] Over the next few years, the appraisals of conservative American intellectuals—Southern Agrarian and University of Chicago scholar Richard Weaver's *Ideas Have Consequences* (1948); ex-communist Whittaker Chambers's *Witness* (1952); Kenyon College education reformer Gordon Keith Chalmers's *The Republic and the Person* (1952); Anglo-Catholic thinker Russell Kirk's *The Conservative Mind* (1953)—rued the decay of Christendom's moral absolutes and the treachery of liberal perfectionism.[30] The neo-evangelicals were not intellectual outliers or drowsy fundamentalists playing cultural catch-up. They were members of the conservative ideological vanguard.

MENTORS OF THE NEO-EVANGELICAL MIND

If neo-evangelical intellectuals spoke a common language of cultural criticism, they did so from a unique theological perspective. When they proclaimed their *Weltanschauung*, they used the word to describe God's intentions for the human race and the Christian obligation to apply the gospel to every sphere of existence. Carl Henry learned that he had a world-and-life-view—and that he ought to fight for it—from a Wheaton College philosophy professor named Gordon Clark. Other neo-evangelicals also studied with Clark and honed their theological training further at Princeton and Princeton's estranged fundamentalist sibling, Westminster Theological Seminary outside Philadelphia. In Clark's care they imbibed a school of Reformed apologetics called presuppositionalism, which emphasized close attention to the assumptions about reality that shape a person's worldview. The notion that a person's basic beliefs about reality and God shape his interpretation of scripture was an old idea, the core of conservatives' suspicions about liberal scholarship for at least a century. Clark and a new generation of Reformed thinkers reformulated this insight in terms that suited the ideological atmosphere of the twentieth century. They gave that seductive word, *Weltanschauung*, a systematic theology.

Abraham Kuyper had been the first to articulate the basic elements of mature presuppositionalist thought in the late nineteenth century as part of the "New Calvinist" theology that he urged Christians to apply to culture and politics. Cornelius Van Til, a Dutch émigré who taught at Princeton and later helped found Westminster, developed presuppositionalism into a complicated line of reasoning more severe than Kuyper's or Clark's versions. Van Til reacted strongly against the Princeton theologians' emphasis on proving Christian truths with the aid of worldly evidence outside revelation. He argued that a nonbeliever cannot interpret such evidence accurately because, without faith, he reasons from the wrong assumptions. Van Til denied the Enlightenment ideal of the pure, objective fact, insisting instead that no assumptions are neutral, and that the human mind can comprehend reality only by proceeding from the truth of biblical revelation. It is impossible, then, for Christians to reason with non-Christians. Van Til shut down open-minded exchanges before they could begin, and "raised the Westminster Seminary principle of separation to cosmic philosophical proportions," historian George Marsden has written. Clark's presuppositionalism allowed a greater role for human reason in bridging the gap between faith and unbelief, but he too denied neutral ground between the Christian and non-Christian world-and-life views. He wrote that true art and literature were only possible when based on theistic assumptions, and suggested that nonbelievers who had no claim to an ultimate source of meaning depended on Christian presuppositions—if only unconsciously—in order to go on living. "If humanists wish to be completely consistent, they ought to kill themselves," he wrote.[31]

The career of another Presbyterian thinker, a New Testament scholar named J. Gresham Machen, demonstrated the odd blend of alienation and engagement—and the potential for an appealing public theology—in this Reformed penchant for taking ideas to their logical conclusion. A well-bred Baltimore native who studied Latin and Greek as a boy, majored in classics at Johns Hopkins University, and trained in the thick of German liberal theology at the universities of Marburg and Gottingen, Machen was both a staunch fundamentalist and a mainstream public intellectual. Although he died five years before the organization of the NAE, his spirit hovered over the neo-evangelicals. Several read his books and admired him from afar, while others studied with him directly at Princeton and later at Westminster. He was convinced that modernist theologians had broken with the premises of traditional Christianity and created a wholly different religion, one that "is only the more destructive of the Christian faith because it makes use of traditional Christian terminology. This modern non-redemptive religion is called 'modernism' or 'liberalism.'"[32]

Once he left Princeton, Machen remained affiliated in letter, if not in spirit, with the moderate Presbyterian Church in the U.S.A. until a controversy over missions in the 1930s led to his suspension from the ministry. The *New York Times* avidly covered his trial. Machen was, after all, a *Times* regular, a prolific writer of letters to the editor whose fulminations against state regulation and "collectivism" in higher education, federally funded roads in his favorite national parks, fingerprinting laws, and other threats to "the remnants of American liberty" regularly graced the Gray Lady's pages.[33] He defended Christian truths to readers of the *Times* in long essays published on the eve of the Scopes Trial. To those hecklers who considered fundamentalists illiterate bumpkins, Machen declared that it was the fundamentalist Christian, not the snooty liberal besotted with modern thought, who was the true intellectual:

> Against the passionate anti-intellectualism of a great section of the modern Church he [the fundamentalist] maintains the primacy of the intellect; he holds that God has given to man a faculty of reason which is capable of apprehending truth, even truth about God.... We refuse,

therefore, to abandon to the student of natural science the entire realm of fact, in order to reserve to religion merely a realm of ideals; on the contrary, theology, we hold, is just as much a science as is chemistry.[34]

Machen defended conservative Protestantism before audiences at Columbia University and the Brooklyn Institute of Arts and Sciences. Luminaries Henry Sloane Coffin and Reinhold Niebuhr heard him speak at Union Theological Seminary in New York.[35] His example proved that it was possible to compel liberal intellectuals and mainstream readers to hear out the case for traditional orthodoxy. Richard Hofstadter, the liberal historian who blamed evangelical religion for much of American anti-intellectualism, exempted Machen from his critique, calling him "the highbrow fundamentalist." To his students, Machen represented fundamentalism's road back to respectability, proof that holding firm to orthodoxy—as a holistic philosophy of life rather than a mere list of doctrines and anathemas—was no bar to mainstream relevance. In an obituary of Machen, fundamentalists' scourge H. L. Mencken, a fellow Baltimorean, worried that most readers assumed "he was simply another Fundamentalist on the order of William Jennings Bryan and the simian faithful of Appalachia. But he was actually a man of great learning, and, what is more, of sharp intelligence . . . Dr. Machen himself was to Bryan as the Matterhorn is to a wart."[36]

A NEW CRUSADE

The neo-evangelical leaders gave every appearance of having moved beyond Machen's taste for church schism, the "come-out-ism" that troubled Carl Henry during his undergraduate days at Wheaton. Over the course of the late 1940s and 1950s, their evangelistic campaigns flourished. The massive crusades of Billy Graham and efforts aimed at young people such as Youth for Christ, Campus Crusade, and InterVarsity Christian Fellowship answered Harold Ockenga's call for postwar revival. The country seemed to be finding its way back to God. In a 1949 radio address, President Harry Truman told Americans that "the basic source of our strength as a nation is spiritual. . . . Religious faith and religious work must be our reliance as we strive to fulfill our destiny in the world." Five years later, in part due to pressure from a grassroots campaign headed by the Catholic fraternity the Knights of Columbus, Congress

added the words "under God" to the Pledge of Allegiance. In 1956 "In God
We Trust" reappeared on all U.S. coins and currency as the country's official
motto. (American coinage had featured the phrase intermittently since the
1860s). Church membership rates climbed. By the decade's end, 65 percent
of Americans belonged to some kind of religious institution, and 90 percent
said they believed in God and the power of prayer.[37]

This rising tide of indistinct religiosity and Judeo-Christian patriotism
did not, however, satisfy those who sought the preeminence of theologically
conservative and academically respectable Protestantism—inerrancy for
intellectuals—in all spheres of life. "Let no representative of Jesus Christ
be misled into believing that, just because church attendance is improving
and the growth of most congregations is better than it has been in years past,
that therefore the world has suddenly come to accept Christianity wholeheartedly...the battle for the souls of men for Jesus Christ is far from won,"
warned Walter Hellman, the head of the American Lutheran Church's
California district. As much as conservative Protestants shared the concerns
that preoccupied other Western intellectuals in the years after World War II,
so far they were only a chorus of echoes, not opinion makers or counselors to
power. And while the norms that Americans espoused in public held steady,
in private more Americans were deviating from traditional church strictures
against drinking and premarital sex. Notions of original sin and human depravity remained convincing in this age of hot and cold war, but at the same time
social scientists and psychologists preached secular interpretations of human
suffering that banished the idea of Christian guilt.[38]

Ordinary Christians have never lived up to their clergy's expectations.
The neo-evangelicals' lament over the state of American culture was not all
that different from the jeremiads of their Puritan ancestors, but they had in
mind a new fix for waning piety. Ockenga called for not only old-fashioned
revival, but revival by means of intellectual renewal. "Unless the church can
produce some thinkers who will lead us in positive channels," he warned,
"our spiral of degradation will continue downward."[39]

Historically, American evangelicals have been inventive and productive
activists. It is in the doing, rather than in intellectual legwork, that their
joint efforts have thrived. The NAE followed the precedent of large-scale,
nondenominational cooperation toward concrete goals pioneered by the
missions associations, temperance leagues, and the other benevolent societies that absorbed so much evangelical energy in the nineteenth century.

But this action-oriented approach was ill suited to the demands of the post-war age of ideology. Gordon Clark warned that

> [evangelicals] have been preaching Biblical sermons and have given themselves to evangelism. And this is essential, necessary, indispensable. But they have neglected the philosophical, scientific, social, and political problems that agitate our century.[40]

Clark worried that if conservative Protestants failed to tackle the philosophical problems of the day, "the thinking world has the choice of going through modernism to communism or of taking the road to Rome." Neo-orthodox theologians like Karl Barth had risen to the challenge by repackaging the doctrines of original sin and God's transcendence for twentieth-century audiences. Catholic thinkers had revived church tradition to arm themselves against the modern age. Even communists, in their dialectical materialism and predictions of class warfare, had a seductive explanation for modernity's problems. Where was the evangelical answer?

Clark's warning appeared in the foreword he wrote for a book he called "a hopeful sign," written by his former student Carl Henry.[41] *Remaking the Modern Mind* (1946) was a neo-evangelical cousin to the other conservative manifestos that would soon appear beneath the bylines of thinkers like Richard Weaver and Russell Kirk. The "dissolution" of the West, Henry argued, was the result of the erroneous philosophy of history that grew out of the Renaissance and made its most recent and powerful gains through the work of Hegel and Darwin: belief in "the inevitability of progress," of mankind's climb toward perfection and away from the biblical worldview. Only the "so-called fundamentalist churches" rooted in the Reformation—and, Henry grudgingly admitted, the Roman Catholics—"seriously questioned the capacity of human nature for complete achievement or self-realization." The fundamentalist churches, however, cultivated pessimism about the present world order and failed to take advantage of the breach in this long tide of optimism about human nature created by the world wars. Orthodox Protestants ceded the intellectual field. "Most creative Protestant thought for the past two generations has been liberal, often much more identifiable with humanism than with traditional Christianity," Henry wrote.[42]

Yet the cataclysm of global war and the relegation of conservative Protestantism to a minority position alienated from much of Western culture was not a sign of final defeat. It was a world-historical opportunity on par with the Reformation. The neo-evangelicals were a remnant, a holy few trapped in exile. God had raised up the remnant in times past. Henry repeated the old Christian promise that spiritual regeneration would redeem the wider culture, but he hinted that the task might require extra work of a different order: "The modern ideology needs to be remade."[43]

From the neo-evangelical point of view, if Christian civilization was to survive the twentieth century, then biblical inerrancy and a reenergized Christian *Weltanschauung* must form its bedrock. Although some of Henry's allies grew up in the orbit of Pietistic churches that emphasized personal religious experience over objective knowledge, a more rationalist, Reformed school of thought dominated their theological training. In this tradition, there was a single proof that one's presuppositions were the right ones, and one acceptable defense for any intellectual position: It was a true reading of the inerrant gospel. The neo-evangelicals championed other theological principles too, but they recognized that conservative Protestants might reasonably disagree on details of doctrine. The NAE had no business taking a firm stand on predestination or exactly when Christ was due to return.

Biblical inerrancy and the totality of the "Christian world-and-life-view," on the other hand, were different. These were not really doctrines at all, but facts: facts that made sense in an age when everyone from Nazis and communists to Catholic theologians and U.S. Foreign Service officers were talking about worldviews and presuppositions. This convergence of intellectual anxieties allowed a small group of thinkers with conspicuously similar Reformed backgrounds—a tiny minority of the variety of Protestants who assembled to join the NAE—to claim the right and the duty to speak for a population of Christians whose opinions outnumbered the hues on Joseph's dream coat.

The trouble was that neo-evangelicals presumed an evangelical solidarity that did not exist. The call for cooperation that began with the NAE would expose discord and ambivalence—not least because, it turned out, the neo-evangelicals' instinctive response to debate was to turn a deaf ear and close ranks. They differed from their fundamentalist forefathers only in the degree of their separatist impulse. The debasement of the Bible's authority alarmed all conservative Protestants, but some looked warily on the neo-evangelical plan for collaboration and considered themselves Wesleyans, Mennonites, or Baptists first, and evangelicals second, if at all. All had suffered in the fundamentalist–modernist battles fought a generation earlier. But if platitudes about the Bible's authority all sounded alike, every church was unhappy in its own way.

Chapter 2

The Authority Problem

W HEN THE FOUNDERS OF THE NATIONAL ASSOCIATION OF EVANGELICALS began to round up support for their new organization, they sponsored meetings in churches around the country to pitch their vision of "ecumenical evangelicalism" to skeptics. J. Narver Gortner, the president of a Pentecostal school called Glad Tidings Bible Institute in San Francisco, attended an early meeting at a Baptist church in Oakland. Around him sat many of his comrades in the Assemblies of God, one of the largest Pentecostal denominations in the country. They doubted that Presbyterians and Baptists—and other churches that had treated them as heretics since the Pentecostal movement began half a century earlier in a wildfire of holy fits, tongues, and other scandals—would now welcome them into the evangelical fold. Yet, to their surprise and cautious pleasure, they were at this meeting by special invitation.

Before long, old hostilities surfaced. A Presbyterian minister from Berkeley stood and demanded to know who, exactly, would belong to the proposed organization. Gortner heard him say that "there are many groups who regard themselves as evangelical and that some of them are very extreme, and he [the Presbyterian] intimated that some among us would not care to be associated with them," he reported to Assemblies headquarters in Springfield, Missouri.

After he had been speaking along this line for three or four minutes Brother Moon who was sitting just behind me punched me in the back and said, "He means us." That was apparent. I did not need to be told. We all knew it. When he sat down there was an ominous silence.

Nobody else seemed to have anything to say; so I rose, and proceeded to make a speech.[1]

Gortner reminded the audience that he and his fellow Pentecostals were present because the meeting's organizers had invited them. He suggested that they defer until after this "formative stage" the delicate question of which churches ought to participate in the association. "If, when the time comes, it seems advisable to exclude us we shall walk out without a murmur, with no hard feelings toward anybody," he said. When Gortner finished his speech and sat down, Harold Ockenga broke the awkward silence: "Brother, I should like to hear you preach some day!" Pleased, Gortner reported the compliment to his wife later that night. "I suppose he thought he had to say something, and he didn't know what else to say," she said.[2]

The National Association of Evangelicals was the first test of the neo-evangelicals' plan to unite America's conservative Protestants. The initial results were disappointing. D. Shelby Corlett attended the association's 1943 meeting in Chicago on behalf of the Church of the Nazarene. He felt uneasy about the tirades of "a few malcontents who were there with an ax to grind, a number of independent tabernacle and radio preachers with representatives of independent publishing outfits, and only a minority of the more substantial men of the evangelical world," he wrote to headquarters in Kansas City. Corlett left the meeting with cautious admiration for its cooperative spirit, but he doubted that the association was a good fit for those loyal to their own denominations. "It was a little difficult for a denominationally minded person to catch the trend of the convention, for most of those in charge were not denominational officials," he noted.[3]

The Nazarenes would not join the NAE until the 1980s. Far more evangelicals stayed out of the NAE than signed up. The Mennonite Church, one of the largest representatives of the Anabaptist tradition and conservative in theology and cultural opinion, declined the invitation. The churches that grew out of the Second Great Awakening and stripped down worship to follow only the explicit commands of the Bible—Restorationist traditions like the Independent Christian Churches and the Churches of Christ—looked upon the growing NAE bureaucracy with revulsion. The immense Southern Baptist Convention, the largest Protestant denomination in the country whose allegiance would have more than quadrupled NAE rolls, felt no compulsion to join.[4]

The NAE's founders underestimated the degree to which many evangelicals still trusted their denominational leaders and viewed a cooperative organization like the NAE as redundant, if not an outright threat to their own churches' authority. Moreover, while scholars in every tradition were struggling to navigate the troubled waters between orthodoxy and modern intellectual life, fundamentalism meant something slightly different in each church. Neo-evangelicals assumed that the battles against modernists in the early decades of the twentieth century had left all evangelicals with the same experience and collective memory. Nothing was further from the truth.

The Independent Christian Churches and the Churches of Christ—Restorationists, for short—fought over the use of musical instruments in worship and the degree of bureaucratic organization permissible for a "New Testament Church." The Nazarenes and Mennonites argued about "worldliness" and abandonment of older customs and styles of dress. Southern Baptists considered both fundamentalism and evangelicalism to be "Yankee words" (though they were sufficiently alarmed by creeping modernism to draft their first "creed," the "Baptist Faith and Message," in 1925).[5] While northern fundamentalists were worrying about biblical criticism, Southern Baptists were distracted by the battle between moderates and Landmarkers who denied the convention's authority and defended an extreme view of the autonomy and purity of each Baptist congregation—a long-lasting yet entirely intramural debate.

The more doctrinaire side of each of these debates could be labeled "fundamentalism," and often metastasized to include the broader concerns about modern thought that split the northern Baptist and Presbyterian churches that nurtured many of the neo-evangelicals. These communities shared the neo-evangelicals' core anxieties, but their leaders had their own ideas about how to translate the Bible into Christian life and worship. At the same time, the call to defend inerrancy was a distress signal that few conservative Protestants could ignore. They might reject inerrancy or redefine it, but they could not dodge the challenge to stand up and testify that the Bible was true. At the same time, the relative success of their denominations in weathering the fundamentalist–modernist wars came with a drawback. For these churches' most ambitious intellectuals, denominational institutions became gilded cages that exalted their message within their own tradition, but hindered their ability to reach evangelicals outside it, let alone to address mainstream America. They were company men, not entrepreneurs like the neo-evangelicals—whose intellectual self-employment came with its own risks.

THE OTHER EVANGELICALS

Henry Orton Wiley personified evangelical ambivalence toward inerrancy-obsessed fundamentalism. Born in 1877 in a sod house on the Nebraska prairie, Wiley moved as a child to a central California ranch, where he helped his father raise hogs and collected rattlesnake skins in his free time. One day while he worked the plow at age thirteen, a spooked horse dragged him along behind and left him with a lifelong limp.[6] Two years later his family moved to Oregon, where he graduated high school thinking he would become a pharmacist. When the drugstore business left him unsatisfied, he returned to California to study at Berkeley and the Pacific Theological Seminary (now the Pacific School of Religion). Wiley fell in with the Church of the Nazarene, a new denomination formed in 1908 by a merger of smaller churches (which themselves sprang from the Holiness movement, a nineteenth-century revival in the older Wesleyan tradition that emphasized the radical change that the Holy Spirit worked in new believers). The denomination's main founder, a one-time Methodist pastor with a passion for the urban poor named Phineas Bresee, tapped Wiley to help transform a Bible school in southern California into a respectable Nazarene college. Wiley became dean of Pasadena College (now Point Loma Nazarene University) and was appointed president at age thirty-six.

Wiley quickly became one of the Nazarenes' most important educators and public intellectuals. He enjoyed the influence of all those institutional tools of authority that Baptist and Presbyterian fundamentalists had surrendered to modernists. By the end of his career, he had served as president of two Nazarene colleges, editor of the *Herald of Holiness*, and author of the church's most important early work of systematic theology, the three-volume *Christian Theology* (1940). An energetic teacher known to pace about the classroom, waving chalk and sketching hasty diagrams on the blackboard, Wiley always dressed and comported himself like a Nebraska ranch hand.

One student attending a college event where Wiley, as president, was invited to speak, wondered why a farmer was sitting onstage.[7]

Despite appearances, Wiley had a subtle theological touch. He was as comfortable in ancient neo-Platonic philosophy and medieval scholasticism as he was in the pages of John Wesley's sermons. In seminary he developed an interest in personalism, a philosophical movement that appealed to many Christian intellectuals in Europe and North America because it emphasized the value of the human individual and the distinctiveness of personal experience as a framework for understanding reality. He was skeptical of modern man's obsession with objective, scientific knowledge. "Our danger is rationalism, which exalts the intellect to the detriment of the affections and the will," he wrote. Wiley defended the Bible's authority. He granted that if Nazarenes were careful in how they defined "inerrancy," they might use the term, but he considered himself a moderate obliged to guide the church through the narrow strait between liberal and fundamentalist errors. He "knew that if Wesleyans fell in with the Calvinistic Fundamentalists on this issue [inerrancy] we would be only hurting ourselves. For to him [Wiley], our ultimate authority is Jesus Christ, the Living and Personal Word. This is revelation in the primary sense," wrote an admiring younger scholar.[8]

Wiley reinforced the old Wesleyan idea that Christians should interpret all scripture through the lens of Christ's incarnation and resurrection, not according to the demands of modern science or the revelations of the latest biblical criticism. "The enthroned Christ becomes the great treasure house, in whom are hid all the treasures of wisdom and knowledge, and the Holy Spirit comes as a Spirit of Truth to conduct us into ever deepening channels of heavenly wisdom," he wrote in 1922. Many Wesleyans objected to fundamentalists' literalist, pseudo-scientific method of reading the Bible. Traditionally, they emphasized the Bible's "sufficiency" as a guide to salvation over its "authority" in matters of fact and granted the Holy Spirit a prominent role in guiding the believer's understanding of scripture: "The Bible is finally and essentially an instrument of revelation, not ultimate revelation itself," one Nazarene scholar has written.[9] Higher biblical criticism was not such a terrifying threat to a tradition that interpreted revelation not in terms of scripture's fixed, scientific meaning, but as an epiphany that occurred at the intersection of text, tradition, experience, and human reason. In contrast to the Princeton theologians' emphasis on an immutable set of presuppositions about what a perfect Supreme Being could and could not do, John Wesley had always been wary of any attempt to define God's nature or intentions.[10]

Yet Wiley watched firsthand as the fundamentalist spell bewitched Wesleyan Holiness churches and transformed their views of a Christian's earthly obligations. In the middle and late nineteenth century, Holiness groups combined evangelism with social work, embedding themselves in poor communities in both the country and the inner city. By the first decades of the twentieth century, however, they had embraced fundamentalist rhetoric about the modernist threat, the decline of American culture, and imminent apocalypse. Social work was no longer so important when the purity of the church was in danger. Holiness churches amplified their emphasis on personal sanctification and distanced themselves from liberal social reformers. They pushed their traditional emphasis on modesty to new extremes, railing against such worldly perils as jewelry, movie theaters, and mixed bathing in public pools. Adopting fundamentalist antagonism toward government "interference," many Nazarenes fled from public education and established their own primary and secondary schools, usually attached to church colleges.[11]

Wesleyan Holiness Christians recognized some familiar themes in fundamentalists' sermons and tracts, particularly their harangues about holy living. Reformed evangelicals, after all, had a holiness tradition of their own. The Presbyterian revivalist Charles Finney, hero of the Second Great Awakening, had emphasized the Holy Spirit's perfecting work on the soul. More recently many evangelicals outside the Wesleyan tradition had come to believe in a second blessing after conversion, when the "indwelling life of Christ" would suppress their sinful tendencies—though not completely eradicate a person's sinful nature, as most Wesleyan Holiness Christians believed—and lead them into a "Higher Life."[12] However, as Reformed fundamentalists insisted on their tradition's rationalistic understanding of biblical authority, and Baptist and Plymouth Brethren pastors preached Reformed ideas about the eternal security of the saved (Wesley taught that saved Christians may fall away from Christ), Wiley and other Wesleyan Holiness leaders tried to steer their churches away from the movement. In 1928, the Nazarene General Assembly distanced the church from mainstream fundamentalism by stressing the Wesleyan doctrines of human freedom and sanctification, in which God does not force Christian obedience.

Rather, humans actively respond and cooperate with divine grace. The amended statement of faith referred to inerrancy, but in a manner that would not satisfy fundamentalists: It declared the Bible "given by divine inspiration, inerrantly revealing the will of God concerning us in all things necessary to our salvation."[13]

Yet reversing a decades-long cultural shift was not as simple as amending a statement of faith. By the time the neo-evangelicals presented their invitation to revamp schism-mad fundamentalism, Wesleyan Holiness leaders like Wiley had an interest in their mission, whether they admitted it or not. Their churches' internal unity was at stake, and so too was the question of how their tradition should speak to the surrounding culture. Bickering over denominational statements of faith did not make for effective public theology.

If any evangelical community seemed to have the resources to sustain a coherent vision of the church and its role in the world, it was American Anabaptists.[14] Their Reformation forebears founded "a prophetic movement in the full-blown biblical sense of that word," wrote C. Norman Kraus, a Mennonite theologian. "Anabaptists were heralds of a new social order," one that called the converted to form a new covenant obedient to Christ above any secular prince, to form a living witness to the most radical implications of the gospel.[15] But the winding paths they followed as they fled persecution in the Old World—combined with the revivals and controversies of American religion and the relentless pace of change in American culture—splintered Anabaptists into rival churches, muddied their knowledge of history, and confused their sense of purpose. The Mennonite Church was no exception. Harold Bender, a contemporary of Wiley and a "neo-Anabaptist" scholar with ambitions that matched those of the neo-evangelicals, stepped forward to straighten out Mennonites' relationship with mainstream fundamentalism—and to remind his fellow believers that while they embraced the same "fundamentals," their tradition interpreted and applied those doctrines very differently.

Here again lurked the problem of the Bible's authority. Traditionally, Mennonites read the Bible for guidance on the practical details of Christian life rather than answers to abstruse theological questions, and they lacked a well-developed theology of biblical inspiration.[16] However, they emphasized a "literal" reading of key passages: Their sixteenth-century forebears alarmed other Protestants by reading scripture even more literally than the

Reformed or Lutherans did, abolishing ancient practices that the Bible did not explicitly endorse, such as infant baptism. When fundamentalists began to argue that the inerrant Bible was under attack, many Mennonites were easily convinced—though few plunged directly into the fray, because at first they perceived little sign of modernism in their own church. Harold Bender's father-in-law, theologian John Horsch, was one of a few prominent Mennonites who actively supported the mainstream fundamentalist movement, publishing *The Mennonite Church and Modernism* in 1924. Horsch and his allies flushed out "modernists" from church colleges. Between 1913 and 1951, seven Mennonite college presidents resigned over such conflicts. Goshen College in Indiana—where Bender was an undergraduate and later returned to teach—was forced to close for a year. By the 1930s, Mennonite fundamentalists had effectively banished the open teaching of modernist theology from their church.[17]

Many Mennonites feared that any trace of so-called liberalism was proof of contamination by mainstream American culture. Fundamentalism, then, appeared to be a way to beat back Americanization and preserve the heritage that their ancestors had brought from the Old World. Harold Bender shared their concern over the temptations and dangers of modernist theology. As a young man he ventured out of the Anabaptist fold for graduate work at Garrett Biblical Institute, a liberal Methodist seminary just north of Chicago, but left the school—under some pressure from Horsch, who doubted the faculty's orthodoxy—to finish his degree at Princeton Theological Seminary. There he took classes with J. Gresham Machen, who convinced him of the perils of liberalism. He later told a colleague that "I owe my decisive theological development to him. . . . He was the best teacher I ever had." Bender accepted a post teaching history at Goshen (the college administration was not sufficiently confident in his orthodoxy to permit him to teach theology and quarreled with him over the style of bonnet that his wife would have to wear). Settling into a career at the church college did not mean retreating from the world. Bender left for a term to complete a doctorate at Heidelberg, but he disarmed his conservative detractors by publishing articles in church periodicals on "Detecting Modernism" and "Biblical Tests of Orthodoxy."[18]

To Bender, the best inoculation against the modernist contagion was not a hasty embrace of "the fundamentals" as understood by other churches, but the recovery of Mennonites' unique heritage. Like the neo-evangelicals, he knew the value of intellectual institutions. At Goshen, he founded the *Mennonite Quarterly Review* and Mennonite Historical Library—the latter stocked with out-of-print books that Bender personally recovered on trips to Europe and visits to rare book shops and the attics of kind old ladies in Mennonite communities across the eastern United States and Canada.[19] He embarked on a mission to transform his church's historical consciousness and attitude toward the Bible's authority in Christian life.

In 1943, Bender delivered a presidential address before the American Society of Church History entitled "The Anabaptist Vision." Anabaptists desperately needed an apologia for their theology of nonviolence during a world war that appeared—at the time—morally unambiguous. Bender helped create the Civil Public Service system to provide conscientious objectors with a nonviolent means to contribute to the war effort, a program that changed Mennonites' relationship to patriotism and American identity. In "The Anabaptist Vision," he matched this political innovation with a paradigm shift in how Anabaptists should consider their history and doctrine, a "loyal rallying to the historical principles of Mennonitism" that he had been honing since the 1920s and was now ready to present before a mainstream academic audience.[20]

Bender dismissed the caricatures of his tradition that had arisen over the centuries, ranging from the confusion of Anabaptism with sixteenth-century mystics and fanatical anarchists to the conclusion of Marxist historians that the movement was merely a pious varnish on the rise of early modern class-consciousness. Instead, he asserted that Anabaptism carried the core principles of the Reformation—voluntary faith and Christlike discipleship—to their natural conclusions. Anabaptism represented what the visions of Luther and Calvin might have become had they not been co-opted by the secular state. The first Anabaptists provoked consternation among the Reformers precisely because their creed was not just a list of doctrines. It was a worldview with implications for daily life and the Christian's relationship to secular powers. Bender quoted the Strasbourg reformer Wolfgang Capito's bafflement at the Swiss Brethren: "I frankly confess that in most [Anabaptists] there is in evidence piety and consecration and indeed a zeal which is beyond any suspicion of insincerity. For what earthly advantage could they hope to win by enduring exile, torture, and unspeakable punishment of the flesh?"[21]

Bender argued that the Anabaptist doctrine of nonviolence and fealty to Christ alone was an ethos that applied to all spheres of life, during wartime and peace (he worried that his church's commitment to pacifism was waning: By 1943 it was clear that almost half of Mennonite draftees were entering military service).[22] This worldview was distinct from that offered by popular fundamentalism. An Anabaptist believer came to knowledge of Christ primarily through a life of discipleship, rather than proof texts from an inerrant Bible. Writing in a popular Mennonite magazine a few years later, Bender lamented the flood of apocalyptic literature and fundamentalist Sunday school lessons that found their way into Mennonite bookstores, "the omnipresent radio with its popular religious programs," the "non-Mennonite Biblical institutes and theological schools, which have been and still are training their dozens of young Mennonites." Yet he saw something different and more promising in the neo-evangelicals. Harold Ockenga was an "outstanding conservative evangelical" whose movement sought to embrace "the full orthodoxy of fundamentalism in doctrine but manifests a social consciousness and responsibility which was strangely absent from fundamentalism."[23]

Harold Bender's address came just three years after H. O. Wiley published the first volume of his magnum opus and the same year that neo-evangelicals founded the NAE. These intellectual and organizational efforts from across the evangelical spectrum had been a long time in the making, and did not coincide by chance. They signaled a shared preoccupation with the problem of intellectual authority in the modern world, piqued by the cultural and moral devastation of World War II and the challenge that fundamentalists issued to all Protestant believers. Now more than ever, that problem demanded a systematic solution.

At the same time that the neo-evangelicals were mounting their defense of the Bible and revival of conservative Protestant intellectual life, thinkers in other theological traditions were tackling many of the same challenges that concerned Carl Henry and his colleagues. In principle, the Reformed-inclined neo-evangelicals acknowledged that their endeavor might benefit from input from the whole spectrum of conservative Protestantism. Yet Wiley and Bender remained church theologians, little known outside their respective traditions. The neo-evangelicals paid almost no heed to their efforts. Instead, in the coming years they laid the groundwork for an ideology that would inflame—and help politicize—the crisis of religious authority that they so hoped to resolve. Why, and how, did this happen?

The answer lies partly where the roots of a broken intellectual culture can always be found: in defective institutions. After the founding of the NAE, the neo-evangelicals' next priority was to found a seminary, the first node in what would become a network of institutions meant to rebut the charge that traditional Protestantism was incompatible with modern reason and critical inquiry. They believed that the pillars of biblical inerrancy and the Christian worldview—the authority of the sacred text and its application to earthly life—would support a nondenominational (but orthodox) framework in which creative thinking would flourish. The neo-evangelicals were refugees from churches conquered by modernists a generation earlier, and this freed them to preach across denominational lines. Yet when it came to institution-building, a separatist hangover combined with the ideological mindset of the early Cold War to dampen any ecumenical spirit.

Scratch a neo-evangelical and underneath you would likely find a fundamentalist who still preferred the comforts of purity to the risks of free inquiry and collaboration. Their efforts did not calm evangelical anxieties over the place of the Bible in modern life: Instead, they institutionalized them. The Wesleyan Holiness churches, Mennonites, and other denominations made a similar choice. They designed their colleges and seminaries as citadels to protect the faithful, not as schools with the confidence to invite all comers and entertain any challenge.

FULLER THEOLOGICAL SEMINARY AND THE PUZZLE OF DISSENT

Charles Fuller was a radio evangelist, not an academic. But he had a keen interest in training the next generation of church servants, and if there was any individual positioned to attract students across the widest possible range of beliefs and dispositions, it was him. By the early 1940s his weekly radio show, "The Old Fashioned Revival Hour," was broadcast over three hundred stations to an estimated twenty million listeners around the world, outpacing secular radio stars like Bob Hope and Charlie McCarthy. Son of a wealthy California orange grower, Fuller was a graduate of Pomona College and the Bible Institute of Los Angeles (Biola) who had demonstrated a taste for fundamentalist separatism early in his ministry. When the pastor of his Presbyterian church grumbled about the popularity of the Bible study class that Fuller was teaching, Fuller led his students out of the church and reorganized them as his own congregation. Yet in the years since then, particularly in his role on Biola's board of directors, Fuller had seen firsthand how infighting could damage the fundamentalist movement. He filled his Revival Hour with simple assurances that "Jesus saves" and promised listeners that they had "a friend in Jesus."[24]

Fuller, Harold Ockenga, Carl Henry, Henry's college roommate Harold Lindsell, and Moody Bible Institute professor Wilbur Smith had worked together to sponsor large-scale nondenominational revival meetings even before the foundation of the NAE. When they decided to found a seminary, they did not think of themselves as separatists. Historical precedent, however, did not bode well for ecumenical tranquility. Most of the neo-evangelicals studied at colleges and seminaries still smarting from the schisms of the previous generation, and they had learned how to build a movement in the context of their mentors' battles against the modernists. Almost to a man, the founders of Fuller Theological Seminary were J. Gresham Machen's students or admirers. Yet they were determined that Fuller would not fall into fundamentalists' bad habits. They would "reform fundamentalism" by hiring a faculty that "saw Christians as having a duty to transform culture in addition to their primary duty to evangelize."[25]

The seminary, its founders hoped, would attract first-rate candidates from a range of conservative Protestant denominations. The faculty would train them in the relevance of the gospel to culture, teach them to withstand the secular-humanist onslaught, and send them back into the world as emissaries for the neo-evangelical worldview. When the faculty discovered they did not agree on the foundation of this worldview—the authority of the Bible—the conservatives knew no way of coping but to exit. Their insistence on biblical inerrancy became a loyalty oath not unlike the pledge against modernism that the Vatican demanded of Catholic university instructors, or the vow to uphold the Constitution required of many American professors during the years of Joseph McCarthy's red-baiting. Such purity tests had long roots in the history of Christian authorities' attempts to exterminate heresy, but they also suited an era when Americans feared subversion and dissent.

A few years after the seminary's founding in 1947 (thirty-nine students enrolled that fall, including Campus Crusade founder Bill Bright), signs of sedition appeared. The brief tenure of Hungarian theologian Bela Vassady, whose doubts about inerrancy and interest in dialogue with liberal Protestants led to his departure, belied the seminary's stated goal of engaging international theological debate. Émigré intellectuals had played key roles in the libertarian and Anglo-Catholic branches of the midcentury American conservative revival, but the neo-evangelicals quickly drove out one of their own.[26] Although the faculty at Fuller claimed to repudiate fundamentalist provincialism, European Protestants who lacked an instinct for navigating the aftermath of the American fundamentalist-modernist fights struggled to find a place.

A few years later, a professor named Charles Woodbridge, a conservative Presbyterian who studied with Machen (and with liberal German theologian Adolf von Harnack), denounced Fuller trustee Billy Graham's practice of cooperating with Roman Catholics and liberal Protestants in his crusades. Woodbridge resigned in 1956 and stepped up his attacks on the school.[27] In 1959 Edward Carnell, then Fuller's president and a brilliant but troubled scholar who had won accolades for his doctoral work at Harvard on apologetics (which he completed simultaneously with a doctorate in philosophy at Boston University), critiqued neo-evangelicalism's fundamentalist heritage in a book called *The Case for Orthodox Theology.* He eviscerated the legalisms and hypocrisies that he saw in modern fundamentalists, their obsession with personal holiness and the end-times that sometimes blinded them to the poor and suffering in their midst. He dismissed fundamentalism as "orthodoxy gone cultic," with no ear for theological subtlety or the lessons of history.[28] The book outraged Fuller's constituents. Carnell was forced to resign from the presidency.

In the late 1950s, a number of Fuller professors—including the founder's son, Dan Fuller—concluded that they could not abide by the seminary's statement of faith on the point of strict inerrancy. They had come to believe that while the Bible remained an "infallible" guide on matters of doctrine, worship, and Christian life, it was not accurate in every scientific and historical fact. By 1961, the atmosphere at Fuller was poisonous. Wilbur Smith, a traditionalist who firmly opposed the "liberal" faction, wrote to Harold Lindsell that he would not attend the rest of the faculty meetings scheduled for that semester: "We have had more disputes, more sharp divisions, and more accusations by one member to another, than I have ever witnessed in faculty meetings in any one academic year in the last quarter of a century." The following year, when one of Fuller's trustees resigned, board member C. D. Weyerhaeuser begged him to consider the complexity of the inerrancy debate. There was a "very real problem of arriving at a precise meaning of the word 'inerrancy,'" he wrote in December 1962. "It would be literally impossible for you or anyone else who has a fairly good knowledge of the Bible to sign our doctrinal statement without at least some degree of reservation... I—along with others—believe the statement should be carefully reviewed by our faculty (dispassionately, I hope!) in much prayer and in the Holy Spirit... the Fuller faculty and board compose the only group I know of in evangelical circles who are *honest enough* to face this matter openly."[29]

The neo-evangelicals had an authority problem. In the secular world, institutions of higher education granted faculty significant freedom to question traditional wisdom without fear of getting sacked or damaging the institution. However, Charles Fuller and his neo-evangelical colleagues viewed the seminary not, primarily, as an academic institution. They understood Fuller as an intellectual extension of the gathered church: the early Christian ideal of the free association of godly men, a congregation of spiritually regenerate "saints" who proved by their testimony that they knew Jesus and lived by the Bible's commands. Although the most conservative Fuller faculty left the seminary in disgust by 1963, leaving the school in the hands of more moderate scholars with a higher tolerance for dissent, the conservative refugees emerged as the leaders of the neo-evangelical movement. They had more prominent reputations and grander plans, and they took the side of purity. Biblical inerrancy was nonnegotiable. To them, requiring a statement of faith in inerrancy was the equivalent of a mathematics department demanding that all faculty agree that two and two is four.

THE AIM OF GODLY STUDY

The mentality of the gathered church, the priority on purity over critical thinking, had long informed most evangelicals' views of higher education and undermined their willingness to support advanced training for their ministers. Historically, most conceded that a college degree was harmless enough. Schooling beyond that point, however, meant reading arcane German theology rather than focusing on the "common-sense" meaning of the Bible. Many Christians across a variety of evangelical traditions worried that overeducation—or the wrong sort of education—weakened a pastor's faith and interfered with his ability to connect with his congregation.

Although the Southern Baptists had founded three denominational seminaries by the time of World War II, as late as the 1980s only half of Southern Baptist pastors actually possessed seminary degrees. The Nazarenes and Mennonites were at first disinclined to establish any seminary at all, preferring to invest in liberal arts colleges. The Nazarenes coordinated a system of regional colleges to prepare youth for a wide range of Christian service, and some of these colleges offered meager and underfunded graduate programs in theology. One early Nazarene college president stressed, however, that "our purpose is not primarily educational as this word is commonly used." The college's main aim, he said, was cultivating students' "holy character."[30]

Yet in the 1940s, as the neo-evangelicals were planning Fuller, both Nazarenes and Mennonites began to revisit the idea of a seminary—for reasons different from those of Carl Henry or Harold Ockenga. While many neo-evangelicals were alienated from their own denominations and found themselves "in a sort of ecclesiastical no-man's land" by the time of Fuller's founding, evangelicals in other traditions retained greater respect for their denominations' authority.[31] Their central concern was rebuilding the dikes that protected their traditions from outside corruption and kept the next generation close. "Moody [Bible Institute] has taken a number of our Brethren students during the past several years, and there has been considerable dissatisfaction over their going to Moody, because they are so often lost to the Brethren Church, because the school seeks to 'undenominationalize' them," wrote church magazine editor Paul Bauman in 1943. He preferred that the young people of his denomination—a more revivalist cousin of the Mennonites—attend the church-affiliated Grace

Theological Seminary in Winona Lake, Indiana. "The loss to the church from those who take seminary work in institutions unfavorable to the fundamental principles of our denomination is too heavy," Nazarene general superintendent R. T. Williams told his church's General Assembly in 1940. "We need to train our men in our own institutions for our own peculiar, God-given task."[32]

Harold Bender lobbied for years to convince his colleagues to establish a seminary, but among Mennonites resistance to an overeducated "hireling ministry" ran deep. In 1944, when Goshen finally separated its fledgling graduate program from the undergraduate college, at first church leaders christened the new institution a humble "Bible school" to avoid any hint of intellectual pretense. Bender, the school's first dean, waged a careful propaganda campaign to persuade skeptical Mennonites—used to selecting ministers by lot from within their congregations—that the graduate program was not a capitulation to worldly standards. He assured them that the curriculum retained a "Mennonite emphasis" on "holiness, love, and separation, which our fathers have taught and practiced from the beginning."[33]

His church—like the Nazarenes, who founded their seminary the following year—borrowed freely from other evangelical schools' curricula, but focused on teaching their own distinctive beliefs. A denominational seminary was a barrier against unwelcome outside influences, as well as a forum in which to settle internal feuds: a place to resolve communal identity and police boundaries. Yet founding a seminary was not just a rearguard action, but a bold act to accommodate mainstream culture. In the 1950s and 1960s, American higher education was rapidly growing in scale and influence. In part, these evangelicals were no different from many other Americans, succumbing to a national mania for the advanced degree.

There was another plan in the works to spark pan-evangelical conversation about how to best defend biblical authority and promote the Christian worldview. The Evangelical Theological Society, founded in 1949, emerged out of the Conferences for the Advancement of Evangelical Scholarship, a series of annual meetings that Harold Ockenga and colleagues in the Boston area hosted between 1944 and 1947. Ockenga envisioned a gathering of "evangelical scholars who would do in apologetics what the NAE was doing in ecclesiology": that is, overcome sectarian differences and recover the core of the Christian message. The ETS was an evangelical alternative to the more secular Society of Biblical Literature and kindred Roman Catholic associations. The society's first president, Calvin Theological Seminary's Clarence Bouma, stressed the organization's diversity in his first keynote address and emphasized that both those who supported the NAE and partisans of the fundamentalist American Council of Christian Churches were welcome. Common "faith in the Word of God as the source and norm of all Theology" would unite scholars of diverse church backgrounds and provide "mutual encouragement in the face of the enemy," modernist Christians who rejected the infallibility of Scripture. The ETS adopted a succinct doctrinal statement, which all members had to reaffirm each year: "The Bible alone, and the Bible in its entirety, is the Word of God written, and is therefore inerrant in the autographs."[34]

The inerrant Word remained at the center of most ETS conferences over the years. Academic quality was spotty. In the early years, particularly in the ETS's southern section, some presentations more closely resembled fundamentalist sermons than academic papers.[35] Some members, like Harold Lindsell, made it their business to smoke out anyone who blinked at the mention of inerrancy. In 1963, an article by Stanford professor and ETS member Richard Bube suggesting that the fundamentalist view of scripture went "beyond the claims of Scripture itself" caused great scandal.[36] By 1965, ETS secretary Vernon Grounds was so concerned about agitation over the society's doctrinal statement that he mailed to ETS officers a copy of a letter of resignation from "one of our active leaders." "I have decided to be honest with my convictions," said the resigning member, whose name Grounds omitted:

> For a long time I have found it spiritually unnecessary and intellectually impossible to accept the last clause of the Society's doctrinal basis as either logically following from the basic preceding statement or as the truth; and I dare say a good many other members of the Society are in the same boat ... to define inerrancy and infallibility in the sense in which many older members of ETS (and of fundamentalism in general) do, is to put the emphasis in the wrong place and for the wrong reasons.... My own long acquaintance with fundamentalism (I grew up in it and, through the Society, have heard its expression for a long time) indicates that a remark to the effect that the "inerrancy" which is

claimed for the Bible is really an inerrancy claimed for fundamentalist interpretations of it, is all too true.

I further object to the arrogant claim, often made only by implication, but still very clearly made, that only those who are in "our" camp are "evangelicals"... or that only those who hold the doctrines as Carl F. H. Henry and company holds them are truly evangelicals. Too many in the Society are glad to be so represented, I fear—and this is revolting to my Baptist soul.[37]

In their call for engagement with the wider culture, for intellectual curiosity and rigor, the cadre of ex-fundamentalists at the center of the neo-evangelical movement tapped into a real sentiment simmering among conservative Protestants. Yet for all the broadminded engagement that they encouraged in theory, their institutions waved the banner of biblical inerrancy without coming to terms with the controversy surrounding this doctrine. In the summer of 1966 Harold Ockenga, dismayed at the discord that afflicted the movement he had hoped would unify conservative Protestants, invited more than fifty evangelical scholars to a conference in Wenham, Massachusetts, to try to settle the question. The meeting adjourned after ten days without any sign of détente between those who considered the Reformed, rationalistic understanding of inerrancy anathema to Christian intellectual life, and those for whom inerrancy was a hill to die on.[38]

The curious thing was that the source of the rift between self-described inerrantists and those who rejected the term was not, in most cases, the question of whether the Bible contained apparent discrepancies. When inerrantists discussed strategy among themselves, with allies who shared their panic that this doctrine was the last levee holding back the surge of secular materialism, they often acknowledged scripture's inconsistencies, such as multiple, conflicting accounts of the same event. They freely admitted that when God inspired the biblical authors to set down his perfect revelation, he did not place them in a divine crow's nest peering over space and time. He left them to write within the boundaries of their mortal perspective.[39] However, when inerrantists granted these problems in scripture, they did so to protect the notion of inerrancy, not to refute it. They asserted that simply because, in our finite human judgment, the evangelists seem to disagree about how many times the cock crowed before Peter denied Jesus, there is no reason to conclude that the first chapter of Genesis is all metaphor, that the Marys did not find the tomb empty—or, more fundamentally, that *scriptura* could truly stand *sola*, that the plain meaning of God's word somehow depended on human authorship or interpretation.

Motive made all the difference. Informed biblical criticism was not the problem. The atheistic presuppositions that lurked beneath it were the real enemy. Conservatives permitted a great deal of slippage in the name of inerrancy as long as these qualifications were offered in the spirit of refuting "modernist" presuppositions and reversing the decline of biblical authority over human thought and life. The battle over inerrancy was a proxy war for something far bigger. The inerrant Bible was a symbol burdened with the centuries-old tangle of faith and reason, and it was beginning to crack under the weight.

Neo-evangelicals were flush with potential allies in their efforts to return the Bible to the center of modern life: thoughtful spokesmen from alternative Protestant traditions who defended the Bible in ways that did not preclude embracing the latest scientific and historical revelations. Yet this insistence on inerrancy often troubled intellectuals outside the neo-evangelical corner of the Reformed tradition, even as rationalistic strains of fundamentalism infected Wesleyan Holiness and Anabaptist churches. The segregated character of evangelical intellectual culture—in which academic institutions served as bulwarks manned by pure and obedient faithful, rather than as open scholarly communities—further stymied collaboration. At the same time, Billy Graham and his more scholarly colleagues commanded attention by declaring themselves the spokesmen for orthodoxy.[40] Neo-evangelicalism became a fun-house mirror in which other Christians were forced to see their own distinctive features in exaggerated form.

When the neo-evangelicals launched their official mouthpiece, a fortnightly magazine called *Christianity Today*, they entered a vast arena of religious media competing for evangelicals' attention, not to mention an array of secular and Catholic magazines offering American readers their own appraisals of midcentury ideas and culture. The neo-evangelicals behind *Christianity Today* did not propose to modernize old-time religion. On the contrary, they were proud defenders of fundamentalism—although they qualified the term. But what about those unreconstructed fundamentalists, the fire-tongued preachers who dismissed the NAE as a nest of idolaters and called on true Christians to unyoke themselves, to separate from the world and spotlessly serve the Lord? If the neo-evangelicals hoped to present themselves as public theologians fit to speak to mainstream America, *Christianity Today* would have to survive a collision with its own past.

Chapter 3

Fundamentalist Demons

L. NELSON BELL, BILLY GRAHAM'S FATHER-IN-LAW, WAS A PRESBYTERIAN medical missionary who spent most of his career as a surgeon in China. The outbreak of war with Japan made missionary work more difficult, but the Bells persisted until finally returning to the United States in the spring of 1941. They settled near Asheville, North Carolina, where Bell continued to practice medicine and grew deeply involved in the doctrinal battles that had overtaken his denomination, the Presbyterian Church in the United States. J. Gresham Machen's indictment of modern Protestantism, *Christianity and Liberalism*, left him stricken. He vowed to safeguard his own church against encroaching liberalism and founded the *Southern Presbyterian Journal* to fortify ministers with orthodox theology. In 1954, Bell began considering how he might start a magazine that could do for "the whole nation what the *Southern Presbyterian Journal* now provided one denomination: a clear, biblical, scholarly voice to combat the dominant theological liberalism, in seminaries and church leadership."[1]

That Christmas, while Bell was chatting with his son-in-law at his home in North Carolina, Billy Graham announced that he too felt the need for a conservative counterpart to the liberal *Christian Century*, "something that will be evangelical, theologically oriented, and will commend itself to the Protestant ministers of America."[2] The idea had struck him months earlier, in the wee hours of the morning. Sleepless with excitement, he drafted a budget and editorial scheme. He and Bell would always insist that they thought of the same title independently—Bell remembered it as the name of a defunct Presbyterian periodical mailed to him when he served in China.

In early 1955, Bell approached J. Howard Pew, the Sun Oil magnate and a devout Presbyterian, to discuss funding. His timing could not have been better. Pew had no history in fundamentalist separatism, but a frustrating term as chairman of the laymen's committee of the National Council of Churches had left him pessimistic about the direction of the Protestant mainline. The previous fall, Pew's committee had adopted a resolution chastising the NCC for "sitting in judgment on current secular affairs" and involving itself "in economic or political controversy having no moral or ethical content, promoting division where unity of purpose should obtain."[3] The resolution was disingenuous: Pew and his allies seemed only to object to clergy who commented on politics when that commentary veered left of their own conservative views.

The leaders of the NCC ignored the resolution. Soon Pew would conclude that "a wide chasm existed between the thinking of the laity and clergy and the executives of the denominational bodies which comprise the national council," he told reporters. The liberal clergy in charge of the NCC failed to take up arms in the ongoing battle for civilization. In their mushy-minded denunciation of Senator McCarthy's anticommunist campaign and America's growing nuclear arsenal, they "might influence the American people to believe that communism is nothing more than a personal economic or political belief and that it is a gross invasion of personal privacy for a congressional witness to be questioned as to whether he is or ever has been a member of the Communist party."[4] When Billy Graham and Nelson Bell proposed a magazine that would offer an intelligent alternative to the liberal Protestant message, Pew was eager to help. Bell closed his surgical practice to offer his full-time services as an editor of *Christianity Today*.

CT's main funder was preoccupied far less with the esoteric arguments of theologians than he was with the ideological battleground of the Cold War. Pew supported the neo-evangelical effort to revive fundamentalism's intellectual reputation and evangelize the world because he was convinced that their mission would aid the fight against communism at home and abroad. The neo-evangelicals already had a strong interest in translating religious doctrine into a worldview with cultural and political implications, but Pew's support turned that project into a pressing financial obligation. In the context of the early Cold War, theology was inseparable from politics. Only a few years earlier, President Eisenhower had approved American fundamentalists' plan to send planes over the Iron Curtain to release thousands of balloons carrying Russian-language religious pamphlets and Bible passages.[5]

CT would come to represent the neo-evangelical brand, to serve as the tribune of these self-appointed standard-bearers of the faith. It could not displace older, established religious media, the church-run magazines and newspapers on which denominational leaders relied to guide their flocks and watch over the porous boundaries between their own traditions and the wider Christian world. The editors did not want to do so: They considered the magazine's peers not the traditional church papers, but the ecumenical *Christian Century* and secular intellectual magazines like the *New Republic* and *Commentary*. The magazine made a bold play for mainstream attention and influence in politics as well as theology. However, the neo-evangelicals' effort to paper over anxieties about faith and reason with a rehashed defense of inerrancy and a rerun of old fundamentalist debates could not match the efforts of conservative journalists and activists outside evangelicalism who were rapidly building a national movement.

The editors at *CT* lacked their knack for infiltrating hubs of political power, building coalitions, and mobilizing the grassroots. More fundamentally, they lacked the political instinct for subjugating means to ends. Quarrels over theology, history, and the meaning of "the fundamentals" plagued *CT* before the magazine could grow beyond the bounds of the evangelical subculture. Yet their efforts were not in vain. The neo-evangelicals were sculpting a crude but compelling public theology, a set of claims about the past, assumptions about the present, and slogans aimed at the future. This theology was not original or even totally coherent. It was sewn together from scraps of old fundamentalist impulses and Cold War conservatism. Yet its lack of sophistication or complexity would eventually prove a great boon—when, decades later, it passed into the hands of believers who did know how to kindle a movement.

"HIGHBROW FUNDAMENTALISM"

In late 1955, desperately working to recruit contributors to *Christianity Today*, Nelson Bell told one candidate that the editors intended to send the magazine free to every Protestant minister in America, Canada, and

Great Britain for the first year: a total of nearly 200,000 readers at minimum, expanded in the magazine's second year to include Unitarians and Universalists. They mailed "outstanding excerpts" of each issue to 600 secular newspapers, and one copy to every columnist in Washington, DC, where *CT* was headquartered in order to be close to the pulse of national politics. The editors reviewed readers' feedback at each board meeting, responded to nearly all letters, and maintained a scrapbook of references to *CT* in the secular press. Carl Henry, *CT*'s first editor-in-chief (though the masthead, much to his irritation, called him merely "Editor"), did not hide his grand vision under a bushel. He had long believed that serving Christ required both savvy marketing and sophisticated thinking—he had followed his ThD thesis on church publicity with a PhD in theology at Boston University—and the magazine provided the perfect platform for both. He declared *CT* to be the culmination of the neo-evangelical effort to reinvent the reputation of orthodox Protestantism. In May 1957, he tried to alert his colleagues to the opportunity at hand:

> In a sense, all that has gone before is a discreet preliminary operation aimed to secure for the magazine the theological respect and intellectual dignity necessary for effective conversation with liberal and Neo-orthodox ministers...our contributing editors indicated that now is the time to become theologically and ecclesiastically more aggressive.[6]

The editors planned to rehabilitate conservative Protestantism's reputation in the eyes of the American establishment and intellectual elite. Contributing editors included Billy Graham and Edward L. R. Elson, Eisenhower's pastor. An ad campaign in the pages of *U.S. News & World Report* assured leaders in business and politics that Christian faith was crucial to the democratic, capitalist way of life: "It was never intended that God be ignored from the business scene, any more than he can be excluded with impunity in world affairs.... Necessary as business and trade journals are, a business leader also needs the help and insight he can receive from *CHRISTIANITY TODAY*, the magazine with a 'world view' approach to today's problems and pressures."[7] The ad decried the false notions of "peace" advocated by the Soviets and lamented the socialist specter of strong labor unions at home. These were not just political perils but spiritual dangers, signs of a civilization drifting from its Christian moorings.

The editors aspired to win readers outside the United States as well. Henry wanted a voice in the theological debates under way in Europe. In one report to the board, he argued that the dominance of neo-orthodox theologians Karl Barth and Emil Brunner had subsided. The liberal theology of Rudolf Bultmann, who was determined to "demythologize" the Bible and reinterpret its supernaturalism in existential terms, was on the ascent. This moment of instability opened the way for CT to enter the fray. Henry recommended that the magazine open bureaus in London and Geneva and publish a German edition (Henry's German roots probably sharpened his desire to enter intellectual debates there). "Such a transition time in theological leadership takes place only once in a generation, and it creates a strategic moment for us," he wrote. "We have a golden opportunity to step into the situation influentially on the evangelical side."[8]

Implicitly, Henry acknowledged that the debates in the halls of Fuller and at Evangelical Theological Society conferences made little impression beyond evangelical circles. He was the most ambitious of the CT staff and saw himself as a public intellectual whose reputation depended on the magazine's reception among Protestant elites. He nursed for years the slightest wounds to his ego. His colleagues grumbled about his tendency to leave the office on international speaking tours for weeks and months at a time and put his own aspirations before the magazine's best interest. His enthusiasm for international bureaus led to an office in London, and for a time CT had a "beachhead office" in Toronto.[9] CT recruited scholarly contributors to engage prominent nonevangelical theologians, but avoided academic jargon in order to appeal to a range of readers—particularly ministers who might find a kernel to smarten up their Sunday sermons.

By the most basic measure, Henry and his colleagues succeeded: People read the magazine. Six years after its founding, 140,657 pastors received the magazine free; only 38,208 paid for it. That number seems small when compared to the circulation of popular magazines like Time, which claimed 2,450,000 readers in 1960. Yet alongside peer publications CT was doing well, with figures topping those of its venerable mainline analog, Christian Century, whose circulation hovered at 37,500, and besting National Review (30,000 in 1960, although NR's numbers were climbing). An independent poll in 1958 determined that CT was "the most widely and most completely and most regularly read Protestant magazine," Henry bragged in his autobiography.[10]

The magazine attracted notice beyond conservative Protestant circles. Despite the myth that mainstream journalists only "discovered" evangelicalism with the rise of Jimmy Carter, the editors at *Time* had an abiding interest in evangelicals throughout the 1960s. They called *CT* "a magazine of evangelical Christianity that tries to make traditional Protestant theology clear and interesting—and nearly always succeeds…a kind of literate, highbrow fundamentalism." (*CT*'s editors must have blushed. From the secular media's perspective, they were the first "highbrow fundamentalists" since J. Gresham Machen.) Throughout the 1960s and 1970s, the magazine's combination of self-promotion and accessible erudition persuaded secular journalists to pay a disproportionate amount of attention to *Christianity Today*. They dubbed it "the leading evangelical periodical" and the "leading evangelical, conservative Protestant magazine" despite the fact that other evangelical magazines boasted higher circulation figures. The nondenominational *Christian Herald*, edited by Daniel Poling, a "gentle fundamentalist" and Norman Vincent Peale's predecessor at New York's Marble Collegiate Church, claimed a circulation of 450,000 in 1964—yet the *Herald*, like other evangelical magazines, "deferred to the authority" of Henry and his colleagues and often reprinted *CT*'s articles, one historian has noted.[11]

Conservative intellectuals outside evangelicalism often disdained Billy Graham as a shallow huckster, but the editors at *National Review* watched the neo-evangelicals with modest interest. The magazine reviewed Carl Henry's edited collection *Basic Christian Doctrines*, noting that the essays were "written in lucid language by eminent evangelical theologians." The reviewer, Bruce Lockerbie—a teacher at the evangelical Stony Brook School on Long Island—described *Christianity Today* respectfully as a "conservative fortnightly with world-wide circulation," and praised Henry's volume for providing

> non-evangelicals the opportunity to read for themselves a statement on conservative evangelical theology. Far from finding the obscurantism they might have been prepared to expect, readers not previously acquainted with evangelical Christianity will find evidence of both faith and reason at work.…*Basic Christian Doctrines* disproves the theory that in Protestant theology intellectualism can only be synonymous with Liberalism.[12]

All the same, nonevangelical conservatives considered *CT*'s intellectual seriousness an exception in evangelical culture, rather than the rule: a handy summary of the "evangelical perspective" rather than required reading on events of the day. Conservative Protestants, for their part, knew that they had allies among secular conservatives and Catholics in the fight against communism. (Even fundamentalist Carl McIntire swallowed his separatist bile long enough to cooperate with Catholics in his anticommunist rallies, although he condemned such cooperation in evangelistic work). However, the 1950s and early 1960s saw little cross-pollination between neo-evangelical intellectuals and their secular and Catholic peers. While Catholic magazines such as *Commonweal* and the Jesuit publication *America* kept overt evangelism to a minimum and appealed to sources of authority outside their own church, *CT* rooted all claims in an exclusively evangelical understanding of the Bible.[13] The magazine failed to sustain outside interest or influence because the editors' notion of intellectual authority was so narrow.

Moreover, the neo-evangelicals (like most Protestants at this time) remained fiercely anti-Catholic. L. Nelson Bell attracted the eye of Internal Revenue Service investigators when the tax-exempt *Presbyterian Journal* of Weaverville, North Carolina, sold 200,000 copies of his anti-Kennedy tract in the run-up to the 1960 election. *CT*'s editors clashed often with their funder J. Howard Pew, who valued the defense of free markets and the rollback of "socialist" government interference over theological debate with Rome. In the magazine's early years, when the editors were convinced that Catholics were conspiring to block the approval of *Christianity Today*'s tax exemption, Pew dismissed their suspicions—and even offered to obtain the Vatican's endorsement of their publication (the editors declined).[14]

CT's efforts to win the attention of those readers that Henry valued most—prominent liberal Protestant theologians—were largely unsuccessful. The neo-orthodox scholars were polite. When the editors solicited an essay from Emil Brunner on the prospect of admitting China into the United Nations, he complied, and Karl Barth's publisher allowed *CT* to print the occasional excerpt from his books.[15] But there is no indication that these men seriously engaged *CT*'s critiques of their work. Liberal pastors greeted their complimentary subscriptions with bafflement or suspicion. "The free flow of subscriptions to 'Christianity Today' continues to surprise my colleagues. . . . Many of my brethren are wondering where all this money is coming from," one liberal pastor wrote the editors. "It seems a sheer waste when I think of those who throw their copies in the waste basket without reading. I choose to read mine because I continue to learn about your devious ways of attack on fellow Christians."[16]

THE POSTWAR CONSERVATIVE REVIVAL

In these years, conservatives of all stripes faced disdain from liberals, many of whom dismissed conservatism—whether secular, Jewish, Catholic, or Protestant—as a psychological abnormality, a state of intellectual arrested development at odds with authentic American ideals. Richard Hofstadter wrote that modern conservatives operated on fantasy and ignorance rather than fact, much like the obsessive anti-Masonic movement of the eighteenth century, or the anti-Catholics who suspected a Jesuit plot around every corner. Along with Louis Hartz, Daniel Boorstin, and others, Hofstadter was one of the era's "consensus historians," nicknamed for their conviction that Americans had always agreed, more or less, on the principles of Enlightenment rationalism and Lockean liberalism, and dissenters from this "consensus" were doomed to alienation and political failure. A cottage industry of books critiqued conservatism from this vantage point, including collaborative volumes *The Authoritarian Personality* (1950) and *The New American Right* (1955), in which the era's leading liberal social critics probed conservatives' "rabble-rousing" and "status resentment" with the condescending interest of psychoanalysts studying a difficult patient.[17]

Nonevangelical conservatives felt just as embattled as the editors at *Christianity Today*. The editors of the *National Review* founded their magazine one year earlier out of a similar desire to rally their cause in a hostile marketplace and overcome liberals' caricatures of the "Neanderthal Right," as William F. Buckley, Jr., put it. He had his work cut out for him. Journalists smirked at the "hundred-odd, letter-writing, right-wing groups that have sprung up since the heyday of the late Joseph R. McCarthy," ranging from the fluoridation-fearing, Earl Warren–hating John Birch Society and grumbling military veterans of Defenders of the American Constitution to the antitax Foundation for Economic Education and even a neofascist group called the National Renaissance Party, "whose current heroes are Castro, Hitler, and Nasser.... How effective have these groups been? Not very."[18]

Midcentury American conservatism featured—on a grander, more tumultuous scale—the same insecurity and discord that the neo-evangelicals perceived in their conservative Protestant world. Its various factions formed a dysfunctional family, clamoring with clashing beliefs and pet obsessions, whose members spent as much time squabbling among themselves as they did lobbying for right-to-work laws or denouncing progressive rulings by the Supreme Court. They felt both marginalized in the corridors of power and exhilarated by their increasingly well-funded drive to take back America (J. Howard Pew's largesse was not limited to *CT*: In earlier decades he backed the anti–New Deal Liberty League, the libertarian journal *Human Events*, and the Foundation for Economic Education; later he offered discreet support to the Birchers and was the "chief financial backer" of the libertarian Christian Freedom Foundation).[19]

Buckley, however, was a master coalition builder. He managed to keep secular libertarians and Catholic traditionalists on the same masthead and maintain a healthy distance from the John Birch Society and other radioactive characters in the movement. This uneasy alliance was the key to his ability to lead an intellectual resurgence that eventually penetrated Washington. Like the neo-evangelicals, Buckley was also interested in higher education. In 1953 he collaborated with the Jewish intellectual Frank Chodorov to found the Intercollegiate Society of Individualists (now the Intercollegiate Studies Institute), a libertarian organization that sprouted chapters on many college campuses. In 1960 he gathered ninety students in his Connecticut home to found Young Americans for Freedom, another student activist group organized to "affirm certain eternal truths" "in this time of moral and political crises."[20]

The following year, one journalist conducted a survey of the shifting climate on college campuses and gave Buckley's organizations the lion's share of the credit for the burgeoning "revolt not only against socialist welfare statism in government, but also against indoctrination by leftist professors.... The conservative student revolt is a campus phenomenon from Stanford and Berkeley on the West coast to the Ivy League, from the University of Washington to the University of Miami." *The Conscience of a Conservative*, Senator Barry Goldwater's libertarian cri de coeur (ghostwritten by Buckley's close friend L. Brent Bozell), was a best seller in many campus bookstores. Membership in conservative political societies and debating clubs was mushrooming, and polls at several Big Ten universities and numerous liberal arts colleges revealed that startling numbers had voted for Richard Nixon in 1960.[21]

Between Buckley's coalition of conservative writers and his vanguard of student followers, he was poised to channel the anxieties of the early Cold War—particularly the dread of godless communism and the rumblings of social change, abetted by Washington and the courts—"to generate a *Weltanschauung* which could galvanize the intellectual, creative, and moral energies of students who had been indoctrinated over thirty years by their teachers to believe that conservatism was merely a highbrow word for the profit system" and to forge a coherent movement from "distinct but complimentary, even symbiotic positions" ranging from Catholic traditionalism to classical libertarianism. Armed with not just a list of doctrines but a fully developed conservative "worldview"—even if, in the interest of pleasing all factions, this worldview was not entirely coherent—Buckley and his allies were ready to prove that conservatism was a philosophy based on "transcendent values," not an array of crabby reflexes at odds with the American character.[22]

Sneering critics at home and an enemy of cosmic proportions lurking abroad encouraged American conservatives to build coalitions. But for evangelicals, that ecumenical spirit had limits. The editors at *Christianity Today* were talking of *Weltanschauungen* before their peers at the *National Review*. However, their world-and-life view emerged from the distinctive stream of Reformed theology that watered Westminster Theological Seminary, and despite their ambitions to draw readers and contributors from across the Protestant spectrum, they had no intention of burying their own theological preferences. "I agree with you that, inasfar as possible, we must follow a strictly Calvinistic policy," Nelson Bell wrote to Gordon Clark, who was then teaching philosophy at Butler University. "However, this must be subordinated to some extent in the hope of reaching as many Methodists and Lutherans as possible." During periods of turnover Bell worked to preserve the "Reformed or Presbyterian" character of the editorial board. The magazine published articles by non-Reformed contributors and tried to maintain a neutral position on sensitive disputes between churches, but the editors were not afraid to express their disapproval if an author betrayed an anti-Calvinist bias. In a letter to *CT* contributor Timothy Smith critiquing his new book on the history of revivalism, Henry chastised the Nazarene scholar for "spank[ing] the Calvinists whenever there is an opportunity."[23]

Some evangelical writers were put off by the editors' connections to Reformed fundamentalism.[24] Even if secular journalists often accepted *CT*'s self-presentation at face value, journalists and scholars more attuned to divisions within conservative Protestantism suspected that the neo-evangelicals were simply fundamentalists' more polite and articulate cousins. Despite Carl Henry's 1947 manifesto decrying fundamentalists' neglect of social justice, *The Uneasy Conscience of Modern Fundamentalism*, he and the other editors toed the conservative line on every significant political and theological issue from foreign policy and civil rights to evolution and the ecumenical movement. Critics suspected that Pew's conservative economic philosophy steered *CT*'s editorial policy. Indeed, the editors depended on Pew, who (along with shoe manufacturing mogul Maxey Jarman) covered an annual deficit that ran to $225,000 in 1962. However, they sometimes chafed at Pew's demands, and by the late 1960s they had subtly drifted from him in their vision for the magazine. Henry, while no liberal, viewed Pew's opposition to social activism as outdated and morally inadequate (Pew, for his part, called Henry a "socialist"). Henry was so frustrated with Pew's interference, exhausted by the workload, and at odds with his colleagues that he resigned (he wrote in his autobiography that the executive committee effectively fired him) in late 1968. Pew made his continuing support contingent on the promise that Henry's successor, Harold Lindsell, would continue condemning "the ecumenical church's political involvement." Henry assured Lindsell that he would remain editor-at-large "long enough to be assured that the magazine doesn't abandon persuasion for polemics and propaganda."[25]

These noisy internal quarrels concealed one remarkable silence: the dearth of conversation with conservatives outside the neo-evangelical bubble. In the magazine's early years, when nearly every issue featured essays lambasting communism, urging a retrenchment of conservative Christian values, and otherwise echoing many themes favored by William F. Buckley and other writers in the rash of new conservative journals, the editors of *Christianity Today* gave little sign that they considered themselves comrades in arms with conservative Catholics, Jews, and repentant ex-socialists. Instead, a different movement continued to occupy their attention: fundamentalism.

A CONTEST FOR HISTORY'S BLESSING

"Let me assure you that this is not a 'Fundamentalist' magazine," wrote *CT* associate editor J. Marcellus Kik to a potential contributor shortly before the magazine's maiden issue in 1956. "We do believe in the plenary inspiration of the Scriptures, and will do our best to show that this is Scriptural doctrine....We feel that there is a drift to the right, theologically and we certainly would like to give it some guidance, lest it become 'fundamentalist' in character." In most of their publications and correspondence, the *CT* editors preferred to call themselves "evangelical," a label untainted by the ghost of the Scopes trial and the ugly church schisms in the early part of the century. When Barth published his American lectures as *Evangelical Theology* in 1962, Carl Henry wrote that *CT* was "all the more responsible in the months ahead for sharply defining the content and meaning of the term 'evangelical.'"[26]

The editors had come not to bury fundamentalism, but to rehabilitate it. Bell was not afraid to use the word in order to win over the pastor of a Bible Baptist Church in Kansas: "Let me assure you that CHRISTIANITY TODAY assumes the complete doctrinal position of fundamentalism," he wrote.

> Our deviation from that position has to do with the *method* of preaching the Gospel. With all our hearts we believe in separation from the world and from apostacy [sic]. However, men who truly believe Jesus Christ to be the Son of God and their Savior from sin are not apostates, although they may be weak in the faith or lacking in knowledge of the Word.[27]

Bell, a worldly-wise missionary and veteran of decades of Presbyterian squabbling, was at heart a pragmatist who believed that his son-in-law's cooperation with liberals, modernists, and Catholics was a reasonable price to pay for packing more warm bodies into the crusade venue each night.

A quarter-century of missions in China had taught him the value of earning the trust of all members of a local community before beginning evangelistic work. However, separatists' accusations that Graham and *CT* departed from "old-time orthodoxy" got his goat. "I am a thoroughgoing evangelical and fundamentalist, *in the old sense of the word*, but I am sick and tired of the type of 'fundamentalism' which is characterized by divisiveness and a spirit far removed from that of Christianity," Bell wrote in a letter to the *Greenville News*, the hometown paper of one of the neo-evangelicals' fiercest critics, Bob Jones.[28]

A circuit preacher from the age of fifteen, with eyes like wet stones and a crowd-carrying voice that made him one of the most famous evangelists in the country, Jones had left full-time evangelism in 1927 to found Bob Jones College with eighty-five students (the school became a university when it moved to Greenville, South Carolina, in 1947, boasting an enrollment of nearly 2,500). "Dr. Bob"—an honorary title that simultaneously aped and mocked the academy—resented the neo-evangelicals' airs of erudition but shared their fear of civilization's collapse.[29]

He believed that cooperating with nonevangelicals, as Billy Graham did, would hasten the demise of the Christian West rather than forestall it. "If I were not to take a position against the [ecumenical] sponsorship Billy Graham has in New York, I would be repudiating the position I have always held," Jones wrote to Bell in 1957. "It is the position primarily held by [evangelists Billy] Sunday, [Reuben] Torrey, [Morris] Chapman, and I knew all of them and worked with all of them. I know how they stood."[30]

Jones brought his vision of fundamentalist separatism to life on the campus of his university. When Nelson Bell mailed a letter defending Billy Graham to every BJU student address he could obtain, he provoked a flood of supportive—and sometimes fearful—replies. A few wrote to describe their interrogation and verbal abuse by Dr. Bob before he expelled them from the school for supporting Billy Graham. His minions opened their mail to monitor their correspondence. They feared that if they tried to raise questions with their teachers in private, their comments would be recorded and used against them. "Two parents from a distance came by to see me after visiting the University and told me that the spying, fear, repression, and mental and spiritual regimentation of their children was something they thought existed only in Soviet Russia," Bell wrote to a BJU trustee.[31]

One distressed student sent Bell a copy of a plea he had mailed to his class-mates at the height of the controversy:

> We are being brainwashed and you know it. We cannot think our own thoughts or make our own decisions. We cannot even pray for a Christian leader like Billy Graham whom God is using so much. . . . I do not mind being laughed at for Christ's sake but this school is becoming a laughing stock and an object of pity on the part of other Christians who know and serve the Lord truly from their hearts and who know what is going on here now. I do not dare sign this letter. As it is there will be an inquisition and the usual Gestapo tactics. "Gripers" and "Disgruntels" [*sic*] will be called on the carpet and some of us fired. God help us.[32]

This is not to say that Bob Jones did not have his own blueprint for cultural renewal. Totalitarians—or would-be totalitarians—always do. When he founded his college, Jones envisioned a great liberal arts institution that would overturn the popular stereotype of fundamentalists as yokels with "greasy noses, dirty fingernails, baggy pants and who never shined their shoes."[33] His mother-in-law, Estelle Stollenwerck, was the matriarch of a prominent Alabama family who tutored BJU students in high culture and etiquette and helped found the BJU Opera Association. Bob Jones, Jr., the evangelist's son, was a fanatic for Shakespeare and Renaissance art. He founded a successful undergraduate Shakespeare company "and assigns himself a top role in almost every play the school puts on," reported *The Nation*. "As a dying Lear, he can mutter a creditable 'Pray you, undo this button.'"[34] Jones, Jr., toured Europe each summer with an allowance from the Board of Trustees to purchase fine works by Renaissance and Baroque masters for the university's growing collection. Fine art proved compatible with BJU's fundamentalism—as long as it remained a foreign language one had to master, rather than a stimulus for free thought. In the minds of the Joneses, art, like history, was a narrative to be preserved, not reinterpreted; a source of authority, not provocation.

Bell, too, invoked the blessings of Dwight Moody, Billy Sunday, and other great revivalists of previous generations. He insisted in letters to Jones and others that Graham's "policy with reference to cooperation and support of his meetings is identical with the policy followed by" the fundamentalist preachers of yore.[35] Bell was largely correct. These evangelists placed far more emphasis on saving souls than enforcing theological boundaries. Charles Finney warned against a "sectarian spirit" and the "janglings and strife of words" that might interfere with saving the lost, and chastised clergy who "have exalted their peculiar views in their own estimation, into fundamental doctrines, and contend for them with as much pertinacity and vehemence as if all must be reprobates who do not embrace them." Billy Sunday welcomed the support of Catholics at his revivals.[36] However, the scale and meticulous organization of Billy Graham's crusades were unprecedented, and he called on the local pastors who sponsored him to give more than their mere assent. Some served on the crusade's executive committee and lent their churches' resources and parishioners to meet Graham's staffing and organizational needs, close cooperation that outraged fundamentalists.

The neo-evangelicals' pragmatic and peace-making approach to revival—their conviction that the "come-outism" of early fundamentalist days had done the cause of the gospel more harm than good—was not a conversion to historical relativism. Bob Jones understood history as the unfolding of divine will and biblical prophecy, God's fixed rules for human life "yesterday, today, and forever." So, more or less, did Nelson Bell. Like traditional fundamentalists, the editors at *CT* saw their own era as the decaying image of a purer and more faithful past. In a long lead article entitled "Who Are the Evangelicals?," Harold Lindsell outlined a quintessentially fundamentalist account of church history, one that, as historian Joel Carpenter has written, "assumed that primitive Christianity had already been restored at the Reformation and revived several times since then." Lindsell declared that "evangelical Christianity has manifested the power and glory of biblical religion in a succession of great men who have followed in the train of the Apostles and the Reformers: Rutherford, Wesley, Whitefield, Edwards, Spurgeon, Moody, Chapman, Torrey, and in our day Graham, to name but a few." He went on to describe elements of that narrative that the fundamentalist movement had ignored, such as the social concern of nineteenth-century evangelicals and the international, ecumenical orientation of groups like the World Evangelical Fellowship, but Reformed or nondenominational evangelists remained his main characters.[37]

Lindsell's essay, published several years after the storm of mutual denunciation between *CT* and Bob Jones had blown over, underscored what was at stake in the neo-evangelicals' clash with separatist fundamentalists: their claim to speak and write with not only the authority of the Bible behind them, but with the gravitas of a historical tradition, a litany of saints, a precedent for reconciling theological purity with cultural relevance. In the 1950s, many conservative intellectuals were in the business of historical rediscovery, reconstructing an intellectual genealogy to support their critique of liberal theories of human progress and individual autonomy. Against modern secular liberalism, they asserted the sacralized and sin-stained worldview of medieval Christendom, the natural law of the ancient Greeks, the civic decrees of Roman philosophers.

The editors at *CT* pondered much of the same history in these years, filling the magazine with reflections on the course of Western civilization and debating among themselves whether "the middle ages compares favorably in respect to culture" to modern times. Sometimes J. Howard Pew weighed in. "For at least 2500 years, many great minds throughout the world have been pointing out that Divine Law, Moral Law, commonly referred to as Natural Law, must be basic to man-made law, if dictators are to be prevented from destroying the freedom of the people....I have had prepared for me a digest on Natural Law, citing the greatest authorities down through the ages, and am enclosing you a copy of it because I thought there was in this material meat for several articles," he wrote to Bell in 1957.[38]

Yet the commitment to biblical inerrancy had warped neo-evangelicals' understanding of the past. Although no godly revivalist's teachings stood on par with scripture, the basic principle of inerrancy—that historical circumstance does not influence human authorship or interpretation, when that human writes or thinks by God's will—seeped into the way they interpreted history outside the Bible as well. They were less interested in understanding ancient thinkers in their own historical context than in linking themselves to a succession of proto-fundamentalist torchbearers, Christians who—even in the "Dark Ages," under Rome's thrall—"believed the Bible" as the neo-evangelicals themselves thought scripture should be read. Their ahistorical view of scripture, their overriding desire to defend their doctrine of inerrancy as ancient, immutable, and God-given, made sensitive scholarship impossible. In the hands of *CT*'s editors history

became a legal brief for inerrancy, a purity test for the present. Their attitude was not so different from that of Bob Jones, who bragged to Bell
about his own historical fastidiousness: For thirty years he had kept a
carbon copy of every letter he wrote, a trove of archival righteousness to
thwart the gripers.[39]

THE DOOMED SCHEME FOR CRUSADE UNIVERSITY

Even as the neo-evangelicals proclaimed their break from Jones-style separatism, they could not escape their inclination to favor sterile certainty over
the hazards of new ideas and allies. This had predictable consequences
for their efforts in higher education, and not only in the neo-evangelical
petri dish of Fuller Theological Seminary. Whereas Buckley and his allies
founded student organizations to plant cells of young conservatives on
secular university campuses in order to subvert the liberal regime—one
historian notes that they deliberately mimicked old communist tactics of
infiltration and sabotage—the neo-evangelicals cordoned off their most
ambitious intellectual endeavors. Evangelistic organizations like Campus
Crusade and InterVarsity Christian Fellowship had great success among
college students, but these groups went out of their way to keep theological and intellectual debate to a minimum in favor of emphasizing the
born-again experience.[40]

A few years after *Christianity Today*'s founding, Billy Graham, Carl Henry,
Harold Ockenga, and several other neo-evangelicals became entranced by
the idea of founding a Christian university near New York, tentatively called
Crusade University. Yet negotiations broke apart over the abiding question of
separatism. Could a world-class university function within the confines of a
traditional evangelical code of conduct? If not, would the neo-evangelicals'
constituency support a school that failed to regulate student speech and
behavior? Given their criticism of separatists like Bob Jones, would founding a university exclusively for evangelical Christians only "perpetuate the
philosophy of false separation?"[41] The neo-evangelicals were torn between
their envy of the cultural esteem and achievement associated with modern
universities, and their loyalty to the medieval model of preserving and trans-
mitting fixed knowledge to obedient pupils.

Crusade University would have been the first evangelical research university, an omnibus institution with undergraduate and graduate programs, churning out original scholarship in the Lord's name. It would have been a powerful victory for the neo-evangelicals, reclaiming the very cultural institution—like higher biblical criticism, invented by the Germans in the nineteenth century—that precipitated conservative Protestants' alienation from academic life. America's two other prominent conservative Christian constituencies, Catholics and Mormons, had managed to found thriving research universities. Both those churches shared evangelicals' fears of the secularization of modern culture, and both, it must be said, struggled with the problems of separatism and academic freedom. But there was an important difference. Catholics obeyed the authority (and ambiguities) of church tradition and Vatican decree, and Mormons accepted an equally powerful magisterium while expecting changing and continuing revelation through their prophet, the president of the church. Neither church entertained the fiction that Christians might understand scripture without guidance or interpretive frameworks.

Human authorities and the dictates of tradition sometimes prescribe strict law, but they can also provide room to maneuver and cajole. Their emphasis on loyalty to the mother church discourages the human tendency to break away from one's opponents. The strength of their central authority fosters the concentration of resources vital to funding and running a university. Catholics and Mormons are not "literalist" in the rationalistic Reformed Protestant style, and separation from fellow believers has always been anathema in both churches. In their efforts at higher education they did not face the evangelical stumbling blocks—the same problems that hampered *Christianity Today*'s mainstream appeal—that crippled intellectual investigation and made it impossible for neo-evangelicals to achieve the financial support necessary to found a first-class university.[42]

Crusade University's advocates could not move beyond enthusiastic memos and glossy brochures. They lacked funds, and they struggled to agree on how to reconcile Protestant orthodoxy with the demands of mainstream academia. The project's failure highlighted an awkward question: How could evangelical intellectual institutions meet secular peers on equal terms when evangelicals could not agree among themselves on how to balance of the contending claims of reason, religious community,

and scripture? The neo-evangelicals had tried to overcome fundamentalist isolationism by building a seminary, academic and evangelistic associations, and a magazine, but their separatist habits sabotaged their ambitions.
In a memo on "evangelical strategy" probably circulated in 1965, the *CT*
editors stressed that their main concerns would remain evangelism, evangelical education, the creeping influences of "ecumenical inclusivism" and
Catholicism, and the old problem of defining and redefining the word *evangelical*. Fuller was in the hands of progressives; debates over inerrancy and
separatism paralyzed the Evangelical Theological Society and torpedoed
plans for an evangelical university; despite the high hopes of *Christianity
Today*'s editors, the magazine seemed destined for parochialism. "It is my
conviction that evangelical Christianity is now at the brink of crisis," Carl
Henry warned. "These next ten years—between now and 1975—will determine whether it survives as a virile force in the modern world or whether it
will be dismissed as a solitary wilderness cult."[43]

Chapter 4

Reform and Its Discontents

IN THE SPRING OF 1955, AS CARL HENRY WAS PREPARING ANOTHER CLASS of Fuller students for graduation and planning the launch of _Christianity Today_, he received a letter from a twenty-seven-year-old Mennonite scholar named John Howard Yoder. Yoder may have been young, but he was bold. He bombarded Henry's dearest convictions, particularly the inerrancy of the Bible. Yoder took offense at the suggestion—implicit in so much of what neo-evangelicals like Henry said and wrote—that only disciples of Reformed fundamentalism were capable of rational argument, while liberal Protestants divorced reason from faith and other evangelicals were lost in a fog of religious enthusiasm or fixated on moralistic ideas of holiness. To Yoder, the neo-evangelicals had made their own assumptions into idols. When Henry responded with a letter defending the neo-evangelical aim to rehabilitate fundamentalism, Yoder slyly suggested that

> Your ultimate criteria are your idea of reason, your judgment of metaphysical realities, your judgment of what is consistent and what contradictory. Those are all philosophical positions which may or may not be good philosophy, but in theology the chances are great that they will get in the way of Christ as the only source of knowledge.[1]

Yoder had hit on the crux of the divide between Reformed evangelicals and many other evangelical traditions. While they claimed to follow scripture alone, the neo-evangelicals interpreted the Bible on the basis of certain philosophical propositions. By contrast, Yoder's Anabaptist heritage emphasized the personal habits and local community through which God's word informed everyday life. Discipleship, more than dogma, was the primary way to follow Christ. Yoder urged Henry to relinquish his obsession with doctrinal details and philosophical rationalism. The *Fundamentals* pamphlet series "was a time-bound polemic strategy" that addressed issues pertinent to the early twentieth century, but could not meet the challenges of the 1950s. "For instance, they included nothing about social ethics, nothing about what Christian Unity is and is not, and further, the polemic strategy then chosen served better to build a barrier than to speak across the gap," he wrote. He defended the World Council of Churches, suggesting that it was no more of a "superchurch" than the NAE. Henry was unmoved: "It seems to me that the fundamentalist position implied and even required what you rather take to be optional, that these doctrines are revealed, that is, that God speaks propositionally."[2]

Yoder was Harold Bender's most precocious student at Goshen College. He had gone on to study in Basel with Karl Barth. The neo-evangelicals' "highbrow fundamentalism" seemed to Yoder to hold both promise and danger for conservative Protestantism as a whole. On the face of it, his interest seemed misplaced. Only a small minority of conservative American Protestants shared the neo-evangelicals' rationalist, Reformed heritage. Most churches continued to emphasize other themes—such as personal holiness, internal transformation, or the gifts of the Holy Spirit—over intellectual assent to philosophical claims about the nature of God. Yet the spirit of Common Sense Realism that shaped the old Princetonians' portrait of the Bible as a "storehouse of facts" was not a Presbyterian quirk. It pervaded American culture in the nineteenth century. During the fundamentalist–modernist battles "inerrancy" had become a watchword in many churches.

The neo-evangelical program concerned Yoder precisely because it was more than fundamentalism warmed over. It was a set of ideas whose time had come, expressed in a language better suited to the marketplace of mainstream America than were the idioms of holiness, spirit-filled enthusiasm, or Christian obedience. In the early twentieth century, disillusionment with modern life spawned a number of ideologies that—while radically different in content—used the tools and structures of Enlightenment reasoning to critique the modern world that the Enlightenment had produced. Fascist ideologues in Germany and Italy waxed lyrical about using modern technology to fulfill the *Volk*'s romantic destiny (or, in Mussolini's case, to resurrect the Roman Empire). They concocted pseudo-scientific theories to justify the racial purification of the nation. Other totalitarian regimes adapted Karl Marx's materialist dialectic and "science of history" to serve imperialist and anti-intellectual ends. "Ideologies are known for their scientific character," Hannah Arendt wrote in 1951. "They combine the scientific approach with results of philosophical relevance and pretend to be scientific philosophy."[3] Now the neo-evangelicals made their modest contribution to the cannibalism of the Enlightenment by using the vocabulary of modern empiricism, by appealing to reason and evidence, in order to defend premodern dogma.

Like their age's array of secular ideologues, the neo-evangelicals promoted not just a set of doctrines, but a grand theory that attempted to explain the foundations of knowledge, the course of global events, and humanity's place in the cosmos. Each of these intellectual systems depended upon an internal logic that invalidated opposing worldviews. Each trained its adherents in a tendentious retelling of history to support its claims. (Observing the Nazis, the Soviets, and the lesser totalitarians who had ravaged Europe, Arendt noted "the emancipation from reality" that came with "the claim of all *Weltanschauungen* to offer total explanations of everything, mainly, of course, the past, present, and future.")[4] At a time when conservative Protestants saw fascism and communism as pressing threats, and keenly felt the damage done to biblical authority by the acids of historical critique, the neo-evangelicals offered a worldview that claimed to be as sweeping and systematic as the former and immune to the latter. They conveyed this ideology in terms of reason, truth, and fact rather than Christian jargon of sanctification, ecstatic experience, or holy life. This is not to suggest that the neo-evangelicals were fascists. The similarities are in form rather than substance. Rather, their theology was one of several antimodern ideologies that, at roughly the same time, came upon the insight that one could manipulate the language and structures of modern science to compel the Enlightenment to devour itself.

Non-Reformed leaders like Harold Bender and H. O. Wiley noticed that champions of this worldview were beguiling their flocks, and they began to push back. The next generation of evangelical intellectuals—in a few cases, Bender's and Wiley's own students—grew more vocal in their concern that a distinctly Reformed style of thought had saturated their churches and separated Anabaptists, Wesleyans, and other evangelicals from their own heritage. As fundamentalist strains of Reformed thinking stirred in their pews and modernist Reformed theologians set the terms of theological debate, evangelical intellectuals in other traditions had no choice but to rethink the essentials of Christian identity. Some discovered in Reformed theology an appealing framework in which to respond to secular science and culture. Others wrestled to purge this influence and nurture internal renaissance—and even to "evangelize" the neo-evangelicals.

PILGRIMS TO THE CLASSROOMS OF EUROPE

John Howard Yoder was born in 1927 in an established Mennonite community in Smithville, Ohio. At Goshen College he imbibed Harold Bender's call for Mennonites to overcome their insularity and recover the inspiration of their ancestors. Yoder earned his ThD at the University of Basel, where he studied with biblical theologian Oscar Cullmann and existentialist philosopher Karl Jaspers. He attended Karl Barth's seminars and developed a reputation for following the theologian around the room at social events, nagging him with questions until Barth swatted him away.[5] While dialogue with Barth and the latest trends in European Protestantism would frame much of his future scholarship, Yoder's time at Basel was formative for another reason: He established friendships with non-Anabaptist evangelical Americans, particularly Kenneth Kantzer, a Harvard PhD who taught at Wheaton College and would go on to become dean of Trinity Evangelical Divinity School and editor of *Christianity Today*, and David Wallace, a graduate of Fuller Theological Seminary and friend of several faculty there.

Yoder, Kantzer, and Wallace exchanged letters about theology, biblical authority, and the future of American fundamentalism long after they left Europe. "I had the opportunity for a good deal of discussion with two representatives of the movement which calls itself 'evangelical' and which outsiders would probably call intelligent fundamentalism," Yoder wrote to a colleague at the World Council of Churches in 1955.

> For me it was educational to discover that, within what looks to be a cast-iron position, there are people asking questions, and willing to submit their own past convictions to examination before anyone who does not ask them to give up God in the prolegomena. Which means that, as far as I can see, theologically, they are in the Oecumene [the global

Christian community]....I hope that, among all the other problems, your study group can keep open a possibility for dialogue with these people. In terms of missionary vitality they are way ahead of the sacramentalists, and let's not forget that the real grandfather of the World Council is D. L. Moody.[6]

Yoder purchased a subscription to the NAE's magazine, *United Evangelical Action*, to stay current on American Protestantism while he was abroad. He wrote at least one article for the magazine, "The Christian Critique of Nationalism," which ran in the October 1954 issue and dissented from the magazine's blindly patriotic editorial line. Despite his stalemate with Carl Henry, Yoder believed that "the NAE is looking for more contacts with Mennonites, to judge from their use of articles and news items in *Action*," he wrote to Christian Hostetter, a Brethren in Christ bishop who probably agreed: Hostetter was serving on the boards of both the NAE's World Relief Commission and the Mennonite Central Committee, the relief agency sponsored by most North American Mennonite churches. "I don't know just what the reason is; whether they think we have money, or are impressed with the quality of our schools, or feel that we really have something to say. At any rate we should use this opportunity while we have it." In writing to the neo-evangelicals, Yoder continued to use the first-person plural. He considered himself not an outside commentator, but a firsthand participant whose own church had much at stake.[7]

The salons of European Protestantism forced Yoder out of the American Mennonite enclave that reared him. Many of the most ambitious American evangelical students from across a range of traditions found their way to European universities during the 1950s and 1960s, and this common academic experience among the evangelical elite sparked dialogue around a shared set of theological questions. These questions had more to do with the Bible's intellectual authority—the neo-evangelicals' central obsession—than with the historic interests of Wesleyans, Anabaptists, or other evangelicals.

Fuller Theological Seminary, now shorn of its hardline conservatives, attracted moderate scholars who had studied in Europe's trendiest theological circles. Paul Jewett, a Fuller professor and one of the pioneers in egalitarian gender theology among evangelicals, studied under Emil Brunner at Zurich. George Ladd and Dan Fuller studied at Basel, the nerve center of

Barthianism. Geoffrey Bromiley devoted most of his career to translating and teaching Barth's corpus. These faculty and others sent dozens of their own students to do the same. "Quite a number of men at Fuller are interested in going to Basel for their Th.D.," Dan Fuller wrote in 1963 to his colleague Robert Meye, a professor at Northern Baptist Theological Seminary and fellow Basel alumnus.[8]

Fuller insisted that the broad perspective that students absorbed in Basel and at the other great universities of Europe was critical to salvaging the reputation of conservative orthodoxy. "One of the things that has impressed me the most since being here is that it is the systematizers, the men who try to give a coherent view of reality, that are really rocking the boat here in Europe," he wrote to Jewett while still a graduate student.

> Barth and Bultmann are really the big wheels here, for they are both proposing an entire worldview based on their distinctive hermeneutical foundations. . . . These men are giving out systems of truth and with such enthusiasm that in [post-Bultmannian scholar Hans] Conzelmann's class they had to bring in extra chairs to hear him existentialize Romans 5:12ff. If the emphasis of our school is simply to putter around in the Hebrew vowel points and quibble over the niceties of exegeting a few sentences in Paul, our future looks most dull.[9]

Neo-orthodoxy (in its various permutations) and Rudolf Bultmann's liberal theology each presented a fully realized vision of humankind's relationship to the divine, a complete and consistent world-and-life view. Evangelicals who spent time at Basel and other European universities usually did not convert to more liberal forms of the faith, but they sometimes revised their views of biblical inerrancy and eschatology. After a year's sabbatical spent studying with Barth, Baptist theologian Bernard Ramm returned to his post at Baylor University convinced that the classic fundamentalist approach to scripture suffered from "intellectual bankruptcy."[10] Dan Fuller and George Ladd both provoked an uproar when they departed from traditional inerrancy and modified their views of dispensational premillennialism, a popular theory of the end-times that divides history into epochs marked by different relationships between humanity and God, and predicts that Christ will return to begin his millennial reign only after a period of great suffering and cosmic battle against the various villains depicted in the Book of Revelation.

In many cases, however, evangelicals who went abroad were clever in selecting schools and faculty advisers who would not radically challenge their presuppositions. Unlike Yoder, most who went to Basel did not study directly with Karl Barth. Oscar Cullmann, a more traditional New Testament theologian, drew them to the university. Cullmann was a leader in biblical theology, a midcentury reaction against liberalism and historical criticism. Biblical theologians embraced the essential claims of the historical critics—they agreed that one should take historical context into account when reading scripture—but they argued that by obsessing over the minutia of archaeological data, historical critics had lost touch with the meaning of the Bible as a whole. In America, biblical theologians defended scriptural authority, but they "bent over backwards to specify that the authority of the Bible lay in its relation to other factors, such as tradition, the Holy Spirit, and the church, lest the emphasis on Biblical authority be taken as a return to Fundamentalism," wrote one scholar. Biblical theology was far more flexible and expansive than the directives of old Princeton and enjoyed a broad following beyond the bounds of conservative Protestantism. But it adhered closely enough to traditional orthodoxy to be the "one movement that has gained their [conservative evangelicals'] sympathetic interest," wrote Arthur Glasser, a Reformed Presbyterian minister and dean of Fuller's School of World Mission.[11]

Biblical theology was also compatible with the traditional fundamentalist method of "synthetic Bible studies" and the "Bird's-eye View of the Bible," which fundamentalists intended to rebut the higher critics (although these methods emphasized the end-times in a way that biblical theology did not).[12] Its appeal stretched across denominational lines. During his tenure as president of Nazarene Theological Seminary in Kansas City, William Greathouse steered the curriculum toward biblical theologians like Oscar Cullmann and neo-evangelicals such as George Ladd. He sent faculty to Europe on sabbatical to study biblical theology. Even Restorationist Christians like the Independent Christian Churches and Churches of Christ, known for their insularity, were aware of Cullmann as a learned and orthodox defender of the faith. John Howard Yoder would draw on biblical theology in his most important scholarship. Stephen Dintaman, another Mennonite scholar who

studied at Basel, noted that "the rise of neo-Anabaptism [the renewal movement associated with Harold Bender] coincided with the rise of Biblical
Theology and fed on it"; this development "brought us into a mainstream
movement, or at least in talking distance."[13]

If American evangelicals wanted to participate in the most exciting
postwar theological conversations, they had to make pilgrimages to the
Reformed—and, occasionally, Lutheran—theological centers of Europe.
Despite the fame of a few theologians of Lutheran background, such as
Bultmann, Cullmann, and Paul Tillich, the Lutheran tradition does not
seem to have held as much allure for American evangelicals, perhaps
because it struck many of them as "too Catholic"; because it emphasized
the paradoxes of Christianity rather than offering a seductive systematic
theology; and because American evangelicals scorned the moribund state
churches that comprised most of European Lutheranism, while in America,
Lutheranism was known as an immigrant faith whose members were, with
some exceptions, somewhat secluded from the rest of Protestantism and
suspicious of ecumenical collaboration.

At the same time, the patchwork of Reformed ideas swirling through
many evangelical circles was just that—a patchwork, not a coherent tradition. Often the resulting theological mix included doctrines—notably, premillennialism—that appalled the classical Reformed churches of
Europe, as well as the Dutch Reformed and more traditional Presbyterian
churches in America. The evangelicals who headed overseas went in search
of intellectual tools, insights (gilded, of course, with European prestige) to
meld with their own "common-sense" reading of scripture and their communities' prevailing beliefs.

In the United Kingdom—a more accessible destination for many
American evangelicals intimidated by the linguistic and cultural barri-
ers of continental Europe—most of the attractive universities and faculty
offered a Reformed (or at least Reformed-inclined) perspective. F. F. Bruce,
a classicist-turned-biblical theologian at Manchester who drew many
American evangelical students, was a member of the non-Reformed Open
Brethren tradition but described himself as "an impenitent Augustinian
and Calvinist."[14] Fuller graduates frequently ended up at the Universities
of Aberdeen and St. Andrews and went to Edinburgh to work with T. F.
Torrance, who studied under Barth. As bastions of conservative Reformed

Protestantism, Scottish universities were especially appealing to American Reformed evangelicals. Escaping to foreign universities allowed Americans to avoid the prejudices and difficult questions that they sometimes encountered at American seminaries and universities, where vague memories of the fundamentalist–modernist fights influenced the faculty's impressions of conservative Protestants.

Plenty of evangelicals also completed advanced degrees at American institutions. Even a casual glance at the faculty rosters and alumni magazines of conservative evangelical institutions in the two decades after World War II belies the notion that evangelicals were "alienated" from mainstream academia, at least in the most straightforward sense. Several neo-evangelical scholars earned PhDs and ThDs at Harvard in the 1940s and 1950s. In the early 1950s at Biola—still very much a Bible college at that time—a few faculty had only diplomas or BAs, but others had PhDs from the University of Southern California, Edinburgh, Johns Hopkins, and Northwestern. Fuller graduates were winning Fulbrights and earning PhDs at places like Stanford, Harvard, the University of Iowa, and the University of Tennessee. As Mark Noll has noted, the problem was not so much evangelicals' failure to excel at secular academic institutions, but rather their ability to compartmentalize their faith from new learning.[15] They tended to position themselves in fields where no one would corner them too aggressively on their views about, for example, how one ought to interpret the creation narrative in Genesis. "American evangelicals would do PhDs at places like Brandeis, and study harmless things like archeology," recalled John Goldingay, a professor of Old Testament at Fuller.[16] They also showed a marked preference for fields like New Testament theology and philosophy of religion. The latter discipline suited Reformed scholars such as Carl Henry and Edward Carnell, who trained under philosopher mentors like Gordon Clark.

While the neo-evangelicals were finding reinforcement for their Reformed perspective in their studies, scholars in other traditions did not have the luxury of such provincialism. Reformed theologians were the pacesetters of European Protestant debate, and, increasingly, Reformed thinkers were guiding mainstream Americans through the spiritual challenges of the Cold War. Reinhold Niebuhr, the son of German immigrants and of mixed Lutheran and Reformed heritage, emerged in the 1930s as an influential social critic who challenged liberals' prewar optimism and faith in human nature by pointing out the power of original sin to warp the best intentions. H. Richard Niebuhr, Reinhold's younger brother and a theologian at Yale Divinity School, wielded equal influence among elites across a wide spectrum of traditions.[17] As ministers, educators, and scholars struggled to interpret the social revolutions that followed World War II and America's changing role in the global order, they were troubled by H. Richard Niebuhr's small, influential volume *Christ and Culture* (1951). The book suggested that while Anabaptists turned their backs on outsiders and Holiness and Pentecostal Christians were preoccupied with otherworldly matters, Reformed Christians knew how to transform society. Some readers begged to differ. Others looked around and wondered if Niebuhr was right.

A THEOLOGICAL VOGUE

There was no way around it: International theological conversation in the mid-twentieth century required fluency in the Reformed tongue. The Niebuhrs, Karl Barth, Emil Brunner, and many of the other neo-orthodox and liberal theologians who framed the great Christian debates of the twentieth century hailed from a heavily Reformed heritage. These theologians upended traditional orthodoxies, but most also shared old Reformed preoccupations: the depravity of man, the complete sovereignty and transcendence of God, the need for harmony between faith and reason, and the responsibility of the Christian church to sanctify the world. (One might even say that Karl Barth—who taught that human knowledge of God derives from revelation alone—advocated an unorthodox version of presuppositionalism.) Non-Reformed evangelicals had no choice but to adapt.

Pressure to think in Reformed terms emanated not just from the ivory towers of international Protestantism, but from domestic grassroots: the legacy of the fundamentalist–modernist battles in conservative churches across America. Biblical inerrancy now seemed to many evangelicals to be a common-sense doctrine. The Reformed insight honed by thinkers like Cornelius Van Til and Gordon Clark—that Christians ought to scrutinize the foundations of knowledge, and accept only claims based on the Bible—exposed the atheistic assumptions that buttressed liberal ideas about scripture's authority. A wide range of conservative Protestants found in presuppositionalist language a handy way to talk back to secular threats.

Restorationist evangelicals were wary of fundamentalist and evangelical empire-builders. The *Christian Standard* and the *Restoration Herald*, published by the Standard Publishing Company and the more conservative Christian Restoration Association, portrayed neo-evangelicalism and fundamentalism as largely malignant developments that caused as much harm to Christian unity as traditional denominations did. Yet these magazines frequently reviewed books published by Reformed publishing houses such as John Knox, Zondervan, and Westminster. A *Christian Standard* feature entitled "The Minister's Library" recommended that every pastor ought to have books by Carl Henry on his shelf, as well as issues of Reformed journals *Evangelical Quarterly* and *Westminster Theological Journal*. The magazine encouraged pastors to embrace their Restorationist heritage—that impulse, born in the Second Great Awakening, to shed theological labels and purify worship of all ideas and practices not found in the Bible—but it also urged them to be informed citizens of the modern Protestant world.[18]

By the mid-1960s, Restorationist churches had found their way to a simplified presuppositionalism. In some cases, specific individuals smuggled Reformed thinking into Restorationist circles: Jack Cottrell, a professor at Cincinnati Bible Seminary, studied at Westminster Theological Seminary and wrote frequently on topics of special interest to Reformed Christians, such as free will. In 1967, a *Restoration Herald* contributor echoed the slogans of Van Til when he lamented the most recent Supreme Court decision declaring that "the public schools must remain neutral in relation to religion": "Neutralism" was impossible in a "religion-oriented society." He also admired the fathers of Princeton-style inerrancy, called theologian Archibald Alexander Hodge a "prophet" in his prediction that public schools would prove to be "the most appalling enginery for the propagation of anti-Christian and atheistic unbelief," and quoted J. Gresham Machen approvingly on the importance of private Christian schools. Without missing a beat, he cited early Restorationist leader Alexander Campbell on the same question, implying that Machen and Campbell were in perfect theological agreement (in truth, they would have quarreled over everything from baptism to the doctrine of original sin).[19]

Pentecostals were for the most part even more distant from Reformed neo-evangelicals than were the Restorationists. But they were early and eager fans of mainstream evangelical radio preachers like Charles Fuller. As Pentecostals poured energy and funds into improving their educational institutions in the 1950s and 1960s, they seemed convinced that in order to obtain the stamp of intellectual gravitas, they had to look outside their own tradition. When Central Bible College and Evangel College, the main educational institutions of the Assemblies of God, merged in 1958, the church invited Wheaton College president V. Raymond Edman to speak. "You were unanimously selected by the committee because of our high esteem for Wheaton College and the wonderful Evangelical Christian tradition that it has maintained," the invitation read.[20]

Edman was no Reformed theologian—he was the revival-minded son of Swedish Pietists—and Pentecostals were late to discover many features of Reformed thought. But they did so eventually. When Pentecostal scholars decided to prove their intellectual maturity by founding an academic association, the constitution of the Society for Pentecostal Studies promised to "study the implications of Pentecostal theology in relation to other academic disciplines, seeking a Pentecostal world-and-life view."[21] That final phrase had a clear pedigree. SPS members had not become disciples of Van Til: They adapted this idea to reflect their distinctive belief in the Holy Spirit's role in believers' lives. But it is of no small significance that they expressed Pentecostal notions in Reformed language. The credo of the *Christianity Today* crowd was becoming evangelicalism's predominant public theology.

The idea of the *Weltanschauung* resonated earlier with Mennonite leaders and scholars because their own heritage, rooted in Reformation history, had natural affinities with Reformed ideas. Linguistically, the word was native to the Swiss-German Anabaptist tradition. In a paper delivered at a Goshen College theological workshop in 1958, professor J. Lawrence Burkholder warned against a fundamentalist reading of the Bible that held scripture to modern scientific standards of accuracy. He also emphasized the danger of tolerating discrepancies between one's rational view of the world and one's religious understanding. "It is not possible to unite Christianity and philosophy when considered as two different world-views. They can only clash," Burkholder wrote.

Parts of various Weltanschauungs can be correlated with each other but as systems of thought they can only contradict each other.... Furthermore, it is dangerous to use a philosophical system as a structure in which one may attempt to pore [sic] Christian content with the hope of getting a Christian philosophy.[22]

American fundamentalists had done just that. Drawing on the work of the Princeton theologians, they embedded the Bible in the framework of nineteenth-century Common Sense Realism, a philosophy that neglected the role of spiritual experience and left little room for Anabaptist ideas of communal discipleship. They treated scripture as a compilation of objective facts. On its face, this obsession with divine "data" contradicted neo-evangelical presuppositionalism, which implies that facts are not objective at all: They depend on an individual's assumptions. The trick was that presuppositionalists' basic proposition, which they readily admitted—God is perfect and incapable of error in his revelation, and therefore no human may contradict that revelation—committed them to a highly rationalistic view of the Bible. Since God could never err, any apparent discrepancy between scripture and scientific knowledge revealed not a mistake in revelation or a rupture between faith and reason, but merely an error in human interpretation. (The neo-evangelicals were not unusual in combining theological principles that appeared to be at odds. In matters of theology, American evangelicals have often valued expedience over consistency.) One of the few evangelical scholars to note the advantages of this blended approach explained: "Presuppositionalists want to begin with God, evidentialists with ourselves; the balanced apologist says start with *both* God *and* ourselves simultaneously, as these cannot be broken apart."[23] The "balanced apologist" could have his science and deny it too.

Mennonite Diplomacy

Mennonite elites encouraged their constituents to rediscover the idea of a Christian *Weltanschauung* and wrest it from Reformed hands.[24] It took nerve to engage world-class European theologians and leading evangelical intellectuals, and John Howard Yoder was not renowned for his personal humility. A colleague who knew him later in his academic career (he taught at Mennonite seminaries and the University of Notre Dame) described his lecturing style as "patriarchal": "Here was a man who seemed never to have changed his mind."[25] Yet if he sometimes fell short of the Mennonite ideal of humility in his own life, he recognized its importance in his church's relations with evangelicals outside Anabaptist circles. He feared the consequences of increasing numbers of Mennonites attending liberal Protestant seminaries and preferred that they study at evangelical institutions that shared more theological and cultural common ground with Anabaptists. Yoder felt that his colleagues judged most of American evangelicalism unfairly, particularly its revivalist elements. "We have come widely to associate Evangelicalism as a theological stance with cultural lag (showing our subservience to the framework of analysis of H. Richard Niebuhr)," he wrote to the Interchurch Relations Committee.

> Having identified a concern for evangelical experience with the culturally retrograde, we had laid the groundwork for leaving behind any concern with experience.... In short, our life as an [sic] denomination was saved in the great awakening of a century ago by borrowings from *evangelicalism* which restored to Mennonitism a dimension of experiential vitality.[26]

Yet many feared that Mennonites who absorbed too much from "mainstream" evangelicals and fundamentalists might abandon the ethic of nonviolence, a cornerstone of Mennonite identity that was increasingly relevant—and under threat—in the context of the war in Vietnam. The Mennonite Central Committee sent aid personnel to Vietnam in 1954, earlier than any other major Protestant group. As the war continued the MCC sustained its relief work, eventually expanding its efforts to include North Vietnam—a step few peace activists were willing to take. The war emboldened church leaders to call on the laity to do even more: "Mennonites no longer are protected by their closed communities, and because of this they face a new era of responsibility and mission when their deeds must say more than their words," one Goshen minister told the church's 1967 General Conference.[27]

If Vietnam sharpened Mennonite leaders' awareness of their obligation to bear witness, it also roused fears that the Mennonite perspective was more vulnerable to corruption than ever before. Ed Metzler, of the Mennonite Central Committee, worried that "there is as much danger that Mennonites will lose their nonresistant testimony from the right as from the left, in fact more so. As an increasing number of Mennonites associate with popular, middle or upper class, evangelical organizations (Christian business men's groups, ICL [International Christian Leadership], Billy Graham, Christianity Today, etc) it will be important that the witness of radical discipleship be heard in those circles." As popular support for the war plummeted and public discussion polarized, it was crucial to cultivate friendships and communication between Mennonites and the conservative evangelical world before the chasm between them opened further. "We may be able to provide a vital key in the search among some of the more thoughtful and creative evangelicals for a larger definition and vision of evangelism which combines the new insights from the left . . . with the biblical passion and radicalness of the traditional evangelistic and mission concern," Metzler wrote.[28]

The Peace Section of the Mennonite Central Committee had been making formal overtures to evangelicals and fundamentalists since the late 1950s. A 1960 panel on "The Christian and War" hosted by the NAE's Social Action Committee proved a failure. It drew low attendance; the prominent evangelical speaker invited, V. Raymond Edman, sent his paper to be read in absentia; and no real discussion followed. Mennonite leaders gave up on official dialogue with the NAE and issued their own invitations for meetings with various evangelical and fundamentalist leaders, particularly college presidents. Perhaps more successful were the personal relationships that Mennonite leaders, especially Yoder, cultivated with evangelicals sympathetic to the Anabaptist position. Arthur Glasser at Fuller was an early friend and used Yoder's writings in classes he taught at Winona Lake Summer School of Theology. Paul Rees, vice president of the growing international evangelical charity World Vision, was another eager ear, as was the well-known Anglican apologist John Stott, who briefly embraced Christian pacifism early in his career.[29]

A milestone in Mennonite efforts at dialogue with evangelicals came, after months of planning, at a 1961 breakfast meeting at the Union League

Club in Philadelphia between Mennonite leaders and Billy Graham. J. C. Wenger, a popular preacher and writer in the church, tried to impress upon Graham the Mennonites' authority to speak on evangelical concerns as "an evangelical body with the usual fundamental doctrines generally accepted by other evangelicals...a daughter of the Reformation but actually a bit ahead of Zwingli and Luther in setting up a church which they considered a true believers' church," the "gathered church" paradigm that had come to define American evangelicalism. He confessed that "after five thousand of our brethren, including many leaders were killed [in the sixteenth century], we lost the vision of evangelism," but more recently the missionary spirit had revived.[30] After an extensive presentation of Mennonite beliefs—particularly the peace witness—and their concerns over the direction of American evangelicalism, they asked Graham's advice on improving their image and outreach among evangelicals.

Graham was the consummate diplomat. He told the group that "he could easily be one of us in about 99% of what has been said," the secretary recorded. "He is deeply disturbed by the way in which the churches have created an antinomianism [neglecting discipleship] that is quite dangerous....He feels that we are rendering a tremendous service to all of the evangelical Christendom." Graham emphasized "that his heart is one with us....He is open to be led and to be taught." By the meeting's end, the Mennonite participants felt encouraged, and hoped to use the event as a springboard to further contacts with evangelical leaders. At the same time, Graham was leery of appearing too chummy with a group that was, as far as the rest of the evangelical world was concerned, marginal. He insisted that no press releases quote him directly.[31]

A NEW AND POTENT HOLINESS

The Mennonites were not the only faith community struggling to find equilibrium in their relationship with Reformed neo-evangelicals. The Wesleyan Holiness churches were divided between scholars and denominational leaders who embraced a Reformed understanding of inerrancy and the "Christian worldview" and those who shuddered at the popularity of such ideas. This conflict crystallized around the Wesleyan Theological Society.

Founded in 1966, the society was intended as a forum where Wesleyan Holiness scholars and others who counted themselves among John Wesley's progeny could discuss questions of special interest to them. It was also meant to assert the maturity of their scholarship—but for some church elites, achieving intellectual maturity demanded a Reformed theological makeover.

The Wesleyan Theological Society took as its primary model the Reformed-dominated Evangelical Theological Society and affirmed biblical inerrancy in its original statement of faith—in large part because one of its founders, Stephen Paine, had also helped to found the ETS. Paine was president of Houghton College from 1937 to 1972 and a member of the Wesleyan Methodist Church. At the church's 1951 General Conference, he spearheaded the effort to insert inerrancy into the Articles of Faith. "Let us...ask what it is that inclines devout intellectuals to weaken and relax their insistence upon the inerrancy of Scripture," he wrote in an article for the *Bulletin of the Evangelical Theological Society* later reprinted in the *Nazarene Preacher*.[32]

Among the Nazarenes, some scholars challenged inerrantists like Paine. These men and women rejected the creeping influence of Reformed evangelicalism, but they also worried that their church's own history of revival had carried it far from the teachings of John Wesley. The Church of the Nazarene, born more than one hundred years after Wesley's death, did not spring directly from his theology but from the nineteenth-century Holiness movement. Holiness preachers stressed instant sanctification, in which God's grace cleansed original sin from the believer's soul. Wesley used the term *sanctification* to describe a process as well as a crisis, but the nineteenth-century Holiness movement placed nearly all its emphasis on an instantaneous "second work of grace" to the near eclipse of gradual sanctification. Twentieth-century Holiness conservatives argued that the Holiness movement had corrected Wesley's errors, while scholars of the "Back to Wesley" movement sought to reclaim the gospel as they believed Wesley had preached it himself.

These scholars were alarmed at the Wesleyan Theological Society's obsession with inerrancy. Conservatives in the Holiness movement's main ecumenical body, the Christian Holiness Association, had revised its principles to better align with the NAE's statement of faith, and now neo-evangelical influences had captured the WTS from its inception. Southern Nazarene University theology professor Rob Staples joined "because the idea of a fellowship of Wesley scholars sounded like a good idea, although I had great reservations about their statement on 'inerrancy,'" he wrote to Elwood Sanner at Northwest Nazarene College in 1968. "I rationalized that since they didn't spell out just what they meant by 'inerrant in the originals' I could interpret it to mean what our Nazarene article on the Scriptures means—'inerrantly revealing the will of God.'" However, when the subject of inerrancy came up at the society's 1967 meeting, Staples asked whether Nazarenes were truly welcome, since their own statement of faith did not mention inerrancy. "A 'Wesleyan' society should make Holiness its main point and not get involved in this fundamentalistic shibboleth of inerrancy," he told the group.[33]

"Most of us at NNC were keenly disappointed in this (as I feel) 'aping' of the ETS and were disinclined to join the society," Sanner replied. For him, the issue was especially pressing because of his new post as senior editor of a proposed church textbook on Christian education, a subject on which Reformed evangelicals had written volumes more than Wesleyan scholars. Just as the tension between Wesleyan and Reformed theology had implications for Nazarene attitudes toward social justice, it also influenced their youth's education. "When we begin to deal with the theological and philosophical bases of CE [Christian education] as we see it, we are certain to run into some controversial material," he wrote. "But I have been raising the question, Do we have the courage to be what we are?"[34]

Mildred Bangs Wynkoop believed the church had to answer yes. Born in Seattle to parents who were charter members of their local Nazarene church, she began her studies at Nazarene institutions but later plunged into the Reformed evangelical world. After two years under H. Orton Wiley's tutelage at Northwest Nazarene College, she followed him to Pasadena College when he became president there. She and her husband served as co-pastors and itinerant evangelists (the Nazarenes ordained women from their earliest days) for about twenty years until Wynkoop decided to pursue graduate studies outside the Nazarene fold. Wynkoop attended Western Evangelical Seminary in Oregon (now George Fox Evangelical Seminary), a school founded by Holiness groups and evangelical Quakers, and in 1955 received her ThD from Northern Baptist Theological Seminary—Carl Henry's alma mater. She wrote her thesis on "A Historical and Semantic Analysis of Methods of Biblical Interpretation as They Relate to Views of Inspiration," diving into the thick of the inerrancy controversy. Afterward she returned to Oregon to teach at Western, where she chaired the department of theology.[35] In 1961 she began teaching in Japan and was the founding president of a Nazarene seminary there. In 1966 she returned to America and directed the department of missions at Trevecca Nazarene College (now University) in Nashville for ten years—rounding off a remarkable record of institutional leadership—before finishing her career as theologian-in-residence at the church's flagship seminary in Kansas City.

Wiley wrote to Wynkoop in 1960 that Nazarenes were obliged to stand up against "so much of this Calvinism and Neo-Orthodoxy that is going the rounds." A few years later, she was corresponding actively with colleagues about the unfair treatment Wesleyans received at the hands of *Christianity Today's* Reformed editorial staff. In 1970, she published *John Wesley: Christian Revolutionary*, arguing that Holiness evangelicals had grown too enamored with Reformed fundamentalism and had severed the link between personal piety and social justice that Wesley strove to maintain. She reasserted Wesley's message of synergy between divine grace and human free will, as well as his insistence on the "perfect love" that fills sanctified believers and impels them to serve humanity. To Wynkoop and her progressive colleagues, these were not abstract dogmas but the foundations of Christian activism. These principles were very different from those she detected in the early glimmerings of the Religious Right, particularly the "ground swell of ultra-rightism (fundamentalism)...[that] has infiltrated the church from Calvinistic evangelicalism."[36]

For the same reason, Wynkoop worried about the inroads that dispensational premillennialism had made among Nazarenes. Obsessive apocalypticism ran contrary to her tradition's respect for the limits of human knowledge and the Nazarene emphasis on personal spiritual experience. "Historically, the Nazarene church has carefully avoided any official position regarding the 'Second Coming,'" she wrote to Westlake Purkiser, editor of the *Herald of Holiness*, after the Nazarene periodical had published three articles defending "radical Plymouth Brethren dispensationalism." This eschatological pessimism sapped social compassion and "stands opposed to the involvement of love which is the very heart of holiness."[37] Wynkoop tried to revive the Holiness heritage of social justice in a book released in 1972, *A Theology of Love.*

Her experience teaching in Japan forced Wynkoop to think through the core message of the gospel that she was trying to translate into the language and assumptions of a foreign culture. She moved away from the traditional Holiness notion of sanctification as the eradication of the "substance" of sin and instead described sin as a wrong relationship with God, corrected at the moment of justification. The Christian life requires nurturing relationships with God and with humanity: Love for others and personal holiness are two sides of the same coin. *A Theology of Love* caused a stir in Wesleyan circles. Conservatives objected to Wynkoop's revision of classic Holiness ideas and disapproved of her fluency in the latest theological debates—while those scholars who had been pushing for a return to classical Wesleyanism embraced the book as exactly the accessible reinterpretation of their tradition that Holiness Christians needed.

Thanks to the influence of seminary president William Greathouse (a mastermind at promoting the "back to Wesley movement" in Nazarene institutions) *A Theology of Love* became required reading at Nazarene Theological Seminary. Church leaders from other branches of the Wesleyan tradition applauded her work. "The book has shaken up the Church of the Nazarene considerably! I hope it will do the same thing for the Free Methodist Church," wrote Paul Ellis, a Free Methodist bishop. "We see it as significant because it puts its finger on what we feel to be the heart of the Wesleyan dynamic," wrote scholars Howard Snyder (a Free Methodist) and Donald Dayton (a Wesleyan Methodist) in an invitation to Wynkoop to contribute to a volume they were preparing on Wesleyan theology. In Dayton's view, Wesley was spurred to lead the Methodist revival not only by the spiritual apathy he witnessed, but by the Anglican Church's indifference to social injustice, particularly the slave trade. The founders of his own denomination, the Wesleyan Methodist Church, broke away from other Methodists in 1843 "over a social issue—abolitionism," he wrote to Wynkoop in a letter emphasizing the need to bring the Wesleyan message to other evangelicals.[38]

Wynkoop's influence trickled down below elite academic circles. In 1975, the director of Curriculum Ministries at the Free Methodist Publishing house, who worked closely with other Wesleyan and Holiness churches to plan Sunday school and Vacation Bible School curricula for seven denominations, gushed to Wynkoop that the "perspective of *A Theology of Love* will be influencing the curriculum materials for these denominations."[39] Within a few years, the book's critique of humanitarian indifference in modern evangelicalism earned fans well beyond Wesleyan churches. "Your book, A Theology of Love, has been a joy to me, and a great help to me in wrestling with controversial issues currently agitating the Seventh-day Adventist church," wrote a professor at Loma Linda University.[40] The ideas of elite intellectuals—if ensconced in institutions and endorsed by denominational leadership—could reverberate beyond the bounds of ivory-tower debate.

The Reformed challenge—in its liberal European, fundamentalist, and neo-evangelical forms—struck a powerful chord across evangelical communities ranging from Pentecostals to Nazarenes. Adopting the hyper-rationalist, totalizing idiom popular among the ideologues of the early twentieth century, Reformed theologians seemed to have answers for all the day's pressing challenges, be it the horror of world war, the communist menace, or the continuing harm that modern scholarship posed to the Bible. Through their roles as seminary and college professors, authors of their churches' formal policies and theological texts, and contributors to church media, non-Reformed leaders conveyed to laypeople a mixed message that both pushed Reformed neo-evangelicalism away and pulled it close. Each denomination's intellectuals, leading journalists, and evangelists rarely agreed among themselves about the relationship their church ought to have to the amorphous community known as evangelicalism, or which aspects of their church history were fundamental, and which were foreign accretions.

This was the more fundamental dilemma: the tangled history within each strand of evangelicalism. Each was a blend of different theologies, personalities, and cultures, irreducible to any pristine essence or single authority. These churches' ambivalence toward the labels "evangelical" or "fundamentalist" arose, like Nelson Bell's battle with Bob Jones, from a deeper contest over history and identity. Reformed ideas about the redemption of culture and the invincibility of the inerrant Bible provided the promise of security in an era of change. But the neo-evangelical proposal to resuscitate conservative Protestant creativity and influence was not the only answer in the Christian tradition. Their gospel won some converts. Yet their campaign also revealed different "evangelicalisms" at odds with one another over the nature of religious experience and the gathered church, and a Christian's place in politics and culture.

Part II

To Evangelize the World

Chapter 5

The Marks of Campus Conversion

"READING THE MAGAZINE, CHRISTIANITY TODAY, I REALIZE OVER AND over the difference between theologians and Bible Institute men," Oregon evangelist Hugh Andrews wrote to Sam Sutherland in 1962. "The theologians would get us all wrapt [sic] up in Ecumenicity and leave us near death for Evangelism. The Word says LOVE ONE ANOTHER, yes, but it also reads, 'Press toward the MARK!'"[1]

Sutherland, president of Biola College in the Los Angeles suburb of La Mirada, was always cheered by letters from alumni. When Andrews was a student, Biola was still the Bible Institute of Los Angeles, snug in its citadel downtown. Students lived in dormitories flanking the Italianate grandeur of the Church of the Open Door, whose red neon rooftop sign proclaimed "Jesus Saves" and whose bells boomed hymns and gospel songs over the screech and honk of Los Angeles traffic three times daily. Sutherland shared Andrews's trepidations about those neo-evangelicals who confused their egghead enterprises with Bible-based revival. "We are most heartily opposed to all of the neo-orthodox, neo-evangelical and, now the latest, neo-conservative positions," he assured a pastor in Massachusetts. "We do have students here who have come from churches whose pastors are neo-evangelical, but we endeavor to point out to these young people in the classrooms here at Biola the dangers of these positions and the inevitable disastrous results to which they lead."[2]

Sutherland disarmed visitors with his toothy smile and taste for flamboyant ties, but he was no academic slouch—he came to Biola with degrees from Occidental College and Princeton Theological Seminary. Yet he was firmly a "Bible Institute man" and not a "theologian": like most of his peers at Bible colleges around the country, he had little time for the men at *Christianity Today* who had appointed themselves the intellectual vanguard of conservative Protestantism. There was something vaguely blasphemous in the neo-evangelicals' demands that Christians fully engage the modern world and seek out the attention of heretics like Karl Barth. Sutherland knew his business was training Christians in the practical tools of evangelism, not chasing after intellectual prestige—but if he believed that he could avoid the questions that preoccupied the neo-evangelicals, he was kidding himself.

Bible colleges were not isolated fortresses. Many Biola alumni regretted that the school's expansion required a new campus outside central Los Angeles—they prided themselves on championing the gospel in the heart of Gomorrah. Although many Bible colleges promised parents that they would insulate their children from godless materialism, they also had to promise an education that would prepare students for careers in a changing America. To maintain their authority in the years after World War II—and their bottom line—Bible schools had to rethink the essence of fundamentalist education. Despite Sutherland's skepticism toward *Christianity Today*, by the time of his correspondence with Hugh Andrews he had spent twenty years positioning Biola to engage mainstream academia and supplement technical training in evangelism with liberal arts courses and a holistic Christian worldview. The savviest fundamentalist educators took advantage of inevitable change—particularly the pressure to professionalize and embrace accreditation—by adopting these changes on their own terms as tools that might, if carefully controlled, strengthen the Bible college movement. By the 1960s, their concessions yielded more radical consequences than anyone anticipated.

The Ascent of Expertise

Professional academic work was a nineteenth-century invention. As an increasing array of professions demanded specialized knowledge, Americans remade their colleges—founded with a heavy emphasis on ministerial training, and offering the same curriculum to all, whether or not the church had called them—to equip students with expertise in their chosen occupation. Beginning with the foundation of Johns Hopkins University in 1876, Americans aped the emerging German model of large research-oriented institutions. They adopted the Germans' high bars of entry, hierarchies of professorships and degrees, array of specializations, and commitment to the discovery of new knowledge over the pious preservation of established truths.

At the same time, a wide range of disciplines began standardizing requirements for those who sought to enter their fields. The American Medical Association was one of the earliest professional organizations, dating from 1847. The American Bar Association organized in 1878. Neurologists organized in 1875; historians in 1884, church historians and American folklorists in 1888. Membership dues, professional journals, and annual conferences gave even the most loosely defined discipline an air of legitimacy, prestige, and scientific rigor. In a fluid democracy like nineteenth-century America, where no king granted titles and no feudal lords had left their mark, self-described professionals manufactured status for themselves.[3] By the end of the nineteenth century, the advanced degree had become their common currency. It was a mark of standing, and a pledge of obedience to the scientific method and peer review as the court of final judgment.

Now that a college degree carried such weight, it would not do to leave its meaning up for grabs. Modern accreditation—the certification and periodic audit of an institution by external assessors—originated in the 1870s and 1880s, when universities and colleges began to help secondary schools structure their courses to meet the demands of college entrance exams.[4] This process encouraged the formation of regional accreditation associations, through which colleges kept pace with their peers and guaranteed mutual recognition of credits and degrees. The North Central Association of Colleges and Schools issued its first list of accredited colleges—which included Wheaton College—in 1913.

Fundamentalists, for the most part, wanted no part of this. Wheaton president Charles Blanchard's decision to seek accreditation was a maverick choice. A small number of schools followed Wheaton's example, but generally few colleges that could be called evangelical or fundamentalist received accreditation before the late 1950s—about twenty years after most Roman Catholic colleges, and thirty to forty years after the first secular and mainline Protestant colleges.[5]

Fundamentalists and conservative evangelicals understood the history of American higher education as a story of decline from holiness to heterodoxy. Their own institutions were oases where the Bible still reigned. Moreover, early Bible college leaders were unimpressed by a self-policing, credentialed elite. They exalted the common sense of the layman whose faith was unmuddled by the mystifications of so-called experts. When the Bible college movement began in the 1880s, its founders expressly set out to train nonordained Christian workers: men and women who planned to devote themselves to full- or part-time evangelism and church service (they later added courses to prepare pastors). Initially, most did not grant degrees, which struck them as overly intellectual and worldly. Instead they issued simple "diplomas" that certified course completion. Some schools' charters explicitly limited the kinds of diplomas they could grant, as if the founders feared their successors' pretentions and wished to enshrine the cult of the amateur.[6]

Their curricula were biblical and practical. Common courses besides doctrine and English Bible (distinct from the study of scripture in original languages, although some schools later added coursework in Greek and Hebrew) included hymnody, child evangelism, basic medical training, and later on—for the daring who hoped to evangelize the darkest reaches of Africa, and for veteran pilots who wanted to put wartime flying experience to God's service—missionary aviation. By the late 1940s, classes offered at Moody Bible Institute ranged from "Sunday School Administration" to "Chalk Illustration" and "Sewing or Cookery." Aspiring missionaries studied "Minor Surgery" and "Pagan Religious Psychology." In contrast to the effete training of "professionals" who refused to work with their hands, Bible school curricula emphasized manual labor, the dirty work crucial to missions and church service. "Neither a college nor a seminary, but a school for intensive Bible study and practical experience in soul-winning— that is Moody Bible Institute," declared Moody's course catalog for 1949– 1950. "Correct methods—the 'know-how' for various fields of Christian service—coupled with a usable knowledge of God's Word are the basis of its curriculum."[7]

Though Bible colleges were small institutions with modest enrollment, they formed a core axis of American fundamentalism.[8] In early decades their clout came not from official accreditation or church affiliation, but from the stature of the crusading commanders who founded them—such as Dwight Moody's institute or William Bell Riley's empire based at Northwestern Bible and Missionary Training School in Minnesota—and from proof of their success in the soul-winning trade: baptism numbers and teeming revivals, networks of weekend Bible conferences and newsletters that equipped pastors and lay believers with the latest godly armaments. Biola and Moody ran vast radio and print media empires that extended their reach far beyond the bounds of campus. Supporting thousands of missionaries, church workers, and radio and print sermons each year, Bible colleges wielded influence equal to that of small denominations.[9]

They sought recognition and status the old-fashioned way: by bestowing it upon each other. Early fundamentalism was a web of mutually legitimating relationships. "I looked over the graduates and feel that it is time that we were honoring someone in the Brethren denomination," wrote Sam Sutherland, then dean at Biola, to Louis Bauman, a pastor in Long Beach. Bauman was dear to his heart: He was a prophecy-minded Anabaptist with a preference for Biola's dispensationalist theology and had recently led a group of like-minded fundamentalists to found the Grace Brethren fellowship of churches. Sutherland planned to award an honorary degree to a Biola alumnus who now taught at the new denomination's flagship school, Grace Theological Seminary in Indiana: "We would like to tie in Grace Theological Seminary and the Brethren denomination that much more intimately with the Bible Institute."[10]

These rituals of reciprocal regard would continue for decades, but from the 1940s onward the terrain of American education began to shift under fundamentalists' feet. New economic boons and the Servicemen's Readjustment Act of 1944—the GI Bill—populated schools with students who had never set foot on a college campus before. The GI Bill offered tuition of up to $500 per year for college or technical school, as well as a modest living allowance, for all 16 million servicemen and servicewomen returning from the war.[11] The federal government, keen to raise up a generation with the skills necessary to win the Cold War, leaned on educators to rethink their curricula. "There is hardly a university or college in the country which has not had a committee at work in these years considering basic educational questions," wrote Harvard president James Conant in the 1945 Harvard Report, which evangelical educators read and cited (the NAE would publish its own report, *Christian Education in a Democracy*, six years later). The Harvard Report favored a general core curriculum over vocational training and reflected widespread concern that Americans needed a moral foundation as much as they needed professional skills. "The war period taught a sharp lesson. It suddenly became clear that boys and girls could become the best specialists and engineers and yet be good Nazis," noted the *Christian Science Monitor*. "Something was very wrong."[12]

Fundamentalist Christians never lacked an explanation of what went wrong: Modern man had tried to raise himself above the authority of the Bible. But if they were confident in their worldview, their methods for proclaiming that worldview were under new pressure by the 1940s. Congress would soon revise the GI Bill to limit funding to students attending accredited institutions. Mission boards showed a growing preference for candidates with more than a Bible college diploma. Christian liberal arts colleges that had once accepted Bible school graduates without reservation now demanded accredited degrees.[13] Many students now arrived with ambitions that ranged beyond foreign missions or conventional church service—and required a bachelor's degree, if not more. Bible colleges' resistance to the professional structures and procedures adopted by secular academia blinded them to just how professionally minded even the fundamentalist world had become. Sutherland lamented that "the world in general has gone, I would dare to say, educationally berserk." The president of Eastern Bible Institute, an Assemblies of God school, complained that his students were no longer content to remain in the world circumscribed by church authority. "A veritable mania is sweeping the whole evangelical and Pentecostal world for degrees that are transferable on the highest levels of education," wrote Milton Wells to Ralph Riggs, the denomination's general superintendent. "Spiritual excellence is being relinquished imperceptibly for intellectual excellence."[14]

After a spike in enrollment during and immediately after the war, plunging numbers confirmed administrators' fears that their institutions were failing to meet student needs. An Assemblies of God survey in the late 1940s revealed that 43 percent of students at the church's schools "said plainly that they were not called to ministry...we should make provision for them here, or elsewhere, and give them something appropriate to them," Ralph Riggs told a gathering of Bible college teachers.[15] Bible colleges and institutes were growing more slowly than the college-age population and failing to match the expansion of public universities or secular private colleges.[16] Wells admitted that Eastern Bible Institute was trying to keep pace with "the raising of educational standards"—which compelled the school to raise fees—but he believed a widespread spiritual malaise, rather than climbing tuition costs, was to blame for plummeting enrollment.

> The American way of life (two cars, expensive television sets, rich wardrobes, a superabundance of food, beautiful home conditions with every modern gadget) is equated with godliness....An overemphasis on higher education, both within and without the Pentecostal movement, is directing youths' vision away from the call of God to preach the Gospel. Higher education of any sort stimulates a keen desire for big earnings, positions of prominence, and a feeling of spiritual complacency...'KNOWLEDGE PUFFETH UP'; it caters to the EGO! Calvary-love builds up and magnifies the Lord. Not a few are distressed that so many graduates of our Bible colleges are leaving the ministry for other more lucrative vocations.[17]

Wells's complaint reflected his church's long-standing ambivalence toward academia. Fundamentalists had no monopoly, of course, on frustration at the encroachment of material concerns upon the life of the mind. "The universities are dependent on the people. The people love money and think that education is a way of getting it," the University of Chicago's Robert Maynard Hutchins had complained in 1936. Writing eighty years earlier, British educator and Catholic convert John Henry Newman lamented, "Some great men...argue as if every thing, as well as every person, had its price; and that where there has been a great outlay, they have a right to expect a return in kind. This they call making Education and Instruction 'useful,' and 'Utility' becomes their watchword...I am arguing, and shall argue, against Professional or Scientific knowledge as the sufficient end of a University Education."[18] Newman noted that his opponents were merely rehashing the demand of seventeenth-century philosopher

John Locke that "utility may be the end of education." One wonders if Socrates got into trouble not so much for denying the gods, but because parents doubted that his ruminations were preparing the sons of Athens for lucrative careers.

THE UNEQUAL YOKE OF ACCREDITATION

Bible college educators had to convince students and tuition-paying families that their schools prepared young people to thrive in the modern world. To do so, they worked together to reinvent themselves. After two years of preparations, the organizational meeting of the Accrediting Association of Bible Institutes and Bible Colleges convened at Winona Lake, Indiana, in December 1947. (The group soon dropped "Bible Institutes" from its title: The term signaled amateurism and disdain for scholarship, even to fundamentalists.) If accreditation was now the governing paradigm of higher education, the Bible colleges would confront it on their own terms by forming a "professional accrediting agency" to "encourage us to build solidly and rightly in order that we may be worthy of the recognition we seek in the educational world." Unlike evangelicals' later political action in the realm of education—the homeschooling and private Christian academies of the 1960s, the civic protests and hostile takeovers of school boards—the Accrediting Association of Bible Colleges was not a weapon of the culture war. The association's founders sought inclusion and parity, not hostile resistance.[19]

As these objectives came into focus, fundamentalist educators' attitudes toward professional academia shifted. In a 1950 letter to a colleague, Sutherland bragged about the fleet of new PhDs on his faculty—a striking sentiment from a man who, only two years earlier, complained that the world had gone "educationally berserk." Like many of his colleagues, Sutherland had realized that there were "safe" ways for faculty members to pursue PhDs. Many completed their doctorates at nearby universities while continuing to teach—avoiding total immersion in a secular atmosphere— and attended schools with a history of welcoming evangelical scholars, such as the University of Southern California and Boston University (both had Methodist roots).[20] Obeying the rules of secular education could enhance Bible colleges' authority within the evangelical world and compel nonevangelicals to take them seriously. "I feel that as our movement grows and becomes established in the American picture, indeed in the world picture, as one of the important religious movements of the world, it will be increasingly desirable and necessary to have more men in our ministry who can hold their own with other men both intellectually and spiritually," wrote Leland Keys, the president of Bethany Bible College, a Pentecostal school in Santa Cruz.[21]

Sutherland insisted on keeping curricular requirements for member schools fairly general. He felt strongly (against the opposition of some colleagues) that the association should not require all schools to adhere to premillennialist eschatology—an important and surprising point of doctrinal flexibility. The dispensationalist form of premillennialism that John Nelson Darby had brought to the United States—popularized by revivalists like Dwight Moody and anchored by the annotations of Cyrus Scofield's Reference Bible—was a doctrine that many feared was under threat as evangelicals adapted to professional academia. This was a sensitive issue at Biola. Suspicions among the school's alumni and fundamentalist critics that the school was insufficiently dispensationalist almost ruined the institute in the 1920s. A friend of Biola wrote to Sutherland with his concern that the Scofield Bible always receive "proper respect." He feared that "some men who are high in the academic realm and who have spent many years in school have not thought themselves through on many of the problems of eschatology. Such men are an easy prey for the A-millenial [sic] boosters who have nothing to build up but are very adept at tearing down."[22]

The Bible college movement was highly eschatological in its origins, dispensing with fancy degrees and admitting all comers. If Christ's return was imminent, little time remained to reach the lost. Premillennialism remained important, but educators increasingly believed that their students needed broader, more professional preparation to carry God's word throughout mainstream culture. Though he worried about the consequences of a vague statement of faith, Robert McQuilkin admitted that "liberty in eschatology" might be necessary to "help correct the present unfortunate dogmatic attitude of some leaders in 'fundamentalism.'" He hoped that his school, Columbia Bible College in South Carolina, would soon "partake of the character of a college, a seminary-college, a Bible Institute," for students should not have to choose between the liberal arts and a Bible-based education. McQuilkin knew the value of a broad curriculum—his bachelor's degree was from the University of Pennsylvania—but he worried where these compromises might lead: "If we lean toward liberal arts, then we are in danger of curtailing our emphasis upon the Bible and Christian doctrine and Christian service."[23]

McQuilkin smarted under his regional accrediting association's requirement that Columbia install two modern science labs and faculty qualified to teach a full program in the hard sciences. Most Bible colleges shared his wariness of drifting too far from their original mission: evangelism. They shared the same disdain for materialistic society and paycheck-fever that compelled Robert Maynard Hutchins and his allies to rally around the liberal arts and "Great Books"—but to fundamentalists, the humanities and sciences were not an antidote to materialism. On the contrary, the liberal arts were like iodine: beneficial in small quantities, but a large dose would poison the Bible college enterprise. As if to reaffirm Biola's commitment to old-time religion in the midst of so much accommodation to secular academia, in 1958 the college sponsored a new edition of the *Fundamentals*, the pamphlet series that helped launch the fundamentalist movement at the turn of the century.[24]

The AABC became a fulcrum of change in fundamentalist and conservative evangelical education. It offered a striking contrast to earlier fundamentalists' efforts to supervise the movement's Bible schools, such as the plan of the World Christian Fundamentals Association (founded in 1919) to select a group of schools loyal to inerrancy and other fundamentals.[25] The AABC attended to orthodoxy, but was equally concerned with academic excellence and marketing the Bible school in mainstream American society. By the early 1960s, its evaluative process had precipitated a top tier of Bible colleges—such as Biola, Azusa Pacific College, and Bethel College—most of which would eventually develop (true to their founders' fears) into full-fledged liberal arts colleges, and even rechristen themselves as universities. By the mid-1960s, the assumptions of secular academe had become so ingrained in the AABC that while the association praised Columbia Bible College for sending 99 percent of its students into church service, it declined to renew the school's accreditation. Officers criticized Columbia's "lack of clarity in academic objectives, low standards in some courses, irregularities in grading, weaknesses in library holdings, deviation from standard college accounting," and an "anti-intellectual" culture on campus. The

AABC took particular exception to the statement in Columbia's course catalog that "Christian doctrines...are the only reasonable truths that man's intellect can accept."[26]

Columbia's trustees responded curtly, noting that the AABC had never before challenged that statement—written by one of the AABC's own founders, Robert McQuilkin. The evaluation committee "should realize that the main thrust of its recommendations has repeatedly destroyed spiritual effectiveness throughout the course of church history." Columbia Bible College eventually withdrew from the AABC altogether. By then, the AABC was itself seeking "supra-accreditation" from the National Commission on Accrediting, whose approval the association hoped would demonstrate "the professional character of the AABC." Yet what looked to critics like weak-kneed accommodation was, rather, the latest iteration of evangelicalism's pragmatic spirit—the adaptable temperament that allowed evangelicals to turn their anxiety about religious identity into a source of vigor, and to reposition their institutions to stand within a changing mainstream culture while holding the authority of that culture at arm's length.[27]

ACADEMIC FREEDOM AND ITS CRITICS

The one thing most crucial to professional higher education was the one thing that most stymied conservative Protestant educators: academic freedom. Behind their hand-wringing over the liberal arts and their resentment of meddling accreditors was the fear that these reforms would encourage teachers and students to prize intellectual exploration over evangelism and prefer the scientific method to proof texts. They would ask questions—and venture answers—that might place their salvation at risk.

"You and I will say that education is not a substitute for the power of God," Ralph Riggs told teachers at Glad Tidings Bible Institute. "We want that down in black and white and clearly understood on the record....We are not educating for education's sake, but rather as a means to an end." At the same time, Riggs spoke for colleagues across the fundamentalist and evangelical academy when he encouraged teachers to embrace intellectual ambition. Their acceptance of Christ as lord and savior specially equipped them—indeed, obliged them—to pursue knowledge. "Men are totally depraved, helplessly lost in sin," he explained.

There is a fundamental premise, that the natural mind, that of the college professor and of us all by natural birth, is darkened by reason of sin, blinded and darkened, and we grope. Look at all the philosophers of the past. They just go in circles, and one contradicts the other.... We have the mind of Christ, Christ is made unto us wisdom, which comes flashing into our intelligence, a divine light which enables us to begin to understand and to learn. Thus we have our path charted for us where we can really begin to understand the mysteries of life.[28]

Riggs told the teachers that the best way to guide students through "the mysteries of life" was by the "inductive method," in which students reasoned from individual facts toward abstract conclusions. This method was "the way the human race has learned," and "cultivates the sense of mental independence."[29] Inductive Bible study had long formed the core of evangelical and fundamentalist pedagogy. Students studied the "facts" of the Bible for themselves. Theology was not a subjective exercise, but a "science" above all others, the explication of God's revelation.

The inductive method appeared to repair the fracture between faith and reason. It restored the Bible to its rightful authority while assimilating—yet restraining—human rationalism. Over the years, conservative Protestants would use it to hold at bay a range of dangerous ideas, condemning everything from Darwin's evolution to inborn homosexual orientation as mere "theories," speculative hypotheses without basis in the inductive study of facts. By this standard, academic freedom as understood in the modern secular university—the liberty to follow scientific observation to its conclusions even if those conclusions flout received wisdom, and the liberty to answer to no other authority than one's colleagues—was not freedom at all, but slavery to human pride that would lead young Christians from the narrow path.

Absent formal tenure processes, the fate of Bible college faculty was usually in the hands of the president and trustees. What oversight there was usually came from a governing church body rather than from within the school itself. Even schools with greater autonomy could not afford to offend their denominational constituencies for fear of jeopardizing their financial support. Some institutions—particularly colleges in the Wesleyan Holiness and Restorationist traditions that had resisted the fundamentalist obsession with fine points of dogma—remained officially mum on the subjects of academic freedom or statements of faith, and relied on campus culture and self-censorship to rein in wayward speech. Administrators at other schools published explicit restrictions: "The naturally sacred right of freedom of expression is, of course, recognized by Central Bible Institute and Seminary as a requisite for effective and intelligent dissemination of ideas," read a 1963 faculty handbook. "Nevertheless...All are expected to show a respectful and sympathetic attitude toward the doctrines of the Church and the American principles of government. Obviously any grave offense against these doctrines and/or principles must be considered just cause for dismissal."[30]

Yet Christian colleges could not win the approval of secular accrediting bodies without raising faculty salaries (traditionally low, for such teaching was, in the words of one college president, "a sacrificial ministry instead of merely a profession"), standardizing tenure, and codifying operating procedures in a way that checked executive power and gave the faculty some voice and opportunity for professional development. Capricious tenure policies and unfair dismissal sometimes continued, but now that their schools were part of interstate associations that included public, Roman Catholic, and mainline Protestant colleges and universities, faculty began to think of themselves as professional scholars responsible not only to their college and church, but to a community of intellectual peers. In the 1950s and 1960s—decades behind their colleagues in secular academia—they began to organize their own academic societies, networks for evangelical historians, psychologists, sociologists, and others who sought to balance standards of professional scholarship with the demands of faith.[31]

This belated organizing was not due to a lack of professional training. Most of Fuller's early faculty held degrees from prestigious American and European universities, and by the 1950s even a Bible college like Biola had its share of impressive PhDs. Through the 1950s and 1960s, however, many of the most talented evangelical scholars spent their careers at Christian colleges that did not encourage them to think of themselves as citizens of a broader intellectual community. Some evangelical academics managed fine careers in secular academe: Timothy L. Smith, an ordained Nazarene minister and prominent historian of American religion who earned his PhD at

Harvard under Arthur M. Schlesinger, taught for decades at Johns Hopkins; Robert Frykenberg, a Baptist born to missionaries in India, trained at the University of London and taught South Asian studies at the University of Wisconsin. Both men were historians whose discipline demanded little public engagement with knotty questions of biblical criticism or science that often stymied evangelicals. Just as important, these men taught not at liberal arts colleges focused on forming the young, but at universities that prized original research—institutions that evangelicals had tried and failed to establish for themselves.[32]

Youthful Defiance

In 1965, when auditors from the North Central Association visited Evangel College, the ten-year-old Assemblies of God liberal arts college in Springfield, Missouri, they acknowledged the difficulties involved in trying to maintain loyalty to old orthodoxies and professional academic standards at the same time:

> In its relations with the denomination, the College may be walking a kind of tightrope. On one hand, the College will probably serve as a major source of change in the denomination, providing leadership as the Church itself becomes more middle class and values education more highly. On the other hand, it is seen by many supporters as a conserver of existing attitudes and institutions, and in some ways it undoubtedly does perform that function.[33]

By the mid-1960s, evangelical educators still had not solved their institutions' crisis of identity and purpose. While college administrators sought to attract students with broader curricula and faculty strained to earn the respect of colleagues outside the evangelical world, parents still expected their churches' schools to insulate—or at least arm—their children against the scandal of mainstream society. Their task grew more complicated in the 1950s and 1960s, when the challenge of professionalization in higher education coincided with the emergence of a self-conscious American youth culture.

The cliché of the college student newly independent from coddling parents and on a quest to find his purpose in life is a relatively recent phenomenon. The notion of "adolescence" entered popular usage in the late nineteenth century, scrutinized by researchers suddenly fascinated by child development and adorned with rites of passage such as the "coming out" ball. In postwar America, however, adolescents no longer occupied a carefully mediated prelude to adulthood, but viewed themselves as individuals distinct from both children and adults, entitled to pursue their own ends. Americans coined the word "teenager" in the late 1940s, with connotations of carefree and sometimes troublesome youth at odds with their parents. Teenagers emerged as major economic players. Hollywood discovered a booming market for "teenpics" in the 1950s, and conservative commentators, hysterical over juvenile delinquency, blamed comic books and movies for corrupting young people. Perhaps most important, by the 1950s high school had become a far more universal experience for American teens, including conservative Protestants. More than 80 percent of teens attended, and segregation with youth their own age for much of the week encouraged them to hone their own subculture, increasingly mysterious to adults.[34] For those who went on to college, higher education no longer meant only professional preparation for adulthood, but the opportunity for self-reinvention and willful disobedience.

Students at Bible schools and conservative Christian colleges lagged behind this cultural shift. Through the 1950s, young people at schools such as Moody and Biola still considered themselves adults-in-training, preparing to take over the older generation's battle against modernism and secularism. The *Moody Student*, Moody Bible Institute's student newspaper (widely read by an international constituency of alumni and supporters), reprinted editorials by senior fundamentalists and conservative evangelicals, such as Harold Ockenga's 1947 challenge, "Can Fundamentalism Win America?" This crisis of purpose and identity was not a fringe notion limited to a handful of neo-evangelicals at Fuller or *Christianity Today*, but one that "must be faced by every intelligent thinking Moody student," the editors noted.[35]

Campus discourse began to evolve in the mid-1960s. In 1964, editor Leith Anderson—who was no separatist, and would go on to serve as president of the National Association of Evangelicals—urged students to tune into current affairs and "become involved in political life." The paper covered the civil rights movement, foreign affairs, and secular philosophy.[36] But *Moody Student* contributors still wrote as lifelong servants of their movement rather than young people struggling to "find themselves" or push back against authority. "We are not here to entertain people for a living," wrote one student who disapproved of humorous skits performed to welcome freshmen during the first week of classes. "We are here as God's ambassadors to make Christianity relevant, practical, and real."[37]

The professionalization of Bible school training—the embrace of secular academic goals and standards—encouraged students to think of themselves not as Christian gentlemen and ladies, but as ordinary college kids who took classes that were no longer so different from those at the public university across town. "Accreditation is bringing a different quality of student to campus," wrote one student on a Biola questionnaire. "The higher tuition is limiting Biola to the more sophisticated, better dressed, more affluent young person." Another worried that the school's spiritual vitality must "be guarded closely now that Biola is accredited. It's easy to lose the Christian emphasis when aiming for academic excellence. History repeats itself. To compete with secular schools toward academic attainment can bring about the downfall of the Christian principle."[38]

By the late 1960s, Bible school students had begun a milder version of the struggle against authority then troubling campuses across the country. At Moody, in a 1969 editorial titled "Moody Student under fire," the editors declared their free speech was under attack: "The student newspaper is not the administration's vocal cords." At Biola that same year, college president Sam Sutherland was obliged to reassure angry alumni that the school remained a biblical bastion despite an article in the student paper, the *Chimes*, lauding 1968 Democratic presidential candidate Hubert Humphrey. Sutherland defended the article—"Well over 80% of the students are Republican, but Biola does have some wonderful students who are Democrats"—but he agreed that another *Chimes* columnist was out of order in advertising a Joan Baez concert and a visit to a local brewery. "Most assuredly, we do not endorse such left-wing folksingers, nor do we endorse the visiting of breweries at any time, especially on a Sunday afternoon," he wrote.[39]

When student writers departed from what Sutherland considered the Biola consensus, he first tried polite cajoling—"Dear Todd: I have just read your column...I found it to be quite interesting. However, I am afraid it gives one the impression that we are quite opposed to the war in Vietnam..."—but he did not hesitate to discipline those who continued to cause trouble. "These are the names that have come to my attention for various reasons," he wrote at the top of a long list of students whose sins included campaigning for Robert F. Kennedy, grumbling about mandatory chapel, and writing for an independent student publication, *The Catacomb*, that challenged the administration. "I believe we could get along very nicely without them, unless they change their attitudes." If the range of academic inquiry had widened, the acceptable results were still strictly limited. "We study these various academic fields, we study these various philosophies so that our students can be aware and talk intelligently about these subjects when they come into contact with other people," Sutherland told a student reporter. "We enroll only those students who accept the ideological pattern of the school, whereby their academic freedom will automatically operate within the pattern of the school."[40]

THE INSIDIOUS LIBERAL ARTS

The chastening example of Wheaton College, the "fundamentalist Harvard," showed what an overdose of academic freedom and liberal arts could mean for Christian education. Although each evangelical college has had its own odyssey, Wheaton is of special importance. It has long had outsized influence in the world of evangelical education—influence that would grow in the last third of the twentieth century as many denominational colleges pruned their distinctive doctrines and adopted the broader "evangelical" label in order to widen their appeal in the marketplace of conservative Protestant higher education. "The Wheaton model has influenced a variety of institutions whose vision has grown beyond sectarian or denominational identities in their search for broader Christian self-understanding," one admirer wrote.[41]

During the early decades of the twentieth century, Wheaton's fundamentalist credentials rivaled Moody's or Biola's. In 1927, when Bob Jones founded his college at College Point, Florida, Wheaton president J. Oliver Buswell, Jr., sent him a gruff letter arguing that America had no need for another fundamentalist college when Wheaton was carrying on the defense of orthodox Christianity well enough.[42] Yet by the late 1940s, Wheaton's new literary magazine, *Kodon*, was cautiously criticizing fundamentalism. "I am a Fundamentalist. And, dollars to doughnuts, so are you," wrote a student named John Stam, who went on to study at Fuller and teach at a seminary in Costa Rica. "But just because all of us are loyal to fundamentalism, that very loyalty should compel us to rigorously examine it and vigilantly guard it against the inroad of dangerous elements." Stam did not fear doctrinal error, but insincere legalisms and empty hymns. He cited scripture—but he also approvingly quoted the liberal mainline *Christian Century*.[43]

Kodon's cover art became increasingly experimental. Each issue featured more adventurous content: editorials complaining about Wheaton's ethnocentrism; ongoing debates over whether Wheaton ought to permit drama classes and performances; even short stories romanticizing Catholic monasticism. In the 1950s both *Kodon* and the student newspaper, the *Wheaton Record*, covered national and international politics. One essay in *Kodon* began boldly, "Capitalism has failed!" Despite edgy letters challenging biblical inerrancy from "Two Neo-Orthodox Students" and editorials chastising the evangelical church for rejecting evolution—"her objections to the progress of science no more stopped that progress than the screaming's [*sic*] of a small child prevent father's escorting him to the woodshed"—President V. Raymond Edman did not move to quash their dissent.[44]

Tensions between student editors and the administration escalated when Wesley Earl Craven assumed the editorship of *Kodon* in the fall of 1962. Craven, who would later earn fame as director of the *Nightmare on Elm Street* and *Scream* horror films, had already made a name on campus with a series of dark short stories subverting traditional Christian sensibilities. When he took the helm as editor-in-chief he announced his intentions with "A Warning from the Editor," in which he explained that the staff had revised *Kodon's* constitution to liberate the magazine from fundamentalism's constraints.[45] After scandalized readers charged that the disturbing and morally complex stories in the fall issue failed to reflect "the true spirit of Wheaton College" and "the attractiveness of the Christian life," the *Record's* sympathetic editors granted Craven space on their editorial page in which to answer his "self-styled critics" who called the magazine's new realism a "naturalistic whine":

> You plead for a return to a "firm Christian stand." We of KODON feel
> it is time the Christian Church stopped "standing" around and began

to regain some of the ground it has...passively surrendered in the past centuries....Certainly there is no ultimate defeat, but any sensitive person can see failure in the life about him, even in his own life. There is much suffering and frustration, pain and uncertainty. Is a response to this a whine? I would not call this whining anymore than I would call Christ a whining naturalist for moaning "Father Father, why have you forsaken me?"[46]

Wheaton's Board of Trustees suspended *Kodon* for the remainder of the year. The magazine resumed publication in the fall of 1963, but Craven was no longer on the masthead.[47]

The experience of Wheaton's undergraduate journalists was not unique. Some scholars suggest that 1963 was the year "precisely when the challenge to the notion of *in loco parentis* began to be felt at virtually all church-related or Christian colleges in the country." Students at Calvin College in Michigan waged a similar battle over their desire to watch and review movies, and in 1968 student Paul Schrader (who would go on to write *Taxi Driver* and *The Last Temptation of Christ*) achieved "full martyrdom" when the administration dismissed him and other staffers from their positions at the student newspaper on charges of "bad taste, insubordination, and misuse of funds." The "radicals" whose essays and editorials questioned the status quo were probably a small minority at Wheaton, as they were on most college campuses. However, between World War II and 1963, Wheaton did for students what it had done for Carl Henry, Harold Lindsell, and their classmates thirty years earlier: It taught them that conservative Protestantism was not a rationale for complacence, or a bar to the world of ideas.[48]

These students had two generations' distance from the fundamentalist–modernist battles, and their concerns lacked the theological rigor of the Reformed bloc at *Christianity Today* and the Evangelical Theological Society. While the neo-evangelicals' mentor at Wheaton was Gordon Clark, a philosopher known for his part in church controversy, the teachers who most inspired the student writers of the 1950s and 1960s were irenic personalities who specialized in art, literature, and the history of ideas. In 1951 Wheaton hired Arthur Holmes, a Wheaton alumnus who earned his PhD at Northwestern, as the college's first professional philosopher since Clark's departure (another Northwestern-trained philosopher who joined Holmes at Wheaton, John Alexander, founded the left-wing evangelical magazines *Freedom Now* and the *Other Side* and inspired a wave of civil rights activism on campus in the late 1960s). Holmes began an annual series of conferences, wrote profusely about Christian education, and urged students to engage with ideas outside their own tradition. He collaborated with Shakespeare scholar Beatrice Batson, who joined the faculty in 1957, to found the "Book of the Semester" program, which encouraged all undergraduates to read and discuss a particular work of literature, cultural studies, or history (the semester before the *Kodon* kerfuffle, they read Arnold Toynbee's *Civilization on Trial*; Toynbee lectured on campus in May).[49]

Interest in the fine arts at Wheaton, anemic during Carl Henry's time, was growing. "Modern art is real and meaningful as an expression of what is in the heart of modern man, a reflection of his *weltanschauung*," Dutch art historian Hans Rookmaaker told students gathered for chapel in 1961. The expansion of course offerings in art at Wheaton, Biola, and other Christian colleges sowed the seeds for a small but determined subculture of evangelical artists who would eventually find each other through organizations like Christians in the Visual Arts, founded in 1979.[50] At Wheaton, the art faculty and students clashed with the administration over resources—the department was housed "temporarily" in a damp basement for more than twenty years—and over controversial subject matter. In the 1970s Professor Alva Steffler, who "unashamedly announced his specialty in erotic art within a few months after receiving tenure," used nude models in his life drawing class, exhibited slides of a plaster cast of his wife's vagina, and was known for the consistent "vulval theme" in his sculpture.[51] (Steffler survived his colleagues' denunciations and retired in 2003.) Despite these altercations, annual "Creative Arts" festivals and enthusiastic coverage by *Kodon* and the *Record* nurtured a lively community of student artists.

Perhaps the most influential member of the Wheaton faculty during the decades after World War II was Clyde Kilby, who had been around long enough to recall the schisms and theological furor of the Buswell administration. Kilby joined the English department in 1935 and taught there for almost fifty years. The youngest of eight children born to a carpenter in eastern Tennessee, Kilby worked his way through the University of Arkansas and earned a PhD in English from New York University. At Wheaton, he inaugurated the college's annual Christian Writers' conference to persuade students that orthodox belief did not limit written expression to Sunday sermons and arid exegesis. On the question of academic freedom, Kilby dissented from the views of Sam Sutherland and V. Raymond Edman. He believed that students needed license to range beyond traditional "ideological patterns": freedom to reason through theological questions on their own, without fear of punishment; and freedom to engage with an array of human achievement and wisdom in all genres and art forms, explicitly Christian or not. Kilby made this freedom his life's mission by championing the work of one unusual Christian: Clive Staples Lewis.[52]

C. S. LEWIS AND THE EVANGELICAL IMAGINATION

A sherry-drinking Oxford don seems a strange match for conservative American evangelicals. C. S. Lewis was an Anglican who did not believe in biblical inerrancy, a devotee of Norse mythology who found his way to faith by way of a moonlit walk with a Catholic—fellow medievalist J. R. R. Tolkien, who convinced him that Christianity is "a true myth." Between his conversion and his death in 1963, Lewis published more than a dozen works of Christian apologetics and nearly as many volumes of fiction. Partly by argument, but mostly by virtue of his erudition and academic status, "a major, if not the chief, service that Lewis performed was to demonstrate that the Christian faith need fear no intellectual assault," wrote one *Christianity Today* contributor. Lewis was also an imaginative storyteller. His *Chronicles of Narnia* became one of the best-loved fantasy series in the English language. Evangelical readers otherwise inclined to agree with fundamentalist A. W. Tozer—"If it's Christian, it's true. If it's fiction, it's false"—could trust Lewis's novels because their author had explained so plainly what he believed. He appealed to believers as diverse as neo-evangelicals at *Christianity Today* and fundamentalists at Moody Bible Institute. No less a fundamentalist than Bob Jones, Jr., was a convert. He emerged from a visit with the don slightly baffled: "That man smokes a pipe, and that man drinks liquor—but I do believe he is a Christian!"[53]

Kilby met Lewis once, in 1953 at the scholar's rooms at Magdalen College, and they corresponded occasionally until Lewis's death. He quickly grasped Lewis's power to counteract the distrust of art and literature that many of his students inherited from their churches. He taught Lewis's books in his courses, and later wrote that by the time Lewis died, the Anglican don was "deeply 'ingrained' at Wheaton College. Some Bible [department] teachers required the reading of his apologetic works. Many students by this time needed no such impetus to read his books but did it joyfully and told others of them." *The Screwtape Letters* (purporting to be correspondence between Wormwood, a junior devil struggling to tempt humankind, and his uncle Screwtape) delighted students. For decades, parodies abounded in the newspaper and literary magazine. Kilby began a seminar on Lewis in his home in 1961 and added one on Tolkien three years later (not long afterward, he spent a summer with Tolkien in an ill-fated effort to help the aging writer finish *The Silmarillion*). Both courses soon outgrew the Kilby living room. He published *The Christian World of C. S. Lewis* in 1964, the same year he set off for England in search of unpublished Lewis texts.[54]

Kilby founded the C. S. Lewis Collection in 1965 with his own personal correspondence from Lewis, a modest number of Lewis's books, copies of a few Wheaton students' theses, and a budget of $500.[55] Until his death in 1986, Kilby devoted most of his spare time to letter writing, phone calls, trips to the United Kingdom, and badgering the college administration for funds in an effort to round up as many of Lewis's scattered letters as he could find. Walter Hooper, Lewis's private secretary and executor, wanted Lewis's papers to go to the Bodleian Library at Oxford and impeded Kilby's efforts. However, his dogged pursuit of every cloistered spinster or remote farmer who may have once written to Lewis—as well as his friendship with Lewis's lawyer Owen Barfield, and with Lewis's brother Warren—helped him obtain a substantial cache of letters and manuscripts. Kilby and his staff devoted equal energy to the books and papers of six other authors: fellow "Inklings" Barfield, Tolkien, and Charles Williams, who convened with Lewis for regular literary discussion at an Oxford pub, the Eagle and Child; nineteenth-century novelist and poet George MacDonald, the Catholic journalist G. K. Chesterton, and the Anglican mystery writer and essayist Dorothy Sayers.

To Kilby, there was something more important than accreditation, liberal arts courses, or any of the other grudging and piecemeal transformations afoot in conservative Protestant higher education: the awakening of the evangelical imagination. This alone would equip students to thrive in modern America; this ought to be the crux of the "Christian worldview." The year that Kilby founded the C. S. Lewis Collection, he wrote a long article for the evangelical magazine *Eternity* lamenting that "evangelical Christians don't understand imagination" and even considered it an "intrinsic evil." He warned that those "who denigrate the imagination should know that they thereby place themselves on this issue in a class with rationalistic philosophers like Descartes and Spinoza." Writing on "The Aesthetic Poverty of Evangelicalism" for the *Wheaton Alumni Magazine*, Kilby complained that evangelicals tended to believe in the divine inspiration of only the content of the Bible, rather than its poetic forms. "Our efforts to keep the Gospel pure and the way of salvation clear have led us almost exclusively to the expository, frontal, exegetical, functional and prosaic. . . . There is a simplicity which diminishes and a simplicity which enlarges and evangelicals have too often chosen the wrong one."[56]

As for those proud sons of Wheaton, the neo-evangelicals who founded *Christianity Today* and supposedly led the charge to regain the movement's intellectual respectability, Kilby had his doubts. He had known Carl Henry since he was a freshman and disagreed "most heartily with his thesis that truth, including Biblical truth, is only reached through propositions," he wrote to a friend. "How can the Psalms be propositional?" Meanwhile, he watched Lewis, Tolkien, and the other "Oxford Christians" awaken his students to the possibility of divine truth in all art forms. "Perhaps I have learned more about Christianity through this course than my Bible ones," wrote one in a course evaluation. "And definitely more about the joy and mystery!"[57]

Evangelical scholars around the country shared Kilby's devotion. Their reforming forefathers may have smashed icons and turned their backs on Catholic saints, but American evangelicals raced each other in pilgrimages to Lewis's Oxford home, collected his holy relics, and built ever more elaborate shrines. Shortly after Wheaton purchased from Lewis's estate the wardrobe that Warren Lewis claimed inspired the magical entryway into Narnia, Westmont College, an evangelical school in southern California, purchased a different wardrobe from the current owners of Lewis's home and proclaimed theirs the authentic model. The controversy of the rival relics continued for years. Later, Taylor University in Upland, Indiana—with the help of a local businessman who made a hobby out of collecting British pub paraphernalia—constructed an exact replica of the Eagle and Child, the pub favored by the Inklings, in the basement of the university library. The beer taps at the bar were just for show. Taylor, like Wheaton, was a dry campus.[58]

For young evangelicals, academic freedom meant not only the checks and balances found in secular universities—which evangelical colleges adopted gradually, and with caution—but the emergence of what one Wheaton professor called "a sacramental sense of life": a culture in which God might be found in all creation, and intellectual exploration was no longer so threatening.[59] Conservative critics worried—and some secular observers crowed—that there could be no mistaking the inexorable triumph of secularization in Wheaton students' interest in art and literature outside the Christian fold, and in the gradual weakening of restrictions on some "worldly" activities on college and Bible school campuses. The trouble with this diagnosis is that it assumed a fixed and orthodox arcadia that never really existed. The history of Christianity, like that of all religions, is one long story of the mutual accommodation between sacred tradition and new cultural contexts, needs, and threats. Bible college students who challenged old restrictions or registered for new liberal arts classes did not perceive themselves to be any less Christian than their forebears. On the contrary, they believed they were more fully Christian, more engaged with God's creation. Sociologists John Schmalzbauer and C. Gray Wheeler have called these changes evidence of the "reenchantment" of earthly life: the very opposite of secularization.[60] What was so outrageous about Wesley Craven's brooding stories in *Kodon* or the Biola *Chimes* ad for a Joan Baez concert was not that these offenses challenged biblical inerrancy or disputed the Second Coming. Rather, these students stepped beyond the imagined perimeter of fundamentalism and into a world in which godliness and darkness mingled.

There were also those evangelical students who disregarded entirely the false sense of quarantine offered by Christian education. For reasons of convenient location, tuition costs, or desire to escape their parents, they pursued their educations at secular colleges. Other students came to college indifferent to religion and found Jesus on the quad or in the fraternity house. While Bible schools and Christian colleges reinvented themselves, evangelical ministries on non-Christian campuses were booming. InterVarsity Christian Fellowship (which established its American arm in 1941) and Campus Crusade for Christ (founded in 1951) bustled with outreach activity. By 1971, one staff member of the Princeton Evangelical Fellowship was complaining that four evangelical groups competed for students there. InterVarsity focused on faculty as well, releasing memoranda on professorial witness in the classroom and condemning the "lingering myth" of "assumed objectivity" in scholarship: A "Christian professor surprises his students by teaching them that everyone has his own set of presuppositions.... When the occasion arises, he shares his presuppositions—his deepest convictions about life—with the class."[61]

Evangelism remained central to the evangelical ethos. All this talk of the "evangelical imagination" was not an intellectual dalliance. It was crucial to being a successful missionary in the modern world. "Imagination provides the willingness and possibility to get on the other side of the fence. Some people think it's a sin to get in another person's shoes. But for so much missionary work that's what you've got to do—have real love and real sympathy, and imagination helps do it," Clyde Kilby told *Christianity Today*.[62] Missionaries, too, faced rapid professionalization, a flood of new learning, and the struggle to maintain doctrinal purity. They could not hole up, saints gathered unto themselves, but had to come to terms with worldviews different from their own, especially among non-Western Christians unacquainted with the fundamentalist–modernist debates or the creeds of the Enlightenment. American evangelicals' encounter with culture and religion in the postcolonial world would highlight just how many of their convictions and anxieties they owed to their own peculiar histories, rather than to the gospel—and would shake those assumptions to the core.

Chapter 6

Missions beyond the West

IN THE WINTER OF 1956, BILLY GRAHAM EMBARKED ON A SERIES OF CRUSADES in Asia, landing in Bombay and then "cutting through India like Gabriel in a gabardine suit," *Time* reported. The evangelist's own account of the trip beamed with his usual optimism. Secretary of State John Foster Dulles had wished him well, hoping the crusade would prove an antidote to Soviet leaders' recent visit to India to cultivate Prime Minister Jawaharlal Nehru. In every city that Graham visited, tens of thousands came to listen, many from hundreds of miles away. At Kottayam, young girls carved a terraced amphitheater in the hillside, and people brought palm leaves to sit upon while they listened. When Graham told them that he had come "to tell you about a Man who was born right here in your part of the world, in Asia...He had skin that was darker than mine, and He came to show us that God loves all people," thousands came forward to make a "decision for Christ."[1]

Most were probably already among the country's small number of Christians. A few were Hindus happy to elevate Jesus alongside Shiva and the Buddha in their pantheon. One Indian journalist warned against exaggerating the crusade's success: "Evangelism in the Western sense is a new phenomenon here and as such is suspect; Dr. Billy Graham's variety especially so," he wrote. "How [to] explain the crowds?...They were, in large measure, the same people who turned out to see Bulganin and Khrushchev." A few months later, Hindu nationalists stepped up their campaign to encourage new Christians to dip into the Ganges and reconvert to "the religion of their souls."[2]

American evangelicals had confidence in the gospel's power to transcend cultural and ethnic boundaries. Yet generations of missionaries had learned firsthand that the message and methods that might win souls in Peoria would not work as well in the Punjab. Resistance to Western evangelists grew stronger with the collapse of Europe's colonial regimes and the rise of nationalism in Africa and Asia. Missionaries struggled with their reputations as agents of the white man's oppression. Liberal Protestants had been losing their evangelistic nerve for decades, a collapse epitomized in 1932 when a Rockefeller-funded committee of clergy and laymen published *Re-Thinking Missions*, a rueful report urging more cooperation with non-Christian faiths. Ashamed of Western missionaries' imperialist legacy, liberals frowned on unenlightened efforts like Graham's.

Evangelicals bristled at liberals' emphasis on good works over the good Word and their dubious concessions to non-Christian belief systems. At the same time, Graham and his fellow evangelicals knew the mission field had changed. They moved to "modernize" their own missions in foreign cultures—and believed their approach was more compassionate and sophisticated than the cringing hesitations of mainline Protestants. This shift in evangelistic philosophy would spawn the Church Growth movement and a growing evangelical love affair with the social sciences that they had once shunned.

The anthropological turn in missions encouraged some evangelical leaders to challenge one feature of their own culture: racial prejudice. As the Soviets waged an unrelenting propaganda campaign to expose the hypocrisy in America's claim to lead the free world while oppressing human rights at home, evangelical missionaries worried over the costs of this bad press among nonwhite populations in the mission field. Leading missiologists urged evangelical Americans to acknowledge the fallibility of the Western worldview and learn a lesson from the empathy of anthropologists.

The insights of modern social science, however, could not wholly explain the future of world Christianity. By the late 1960s, American evangelicals were startled to realize that the Christians winning the most converts in Africa, Latin America, and elsewhere—charismatics and Pentecostals, performing demon exorcisms, speaking in tongues, and surrendering to the Spirit—defied all modern, rationalist, Western logic. The rise of global Pentecostalism challenged American evangelicals to rethink what it meant to rebuild their tradition's intellectual authority or redeem civilization. Scholars of American religion have described how the domestic upheaval of the 1960s radicalized conservative American evangelicals and altered their view of culture and politics. However, the civil rights marches and college campus riots at home only tell part of the story. American evangelicals consistently spent far more money on missions than on political activism and saw the two as inextricably linked.[3] During the 1960s and 1970s, they scrambled to reassess the interaction between culture and the gospel. The mandate to evangelize the world required nothing less.

The Science of Missions

Most evangelicals believe that rebirth in Christ is an inscrutable matter of the heart. Yet as long as evangelicals have been preaching the gospel to the lost, they have studied the "science" of evangelism and revival. In Jonathan Edwards's day "natural science" was not yet distinct from natural philosophy or theology, but his *Treatise Concerning Religious Affections* (1746) offered a rigorous empirical analysis of the conversions that he witnessed during the Great Awakening. In the nineteenth century, the discipline of *Missionswissenschaft* bloomed. "The science of Missions, unchanging in principles, is ever multiplying its details, and accumulating its facts," wrote William Clarkson, a missionary working in India a century before Billy Graham's arrival.[4]

In the aftermath of the fundamentalist–modernist battles, conservative Protestants viewed the social scientific disciplines as unsavory bedfellows of evolutionary theory and higher biblical criticism. Sociology and anthropology were the atheistic purview of German theorists and liberal sociologists of religion who viewed Christianity as a cultural phenomenon not fundamentally different from other world religions. Nevertheless, evangelicals began to study these fields not to document "primitive" cultures, as secular anthropologists hoped to do, but to transform those cultures, to understand them well enough to bring them to Christ. The rationalist strain in communities that subscribed to biblical inerrancy—the same turn of mind that mined the Bible for hard historical facts and scientific data— gravitated naturally (for nature is not without a sense of irony) to these empirical and method-based disciplines.

It seemed only reasonable to treat evangelism as a science: all the more so in an era when the social sciences and quantitative analysis had begun their ascent in the halls of elite academia and Washington. Anthropology was an early and popular major at Wheaton College, especially among aspiring missionaries. Students flocked to classes taught by "Griggy," a Russian-born, German-trained professor named Alexander Grigolia. He was a round and compact man with a tidy mustache, multiple doctoral degrees, and a some-what mysterious past—undergraduates whispered that he had fled Russia by hiding in the coal bin of a Mediterranean steamer. The first Wheaton anthropology majors graduated in 1939. Gordon H. Smith, a missionary in French Indochina and fellow of the Royal Geographical Society, praised Wheaton's program. In his 1945 book *The Missionary and Anthropology*, he recommended that Bible schools include cultural anthropology in their cur-ricula and missions boards require candidates to take courses in the social sciences. He quoted Robert Glover of the China Inland Mission: "The time for the ordinary rank and file of missionaries is past. They must be specialists."[5]

By 1953, the year that anthropology professor Robert Taylor helped found the journal *Practical Anthropology* with the sponsorship of the American Bible Society, 200 students had graduated from the Wheaton program. Wheaton's most famous anthropology major, Billy Graham, later wrote that he chose the field for "a liberal arts education in the best sense, obliterating any condescending notions I might have toward people from backgrounds other than my own." In 1954, American Bible Society translation consultant Eugene Nida published *Customs and Cultures: Anthropology for Christian Missions*, a guide for missionaries based on his travels in seventy-five coun-tries (students were still reading the book in missions and anthropology courses two generations later). "Biblical relativism is not a matter of incon-sistency," Nida wrote, "but a recognition of the different cultural factors which influence standards and actions."[6]

Evangelicals' enthusiasm for finding new ways to communicate the gospel in non-Christian cultures was strong enough to override some of their oldest prejudices. By the early 1960s, they had recognized that Roman Catholic scholars were producing insightful volumes of anthropology and missiology, and read them eagerly. Catholics began to enroll in the evangeli-cal Wycliffe Bible Translators' Summer Institute of Linguistics, an inten-sive two-year course in scripture translation conducted at the University of Oklahoma. Catholic participation was possible partly because of the Vatican's recent approval of interconfessional Bible work, but Catholics also attended because evangelicals viewed language study, like cultural analysis, as a "science" whose pursuit did not require theological agreement between Christian colleagues committed to evangelism. SIL "actively cultivated its image as a scientific and service organization rather than a missionary organization," wrote one evangelical anthropologist.[7]

In the hands of liberal Christians, these disciplines could be dangerous. Evangelicals lambasted mainline Protestant missiologists, "advocates of the new 'secular Christianity' [who] condemn a 'supernaturalistic' view of revelation," wrote one *Christianity Today* commentator in 1966. "Having disposed of the God Paul preached, they proceed to canonize social science."[8] God intended social science to be a tool, not an idol. While liberal and secular scholars used these methods to develop an atheistic portrait of humankind that replaced the soul with psychological suggestion and God's providence with tribal kinship and economics, evangelicals vowed to study their fellow humans to help them find their way to Christ.

THE CHURCH GROWTH MOVEMENT

American evangelicals' embrace of the social sciences had a radical—though not immediate—impact on their strategies for spreading the gospel. In the years after World War II, two central models of evangelism reigned: "crusade evangelism," exemplified in the revivals of Graham and other celebrity evangelists, and "evangelism in depth," which mobilized a community of believers to reach as many individuals as possible, usually armed with a structured program to guide the unsaved to Christ (such as Campus Crusade's "Four Spiritual Laws"). Evangelicals employed both methods abroad and at home, with significant success. Then in 1955, a missionary named Donald McGavran told them they were going about it all wrong. His book, *Bridges of God*, articulated the fundamentals of a new school of evangelism that missiologists would soon christen the Church Growth movement.

Crusades and evangelism in depth both emphasized the traditional evangelical "sacrament": the personal decision for Christ. McGavran pointed out that throughout Christian history God had grown the church by converting entire peoples to Christianity en masse and then guiding them to make the faith their own, rather than bringing one individual at a time through a prefabricated program of canned speeches and Bible studies. The most effective evangelism required close study and accommodation to the host culture, be it Los Angeles or rural Tibet. McGavran argued, contrary to most American evangelicals' assumptions, that Western individualism was a barrier to understanding how people throughout church history have become Christian. "To Christianize a whole people, the first thing *not* to do is to snatch individuals out of it into a different society," he wrote. "Peoples become Christians where a Christward movement occurs *within that society*." McGavran noted that throughout the Book of Acts, families joined the church, rather than individuals. When the communities at Lydda and Sharon converted, "they preserved their social structure entire. The village elders remained the leaders. Relationships remained undisturbed."9

McGavran did not yet advocate applying anthropology or sociology in the mission field. He did not have a sophisticated grasp of these disciplines. His PhD, from Columbia, was in education. He was simply reacting to problems he saw in the traditional models of Christian witness practiced in rural India, where he was a career missionary with the Disciples of Christ, a relatively liberal denomination. Rather than running hospitals and schools to improve local living conditions, educating the native "intelligentsia" in the principles of Christianity, and recruiting residents to serve a mission church administered by Westerners, missionaries ought to turn the churches over to local Christians, McGavran suggested. Visiting missionaries should focus on evangelism—which meant translating the gospel into cultural terms that their audience could understand and aiming to convert entire peoples.

This approach to evangelism was not new. It was as old as the Christian Church itself, and that was McGavran's point. St. Paul urged Christians to "become all things to all men" in order to communicate the gospel. The Frankish monks dispatched by Charlemagne to Christianize the pagan Saxons in the ninth century rewrote the gospel story in terms that Saxon warriors could understand: Christ became "the Chieftain," his apostles "warrior-companions." In later centuries, the Jesuits earned notoriety for the lengths they were willing to go in order to make Christianity palatable

to cultures of the Far East. They donned native garb and refashioned cru-
cifixes with the Buddha, rather than Christ, at the center. More recently,
nineteenth-century German missiologists like Bruno Gutmann stressed the
importance of understanding *Völkerpsychologie*, the "psychology of peoples." He suggested that missionaries should respect tribal social structure
and treat the God-given bonds between people as the basis for their new
lives in Christ.[10] *Bridges of God* asserted a familiar and fundamentally premodern thesis, criticizing the rise of excessive individualism and minimizing the importance of the intellectual as thought-leader in a community.

Yet the tools that evangelicals had closest at hand for implementing
McGavran's advice were the quintessential implements of the modern age,
the crowning achievements of humankind's conquest of the natural world.
McGavran's premodern insights transformed—with his blessing—into a
data- and research-driven movement. To render the gospel accessible in
foreign cultures and perfect the recipe for "people movements," McGavran
and his colleagues embraced the latest developments in social science
research. By the time Fuller Theological Seminary invited McGavran to
serve as the founding dean of their School of World Mission and turn Fuller
into an international Church Growth mecca—ten years after he published
Bridges of God—the movement had morphed from a subversive critique of
the modern missionary enterprise into a thoroughly, even naïvely modernist
campaign to marshal the latest statistical data and case studies in the name
of converting "homogeneous units" (Church Growth jargon for the missionary's target, social groups within a larger community).[11]

At a time when the collapse of colonial rule in the developing world had
upended the regimes under which missionaries had operated for centuries;
when national independence among colonies in Africa and Asia granted
instant authority to indigenous cultures and beliefs; when liberal Christians
were wringing their hands over Western missionaries' "imperialism" and
the credibility of the entire Christian evangelistic project was in jeopardy,
Church Growth provided evangelicals with an appealing strategy. They
believed this new paradigm was culturally sensitive and nonideological,
centered on the close observation of a society before any attempt to evangelize. McGavran promised that his school would teach only those methods
that proved successful. "Church growth came first," George Marsden wrote
of the Fuller program, "and anthropology was to be used in its service."
For this reason, evangelical missiologists, even those with doctorates in

anthropology, would fail to produce "high-quality research based literature" that passed muster in the guild of mainstream academic anthropology, one evangelical professor of missions has lamented.[12] In a broad sense, the discipline appealed to evangelical intellectuals for the same reasons that pre-suppositionalist apologetics often did, even if Church Growth's claims of scientific objectivity seemed to contradict Van Til's old objection that such impartiality was impossible. Both systems of thought equipped evangelicals to embrace the modern vogue of cultural relativism—to acknowledge that human beings' worldviews arose from culturally informed assumptions—without relinquishing the ultimate truth of Christianity.

Fuller students researched case studies of successful church growth for their dissertations. Faculty circulated a lengthy missionary questionnaire focusing on communications theory and sociology, discussing what they could learn from the Brigham Young University scholars who crafted it (they made no mention of Mormon heterodoxy—which had no bearing on the data, apparently).[13] "The secular world pours millions of dollars into research, considering it essential to progress in today's changing world," McGavran argued.

> It is high time for the Church to channel 5 per cent of what it spends for missions into research in church growth [receptive populations, etc]. Until this is done, missions will not see or develop the full potential for growth at which the finger of God now points. Once research uncovers methods God is blessing in various communions, the new era of good feeling among the churches should issue in willingness to use these methods.[14]

Throughout the 1960s and 1970s, Church Growth institutions sprouted up all over America and around the world, sponsored by a range of denominations. A student of McGavran named Win Arn founded the Institute for American Church Growth in Washington, DC; Methodists at Asbury Theological Seminary started the E. Stanley Jones School of World Mission and Evangelism; another Fuller graduate founded the Church Growth Research Association in India; Lutheran and Pentecostal churches founded their own Church Growth organizations and co-hosted seminars on the subject. The Assemblies of God made Church Growth and cultural anthropology cornerstones of their new graduate school curriculum, and Restorationist magazine editors published McGavran's articles. David Yonggi Cho, pastor of the largest church in the world, Yoido Full Gospel Church (Assemblies of God) in Seoul, was an early and ardent advocate. He established Church Growth International in Seoul and spoke frequently at international conferences. McGavran and his colleagues produced an avalanche of literature on the science of how one grows a church and traveled frequently to regale missionaries at summer seminars.[15]

Culture's Despisers

Conservatives blasted the movement's enthusiastic ecumenism. After learning that Arthur Glasser, a minister in the Reformed Presbyterian Church, Evangelical Synod, had attended the World Council of Churches' 1972 Bangkok Congress as a voting member, his presbytery launched a formal investigation of his cooperation with the liberal ecumenical movement. Although church officials ultimately cleared him of any wrongdoing, he continued to receive hostile mail. One fellow minister was horrified to hear that Glasser had given a presentation on Church Growth for Catholics. "Did you in fact go with the intention of helping them build up the Roman system?" he demanded. "If so, is this not a clear violation of the prohibition of helping the ungodly, and a failure to maintain separation from unbelief which is commanded in Scripture?" Arch-separatist Carl McIntire ran an article in his *Christian Beacon* headlined "Dr. Glasser: Fundamentalist Turned Ecumenist."[16] Fundamentalists believed that any evangelistic strategy permitting cooperation with Catholics in evangelism (as opposed to collaborating in anticommunist activism, which was tolerable) offered converts a doctrine so dilute that it was not orthodox Christianity at all.

More thoughtful criticism came from evangelicals who were not fundamentalists—who saw no harm in cautious cooperation with other Christians—but who did not share Church Growth proponents' theological assumptions. The data-driven movement that its founders believed was wholly "objective" was in fact not neutral at all—nor, according to critics, was it true to Christ's intentions. Although Church Growth had fans in all corners of evangelicalism, it was grounded in the Reformed tradition's emphasis on the potential goodness of all human culture as part of God's creation. Yet in their race to boost baptism rates, Church Growth advocates had become inconsistent Calvinists, celebrating human agency and ignoring the Fall. Nazarene scholar Rob Staples wrote that their rosy view of human culture "sounds more like nineteenth century liberalism than what one would expect to hear from a Fuller Seminary professor." Lesslie Newbigin, a British missionary and bishop of the Church of South India, worried that the movement's messengers were too easy on non-Christian culture. "It seems to me that we shall always have to have a tension between the obligation to ensure that cultural pecularities [*sic*] do not make a barrier for the gospel and the obligation to ensure that Christ is seen as Lord over all cultures," he wrote.[17] Christians were called to be in this world, but not of it. (McGavran had many critics who said the same right next-door on his own campus—primarily in Fuller's School of Theology, staffed with scholars skeptical of Church Growth's priority on baptism numbers over theological orthodoxy.)

At a Fuller conference on Church Growth in 1977, John Howard Yoder challenged the notion that a missionary ought to overlook a group's "sub-Christian" moral practices in the interest of making the gospel more acceptable to them—as Charles Kraft, a Wheaton anthropology graduate, Fuller faculty member, and former missionary to Nigeria, had done when he recommended the baptism of polygamous tribe members (a decision that got him fired from the Church of the Brethren mission he was serving).[18] Yoder argued that the Church Growth approach to culture ran contrary to "the classical evangelical doctrine of regeneration." He attacked the movement as the apotheosis of the overly professionalized missionary, a caricature of the very tendencies that evangelicals criticized in liberals. To Yoder, missions ought to be the duty of the whole church, not merely "the specialist sent overseas."[19]

These elite theologians and fundamentalist polemicists agreed on very little, but both saw Church Growth as a kind of anti-intellectualism, successful only because it reduced Christian doctrine to a malleable husk. The critics wrote with such vexation because the tentacles of Church Growth already encircled so many missionary operations far from the palm trees of Fuller's Pasadena campus—where good-hearted evangelicals embraced Church Growth because it promised the latest sociological analysis and skyrocketing baptism rates.

Ideas that hatched in the mission field came home to roost. Evangelical organizations ranging from *Christianity Today* to InterVarsity Christian

134   To Evangelize the World

Fellowship and colleges like Biola recruited career missionaries to return to America and staff or direct their institutions.[20] In the evangelical world, missionary service earned credibility and opened doors just as military service smoothed the way for a political career in Washington. Church planters began to apply the Church Growth movement's principles at home, building houses of worship that looked like shopping malls and movie theaters and blended into American indigenous culture: the "seeker-sensitive" megachurches that would come to dominate the evangelical landscape. These churches drew on therapeutic trends in Christian counseling that emerged from American clergy's widespread adoption of insights from modern psychoanalysis and behavioral science.[21] In place of unpleasant doctrines like hell, human depravity, and a distant, wrathful Jehovah, seeker-sensitive pastors preached a message more attuned to twentieth-century American culture. They sermonized on self-actualization, urging believers to love Christ, confide in their savior like a friend, and trust that the best would come to pass. When pressed, most affirmed the Bible's apocalyptic prophecies, but did not dwell on them.

The Church Growth movement was wildly successful in its primary aim. Yonggi-Cho, who shepherded 830,000 church members as of 2007, was the movement's poster child. Regardless of critics' unease about spineless doctrine, the hubris of experts, or the conquest of Reformed cultural theology, Church Growth owed its success to an increasingly professionalized ethos and an infrastructure wired to consecrate culture wherever possible. The movement's network of academic centers, seminar programs, publications, and traveling speakers was, in some ways, merely an updated version of the classic fundamentalist media-driven subculture that historian Joel Carpenter has described. But the Church Growth pastors and evangelists of the 1970s were not insular, alienated fundamentalists. The principle of "people movements" encouraged them to embrace and conquer mainstream culture, rather than despise it; to gather statistical data in order to perceive a community's needs, and then to convert and organize its citizens. If these skills sound like they might come in handy in the realm of political activism, they soon would. Church Growth advocates claimed to be apolitical, but only because they did not fully grasp the implications of the theology that undergirded their movement. As the Dutch Reformed theologian Abraham Kuyper once proclaimed, "There is not a square inch in the whole domain of our human existence over which Christ, who is sovereign over all, does not cry: 'Mine!'"[22]

MISSIONS AND THE COLOR LINE

Critics of Church Growth worried that honing an anthropologist's eye could blind missionaries to their duty to challenge "sub-Christian" culture. However, some evangelicals drawn to the social sciences were quick to challenge their own community's terrible record of racial injustice. In *Customs and Cultures*—published the same year that the Supreme Court ruled segregated schools unconstitutional in *Brown v. Board of Education*— Eugene Nida chastised his readers: "The Protestant church, especially in its more theologically conservative branches, is the most racially prejudiced institution in American life." He noted that both Islam and communism welcomed all races—and were bursting with new converts, particularly in Africa. Nida urged Western Protestants to develop an awareness of their own cultural conditioning as well as sensitivity to the foreign cultures in which they worked. His book became a mainstay of seminary and Christian college reading lists, which makes its radicalism even more remarkable. "The missionary's confusion of Christendom with Christianity, of Western culture with the gospel of Jesus Christ, has been the basis of tragic misunderstanding and frustrating endeavor," he warned toward the end of the book. "White supremacy and superiority have been assumed by many and even defended as Biblical."[23]

Nida was not a lone voice. Missionaries ought to "discard the crude and distorting lenses of western culture," wrote staunch inerrantist Harold Lindsell in 1955. Lindsell's first vocation was the mission field, but poor health compelled him to choose graduate school instead. He taught the first missiology courses at Fuller, where he echoed Nida's warnings against "caste or race prejudices. These are fatal to evangelism and reveal the failure of the missionary to control the myths of race superiority or the biblical truth that all men are the created children of God who are equal in the sight of God and precious."[24] Both Nida and Lindsell concluded their books with extensive reading lists packed with anthropology: not the untrained treatises of missionary-observers, but volumes by secular titans Franz Boas,

Bronislaw Malinowski, Paul Radin, Ruth Benedict, Melville Herskovits, and other great social scientists of the day. Lindsell added many books meant to break evangelicals of racial prejudices, from Boas's *Race and Democratic Society* to Bruno Lasker's *Race Attitudes in Children*.

During the early Cold War, more than ever before, evangelical leaders began to realize the costs of prejudice in the mission field. Washington's rhetoric cast Americans as the saviors who had snatched Europe from the maw of ethnic hatred and self-ruin and were now defenders of the free world against communist oppressors. But skeptics denounced America's domestic civil rights record. Kremlin propagandists, eager to win the loyalties of newly sovereign nonwhite peoples, persistently publicized the contradiction between Washington's slogans of liberty and the realities of the Jim Crow South. Although the Soviets had been railing against America's racist hypocrisies for decades, the high stakes of the Cold War added new sting to their barbs and galvanized the White House's commitment to civil rights at home.[25]

Evangelical missionaries had been in the business of evangelizing strange lands with their own message of liberty far longer than any Cold Warriors, and they began to worry about the costs of American hypocrisies as soon as the ashes of world war settled. As an international spotlight fixed on growing racial unrest in the United States, "the whole world expects America to prove her democracy by her treatment of minority groups," wrote Southern Baptist Myrtle Robinson Creasman in a Women's Missionary Union magazine. Historian Alan Scot Willis has shown how Southern Baptist theologians and missionaries became the vanguard of changing attitudes toward race in that denomination, motivated in no small part by their frustrations in African mission fields, where Muslims won converts by declaring Christianity a "white man's religion" and Islam "the only religion fit for the African."[26]

Missionaries complained loudest that segregation cost souls abroad, but clergy at home—who marshaled large donations to support missions and invited missionaries on furlough to speak to their flocks—worried about their congregations' role in the evangelism of the world. In 1965 Herschel Hobbs, pastor of First Baptist in Oklahoma City, admitted the church's first black member, hoping "it will not only be an example, but an encouragement to others. We are facing this, and we may just as well do it gracefully." He lamented recent protests in New Orleans against the appointment of a black Catholic bishop: "That will be flashed around the world, and will do more harm to our Foreign Mission program and foreign policy than most anything we could imagine."[27]

There is no denying the cognitive dissonance common in American churches, where white evangelicals' magnanimous feelings on converting the "noble savage" thousands of miles away did not always temper their reactions to African-American children bound for their own neighborhood's newly integrated school. Yet as David Chappell has argued, white southern clergy across all denominations were reluctant to offer meaningful public support to segregation (in contrast to their enthusiastic quotation of scripture to defend slavery a hundred years earlier). If they still harbored racist sentiments and frequently suspected that communist agents on Soviet payrolls masterminded civil rights unrest, they balked at the prospect of using the Bible to defend Jim Crow—partly because they knew the costs of Christian racism in the mission field. L. Nelson Bell, a southern Presbyterian who was no fan of marches on Washington and favored "voluntary segregation," admitted in a 1956 *Life* magazine forum that "Christians should recognize that there is no biblical or legal justification for segregation." His son-in-law held his first formally desegregated crusade in 1953. Billy Graham, the anthropology major and international evangelist, understood the harm white pride did to the gospel.[28] The ethos of Church Growth and the anthropological turn in missions gave evangelical leaders a framework for coaxing their followers out of old prejudices. Even the most recalcitrant could not argue with baptism numbers.

Cultural attitudes evolve slowly. Some fundamentalists continued their public stands against civil rights. In 1970, Bob Jones University informed its alumni that it would rather risk the school's tax exemption than admit black students (the school soon changed its policy to admit married blacks, but continued to enforce segregation on campus). That same year, John R. Rice opposed interracial marriage in his fundamentalist newspaper, *The Sword of the Lord*—prompting William Culbertson, the president of Moody Bible Institute, to disinvite him from an upcoming conference (Culbertson probably had on his mind recent student protests over bigoted remarks made by a member of his own administration).[29] Nevertheless, by the end of the 1960s, the moderate middle of evangelicalism had not only accepted the victories of the civil rights movement, but seemed to have experienced a genuine change of heart about the meaning of skin color.

Christianity Today's views evolved from a nervous editorial on interracial marriage in 1963 to a 1969 reading list that urged evangelicals to study *The Autobiography of Malcolm X*, Stokely Carmichael's *Black Power*, and James Baldwin's *The Fire Next Time*. By the mid-1970s, seminaries ranging from Fuller to Gordon-Conwell in Massachusetts were offering courses in black studies and black theology.[30]

"Look Out! The Pentecostals Are Coming"

The reports rolling in from mission posts around the world were impossible to ignore. Many of those postcolonial peoples for whose souls missionaries strove were flocking to revivals laced with glossolalia, healing, and prophecy. Black Christians played a prominent role in the early history of Pentecostalism in America, and for many white evangelicals "holy-roller" worship had carried racial connotations ever since the shocking origins of modern Pentecostalism in the integrated revivals of Azusa Street. From the movement's earliest years some white Pentecostal denominations flourished, such as the Assemblies of God, but black Pentecostal churches still outnumbered white Pentecostal congregations decades later. Yet if white evangelicals had long policed the boundary between themselves and those who babbled in tongues, the momentum of global revival was about to overpower them.[31]

By the 1970s, many of the world's fastest growing churches—of all colors—were Pentecostal. Yonggi-Cho's church in Seoul was affiliated with the Assemblies of God. Missionaries returned from Latin America and Africa with stories of booming Pentecostal congregations. In an effort to respond to the changing circumstances of foreign missions in the developing world, and to rebut liberal Christians' charges of imperialism and prejudice, evangelicals had adopted a form of evangelism that they believed was scientific, culturally neutral, and color blind. Church Growth soothed its advocates' anxiety over reconciling faith and new learning because it appeared savvy by the standards of modern scholarship while still true to the Bible's Great Commission. The surprising thing was that their data on conversion, their cutting-edge social science, encouraged them to embrace a thoroughly "premodern" Christianity. The international rise of Pentecostalism forced American evangelicals to revise their assumptions about the limits of spiritual experience and the walls that had long divided Christians from one another.

The "charismatic renewal movement" is a catchall term for the world-wide phenomenon of revivals, individual conversions, and Spirit-saturated prayer meetings that began in the late 1950s and started to level off a decade and a half later. The movement was remarkable for its scale and duration, and also for its manifestation in almost every Christian confession and denomination around the world—including those churches historically hostile to speaking in tongues, healings, and the very suggestion that the Holy Spirit continued to work miracles after the apostolic age. Sparks of charismatic renewal appeared in America as early as 1956, when the Holy Spirit alighted upon five Lutheran ministers attending a Minneapolis meeting of the Full Gospel Business Men's Fellowship International (a Pentecostal men's organization), and the rector of Trinity Episcopal Church in Wheaton, Illinois, began a charismatic prayer group. In 1958, congregants spoke in tongues at the Church of the Holy Spirit in Monterey Park, California (another Episcopalian parish). Observers began to wonder if real revival was afoot with surges of glossolalia in prayer groups affiliated with St. Mark's Episcopal Church in Van Nuys, California. On Passion Sunday, 1960, rector Dennis Bennett announced from the pulpit that he and many church members had received the gifts of the Spirit. Episcopalians in Baton Rouge reported revival the next year; tongues had reached Anglicans in Toronto by 1963. That same year, one church journal reported that in the whole state of Montana, only a single American Lutheran pastor had not yet experienced the gift. A Presbyterian pastor in Oklahoma named Brick Bradford founded a "Charismatic Communion" of "Spirit-Filled Presbyterian Ministers" in 1967, and counted at least 156 members.[32]

Charismatic renewal received a boost from a new generation of Pentecostal revivalists who eschewed narrow sectarianism and built national ministries to bring their message of divine healing and miraculous gifts to the widest possible audience. Oral Roberts, a small-town preacher from Oklahoma who became perhaps the most famous televangelist of the twentieth century, launched his healing ministry in 1947 and was preaching to packed audiences in his 12,500-person tent a few years later. To enhance his mainstream appeal, he left the Pentecostal Holiness Church to affiliate with the more respectable Methodists. In 1962 he began construction of Oral Roberts University, a "University of Evangelism" that Roberts hoped would attract students of all races from a wide swathe of evangelical denominations, particularly black Pentecostals. His effort to reach across racial lines proved relatively successful. By the 1990s, ORU would boast that 19 percent of its students were black: the highest proportion among the hundred schools affiliated with the Council for Christian Colleges and Universities.[33]

Kathryn Kuhlman began as a traveling healing evangelist who lived on handouts and slept in haystacks. Her talent for charming a crowd made her the most prominent female evangelist in the country by the 1960s, with a flourishing radio ministry, massive revivals, and attention from mainstream periodicals such as *Redbook*. Like Roberts, she rebelled against racial taboos by inviting black musicians to open some of her services. Kenneth Hagin, a soft-spoken Texan who began his career in the Assemblies of God, built a sprawling radio, television, and print ministry that reached across denominational lines—by the end of the century, Kenneth Hagin Ministries claimed to have sold 60 million copies of his 130-odd books. In 1974 he opened Rhema Bible Training Center and took pride in mentoring many black evangelists and pastors. David Wilkerson, a Pennsylvania "country preacher" called by the Holy Spirit in 1958 to go to New York City, founded a street ministry to help young gang members and a drug addiction recovery program affiliated with the Assemblies of God. In 1962 he published *The Cross and the Switchblade*, an account of his ministry that sold more than fifteen million copies in thirty languages and reached fifty million more in the 1970 film version, which starred Pat Boone and Erik Estrada.[34] Wilkerson's story reverberated well beyond Pentecostal circles and convinced many skeptical evangelicals that the Holy Spirit was working miracles in the heart of modern Babylon.

Charismatic renewal warmed white Christians with the fires of Pentecost—and in America the revival remained a largely white phenomenon until the 1980s.[35] The Church Growth movement, with its assumption that Christians prefer to attend church with people like themselves, may have slowed the pace of integration in many evangelical congregations—an ironic twist on its spirit of cultural accommodation. But if the complexion of white evangelical churches changed little, the character of their worship would never be the same. Throughout church history, theology has evolved alongside Christians' lived experience. Nowhere was this clearer than in evangelicals' changing ideas about God's plan for human history. Pentecostal success abroad and the mellowing of old social and racial prejudices at home were, alone, insufficient fuel for charismatic revival. Evangelicals' theology of the miraculous had to change.

Through the first half of the twentieth century, most American evangelicals dismissed the "full gospel" of the Pentecostals because they believed that God forbade it. They read the Bible through the scheme of dispensational premillennialism, which divvied up history into epochs, or dispensations, in which God dealt differently with his creatures. Traditionally, dispensationalism confined speaking in tongues and other miraculous gifts of the Spirit to the time of the apostles. "Unfortunately so much of our evangelical fundamental theology is 'dispensational,' that is to say, it teaches that these spiritual gifts were only for the early church and they are not necessary to-day," wrote H. A. Maxwell Whyte, a Canadian minister who specialized in exorcism.[36] Many Pentecostals had absorbed the dispensationalist view of the end-times from mainstream fundamentalism and adapted the theology to accommodate their experiences, but non-Pentecostal dispensationalists continued to frown on tongues and boasts of divine healing.

By the late 1960s, however, there were signs that dispensationalist circles were reconsidering the notion of present-day miracles. Fuller professor George Ladd had spent more than a decade advocating an alternative theory of the end-times, called historic premillennialism, which persuaded some dispensationalists to abandon the idea of a strict divide between biblical times and the current "church age." In 1967, just as the charismatic renewal movement was rising to a crest, Oxford University Press released a revised version of the classic dispensationalist edition of scripture, the *New Scofield Reference Bible*. The list of editors read like a who's who of midcentury American evangelicalism and fundamentalism, from Frank Gaebelein, headmaster of Stony Brook School in New York and an editor at *Christianity Today* and *Eternity* magazines, to William Culbertson, the president of Moody Bible Institute. While the new edition affirmed many elements of classic dispensationalism, the editors fudged Cyrus Scofield's sharp distinction between the Kingdom of God—which includes all true Christians alive or dead—and its messianic manifestation on earth, which classical dispensationalists confusingly call the "kingdom of heaven." This change dovetailed with the common dispensationalist belief that biblical prophecy regarding the in-gathering of the Jews to their ancient homeland was partly fulfilled by the 1948 creation of the state of Israel, convincing many that God did not strictly separate present times from past and future epochs.[37] The Holocaust and the creation of Israel also chastened non-dispensationalists, who historically contended that God's plan of salvation treats Jews and Gentiles as one people, and that the Church, as "New Israel," inherited the covenant that God made with the Jews. The events of World War II made recognizing the Jews as a distinct people in God's plan a political and moral imperative. Nondispensationalist and dispensationalist Protestants drifted closer together.

Charismatic revival coincided with—and reinforced—these subtle shifts in evangelicals' views of how God deals with his people. Many continued to hold traditional dispensational premillennialist views of the Rapture, tribulation under the rule of the Antichrist, and Christ's thousand-year reign on earth, but they became more receptive to the possibility that God might bless twentieth-century Christians as he did his first-century servants.

Suburbanites and Jesus People

As charismatic renewal spread through mainline Protestant and evangelical churches, converts mainstreamed and "modernized" practices long exiled to the margins of Christianity, supposedly the purview of snake-handlers who had resisted the taming of the Enlightenment. As the revival progressed, glossolalia and ecstatic worship became—with a bit of spiritual editing—middle-class and seemly. In his memoir of the revival in his church, Dennis Bennett wrote that initially he was dismissive: "There was no 'emotionalism' in our church! We were Episcopalians, and prided ourselves on our cool, even somewhat ironical approach to our faith." When he reluctantly agreed to pray for the Lord to grant him the gift of tongues, he was "self-conscious, and determined not to lose my dignity!" Journalist Richard Ostling described a healing service at St. Stephen's Episcopal Church in Philadelphia, where "there were no collections, no overwrought music, no shouted pulpit appeals," simply a line of respectable-looking seekers making their way to the altar rail, where priests laid hands upon heads and murmured a blessing. Compared to an outsider's stereotype of a Pentecostal healing service—a charlatan conning a tent-full of unwashed yokels—services like the one at St. Stephen's indicated "a new clientele." The rector told Ostling that "middle-class people are the most neglected spiritually. Without emotionalism, we appeal to a group which wouldn't get help in a tent."[38]

Evangelicals and mainline Protestants partly succeeded in domesticating charismatic practices, but the renewal movement's revolutionary approach to praying and glorifying God appealed to so many believers—especially young people—that even skeptics had to admit that worship would never be the same. If the Church Growth movement was the embodiment of Western rationalism, the charismatic renewal movement represented a visceral reaction against the dictates of modern, Western reason. Young evangelicals such as the Jesus People, a movement that began in the late 1960s within the hippie counterculture of southern California and the Bay area, helped lead the revival of ecstatic experience in Christian worship. These converts were not interested in systematic theology or social science. They had turned away from the drug culture to "get high on Jesus" and had little regard for creeds or rules. Many reckoned that mainstream churches were not only uptight and uncool, but manmade temples of apostasy that should be torn down to make way for a revival of first-century Christianity in these last days before Christ was due to return (some, wide-eyed at the threat of nuclear apocalypse, gravitated toward the end-times prognostications of Hal Lindsey's *The Late Great Planet Earth* [1970]).[39] Faith healing and signs and wonders appealed to these young people. Their new Christian identity demanded as close an approximation of the Book of Acts as possible.

Even if the Jesus People were a relatively small sect whose hairstyles and habits amused or alienated many evangelicals, they had an outsized impact on mainstream worship by setting charismatic renewal to music. Staid Sunday services began to resemble rock concerts. Calvary Chapel and the Vineyard Churches, two denominations (though they both resisted that label) connected to the Jesus People movement, revolutionized evangelical worship music by substituting guitars and drums for the traditional pipe organ, piano, and four-part harmony.

Christian composer Ralph Carmichael drew on his success in mainstream pop and jazz (his big break had come with arranging Nat King Cole's

1960 Christmas album) to found Light Records, which blended gospel with guitars and trendy pop melodies that beguiled young people. Larry Norman grew up in a strict Baptist home that frowned on rock 'n' roll, but his early love for Elvis Presley and black gospel stars like Mahalia Jackson propelled him into a freewheeling career of singing, songwriting, and street ministry in southern California, an epicenter of the Jesus movement. For more than thirty years he produced a stream of records that combined iconoclastic politics and folk-rock rhythms with classic Christian themes, winning over a generation of younger fans. Norman "seemed to be reclaiming Jesus from the Pharisees and universities and bringing Him back to the streets," wrote one observer. Artists like these "turned it [worship music] upside down," said Sherwood Lingenfelter, professor of anthropology at Fuller Theological Seminary. "They played totally new songs, used a lot of guitars, and there was a lot of emotion expressed. People had their hands in the air...when I was young, bodily expression was not a part of worship. You kept your hands at your sides."[40]

Drawing on rock 'n' roll—a musical genre with roots in traditional African-American blues, jazz, and gospel music—the Jesus People invented Contemporary Christian Music, or CCM, which now plays a dominant role in evangelical worship across most denominations. At the Vineyard, this casual, upbeat praise style had cross-cultural appeal. In the church's southern California birthplace, the Vineyard had more success than most white Protestant denominations in attracting Latino Christians. Many were cradle Catholics grateful that no one at "La Viña" demanded that they formally renounce Rome, and others appreciated the Vineyard's departure from the strict legalism and formal Sunday dress of traditional Latino Pentecostal churches.[41] Even if most churches that adopted CCM remained largely white, their worship music was "integrated" whether they realized it or not. The advent of CCM freed churchgoers to murmur in tongues and hold their hands in the air while the worship leader paced the stage. They could dabble in religious enthusiasm without falling to their knees or quaking in the aisle. CCM offered a medium for nonthreatening religious experience, inviting because it so closely echoed contemporary secular culture.

Charismatic renewal was, in part, a youth movement in a decade of youth movements, and raised hard questions about what sources of spiritual authority would beckon young people into the church and keep them there. At the September 1971 meeting of the Committee on Overseas Evangelistic Strategy in Dallas, evangelical leaders in the orbit of Fuller and *Christianity Today* pondered whether these young charismatics were the future of evangelism. Ted Engstrom, of the global charity World Vision, said he "was impressed by the Jesus People. While there is a real doctrinal lack, and this is risky, they are doing what we should have known and done...they are ready to witness, to express their experiences, which admittedly are emotional but nevertheless very real." He worried, however, that the Jesus People "have no sense of history—they are not interested in continuity. They are an existentialist culture, the NOW generation." In *Christianity Today*, a campus minister named Donald Williams agreed that the movement responded more to the crises of the present moment than the expectations of church history. The young peoples' "apocalyptic attitude is as much cultural as theological. Despair over the population spiral, hydrogen stockpiles, and pollution is easily met by Christian hope, especially for youth who have dropped out."[42]

Just as Church Growth principles dictated that the gospel would take on a new form appropriate for hill tribes in Africa or jungle-dwellers in the Amazon, the Jesus People represented the perfect incarnation of the Christian message in 1960s youth culture. "The movement, thus far, centers in Jesus," Billy Graham wrote. "It may be the answer to the prayers of millions of Christians who have been praying for a spiritual awakening."[43]

TESTING OLD TABOOS

Even if the Jesus People had Billy's blessing, some worried that the revival had encouraged dangerous excess. John Wimber was an evangelical Quaker pastor and musician who helped found the Righteous Brothers before he emerged as a leader in the Vineyard church association. In 1974 he came to Fuller to direct the new Department of Church Growth at the Fuller Institute for Evangelism and Church Growth. Over the next few years, he developed a gift for "power evangelism" that won converts not by rational argument, but by demonstrating God's power through healing, prophecy, or

other miraculous intervention. Wimber began to push his encounters with
the supernatural well beyond the quiet healing prayers and inoffensive mum-
bling that the charismatic movement had brought into so many churches.
He believed that most American evangelicals had gotten too comfortable.
They took the materialist and rationalist veneer of modern Western life for
the whole reality of existence. "The difficulty in the Western Church is that
most people don't know that there is a war going on," Wimber later wrote in
a reflective essay on his work.

> They do not see the relationship between God and Satan that the Bible
> sees. They are only minimally aware of the conflict between the two
> kingdoms, and, due to their secularized, empirical perception of the
> Christian experience, they believe that they are living in a world unaf-
> fected by the two kingdoms and their existences. . . . This world view gap
> has led to the erroneous assumption that the spirit world is somehow
> less real than the tangible, materialistic one in which we live.[44]

The Church Growth movement, launched in the thrall of social science,
had boomeranged upon itself, convincing some of its most ardent advocates
that God would not be praised in the temple of reason. Two decades after
charismatic renewal had begun to transform evangelical worship, Wimber's
Fuller colleague Charles Kraft complained that Western prejudices still
crippled the growth of churches in cultures where spirits and demons were
peoples' most pressing concern. "We've been Westernizing first, then trying
to convert them to a supernaturalistic Christian point-of-view within their
Westernization," Kraft wrote. "It results, very often, in quite a superficial
kind of nominal Christianity." Wimber complained that "scientism" had
"captured the Western mind" and blinded Christians to the reality of spiritual warfare that surrounded them. The more moderate faculty at Fuller
watched in alarm as Wimber and C. Peter Wagner began co-teaching a
class in 1982 called "Signs, Wonders, and Church Growth" that included a
regular "laboratory" session in which students practiced divine healing and
casting out demons. When the administration canceled the popular course,
Wagner accused his colleagues of standing in the way of church growth and
"siding more with western worldviews in minimizing the spirit world than
the peoples of the Two Thirds World, who take it quite seriously."[45]

The Signs and Wonders class caused such scandal because it undermined the presuppositions of conservative Protestantism in the classroom of Fuller, the bosom of Church Growth and neo-evangelical ambition. It was an antirational marvel that challenged the authority of Enlightenment reason. Charismatic revival was, from one perspective, simply the most recent pulse in a rhythm of spiritual enthusiasm that has periodically rocked the church since the first century.[46] But the movement was also a response to the global traumas of the 1960s, and an indictment of the failure of scientific, rationalist responses to the world's problems. The collapse of old colonial and racist social orders, the daily fear of mutually assured destruction, and the subversion of new iconoclastic philosophies primed many communities for religious enthusiasm. It was no accident that charismatic revival coincided with the heyday of New Age spirituality and growing Western interest in the religions of the East. One anthropologist has suggested that charismatic churches taught believers that religious belief is "more like learning to do something than to think something...people train the mind in such a way that they experience part of their mind as the presence of God."[47] What better way to halt a trembling world than to hear the Lord's guidance in your own thoughts and feel the Holy Spirit on your tongue?

Chapter 7

Renewing the Church Universal

DURING THE FALL OF 1969, MONKS AT THE ABBEY OF NEW CLAIRVAUX IN Vina, California, grew curious about Pentecostals. After hearing stories of divine healing and meeting a friendly pastor who spoke in tongues, one day in late September the monks—Cistercians, an order known for keeping mostly silent—learned of a weekend prayer conference hosted by a local Pentecostal group. Four monks "in varying degrees of eagerness got permission from our abbot to go," wrote one named Father Paul.

> As we clicked off the few miles our feelings became more mixed as we approached this "hotbed" of Pentecostalism. We soon learned that we had walked into the Chico regional convention of the Full Gospel Business Men's Fellowship International.... Our presence and monastic identity were sounded abroad, and in short order we found ourselves handshaked and blessed half-to-death, and welcomed like the proverbial long lost brother. After attending the two afternoon conferences, we were loaded down with books and booklets... and were warmly pressed to stay for the evening banquet. Our hesitations were swamped by the presentation of tickets, and we were ushered into the dining room ... the eating intermingled or interspersed with the singing of hymns, witnessing, and spontaneous praying, unfolded as an unusual spiritual experience! And as the meal concluded we were feeling quite at home, and somewhat pentecostal.[1]

What, exactly, had just happened? Neither the tongues-speaking businessmen nor the white-cowled monks probably knew for sure, but both must have sensed that the walls between their two confessions were no longer so high as they once had been. The 1960s and 1970s were years of realignment in American Christianity. Most scholars have traced this transformation through new political alliances between conservative Catholics and Protestants who found themselves on the same side of pressing social questions, such as youth rebellion and the sexual revolution. The sociologist Robert Wuthnow named these changes the "restructuring of American religion."[2] Yet rapprochement between Catholics and Protestants went deeper, and began earlier, than the political exigencies of the culture wars.

Charismatic renewal eroded old boundaries at a time when upheaval in global politics and new challenges in the mission field had transformed evangelical ideas about the relationship between the gospel and culture. If old assumptions and prejudices were changing, so too was the feel of the faith: the sights, sounds, and smells of worship. Catholics and mainline Protestants drew on centuries-old Christian practices to revise their liturgies, and evangelicals began to show a tentative openness toward corners of the Christian tradition that were off-limits to their forebears. Had world events—and the breath of the Holy Spirit—eclipsed American evangelicals' squabbles over biblical inerrancy? To some observers, it seemed as if the most potent sources of spiritual authority lay elsewhere: in ecstatic religious experience, in missionaries' efforts to meet the needs of the developing world—and in the church's reservoir of ancient mysteries.

THE OPENING OF ROMAN CATHOLICISM

By the time faculty and students at Duquesne University, a Catholic school in Pittsburgh, signaled the arrival of Catholic charismatic renewal by reporting their "baptism with the Spirit" at a retreat in 1967, broader cultural developments had paved the way for détente with evangelical Protestants. Successive waves of new immigrants, new racial and ethnic minorities, had replaced Catholics as targets of resentment. By the 1960s—in part thanks to the accessibility of higher education through the GI Bill—Catholics of European descent had begun to accrue wealth and leave their ethnic ghettoes: a modest economic leavening that helped reduce historic antagonisms between Catholics and Protestants. With the rise of the civil rights and women's liberation movements, student unrest, and other signs of cultural upheaval, a host of new concerns competed with the old "Roman menace" for evangelical attention.

None of this meant that American evangelicals developed a sudden affection for the bishop of Rome. Although John F. Kennedy's relatively secular presidency would do much to allay fears that all Catholics kow-towed to the Vatican, the Roman hierarchy still struck most Americans as undemocratic and impervious to reform. In 1960, John XXIII surprised many non-Catholics by extending an ecumenical olive branch. Rome had remained aloof from the Protestant-led World Council of Churches since its inception in 1948, but now the pope established a Secretariat for Promoting Christian Unity with a mandate to pursue interchurch dia-logue. The following year, when John XXIII formally summoned the sec-ond world council of the Catholic Church in modern times, Protestant observers awaited the results with a combination of skepticism and cau-tious hope. Some attended in person: John XXIII took the unusual step of inviting non-Catholic observers to the proceedings.

The Second Vatican Council represented the church's attempt at rec-onciliation with modern democracy and the needs of an expanding flock in the non-Western world. The council radically revised Rome's official posi-tion on Protestants, declaring them "separated brethren" who, while not in communion with the mother Church, were nevertheless fellow believers rather than hellbound heretics. The council reaffirmed the power of bish-ops against exaggerations of papal primacy and encouraged lay participa-tion in worship. Most pertinent to the experience of ordinary believers, the council expanded the use of vernacular language, rather than Latin, in the liturgy. Some observers heard echoes of biblical inerrancy in the council's statement on divine revelation, *Dei Verbum*, which declared that scripture teaches "solidly, faithfully and without error that truth which God wanted put into sacred writings for the sake of salvation."[3]

While the reforms of Vatican II offered a new basis for theological con-versation between Catholics and evangelicals, the Catholic charismatic movement—a worldwide phenomenon equal to if not more extensive than its Protestant counterpart—exposed evangelicals to new common ground with Catholics in daily spiritual life. "Evangelicals tend to look hopefully at new stirrings and alignments within this ancient Church," wrote Arthur Glasser in the early 1970s. "They have increasingly been finding Catholic brethren of like faith and similar evangelistic commitment within the charismatic movement." The National Catholic Charismatic Renewal Service Committee, based at Notre Dame, actively supported renewal efforts in Protestant churches. At the same time, the movement of large numbers of Latino immigrants into the American South—and with them, a fast-growing Catholic presence—meant that conservative evangelicals in the Bible Belt personally encountered Catholics more often and began to grudgingly accept their new neighbors. Just as the Vatican was establishing a new diocese in Memphis in response to an exploding Catholic population there, the Southern Baptist Convention's Home Mission Board sponsored a "Baptist—Catholic Regional Conference" focused more on cooperation than conversion.[4]

In late 1969—only a week after the Cistercians' immersion in the full gospel—Ray Bringham, a Pentecostal pastor who ran a parachurch organization called the Inter-Church Renewal Ministry, described a visit by two Claretian fathers to a prayer meeting at an Assemblies of God church in Hollywood. "One of them got up and asked the whole church to pray that he would receive the Baptism in the Spirit. You can imagine what this did to the church," he wrote to Pentecostal evangelist (and observer at Vatican II) David du Plessis. "I'm grateful they are learning to relate to Catholics." On another occasion Jean LeClercq, a Benedictine monk and scholar, was persuaded to visit a charismatic retreat center despite his skepticism of glossolalia (LeClercq protested that he "already spoke several languages"). "After a bit of discussion he agreed to having prayer, and . . . burst out in a heavenly language," an elated Pentecostal pastor wrote.[5] Monastic spirituality has always centered on constant prayer and intimacy with the divine, and so it was not so surprising to find Catholic monks receptive to Pentecostal ideas of the gifts of the Spirit. Cowled heads bowed together in chapel and singing the Divine Hours may seem a world removed from charismatic evangelicals in blue jeans delirious with the chaos of tongues, but these are two variants of the same desire to be nearer to God.

The Roman hierarchy adopted a cautious but ultimately supportive view of charismatic renewal. In 1968, one year after charismatic revivals first broke out at Duquesne and Notre Dame, the U.S. Conference of Catholic Bishops directed its Committee on Doctrine to investigate. The committee's report noted the movement's "strong biblical basis," though it warned against the sectarian and overly enthusiastic "mistakes of classic Pentecostalism." At first, Catholic clergy were hesitant to attend Notre Dame's yearly international conferences on charismatic renewal. Some even went incognito. But by 1973, 500 priests were there to celebrate Mass.[6] Rome had weathered many renewal movements before, and—unlike evangelical churches that divided over the issue—Catholic ecclesiology called for discipline, not schism. Moreover, charismatic renewal's success in the developing world was not lost on a Roman hierarchy eager to strengthen fledgling churches in Africa and Asia and stanch losses to Pentecostals in Latin America.

The informal fellowship that grew out of this common religious experience inspired a series of formal ecumenical dialogues that lasted more than ten years. After two years of exploratory contact between Pentecostal and charismatic individuals and the Vatican's Secretariat for Promoting Christian Unity, in 1971 a steering committee assembled to develop a five-year program for annual meetings to discuss theological questions ranging from the meaning of "Baptism with the Spirit" to the relationships between experience, charisma, and church hierarchy. Rome was eager to avoid "great publicity" and stressed that the meetings would aim not toward institutional union, but only shared "prayer, spirituality, and theological reflection." Fr. Jerome Hamer, O.P., secretary to the Secretariat, stressed that Rome preferred not to use the term *dialogue* to describe their meetings, as the word was ecumenical jargon for pursuit of institutional unity. The meetings were equally controversial among Pentecostals, in no small part because of their fraught history with Catholics in much of Latin America (more than half of the worldwide membership of the Assemblies of God were ex-Catholics).[7]

Evangelicals observed Catholic charismatic renewal with a degree of smugness, assuming that, newly awakened by the Holy Spirit, most would desert Rome. Some did: In Donald Miller's survey of "new paradigm churches" (his term for neo-charismatic Protestant churches such as Calvary Chapel and the Vineyard), 28 percent of churchgoers were raised Catholic. But evangelicals were shocked to see that Catholic charismatics often became "more Catholic." "I find Catholic charismatics putting more emphasis on their church identity and heritage than ever before," wrote Nick Cavnar in *New Covenant*, a Catholic renewal magazine. "Wherever I go…Catholic charismatics are talking about a rediscovery of Mary, the sacraments, the rosary, the saints, and other traditional Catholic beliefs and practices." He added that there was no pressure from Rome. This was a grassroots movement of Catholics rediscovering church traditions as "channels through which we have encountered the living Jesus. Historically, many of the devotions and special practices of the Catholic Church actually developed with the purpose of helping ordinary Christians grow closer to God."[8]

A DIFFERENT SORT OF REVIVAL

Catholic charismatics' enthusiasm for traditional worship vindicated a half-century of efforts on the part of the Vatican, local bishops, and religious orders to revive laypeople's interest in the ancient rituals of the church. Liturgical renewal had long roots. In the mid-nineteenth century, some Catholic intellectuals grew frustrated at the embellishment of the liturgy and the proliferation of musicians and soloists who had transformed the Mass into an ostentatious music-hall concert performed for a mute congregation. In his 1903 "Motu Proprio on Sacred Music," Pius X condemned the lack of lay participation and encouraged a return to older, more communal worship practices. Monastic orders, particularly the Benedictines, relished this mandate to resurrect their medieval liturgical heritage. In the 1940s, the proliferation of vernacular hand-missals enabled the laity to follow along as the priest celebrated Mass (the Vatican had forbidden lay Catholics from possessing the text of the liturgy in their own languages until 1897, although some vernacular missals were in circulation for much of the nineteenth century). In December 1963, Paul VI promulgated the *Constitution on the Sacred Liturgy*, the first document of Vatican II and the culmination of more than sixty years of momentum toward liturgical renewal. It called for the "promotion of liturgical instruction and active participation" of the laity, stressed the importance of close study of the liturgy in seminary curricula, and extended the place of the vernacular language in worship.[9] Catholic critics of the changes complained that the encyclical reflected the "Protestantization" of Rome, but advocates viewed the reforms as a restoration of practices that had a long history prior to the Reformation.

At the same time, a revisionist spirit was moving through mainline Protestant denominations in America. Proponents of liturgical renewal in the Protestant churches advocated just what their Catholic peers desired: a recovery of tradition stripped of modern accretions, combined with more accessible language and participatory worship. In 1942, a Baptist minister named Samuel Arthur Devan published *Ascent to Zion*, outlining the history of American Protestant worship and calling for greater attention to the use of symbolism, music, decoration, and space in liturgy. Four years later, Henry Sloane Coffin, who had served as president of Union Theological Seminary and moderator of the Presbyterian Church U.S.A., published *The Public Worship of God: A Sourcebook*, and that same year his church revised their *Book of Common Worship*. Several Lutheran churches collaborated on a new common liturgy and hymnal. The Episcopal Church was at work on a series of *Prayer Book Studies* and began revision of the *Book of Common Prayer* in earnest in the 1960s—as did the Methodist Church on its *Book of Worship* and *Hymnal*. Mainline seminaries increased course requirements for the study of liturgy just as Catholics were founding new degree programs in liturgical studies.[10]

In both Protestant and Catholic confessions, liturgical renewal was often—though not always—associated with social liberalism. Leaders of mainline Protestant renewal responded to the new cultural pluralism of the civil rights era by including songs from African-American and other Christian traditions in new hymnals. Dom Virgil Michel, a Benedictine monk at St. John's Abbey in Collegeville, Minnesota, who is often credited with sparking liturgical renewal among American Catholics, considered social justice inseparable from reform of worship.[11] The revived notion of the Mystical Body of Christ, encompassing all believers, required full lay participation in the liturgy as well as care for one's fellow man.

At the same time, both Protestant and Catholic renewal movements featured a certain elitism, an enthusiasm for ancient church heritage as a way of purging contemporary worship of "ignorant" popular customs. In 1947, Pius XII chastised this snobbery (particularly among the monastic orders) in his encyclical *Mediator Dei*. As much as renewalists sought to involve laypeople in worship and make the mysteries of the Eucharist accessible, their revival of ancient prayers and rituals implicitly criticized twentieth-century Western Christianity. The Lutherans, for example, borrowed from the Greeks and from Rome, resurrecting the Liturgy of Peace written by fourth-century Archbishop of Constantinople John Chrysostom. Several denominations borrowed from the Catholic lectionary cycle.[12] In the chaos of modern times, they sought premodern authority, even if that meant rejecting the songs and forms of their youth.

The growth of evangelical megachurches and seeker-sensitive services represented an indigenous strain of evangelical liturgical renewal. Usually defined as a church that attracts more than 2,000 worshippers each week-end, the megachurch dates back at least to the nineteenth century. The sprawling, mall-like complex in the suburbs featuring a coffee bar and café, an auditorium equipped with movie-theater seats and massive video screens, all surrounded by acres of smooth blacktop to accommodate hundreds of minivans and SUVs—the megachurch that most Americans would recognize by the turn of the twenty-first century—rose to cultural dominance in the 1960s and 1970s, at the same time that the Catholic Church and mainline Protestant denominations were revising their ideas about worship. During these years, a new generation of business-savvy evangelicals began to rethink church. At a time when Americans were growing used to the prominence of large institutions in their lives, these pastors applied Church Growth principles and modern marketing insights to build churches nearly as big as the shopping malls, community colleges, and office parks that now dotted the suburban landscape. They did it by reeling in those passersby who felt alienated or bored by more traditional worship.[13]

Robert Schuller, an Iowa minister of Dutch ancestry who moved to California and founded a church in a rented drive-in movie theater in 1955, was the grandfather of seeker-sensitive megachurches. In 1980 Schuller moved his congregation into the Crystal Cathedral, a space-age building designed by the architect Philip Johnson. The church, constructed with 10,000 panes of glass, blinding on a sunny day amid the surrounding palm trees, is a monument to the partnership between megachurch worship and modernism. Through his *Hour of Power* television show and numerous books, Schuller popularized an amalgamation of modern pop psychology and feel-good theology that he adapted from his mentor Norman Vincent Peale.[14] He upended the traditional revivalist tactic of railing at sinners until they cried out for redemption.

Bill Hybels, who founded the flagship of American megachurches, Willow Creek Community Church, in 1975, applied Schuller's insights more systematically. Before Hybels set out to transform his humble youth ministry at South Park Church in Park Ridge, Illinois, into an autonomous church in the wealthier northwest Chicago suburbs, he surveyed the local population to determine why those who did not attend church stayed away. Many respondents complained that the church was always asking for money; others cited the bad music, irrelevant and guilt-inducing sermons, and boring church services that don't "meet my needs." Hybels designed seeker services aimed expressly at the unchurched, eventually drawing 20,000 people each week. George Barna, the evangelical pollster who would popularize seeker-sensitive methodology in books like *Marketing the Church* (1988), developed his theories while living in the Chicago suburbs in the 1980s and attending Willow Creek. He urged pastors to look to companies like Chrysler, which rebounded from the brink of bankruptcy by revamping its marketing strategy. Good business sense, Barna wrote, is biblical: "Jesus Christ was a communications specialist.... Notice the Lord's approach: He identified His target audience, determined their need, and delivered His message directly to them."[15]

Willow Creek would soon become a quasi-denomination in itself, ensnaring smaller churches in its gravitational pull and pioneering trends in American evangelical worship. The Willow Creek Association now boasts a vast publications ministry and more than 7,000 member churches representing 90 denominations in 85 countries.[16] The Willow Creek approach to worship is a fair measure of megachurch "liturgy" nationwide (a worship style that has spread into smaller evangelical churches and infiltrated parts of the Protestant mainline). Worshippers stream into a gaping auditorium lined with acoustical panels, where the sequence of a few prayers, announcements, and a sermon is secondary to the deafening din of a "devotion" led by jeans-wearing musicians on drums and guitars (they are usually as polished as any professional act—indeed, their albums are often for sale in the church's café or bookshop). The Vatican decried the Victorian Mass for its resemblance to pagan spectacle, but megachurches found that they could reap converts by bringing worship into line with popular culture.

Megachurches quickly became outsiders' shorthand for all of American evangelicalism, but they turned off many believers who saw Willow Creek as the apotheosis of modern evangelicalism's worst features: hyperindividualism, mushy theology, and middlebrow taste. (Today, the stereotype is somewhat unfair: Once seekers decide to become members, some of these churches require a rigorous course of doctrinal education.) Backlash against megachurches helped spur widespread rediscovery of much older ritual and tradition. This renaissance, however, was already in progress.

Years before Hybels's innovations, some evangelicals had begun to act on their frustrations with old-time religion.

SMELLS AND BELLS

By the early 1960s, there were small signs that evangelicals were curious about incense, vestments, monastic contemplation, and other elements of high-church Protestant, Roman Catholic, and Eastern Orthodox tradition that they had largely shunned in the past. Baptist pastors traditionally eschewed clerical garments in favor of a suit and tie, but across Baptist churches (particularly in the North), pastors had begun to preach in robes. The laity requested more stately worship that would help them "meet God" and "not just have a chatty time of it." "Baptist services are becoming more formal and adorned, and less and less spontaneous," complained one conservative pastor in the pages of the *Watchman-Examiner.* "We could not be vital, so we became artistic." In 1963, at the eighth meeting of the Southern Baptist Religious Education Association, a pastor named John R. Claypool delivered a paper entitled "The Lost Chord of Worship." He noted that Southern Baptist churches were "losing some of our very finest young people" to denominations that offered more elaborate, majestic worship and called for "'an agonizing reappraisal' of this lost element in Baptist life—the practice of meaningful worship." (Claypool himself was so frustrated by his church's low view of worship—in his opinion, Southern Baptists saw their Sunday meetings as only an evangelistic tool, rather than a time to glorify God—that he later sought ordination in the Episcopal Church.)[17]

In these heady days of the Second Vatican Council, even conservative evangelicals who were skeptical of Roman claims to reform spoke in vague terms of the need for renewal in all Christian churches, including their own.[18] "Renewal" could mean many things, from more social service and more lay involvement in worship to evangelistic zeal. The neo-evangelicals had tried to rekindle intellectual rigor and reconnect with their own churches' early history. Some evangelicals, however, began to think that they ought to reach even further back, before the time of Protestant confessions and hero-evangelists.

Charismatic renewal, which touched churches of every confession, convinced many low-church evangelicals that spiritual vigor could be found amid smells and bells and even celibate nuns and priests. However, polite respect for one's Catholic or Orthodox neighbor was one thing. The desire to share his history, saints, and rituals was something else entirely. "Tradition to him [the evangelical] means corruption and infidelity that must be avoided like the plague," the *Christianity Today* editors wrote in an issue devoted to the subject of Protestant–Catholic dialogue in 1964. "Yet, since he lives in the world of the 1960s, he has to face the problem....Is his flat denial of tradition proper, and is it in accord with the facts, even of his own Christian faith?"[19] Evangelical intellectuals recognized that the modern Western culture that nurtured their churches was not a neutral environment. It contained, as Reformed scholars had taught them to say, its own "presuppositions" with as much poison as promise.

Earlier Protestant experiments in pre-Reformation tradition, at first marginal and hardly known outside their own small circles, began to attract the attention of evangelicals searching for ways to rethink their relationship to the church catholic. Evangelical bookstores began selling admiring studies of early "Protestant monasticism," such as the Iona Community, an ecumenical community founded in 1938 at St. Columba's landing place in the Inner Hebrides; Koinonia Farm, a Georgia monastic commune founded by Baptists in 1942 (and later the birthplace of Habitat for Humanity); and Taizé, a French community founded during World War II whose Rule (based on the Rule of St. Benedict, and including a vow of celibacy) earned fans and imitators around the world.[20] Roger Schutz, "Brother Roger" and Taizé's founder, called himself a "Calvinist student of theology" but wrote his master's thesis on St. Benedict. He described Taizé as an alternative to the "Christian ghetto" in which most Protestants lived:

> The juridical turn of mind which we have inherited through European Christianity from ancient Rome is a poor preparation for this highpoint of the interior life, contemplation. In the Eastern Churches, in contrast, this reality is still lived intensely in our day....We force our faith to rationalize itself. By so doing we risk robbing the salt of its savor.[21]

Taizé's message was alien but intriguing. Personal contemplation based loosely on traditional Catholic practices began appearing in evangelical circles in the 1960s. When Brother John, a Taizé member, visited the

Moody Bible Institute in 1967, students crowded around to ask questions about prayer, meditation, and celibacy. The Lilly Endowment sponsored prayer retreats for Southern Baptists and other churches. One Southern Baptist pastor, David George, recalled that as a student he participated in a retreat led by a liberal Episcopalian: "He was too catholic and monastic to suit me and was hung up on Francis of Assisi, but he knew how to teach people to pray, and prayer was more real to him than philosophy—which at the time was the most real thing to me."[22] George urged his colleague to read *Prayer in Practice* by Romano Guardini, a prominent Roman Catholic professor-priest.

The image of the Catholic monk—devoted to a cloistered life of fasting and prayer, his scalp tonsured, his form hidden in the folds of his tunic—had long provoked the disdain of Protestants. Their forefathers denounced the monastic life. True Christians, the Reformers said, lived wholly in the world, spent their time reading the Bible rather than chanting in Latin, and accepted that God saved them by his grace alone, not as reward for prayers, fasting, or good works. Martin Luther called monks and wandering friars "confounded lice" who "howl and growl day and night like fiends" and carry the pope "as the rats carry their king."[23] Of all Protestants, American evangelicals in particular—activist, family-oriented, and more concerned with evangelism than solitary study or contemplation—historically viewed monks as an alien species, a grotesque caricature of Roman error.

Yet some evangelicals wondered if Luther's judgment was too hasty. A small but highly visible minority of evangelicals ventured further into Catholic and Orthodox spirituality. Some prayed the Divine Office at home and read biographies of saints, while others gravitated toward a communal and semimonastic lifestyle inspired by pre-Reformation practices. By the late 1960s, the founder and director of the Institute for Ecumenical and Cultural Research affiliated with St. John's Abbey, Kilian McDonnell, O.S.B.—who had come to know many evangelical and Pentecostal leaders through his participation in the charismatic movement—was eagerly recruiting Fuller professors to study liturgical renewal there. Catholic faith and works held a particular fascination for progressive evangelicals. The left-leaning magazine the *Post-American* featured Trappist contemplative Thomas Merton on its cover and ran frequent articles about Roman Catholic theology of prayer. *Sojourners*, *Post-American*'s successor, continued this emphasis, printing advertisements for books on ancient Egyptian monasticism and George Woodcock's *Thomas Merton: Monk and Poet* alongside ads for books by and about Dorothy Day, co-founder of the Catholic Worker movement. Henri Nouwen, a Dutch Catholic priest and popular author on spirituality, had a regular column, and the magazine published admiring articles about older Protestant monastic communities in Europe. Catholic practices held some allure for conservatives too: *Christianity Today* ran frequent articles on prayer and worship, and in 1974 Sherwood Wirt, then editor of the Billy Graham Evangelistic Association's magazine *Decision*, wrote an editorial entitled "Let's Lengthen Lent."[24]

Catholic and Orthodox spirituality did not remain the purview of elite activists and intellectuals. In 1978, evangelical Quaker and Fuller graduate Richard Foster published *Celebration of Discipline*, which recast meditative prayer, fasting, and elaborate worship for a mainstream evangelical audience. The book sold over a million copies in the next thirty years, launching a cottage industry of evangelical contemplative spirituality. Although most evangelical pastors found the idea of a headfirst plunge into monasticism unsettling, some began to take an occasional cue from the movement, encouraging youth groups to explore contemplative prayer or think like Franciscans at their weekly soup kitchen.[25]

Those evangelicals drawn toward non-Protestant practices learned from popular Catholic intellectuals like Thomas Merton and contact with Catholics in charismatic circles. In the early 1970s Archer Torrey, an Episcopalian priest and son of the great American revivalist R. A. Torrey, founded a charismatic retreat center called Jesus Abbey among "Catholic Pentecostal friends" in Korea. Charismatic Catholic communities like the Mother of God Christian Community, outside of Washington, DC, drew some Protestants. Conspicuously, however, evangelicals tended to idolize contemplatives and friars who ran against the Roman grain. The ancient Egyptian founders of monasticism, like St. Anthony, who wrestled demons alone in the desert; the Celtic monks, who were largely cut off from Rome after the collapse of the European continent to barbarian rule and worshipped for centuries by their own rite; the Franciscans, who rebelled against a worldly papacy: these were the examples that most appealed to modern American evangelicals, perhaps because they permitted evangelicals to sample Catholic tradition without condemning the Reformation.[26]

For many evangelicals attracted to this jumbled renaissance, which came to be known as "New Monasticism"—and the wider enthusiasm for pre-Reformation spirituality dubbed "Ancient-Future"—to embrace Catholic and Orthodox traditions of worship and contemplation meant rebelling against the nonliturgical, revivalist, or megachurch culture in which so many had grown up. Some New Monastic communities grew out of the countercultural Jesus People Movement and approached Catholic and Orthodox resources as possible roots for their revolt. What better way to irk one's evangelical parents then by praying the Divine Hours and carrying around a biography of St. Francis?

Catholicism and Eastern Orthodoxy offered not only strange rituals and saints, but alternative worldviews. They suggested a deep critique of evangelical assumptions about Christian fellowship and communion with God. John Howard Yoder perceived this awkward amalgam of doctrine and history and questioned its theological integrity. Monasticism represented "one end of the spectrum of divided Christendom," he wrote in 1966 to Father John Michael of the Brothers of Christian Unity, a New Monastic group in Missouri that reached out to Mennonites. "The monastic pattern is fully at home in Roman Catholicism, somewhat less so in Anglicanism, barely present within continental Protestantism, and completely foreign to the free church tradition." He pointed out the profound divide between clergy and laity inherent in monasticism and so alien to Anabaptists. Father John Michael protested that a Mennonite might live as a monk without acting in a way "contrary to his theological outlook...there are some who might be willing to add to their traditions, to find this new mode of expression for it and thus bring their Church which they love to a new and higher plane."[27]

It was evangelicals' sense of rudderlessness—their desire for an authority to guide them in questions of dogma, life, and worship—that led them to rediscover liturgy and history in the first place. The irony was that in their smorgasbord approach to non-Protestant tradition, in their individualistic rejection of the rules of any one church in favor of a free run of the so-called church universal, in their repudiation of American nationalism in favor of cosmopolitanism, young evangelicals were being quintessentially evangelical and stereotypically American, doing as they pleased according to no authority but their own. The principle of *sola scriptura* was far clearer in theory than in practice. No matter evangelicals' faith that, with the "illumination of the Holy Spirit," "Scripture could and should interpret itself," too many illuminated believers came to different conclusions about what the Bible meant.[28] Inerrantists who asserted their "literal" interpretation with absolute certainty could do so only by covertly relying on modern, manmade assumptions. Other evangelicals were now searching for similar assurance in the authority of church history and the mysteries of worship.

SCANDALOUS CONVERSIONS

Some evangelicals came to more candid terms with their desire for extra-biblical authority—though when they spoke to the friends they left behind, they justified their submission to church, history, and ritual by appealing to the Bible itself. For them, Canterbury, Rome, and Constantinople called as to a prodigal son. The Anglican tradition presented the shortest leap. Although the evidence is spotty, a number of evangelicals—particularly college students, academics, and other intellectuals—began to worship in Episcopal or other Anglican churches during the 1970s and 1980s. Robert Webber, the son of Baptist missionaries, a Bob Jones University graduate, and an ordained minister in the Reformed Presbyterian Church, found himself in a crisis of faith shortly after he began teaching at Wheaton College in 1968. When he considered "where evangelicals are going in the 1970s," he found himself pondering a narrative of decline, but could not offer his students a solution. He rejected the Christianity that he had imbibed at Bob Jones, "a proof-texting Christianity...a Christianity based on scientific inquiry. Christianity was no longer a power to be experienced but a system to be defended." Yet he was also put off by evangelicals who embraced the political Left, whom he felt carried "ethical spirituality" too far at the expense of other dimensions of the faith.[29]

Webber attended Easter Vigil at a local Catholic church and was unexpectedly moved. He began reading the Church Fathers on worship and the sacraments. On Reformation Day (October 31) 1972, invited to speak to the Wheaton student body at Edman Chapel, he listened to the college president introduce him, telling students that Webber "is going to speak to us today on the glories of the Reformation." Instead, Webber quoted Lutheran scholar Jaroslav Pelikan on the "tragic necessity" of the 95 Theses

(Pelikan would eventually convert to Eastern Orthodoxy). The following Sunday, Webber "walked into an Episcopal church to stay" (he remained at Wheaton until retiring in 2000).[30]

Gone were the days when *Kodon* short stories described Episcopalian worship, the congregation's "aristocratic, lifted noses" and "stinging brown wine," with mocking fascination. Student conversions multiplied. Even the curator of the Billy Graham Museum was now Episcopalian.[31] In 1985 Webber published *Evangelicals on the Canterbury Trail*, a collection of profiles of several prominent evangelical converts he knew—including David Neff, a former Seventh-day Adventist who would go on to become editor in chief of *Christianity Today*. These evangelicals and many others, Webber wrote, had drifted into the Anglican Communion because their home churches failed to awe them with God's mystery, provide a sense of membership in the church universal, or nurture a holistic spirituality that included private contemplation and intellectual engagement as well as evangelism and activism.

In 1977, Webber helped organize forty-six likeminded scholars from fourteen evangelical colleges and seminaries to meet at a retreat center in the Chicago suburbs and issue a manifesto. (Manifestos were rather un-Anglican and left Catholics and Orthodox bemused, but they were the evangelical way.) The "Chicago Call" stressed the need for evangelicals to put aside their "sectarian" disagreements over biblical authority and redis-cover the theology and practice of historic Christianity. Reporting on the event for *Newsweek*, Ken Woodward noted the subtle "but significant drift among some [evangelical] scholars and students toward more traditional forms of Christianity." The Call reflected "a growing effort among educated Evangelicals to find deeper roots. Some feel cramped by Evangelicalism's low regard for reason and high tolerance of boisterous Biblicalism."[32] Self-criticism and a new taste for history were all very well, but would an evangelical ever follow these sentiments all the way to Rome?

Thomas Howard, who joined Webber on the Chicago Call planning committee, was a true member of the evangelical aristocracy. His father, Philip Howard, edited the stalwart fundamentalist paper the *Sunday School Times*; his sister, Elisabeth Elliot, served as a missionary in Ecuador for years after natives there murdered her husband and became a best-selling author and icon of evangelical womanhood; his brother, David Howard, had a sterling career in missions that would eventually land him at the head of the World Evangelical Fellowship. Thomas himself began to feel ill at ease in evangelicalism during his time as an undergraduate at Wheaton. He drifted toward the Christianity of C. S. Lewis and the other Anglicans whose works he read in English class. After college he studied in England and there was received into the Anglican Church. "And this does *not* represent a departure from the evangelical womb for me," he assured his mentor at Wheaton, Clyde Kilby. "The C. of E. is jammed with raving evangelicals."[33] Kilby could not have been surprised. Howard had been dating his letters with saints' feast days for some time.

Howard went on to do a PhD in English at New York University, where he wrote his dissertation on the British novelist (and devout Anglican) Charles Williams. In graduate school he wrote a memoir of his conversion, *Christ the Tiger* (1967), and later heard that Wheaton's president had commanded the campus bookstore manager to remove it from the shelves—despite the college's growing contingent of Anglicans, and even high-church Anglo-Catholics ("they're there now; Wheaton better pull its socks up"). "I am sure I shall get myself a reputation as . . . the *enfant terrible* of Evangelical Letters," Howard wrote.[34] He took a job at Gordon College, where he shepherded likeminded students into the Anglican fold. He wrote to Kilby:

> One of my erstwhile students is being confirmed at the Easter Vigil on Holy Saturday evening, just before the (midnight) First Mass of Easter at the Church of S. Mary the Virgin, known to its friends as Smoky Mary's, or to one of my friends as Our Lady's Very Own Anglican Shrine. Her parents are fundamentalist Baptists, and she hasn't told them yet. I may find myself at gunpoint here one of these days. She is a brilliant girl, a lit major (you have had hundreds of this type), and was *desperately* unhappy with the more frenzied and random types of religion popular in her home circles.[35]

Howard's relationship with establishment evangelicalism ran hot and cold. Despite discouraging students from reading his memoir, Wheaton College (at Kilby's behest) later offered Howard a position as writer in residence, which tempted him sorely. He wrote occasionally for *Christianity Today* and was listed on the masthead as a contributing editor, yet was constantly at odds with the staff and their "turgid Teutonic theological minds."

CT ran a glowing review of *Christ the Tiger*, but rejected so many of his articles on liturgy and other subjects that he demanded to be removed from the masthead. Yet Howard had few kindred spirits among progressive evangelicals, despite their common frustrations with traditional Protestantism. He dismissed the *Post-American* as an "evangelical left-wing rag." He submitted an article critiquing women's liberation, which the magazine published—along with a rejoinder, which Howard found "amusing, in that the main argument in the whole thing is that I'm high-church (along with CSL & co), which is of course a Bad Thing."[36]

At Easter 1985, Howard was received into the Roman Catholic Church. Gordon College pressured him to resign. He went on to write books and articles explaining his decision to his evangelical kinsmen, the first of which he published on the eve of his conversion, *Evangelical Is Not Enough: Worship of God in Liturgy and Sacrament* (1984). Howard's books were among the first in a growing number of memoirs and apologetics by evangelical converts to Catholicism that swelled to a steady stream by the 1990s. By 1996, at least 150 Gordon College alumni—many of whom Howard taught—had converted to Rome.[37]

There was one destination more remote than Rome: Constantinople. For a small number of evangelicals fed up with the presuppositions of modern, Western Christianity, Eastern Orthodoxy offered the only respite. A handful of broad-minded evangelicals had reached eastward in the past. John Wesley was deeply interested in Orthodoxy and incorporated some of its elements into his own theology. But for most American evangelicals, Orthodoxy was an unknown country until the 1970s, when a small number began to dabble in Eastern theology as a means of understanding and critiquing their own tradition. Thomas Howard, though he never found his way to converting, understood the appeal—as did his conservative sister, Elisabeth. "We're all becoming Russian Orthodox, having read Timothy Ware's (Penguin) *The Orthodox Church*," Howard wrote in 1971. "As Betty [Elisabeth] said, at every point where they differ from Western Xdom [Christendom], *they're* right!" Four years later Peter Gillquist—an alumnus of Dallas Theological Seminary and Wheaton College, veteran Campus Crusade evangelist, and editor at the influential evangelical publishing house Thomas Nelson— organized the New Covenant Apostolic Order. Frustrated by his efforts to evangelize the University of California at Berkeley in the late 1960s, Gillquist and his colleagues had begun reading the early Church Fathers in search of an ancient approach to worship that might feel more "authentic." In 1979 they reorganized their movement as the Evangelical Orthodox Church and grew to include about twenty parishes. Further study convinced Gillquist and his band of refugees to repudiate the tradition that raised them in favor of icons, incense, and polyphonic chants. In 1987 he led nearly two thousand evangelicals into the Antiochian Orthodox Christian Archdiocese of North America.[38]

There is no hard data on how many evangelical Protestants have converted to Roman Catholicism or Orthodoxy over the past thirty years, and it is almost certain that they are still outnumbered by Christians leaving those ancient confessions for evangelicalism. However, evangelical converts were often prominent members of their subculture's intelligentsia. Howard taught at Gordon College, the Wheaton of the East. Scott Hahn, another prolific convert to Catholicism, was a Presbyterian minister and professor at Chesapeake Theological Seminary before his 1986 conversion. Gillquist's 1987 mass conversion included many former Campus Crusade staff and long-time servants of the evangelical cause. More recently, Baylor University philosopher Francis Beckwith caused a stir in 2007 when he returned to the Catholic faith of his childhood—in the middle of his tenure as president of the Evangelical Theological Society (he remained at Baylor). These elite converts and their spiritual trajectories are exceptional stories within evangelicalism, but only in the radical degree and public nature of their transformation—not in the spirit of their reappraisal of evangelicalism or their new regard for the authority and mystery of pre-Reformation tradition, which many evangelicals shared.

Charismatic renewal and liturgical renewal did not coincide by chance. They were two dimensions of the same search for authentic spiritual experience, for supernatural and timeless authority that could offer certainty in an era when worldly powers seemed unable to do so. These movements were not unique to evangelicalism. Evangelicals' new taste for the Holy Spirit and ancient ritual placed them squarely in the Christian mainstream. However, such renewal posed unique opportunities and challenges in a subculture in which there was no magisterial authority to rule on right worship, genuine contact with the divine, or the fraught question of how to separate the treasures of church history from heterodox accretions. In some sense, charismatic and liturgical renewal represented the global revival for which the neo-evangelicals had called decades earlier. But to Billy Graham and his colleagues, tongues and chants and friendly relations with Catholics were hardly a substitute for a worldwide refreshing of orthodox, born-again faith, a "spirit-filled" push to unite conservative Protestants the world over.

Unity in an Age of Fracture

The term "ecumenical" derives from the Greek word *oikoumene*, meaning "the inhabited earth," or in the context of Christianity, "pertaining to the whole church." In the twentieth century, ecumenism came to denote efforts toward institutional reunification of churches and also implied cooperative good faith. This "ecumenical age" revived time-honored ambitions. Christian history is full of efforts by churchmen and princes to mediate between mutually antagonized groups of Christians (usually for rather worldly reasons). American evangelicals, for their part, had never been overly eager to heal schisms. They thought that most schisms happened for good reason, and there was no higher authority to tell them otherwise. Yet despite their proclivity for infighting and separation, for rivalry and "sheep-stealing," they had an instinct for cooperation in the practical business of saving souls.

Billy Graham raised the idea of cooperative evangelism to a new level of sophistication, but he did not invent it. The voluntary societies of the nineteenth century brought evangelicals from diverse church backgrounds together in joint efforts to eradicate vice from society and urge sinners toward the Lord. Later, though fundamentalists savored the boundaries between churches, they also nurtured an international network of Bible colleges, radio ministries, and prophecy conferences that brought together a spectrum of denominations and sometimes actively discouraged participants from exclusive loyalty to their home churches. From the evangelical point of view, liberal organizations like the World Council of Churches did not invent ecumenism, but clericalized and perverted it. A thoroughly evangelical impulse—the desire to preach the gospel to the world's lost—sparked the modern ecumenical movement when it began with a gathering of missionaries in Edinburgh in 1910. Since then, however, evangelicals believed that liberal theology, the triumph of secularist assumptions, and a protracted crisis of confidence had eroded the movement into a feeble and heterodox effort to enact the Kingdom of God through social justice campaigns, rather than to convert and disciple the nations.

To evangelicals, the liberals' theology of mission was not the only problem. The WCC's emphasis on churches as the only Christian institutions capable of ecumenical action seemed out of touch, if not unbiblical. In 1973, when the general secretary of the WCC wrote Fuller dean Arthur Glasser requesting his thoughts on the ecumenical efforts of the past twenty years, Glasser replied that "the WCC needs to be a World Council of Christians, not just a council of Churches." Glasser, like many evangelicals, perceived the WCC as an exercise in ecclesiastical egoism, old-fashioned and churchbound at a time when the most innovative collaboration between Christians was happening through parachurch organizations. He was convinced that a "silent majority" of evangelicals sat muzzled in WCC-affiliated denominations, consistently betrayed by their liberal pastor-representatives to the WCC. One *Time* reporter noted a few years earlier that in the American affiliate of the WCC, the National Council of Churches, "at least one-third of its 39 million Protestant members, according to modest estimates, still maintain evangelical attitudes, forming strong blocs within their denominations." That tally, combined with the estimated 27 million evangelicals outside the NCC, made evangelicals a significant majority among America's 67 million Protestants—one that deserved, Glasser believed, a louder, more unified voice in global Christian affairs.[39]

American evangelicals made a few preliminary efforts to mobilize like-minded Christians around the world. At Chicago in 1960, Wheaton and Berlin in 1966, and in Minneapolis in 1969—partly at the urging of the neo-evangelicals behind *Christianity Today*—evangelicals attempted to "stimulate somewhat of an ecumenical return to that noble heritage" of the movement's early days, Carl Henry wrote in a memo on the eve of the 1966 World Congress on Evangelism in Berlin. In the summer of 1970, evangelical theologians gathered in Germany—the hothouse of liberal theology—to rebut the WCC's further secularization of Christian mission at its 1968 conference in Uppsala, Sweden. The resulting Frankfurt Declaration rejected universal salvation, reasserted the primacy of evangelism over social justice, and "force[d] the World Council into a face-to-face confrontation...to challenge its basic assumptions," wrote Harold Lindsell.[40]

When 2,300 evangelical leaders from 150 nations and dependencies met at Lausanne for ten days in July 1974, much of their discussion centered on the most efficient way to evangelize communities that had not yet heard the gospel. Donald McGavran delivered a paper on "The Dimensions of World Evangelization," and his colleague at Fuller, Ralph Winter, spoke on "The Highest Priority: Cross-Cultural Evangelism." The congress organizers based much of their framework on Church Growth strategies.[41] However, a broader theological discussion surrounded these debates about tactics. The most prominent speakers at Lausanne raised a theme that certain neo-evangelicals had stressed ever since Carl Henry published *The Uneasy Conscience of Modern Fundamentalism* in 1947: evangelicals' poor record on social justice and this-worldly welfare.

Billy Graham told the gathering that while he hoped the congress would reaffirm the orthodox theology of the ecumenical movement's founders, he did not wish to turn back the clock "politically or sociologically." The Reverend John Stott, a leading Anglican evangelical and a chaplain to Elizabeth II, urged "evangelical repentance." "We have some important lessons to learn from our ecumenical critics," he said. "Some of their rejection of our position is not a repudiation of biblical truth, but rather of our evangelical caricatures of it." Behind celebrities like Graham and Stott stood a legion of Lausanne delegates from the developing world who insisted that the congress's official statement affirm "Christian social responsibility" and acknowledge that "evangelism and socio-political involvement are both part of our Christian duty. . . . Faith without works is dead."[42]

Graham hoped that by issuing a centrist statement adopting—with important caveats—some key "liberal" positions, evangelicals could attract moderates affiliated with the WCC.[43] Yet the conference's official statement, the Lausanne Covenant, also affirmed the inerrancy of the Bible. An undercurrent of recalcitrance ran through some of the plenary addresses: There could be no compromise between orthodoxy and the secularized worldview of liberal Christians. This insistence that evangelicals could brook no neutrality on questions of biblical authority owed something to the Reformed presuppositionalist tradition, but by the 1970s that sentiment also reflected the Pentecostal theology of spiritual warfare. Pentecostals emphasized the Christian duty to follow the example of Christ and his apostles by resisting and defeating the efforts of the Devil and his minions as they tempted and deceived humans. The charismatic renewal movement had popularized the principles of spiritual warfare throughout the evangelical world. Peter Beyerhaus, a German theologian from the University of Tübingen and one of the organizers of the earlier meeting at Frankfurt, declared at Lausanne that "the world which is to be won for the Kingdom of Christ through evangelism is no neutral territory. It is in a state of active rebellion. The idolatrous religions of men are ways in which Satan seduces the heathen to worship him. . . . Their personal, cultural, and social life is under demonic captivity."[44]

The charismatic worldview, while not mutually exclusive with certain principles of Reformed theology, framed the dangers and dilemmas of the modern age in terms very different from those preferred by the neo-evangelical intellectuals who built Fuller Seminary and *Christianity Today*. Few of the organizers had expected a harmonious meeting that would satisfy everyone. Two years earlier, Graham lamented the difficulty of pleasing the "more theologically and intellectually inclined Europeans" while still reaching out to evangelicals from the developing world who emphasized experience and spirituality.[45] Now the congress—with its alternate notes of contrition and confidence, its strains of Western rationalism and spiritual warfare—suggested that the world's conservative Protestants had as much to argue about as they shared in common.

A handful of WCC staff members were invited to attend Lausanne as observers. Gerhard Hoffmann, one WCC representative, went with "rather pessimistic expectations" but admitted that he was pleasantly surprised: "Though a congress of this magnitude has to be (unfortunately) strictly and professionally organized and so, to a certain extent, does not allow for fighting out conflicts on the stage and in plenaries, there was room and freedom enough for Pentecostalists and fundamentalists, for revivalists and cross-cultural missionaries, for church growth organizers and for those deeply concerned with the societal political implications of our faith." Hoffmann was pleased by the conference precisely because of the internal divisions that he detected. The evangelical organizers, on the other hand, hoped to present a united face to the rest of the world—particularly to liberal Protestants. In the lead-up to Lausanne, John Stott had complained to Billy Graham that "we were all rather too self-conscious at [the Congress on World Evangelism at] Berlin. We seemed all the time to be looking over our shoulders to see if members of the World Council were watching and listening! We did not so much lay realistic plans as talk to one another in a loud enough voice for ecumenical observers to hear us."[46]

Although the Covenant affirmed inerrancy and the importance of proclaiming the Word, its acknowledgment of past mistakes struck some conservatives as capitulation. In his postmortem of the conference for *Christianity Today*, guru of spiritual warfare C. Peter Wagner was alarmed by the congress's emphasis on social concern and ecumenism. He called these issues "torpedoes" that had almost wrecked the evangelical enterprise altogether. The next summer, conservative Protestants in Norway were up in arms "because they think that the LM [Lausanne Movement] is not speaking clearly enough against the WCC and that our movement is in danger of being neutralized by the WCC's positive policy towards the LM." One Norwegian pastor called for Lausanne's organizers "to clear the thick fog concerning the movement's policy towards the WCC."[47] He worried that, in the interest of winning converts and enhancing the position of evangelical Christianity in the developing world, the neo-evangelical leadership behind Lausanne had gotten carried away with theological peacemaking and cultural accommodation.

Organizers established an elaborate post-congress bureaucracy to carry out the ideas and initiatives that the delegates had produced in their ten days at Lausanne. The "Strategy Group" alone oversaw twelve subgroups, such as the "Theological Education and Evangelization" subgroup, which was tasked with establishing research centers around the world to explore how to translate biblical concepts into different cultures, to analyze "competing ideologies which tend to discredit the authenticity and relevance of the gospel, such as Neo-Marxism, religious syncretism, etc.," and to prepare studies of local culture, history, and politics. Revealing the imprint of Church Growth, many of Lausanne's continuing projects emphasized research to aid in "indigenizing" the gospel in local non-Christian cultures around the world. Under the stewardship of evangelist (and Billy Graham's brother-in-law) Leighton Ford, the International Committee on World Evangelization oversaw all continuing Lausanne operations and sponsored a myriad of conferences in America and abroad. Carl Henry told A. J. Dain that Lausanne would have to succeed where earlier neo-evangelical efforts to revive the mainstream authority of Protestant orthodoxy had fallen short: "*Christianity Today* garnered leadership and initiative in the contemporary theological ferment, but has since lost it, and while its circulation is now again recovering, it does not have the precision theologically to serve here."[48]

The trouble was that the Church Growth movement, charismatic renewal, and ecumenical dialogues offered as much hindrance as help to the neo-evangelicals' original ambitions. Church Growth encouraged rapprochement with the social sciences, stimulated cooperation with Pentecostals and Catholics, and yielded a sophisticated body of thinking on matters of culture—but it also propelled the rise of modern megachurches. These churches were often more diverse and theologically mature than their critics suggest, but they were no vanguard of intellectual renaissance. Charismatic revival vaulted enthusiasm over reason. Liturgical renewal awakened a historical consciousness among some evangelicals, but their new taste for the divine hours and the church fathers did not mean that they were suddenly and searchingly aware of themselves (and their approach to the Bible) as historical creatures. Meanwhile, the world's focus on change in Rome stirred up those fundamentalists who remained as staunchly anti-Catholic as ever, and sometimes had the undesirable effect of luring a few of evangelicalism's most creative intellectuals across the Tiber.

Lausanne and later meetings produced thousands of pages' worth of thoughtful prose and an impressive edifice of conferences, working groups, and follow-up conferences. But they did not solve the underlying problem. The congress and its successors did not discover a way through the unresolved debates over biblical authority still stewing all these long years—the anxiety over the Bible's clash with human reason and modern pluralism that made conservative American evangelicals so skittish around any perceived concession to worldly life or the whims of the Spirit.

One thing was certain: Evangelicals had a habit of acting on their ideas. They wanted to change their world, evangelize the lost, and bring about God's kingdom. Few were quietists content to pray in private, and so their conflicting beliefs about intellectual authority, authentic conversion, and the lessons of history had political consequences. The rise of the Christian Right was one result of this midcentury ferment, but the Moral Majority was not the only political expression of evangelicals' struggle to reconcile their faith with a changing society. By the final decade of the twentieth century, commentators who insisted on drafting all American evangelicals into "red state" ranks did so only by ignoring the diversity, ambiguity, and contradiction among believers who had learned to produce so many versions of their own history that one self-described "evangelical" barely resembled the next.

The National Conference for United Action Among Evangelicals in St. Louis, April 1942. The National Association of Evangelicals—the first major institutional effort by the neo-evangelicals—formally organized the following year. (*Wheaton College Special Collections*)

Carl F. H. Henry (1913–2003), first editor in chief of *Christianity Today* and one of the architects of the neo-evangelical mission to restore conservative Protestantism's intellectual respectability. (*copyright Fabian Bachrach*)

Cornelius Van Til (1895–1987), professor of theology at Westminster Theological Seminary and grandfather of presuppositionalism, a theology that heavily influenced American evangelicals' thinking about culture and politics. (Christianity Today *archives*)

Charles Fuller (1887–1968), radio host of *The Old Fashioned Revival Hour* and founder of Fuller Theological Seminary. (Christianity Today *archives*)

L. Nelson Bell (1894–1973), left, co-founder of *Christianity Today* and Billy Graham's father-in-law, with J. Howard Pew (1882–1971), Sun Oil magnate and the magazine's main funder. (Christianity Today *archives*)

Harold Lindsell (1913–1998), second editor of *Christianity Today* and stalwart defender of biblical inerrancy. Lindsell taught missions at Fuller Theological Seminary before the conservative exodus from the school in 1963. (*Billy Graham Center Archives*)

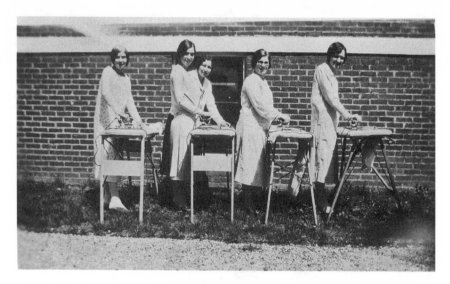

The "ironing crew" at Central Bible Institute in Springfield, Missouri, 1928. This Assemblies of God school shared the practical, anti-professional ethos of the Bible college movement. (*Flower Pentecostal Heritage Center*)

The founding
members of
the Accrediting
Association of Bible
Institutes and Bible
Colleges at their
inaugural meeting
in Winona Lake,
Indiana, 1947.
(*Flower Pentecostal
Heritage Center*)

Henry Orton Wiley (1877–1961), Nazarene churchman and educator who helped his church navigate the difficult strait between fundamentalism and modernism, at Pasadena College ca. 1930. (*Church of the Nazarene Archives*)

Mildred Wynkoop (1905–1997), Wiley's student and an influential theologian and educator in her own right, shown here in the 1960s at Central Taiwan Theological College, where she taught briefly before serving as the founding president of Japan Nazarene Theological Seminary in Tokyo. (*Church of the Nazarene Archives*)

Staff at the Wheaton College *Record* hard at work in the 1940s. (*Wheaton College Special Collections*)

By the 1970s, the dress code at the *Record* office had relaxed, although the editors' commitment to hard news and controversial material had grown stronger over the years. (*Wheaton College Special Collections*)

Clyde Kilby (1902–1986), professor of English at Wheaton College, opens a shipment of C.S. Lewis material for the college's new collection, ca. 1965. (*Wheaton College Special Collections*)

Evangelicals from around the world discuss the future of global Christianity at the International Congress on World Evangelization in Lausanne, Switzerland, 1974. (*Billy Graham Evangelistic Association*)

Billy Graham (born 1918) greets students at Lausanne, 1974. (*Billy Graham Evangelistic Association*)

Peter Gillquist (1938–2012; fifth from left), presiding bishop of the Evangelical Orthodox Church and former Campus Crusade evangelist, greets Antiochian Orthodox Metropolitan Philip Saliba in 1986. The Antiochian Orthodox Christian Archdiocese of North America would absorb Gillquist's fledgling denomination the following year. (Christianity Today *archives*)

Jim Wallis (born 1948), founder of *Sojourners* and liberal evangelical activist, cut a new path for politically minded evangelicals disillusioned with the Christian Right. (Christianity Today *archives*)

Francis Schaeffer (1912–1984), political activist and founder of L'Abri, taking questions from fans in 1982. He is wearing his distinctive Swiss hiking knickers and knee socks. (*copyright Gary Gnidovic*)

Rousas John Rushdoony (1916–2001), Orthodox Presbyterian minister, adviser to the Christian homeschooling movement, shadowy guru to some conservatives in Washington, and father of Christian Reconstructionism. (Christianity Today *archives*)

Cliff Barrows, music director for the Billy Graham Evangelistic Association, leads a 4,000 voice choir in singing "Amazing Grace" at the 1979 Southern Baptist Convention, where conservatives elected the first in an unbroken succession of conservative convention presidents. Photo by David Clanton. (*copyright Southern Baptist Historical Library and Archives*)

Southern Baptist missionaries parade before an estimated crowd of 48,000 at the 1979 Southern Baptist Convention. Photo by Mark Sandlin. (*copyright Southern Baptist Historical Library and Archives*)

Ronald Reagan declares the Soviet Union an "evil empire" in his address to the annual convention of the National Association of Evangelicals in 1983. Near the end of the speech he quoted from the *Screwtape Letters* by the beloved C.S. Lewis—his speechwriters gauged his audience well. (Christianity Today *archives*)

John Howard Yoder (1927–1997), Mennonite theologian, educator, and envoy to "mainstream" evangelicals, with his family ca. 1962. (*Mennonite Church U.S.A. Archives*)

Shane Claiborne (born 1975), founder of the New Monastic community The Simple Way in Philadelphia, draws inspiration from Yoder's Anabaptist tradition—updated for Generation X and the Millennials. He is shown here speaking to students at Goshen College in 2009. (*copyright Jodi H. Beyeler/Goshen College Public Relations Office*)

Part III

Let Them Have Dominion

Chapter 8

The Gospel of Liberation

THE CULTURE WARS OF THE LATE TWENTIETH CENTURY BEGAN, IN PART, AS a civil war within evangelicalism. This battle has proved just as important to the shape of American society as the clash between religious conservatives and secular liberals. Faced with the turmoil of the 1960s, some evangelicals looked to church history for guidance. There they found a powerful set of precedents for Christian politics, from the first-century martyrs of Rome to Reformation-era communes to the social welfare crusades of the nineteenth century. Conservatives dismissed these left-leaning evangelicals as fools and traitors who abandoned the literal truth of the Bible and fell for the deceptions of modernist theology. Yet to the young Christians who formed communes amid inner-city blight, or protested the Vietnam War on the basis of newfound Anabaptist principles, or yearned for the pre-Constantinian purity of the persecuted church, it was the fundamentalists who were guilty of excessive compromise with modernity, who insisted on subjecting two-thousand-year-old scripture to the strictures of science and made the Bible conform to their political preferences, rather than the other way around. "They are the true modernists of our time, trying to create a political, economic, social, and religious nation in which to enthrone Christ who said, 'My kingship is not of this world,'" preached one Southern Baptist shortly after conservatives conquered his denomination.[1]

THE OLD EVANGELICAL LEFT

During the early and middle decades of the nineteenth century, the American Protestant mainstream consisted of a loose coalition of evangelicals bent on improving humanity's earthly lot. Protestants who shared the dogmas of their fundamentalist progeny—faith in the authority of scripture, the Virgin Birth, Christ's atonement for the sins of humankind, his Second Coming, and the necessity of the born-again experience—led the great Victorian social reform movements. They combined evangelistic enthusiasm with zeal to reshape a society convulsed by industrialization, immigration, and war. They aimed to usher in the Kingdom of God by providing every sinner a warm bed, a meal, and a moral education—while also urging him toward Christ.

This commitment to service and justice never disappeared from conservative Protestantism. However, by the early twentieth century, social concerns seemed less firmly fused with evangelical identity. The spread of premillennialism—the belief that this world will fall into greater misery and chaos before Christ's Second Coming—dampened evangelical enthusiasm for collaborating with secular authorities to reform society (they retained much of their passion for "mercy ministries" aimed at individuals). After all, social decay was a sign that Christ's return was drawing near. In the context of the fundamentalist–modernist controversy, large-scale social activism was contaminated by association with the enemy: those heterodox liberals who did not merely live out the gospel through good deeds, but seemed to believe that good deeds might replace the gospel altogether. In a massive shift that evangelical sociologist David Moberg later called "the Great Reversal," many conservative Protestants began focusing more energy on evangelism, personal moral crusades (pressing for Prohibition rather than fighting poverty), and denouncing modernism, all at the expense of social reform.[2]

The resolutions of the National Association of Evangelicals' Commission on Evangelical Action, organized early in the NAE's history, give some measure of what "social action" meant to mainstream evangelical leaders in the early 1960s. At the commission's September 1960 meeting, members discussed the top challenges facing American evangelicals: communism, "the Roman Catholic situation," IRS pressure on ministers who preached politics from the pulpit, the provision of alcohol to passengers by airlines, and Hollywood's recent "attacks on evangelical Christianity in such films as 'Elmer Gantry' and 'Inherit the Wind.'"[3] The NAE supported a World Relief Commission dedicated to alleviating starvation, but avoided head-on engagement with civil rights issues or systemic approaches to poverty and human rights abuse. For the first twenty-five years of its existence, the NAE's domestic social concerns revolved around personal morality and patriotism.

Some evangelical intellectuals had long objected to these priorities. A few prophetic professors of ethics at evangelical seminaries, such as T. B. Matson at Southwestern Baptist Theological Seminary, J. B. Weatherspoon at Southern Baptist Theological Seminary, and Richard Caemmerer at Concordia Seminary (Lutheran Church—Missouri Synod), advocated a broader view of evangelical social concern as early as the 1930s.[4] Thirty years later a wider range of evangelical academics—Vernon Grounds, a Conservative Baptist ethicist and longtime secretary of the Evangelical Theological Society; Richard Pierard, a historian who taught at Indiana State University and Gordon College; David Moberg, a sociologist at Marquette University; and Timothy Smith, the Nazarene who taught history at Johns Hopkins University, to name a few—were speaking and writing on evangelicals' failure to carry out Christ's social teachings.

Carl Henry published the neo-evangelical clarion call, *The Uneasy Conscience of Modern Fundamentalism*, in 1947. Three years later, Youth for Christ missionary Robert Pierce founded World Vision, which cared for poor children in developing countries and would become one of the world's largest faith-based charities. In 1957, Timothy Smith published *Revivalism and Social Reform*, which traced the roots of nineteenth-century social progressivism, normally associated with liberal Protestant theology, to earlier evangelical revivals. A small number of evangelical politicians broke ranks with conservative Republicanism. Illinois congressman John B. Anderson, a member of the Evangelical Free Church who began his career as one of the most conservative members of the Republican caucus, moved gradually to the left to become a "Rockefeller Republican" and ran as an independent in the 1980 presidential campaign. Senator Mark Hatfield from Oregon, a Baptist and a contributor to *Christianity Today*, was an outspoken critic of the Vietnam War.

In 1966, Wheaton College hosted a conference sponsored by the Evangelical Foreign Missions Association and the Interdenominational Foreign Missions Association, a gathering of church leaders, pastors, and missiologists intended to evaluate evangelicals' work abroad in direct comparison to that of liberal churches. The resulting Wheaton Declaration was a study in self-flagellation, lamenting that evangelicals "have sinned grievously. We are guilty of an unscriptural isolation from the world....We have failed to apply scriptural principles to such problems as racism, war, population explosion, poverty, family disintegration, social revolution, and communism." The 1969 U.S. Congress on Evangelism in Minneapolis reiterated these themes.[5] In a volume called *The Social Conscience of the Evangelical*, Sherwood Wirt, a long-time staffer at the Billy Graham Evangelistic Association, raised the difficult question of how to translate scripture into action when no two evangelicals seemed to agree on what "the Bible alone" prescribed for earthly social ills. "Even as he [the evangelical] opens his Bible and draws on the spiritual resources that are available, he is tossed on the horns of a dilemma," Wirt wrote.

> For if he chooses one position, he chances being branded as a Himmler-type reactionary; but if he chooses the opposite, he risks being herded with atheistic pinks and homosexuals. If he proposes to make the Bible his touchstone and guide, he is engulfed by a torrent of literature purporting to show that the Bible's social teaching sanctions everything from state lotteries and genocide to ship-picketing, blood donations to the Viet Cong, and tossing Molotov cocktails at heads of state.[6]

Until evangelicals could agree on a method by which to interpret scripture's application to modern society, large-scale "Bible-based" social reform was difficult. Evangelical leaders like Wirt were not deaf to liberal criticisms of their social apathy. But by the late 1960s, the left side of the American evangelical political spectrum was a rump of what it had been a century earlier.

YOUNG EVANGELICALS

To a loosely knit group of young evangelicals, this hand-wringing was not enough. "Motivated by the positive elements of student protest, the hypocrisy of the [evangelical Protestant] Orthodox churches, and the slow death of the liberal denominations, the Young Evangelicals have been equipped to be the vanguard of a revolution in Orthodoxy under the leadership and in the power of the Liberator who promised to set men and women free from every kind of oppression," wrote Richard Quebedeaux, who counted himself among their number, in his 1974 book *The Young Evangelicals: Revolution in Orthodoxy*. This new generation of evangelical activists combined the rhetoric and tactics of the secular New Left with subversive elements of Christian tradition. During the 1960s, scattered evangelical students and professors volunteered with civil rights groups like the Student Nonviolent Coordinating Committee. After the 1963 bombings of black churches in Birmingham, Calvin College students marched in protest, and the following year civil rights supporters at Wheaton greeted a Barry Goldwater rally with picket signs.[7]

A small but determined protest effort against the war in Vietnam emerged a few years later among students at the conservative seminary Trinity Evangelical Divinity School in Deerfield, Illinois. In 1971, a student named Jim Wallis—raised in a Plymouth Brethren family in Detroit, and an alumnus of Michigan State University, where he was a leader in the campus chapter of Students for a Democratic Society—organized like-minded students into the People's Christian Coalition. Wallis had grown disillusioned with the secular New Left's violent tactics after he watched his friends join forces with the Weathermen to smash East Lansing City Hall in the spring of 1970, when college students across the country erupted in protest against the U.S. invasion of Cambodia and the shooting of four Kent State University students by the Ohio National Guard. He came to Trinity eager for a Christian alternative to SDS's brutality and moral disarray. Wallis found classmates who shared his outrage at domestic poverty and America's sins in foreign wars—and his frustration that prominent evangelical spokesmen ignored the former and cheered the latter. In their free time they discussed politics over beer and peanuts at Bill's Pub and passed out anti–Vietnam War leaflets in Trinity's halls. In 1972 they traveled to a Campus Crusade rally at the Cotton Bowl in Dallas: "A dozen hirsute dissenters in a sea of fresh-faced youth, chanting 'Stop the War!' until Dallas police persuaded them to stop," wrote one observer.[8]

Wallis tried to bring his call to action to the pages of *Christianity Today*. The editors rejected his submissions as "more political than religious," and suggested that the young radical and his comrades, in their plans to inaugurate the Kingdom of God through social activism, "overlook[ed] the problem of evil." One *CT* reader referred to Wallis and company as the "kooks on the left." Wallis never had great hopes for the mainstream evangelical media. The People's Christian Coalition founded a magazine called the *Post-American* (later *Sojourners*), its title implying that Christians had to move beyond blind patriotism and commit themselves to universal human welfare. Like the presuppositionalist thinkers who preached anticommunism and inerrancy, Wallis demanded disclosure of foundational assumptions: "We don't believe in the kind of objectivity that says you find truth best from the standpoint of pure detachment and pure observation. We regard events and news from a particular perspective that we think is biblical or Christian," he told an interviewer in 1978. "I think that we are really more honest than other journalists...we tend to state our bias." Wallis's friend, the Wheaton philosopher John Alexander, started a similar publication, *Freedom Now*, later called *The Other Side* (the two editorial boards had a falling out in later years).[9] Similar (and often short-lived) magazines proliferated, self-published and photocopied on cheap paper with hand-drawn illustrations, for handing out on street corners and stuffing in church vestibules, in the great tradition of student movements.

Although its circulation remained modest—by the mid-1980s, *Sojourners* would near the 60,000 mark, with half of its paid subscriptions going to Catholics—the magazine had impact beyond its numbers.[10] In 1977, Krister Stendahl, a prominent New Testament scholar at Harvard Divinity School, called it "the" journal of the 1970s and 1980s, its influence on par with that enjoyed by the *Christian Century* in earlier decades. Two years later, *Time* featured Wallis in its list of fifty rising young American leaders. His plucky little monthly's regular criticisms of the Reagan administration's policies caused such irritation in the White House that in 1984 Wallis found himself detained by customs officials at the Canadian border. The officials informed Wallis that "the FBI had a thick file on him." A year later, *Sojourners* staff learned that the magazine, a nonprofit, was subject to an IRS audit on the grounds that its articles were politically biased against the administration. If the audit was a deliberate attempt to intimidate critics—not unlike the Nixon administration's efforts to bully opponents of the Vietnam War—the tactic backfired, earning *Sojourners* even more attention from the national media.[11]

In 1975, Wallis and a few friends relocated to Washington, DC: first to the gentrifying Mount Pleasant area, and then to the poorer, largely black neighborhood of Columbia Heights. They rented a tumbledown house and lived communally with the aim of learning "to minister to the poor."

Over the next few years, the magazine published many letters from readers living in similar urban communes, building on the example of earlier Jesus People (and Roman Catholic orders like the Franciscans). By the end of the decade, their office card file included records of 130 like-minded "communities, house churches, resistance groups, and emerging fellowships" around the country. Groups like *Sojourners* made a point of living in black communities to contribute to "the struggle for a unified church" and "reconciliation between black and white." Everyone lived, worshipped, and served together, erasing traditional lines between clergy and laity. Up the coast, Yale-trained historian Ron Sider, a Canadian who grew up in the Anabaptist and holiness ferment of the Brethren in Christ, accepted an invitation from Messiah College (a Pennsylvania school affiliated with the Brethren) to teach at its new satellite campus in downtown Philadelphia. Sider's work with Messiah students in the Philadelphia ghetto inspired his 1977 best-seller *Rich Christians in an Age of Hunger*. Westmont College in southern California—a more mainstream, nondenominational school— began a similar program in San Francisco.[12]

THE PUZZLE OF EVANGELICAL FEMINISM

Since the rise of the first women's movement in the nineteenth century, conservative Protestants had looked on feminism as godless modernism's infection of family life. Bobbed hair, rising hemlines, and demands for women's suffrage were signs that the virus had penetrated to the heart of Christian civilization and threatened to overturn biblical authority in the home—a sacred space, a man's bulwark and "retreat in time of battle," Bob Jones said in 1920.[13]

For most of Christian history, theologians advocated Aristotle's view that a woman is essentially a defective man, inferior by nature. By the early nineteenth century, most Americans had come to believe that women were physiologically and psychologically different from men—and with those differences came both gifts and limitations that suited men and women for different vocations. As conservative evangelicals responded to second-wave feminism in the 1960s and 1970s, they built upon this Victorian notion of "separate spheres" for each sex. They made a point of emphasizing that women and men were fully equal before God but ordained for separate and complementary roles at home and in the world. In a surprising way, they echoed early secular theories of "relational feminism" that imagined the heterosexual couple as the basic building block of society, but added new emphasis on "male headship."[14]

A Christian wife was to submit to her husband. But in practice, as long as her community perceived her as a devoted mother and she paid lip service to her husband's authority, she could work outside the home and cultivate a balanced relationship with her spouse. The Christian Right's most powerful weapons in the fight to roll back "secular-humanist" feminism were women like Phyllis Schlafly and Beverly LaHaye, who used their unimpeachable résumés as "homemakers" (Schlafly had six children; LaHaye had four) as a launchpad for hard-driving activism. Schlafly's Eagle Forum and LaHaye's Concerned Women for America would help defeat the Equal Rights Amendment—while both activists looked, to critics, a lot like the feminist "career women" they were trying to stop.

Even if the lives of most conservative Christian women were more liberated than evangelical leaders cared to admit, they continued to clamor against feminism. A Christian woman might pursue education and work, but she should never value her career as a golden calf above faith and family. Without biblical guidance, the feminist movement threatened to invert God-given hierarchy and encourage the degeneration of the distinct sexual identities imbued in Adam and Eve. Gender was not a choice or an act, but a gift from God. Yet while conservative evangelicals condemned feminism, they discreetly assimilated it. "Biblical feminism" and "complementarian" theology affirmed women as equal to but separate from men and unsuited to the highest formal leadership roles. It enlisted evangelical women on the right side of the culture wars.

Conservatives recast the Christian woman's identity as a "liberated mother" and sexually fulfilled housewife.[15] These were the burgeoning years of the evangelical marriage therapy industry. In books like *How to Be Happy Though Married* (1968) LaHaye and her husband, Tim, the power couple of Christian psychology, assured evangelical women that a "godly" domestic and sex life was far more satisfying than so-called feminist liberation—before best sellers like *Our Bodies, Ourselves* (1971) and *The Joy of Sex* (1972) could tell them otherwise. (Once again, conservative evangelicals proved they were not provincials out of touch with America—if anything, they were slightly ahead of the cultural curve.) Bill Gothard's

Institute in Basic Youth Conflicts taught a "chain of command" theory of the Christian household that stressed freedom within wifely obedience. One of the decade's best sellers, Marabel Morgan's *The Total Woman: How to Make Your Marriage Come Alive!* (1973), adapted feminist themes of self-discovery and authenticity in a book-length companion to her pop psychology course of the same name. It remained in print thirty years later. Cecil Osborne's *The Art of Understanding Your Mate* (1970); Kenneth and Floy Smith's *Learning to Be a Woman* (1970); Bob Mumford's *Living Happily Ever After* (1973): in this crowd of soothing treatises on how a Christian woman might find fulfillment in her family role and even begin to enjoy "the marriage act" (often with the help of anatomical diagrams), evangelical publisher Word Books dropped a theological bombshell—*All We're Meant to Be: A Biblical Approach to Women's Liberation* (1974), by Nancy Hardesty and Letha Scanzoni.

Scanzoni was an independent scholar who had written on adolescence and sex education and published a milder version of the book's argument in *Christianity Today* the previous year. Hardesty worked as an editor at *Eternity* magazine and taught at Trinity College in Illinois before leaving to pursue a PhD in the history of Christianity at the University of Chicago. The authors challenged evangelical assumptions about gender roles, quoting Simone de Beauvoir and highlighting contradictions in biblical passages regarding the relationships between men and women. They candidly discussed single women's "sexual needs" and female masturbation, assuring readers that "the only harm caused by masturbation is guilt produced in those who have been taught it is wrong."[16]

The book appealed to the mild discontent that had been festering for some time among young evangelical women. Ten years earlier, the *Wheaton Record* had begun printing editorials with headlines like "Women, Awake!" and a "woman's page" feature that sympathetically reviewed Betty Friedan. But by the mid-1970s, bold undergraduates were not the only evangelicals who were curious about feminism—or who, at least, recognized that feminism was here to stay. Reviewers at *Eternity, Christianity Today, HIS,* and other evangelical magazines urged the book upon their readers. One prominent evangelical bookstore in Chicago found that it was outselling *Total Woman* six to one (though *Total Woman* was America's number-one nonfiction bestseller in 1974, according to *Publishers Weekly*). Four years after publication *All We're Meant to Be* entered a seventh printing.[17]

Like-minded women organized the Evangelical Women's Caucus as a platform for an egalitarian form of Christian feminism that rejected conservatives' insistence on the sexes' fixed, complementary roles. Lucille Sider Dayton (sister of Ron Sider and wife of Wesleyan Methodist scholar Donald Dayton) founded a newsletter called *Daughters of Sarah*, which would remain in circulation for over twenty years. "We are Christians; we are also feminists," the first issue proclaimed. "Some say we cannot be both, but Christianity and feminism for us are inseparable." On the next page, Dayton inaugurated a feature titled "Our Foremothers," which profiled female leaders from earlier ages of church history (she began with Catherine Booth, co-founder of the Salvation Army) and argued that feminism was no modern innovation, but an evangelical tradition. In 1975, she and her husband co-authored a similar article, "Women as Preachers: Evangelical Precedents," for *Christianity Today*—a prelude to a series of articles the magazine published on the debate over women's ordination.[18]

Several prominent evangelical feminists hailed from the Wesleyan tradition, and they found the best examples of early female church leadership in Wesleyan, Methodist, and Holiness churches, some of which ordained women as early as the mid-nineteenth century. The perfectionist strain in Wesleyan and Holiness theology—the conviction that Christ's atonement set the stage for humanity's gradual improvement and sanctification over time—encouraged evangelicals in these traditions to view the New Testament's restrictions on female leadership as constraints suited to the young church of the first century but inappropriate for modern Christians. While Reformed evangelicals, such as the Princeton godfathers of the modern doctrine of inerrancy, taught that women's subordination was inherent in creation and that Paul's teachings ought to be strictly obeyed for all time, Wesleyan Christians viewed women's subjugation as the result of the Fall, a condition that God intended humanity to overcome.[19]

In the mainstream of evangelicalism, where female senior pastors were often unwelcome, most leaders and laypeople had adopted the conservative Reformed view of gender and had forgotten (or never knew of) women's leadership in the moral crusades of the nineteenth century, or even their prominence as Bible teachers, relief workers, and missionaries prior to the 1930s. The battles against modernists had transformed female religious leadership into a political symbol, and drove many fundamentalist churches to crack down on women's authority in missionary unions and service societies and to restrict female enrollment in Bible schools.[20] Even Wesleyan Holiness churches grew ambivalent about women's roles in church and society. Now, fifty years later, feminists urged evangelicals to realize that inerrancy and complementarian gender theology were not undisputed biblical truth, but human interpretation—and to rediscover an alternative heritage.

It came as something of a surprise, then, that evangelical feminists found one of their most prominent defenders in a scholar who studied at Westminster Theological Seminary and once called Gordon Clark his mentor—just as Carl Henry and Harold Lindsell had done.[21] In 1975, Fuller Theological Seminary's Paul Jewett published *Man as Male and Female* with Eerdmans (a Dutch Reformed press that had long taken pride in publishing "a myriad of responsible viewpoints").[22] The volume marshaled texts as diverse as the letters of Paul, John Calvin's *Institutes*, and de Beauvoir's *The Second Sex* to argue in favor of women's ordination. Jewett's most scandalous charge was his assertion that the letters of Paul and his comrades promoting the subjugation of women were not misunderstood or culturally relative, but simply wrong, based on faulty rabbinic interpretations of Genesis. Paul himself superseded these statements in his own declaration that "there can be neither Jew nor Greek, there can be neither bond nor free, there can be no male and female, for you are all one in Christ Jesus" (Galatians 3:28).

The book cut to the core of the debate over women in the church. This was, at root, an argument about the Bible's authority. Progressives rallied behind *Man as Male and Female*, while for conservatives, it was another sign of creeping heresy at Fuller, where the academic affairs committee was considering courses on "Christian Sexuality" and rumor had it that the (female) student body president prayed to "Our Mother."[23] Feminists' victories at Fuller had limited impact. Conservatives had long ago recognized the progressive drift of that neo-evangelical experiment. While Schlafly and LaHaye had helped mobilize conservative evangelical women into a potent political force, their feminist counterparts floundered, unable to translate their publications and gains in some moderate churches into a move from the margins to the evangelical mainstream. Most women preferred to negotiate their roles at home and in church quietly, gaining gradual independence and influence while remaining outwardly loyal to the slogans of submission and male headship.

EVANGELICALS FOR MCGOVERN

The new evangelical Left, then, was a hodgepodge of scholars chafing at restrictions on academic freedom, antiwar protesters, civil rights activists, frustrated feminists, youth at odds with their parents, and individuals who were simply fed up with some or all of the presuppositions of evangelical culture. These groups coalesced around George McGovern's campaign for president in 1972. The senator from South Dakota was not an evangelical, but he was the son of a Wesleyan Methodist minister, grew up in a poor farming town hit hard by the Great Depression, and studied for the ministry before turning his energies to academia and then to politics. In 1972, McGovern ran as the Democratic nominee on a platform of withdrawal from the Vietnam War, a massive reduction in defense spending, and a guaranteed minimum income for all Americans.

In Evangelicals for McGovern literature, the organization was careful to avoid theocratic language. "Clearly nobody has a direct word from our God on how Christians should vote in November," read a mass mailing two months before the election. "Through the prophets and our Lord, however, God has revealed some fundamental principles about the nature of a just society....If Jesus is to be Lord of our entire life, then he must be Lord of our politics." The letter promised potential donors that McGovern would "close the [tax] loopholes and make the rich pay their fair share"; he took "a courageous stand for racial justice" and recognized that "Vietnamese boys mean as much to God as American boys....The honesty of George McGovern's Wesleyan Methodist parents has helped produce a candid, decent man, who can restore credibility to the office of the Presidency and reorder our national priorities."[24]

In October 1972, the group invited McGovern and Nixon to debate at Wheaton College. Nixon demurred, but McGovern came—and at the end of his speech some students gave him a standing ovation (others booed and heckled). A mock election at Gordon-Conwell Theological Seminary, a nondenominational evangelical school in Massachusetts, ended in a dead heat. When it came to funds and votes, support was meager: 358 people contributed $5,762. Yet *Newsweek*, *Christianity Today*, and several other newspapers and Christian magazines noted the effort with surprise. *Christian Century* marveled that "liberal evangelical" was no longer a contradiction in terms. "To be sure, this mood is a minority one in contemporary evangelicalism. But it is one that seems to be gaining momentum," wrote Richard Mouw, a professor of philosophy at Calvin College (and later president of Fuller) who was working to apply Reformed theology to social justice and American foreign policy. More important than the media attention was the fact that Evangelicals for McGovern prompted energetic liberal evangelicals around the country to form a "marvelous network" of young activists "that spreads out across the land and encompasses positions of power in the highest councils of government and church life, not to mention some of the leading magazines," wrote another *Christian Century* correspondent. "It is apparent that Billy Graham is losing his grasp as the key spokesman for the evangelical community so far as concerns the political dimensions of Christian witness."[25]

The *Christian Century* was indulging in a bit of wishful thinking, but the veterans of Evangelicals for McGovern made the most of their momentum—and reached out to the neo-evangelical old guard as well. In 1973, a group of evangelical intellectuals (including Carl Henry, fellow *Christianity Today* editor and educator Frank Gaebelein, and Carl McIntire's decidedly nonfundamentalist son, Carl Thomas McIntire) met at a dingy YMCA in Chicago. In the resulting manifesto, the Chicago Declaration of Evangelical Social Concern, they declared that "God requires justice. But we have not proclaimed or demonstrated his justice to an unjust American society. Although the Lord calls us to defend the social and economic rights of the poor and the oppressed, we have mostly remained silent." The statement went on to deplore racism, world hunger, war, and violence and express the hope that evangelicals would see that social justice should not concern only liberals.[26]

Coordinators of the meeting tried to avoid "denominational bias" by including Southern Baptists, Mennonites, Pentecostals, Lutherans, Reformed, Episcopalians, and others. They made a point of inviting William Pannell (a black evangelist), William Bentley (president of the National Black Evangelical Association), and Clarence Hilliard of Chicago's inner-city Circle Church to "help the other participants overcome a purely white outlook." (They did not make a concerted effort to include southerners. The list of original signers included only one individual who was from the South and continued to reside there: Foy Valentine, director of the SBC's Christian Life Commission.) Early drafts show that participants even considered abandoning the label "evangelical" entirely and speaking as mere "Christians."[27]

Like Evangelicals for McGovern, the Chicago Declaration generated a brief flurry of attention. A few prominent church groups added their signatures immediately, ranging from the Baptist General Convention of Texas (one of only two Southern Baptist state conventions that would resist conservative conquest in the 1980s) to the Christian Holiness Association. Privately the mainline National Council of Churches offered encouragement, leading to "off-the-record dialogue" between the NCC and the organization that emerged from the Chicago meeting, Evangelicals for Social Action. Criticism came from other corners: Lester DeKoster, an editor of the *Banner*, a Reformed periodical, noted that the declaration granted no clear role to the institutional church, and reflected "the guilt and aspirations simply of fifty individual Christians of undoubted sincerity, whose views could easily be qualified or even largely contradicted by fifty, or say a hundred, *other* individual Christians of equally unquestioned integrity— should someone care to go to the trouble of getting them together and issuing a news release." He called the declaration a "pale copy" of papal social encyclicals going back as far as Leo XIII's defenses of the common man in the late nineteenth century. In DeKoster's view, evangelicals' crucial problem was not their social apathy, but individualism run rampant. Other evangelicals, such as Paul Jewett, refused to sign because the document failed to articulate specific plans or go far enough in self-criticism.[28]

Evangelicals for Social Action responded to Jewett's complaint (they mostly ignored DeKoster's), following up over the next few years with further conferences, "action workshops," publishing projects, regional seminars for local pastors, training for black evangelical leaders, reviews of possible gender bias in Sunday school literature, and a host of other endeavors. However, by ESA's third national conference in 1975, the organization was fracturing along predictable lines. Black participants began to denounce the conference's approach as "purely white and totally irrelevant." Scholars belittled the activists. Feminists objected to "sexist language" in ESA literature. Anabaptists, with their emphasis on nonviolence and personal discipleship, clashed with Reformed evangelicals with very different strategies for political action and cultural transformation. ESA represented a tenuous coalition of dissenters who found it easier to agree on what was wrong with mainstream evangelicalism than to find a common vision for reform—though even outspoken conservative Harold Lindsell admitted that while the declaration did not reflect evangelical consensus, it did offer "leadership."[29]

Historian David Swartz has suggested that as late as the mid-1970s, the political prospects of the evangelical Left seemed nearly as bright as those of their peers on the Right. Evangelicals' ambivalent opinions on social policy, gender equality, and abortion rights had not yet hardened into the slogans of the Moral Majority. Activists like Jim Wallis tried to counter the momentum of the New Right with a notion borrowed from Catholics, a "consistent life ethic" that opposed war, poverty, and patriarchy as ardently as abortion. But the Left's nuanced arguments were no match for cries that "abortion is murder" and "family values are under attack," and progressive activists received little help from secular Democrats eager to make abortion rights a central plank of their party platform.[30] By the standards of a conventional political movement, the evangelical Left failed. They generated much noise but little action.

Groups like Evangelicals for Social Action and Evangelicals for McGovern failed at essential political tasks like fundraising and election-year organizing—not because they overestimated the average American evangelical's concern for the poor or for Vietnamese civilians, but because they underestimated their fellow believers' anxieties over cultural change and the specter of creeping socialism. They were too divided among themselves to offer a grand narrative that could compete with the plotline emerging on the Right: an account of American history that began with pious Puritans and Bible-believing Founding Fathers, culminating on the Manichaean battlefield of the Cold War. Now divinely anointed Americans defended civilization from godless communists—and good Christians helped hold the line at home, despite Soviet agents lurking within every civil rights protest and among the hordes of ungrateful college radicals, brainwashed by their professors, dodging the draft and protesting the Vietnam War. Too often progressive evangelicals ended up cast as unwilling characters in the conservative narrative rather than as authors of their own: agents of "Soviet-style communism," "pseudo-evangelical" saboteurs who are "to evangelicalism what Adolf Hitler was to the Roman Catholic Church."[31]

Even if progressive evangelicals failed to popularize their own account of American evangelicals' role in world history, they grasped the potential for intellectual authority that lay in history—if carefully told. They revised the Right's narrative of decline—the jeremiad lamenting the moral degeneration of "Christian America"—to protest, instead, American evangelicals' decline from forebears who crusaded for justice, balanced personal holiness with care for the needy, and made room for women to help lead the way.

INTELLECTUAL ORIGINS OF DISSENT

Left-leaning evangelicals were more than just gadflies on the gnarled hide of the Christian Right, with no substantial ideas of their own. Three main sources fueled their movement: the scholarship of progressive evangelical scholars, especially at Fuller Theological Seminary; contemporary Swiss and German theology; and the traditions of non-Reformed churches (and even Roman Catholics) that many American evangelicals had long ignored or disdained.

Since the exodus of conservative faculty members in the early 1960s, Fuller had become one of the primary points of contact between traditional evangelical dogma and twentieth-century European theology. Richard Quebedeaux emphasized the school's influence: "By their stature, teaching, publications, and their loyalty to the institutional church and the Church universal, the faculty of Fuller Theological Seminary has provided a model...of what modern biblical Orthodoxy can be—of its explicit revolutionary potential." Paul Jewett was a leading proponent of egalitarian gender theology, while a number of scholars at Fuller's School of World Mission (now the School of Intercultural Studies) were training missionaries sensitive to non-Western worldviews and the ways in which ancient Near Eastern culture influenced the text of the Bible. George Ladd, professor of New Testament, argued that evangelicals could embrace the latest biblical scholarship while continuing to affirm a premillennialist vision of the end-times—as long as they moved away from some classic dispensationalist teachings.[32]

Ladd's views, best articulated in *The Gospel of the Kingdom* (1959) and *A Theology of the New Testament* (a popular textbook at evangelical seminaries since its publication in 1974), along with the work of other scholars such as Clarence Bass at Bethel Theological Seminary, freed young evangelicals to moderate their assessment of how predictions of Armageddon ought to affect Christian care for humanity here and now. During the 1980s and 1990s, young scholars calling themselves "progressive dispensational-ists" would continue to question the theology they had inherited, gravitat-ing away from the "grammatical historical method" of reading the Bible (a euphemism for literalism) to a more flexible interpretation that drew on literary theory and allowed that some parts of prophecy might be figures of speech rather than precise predictions.[33]

While Ladd urged his students and readers beyond the comfortable assumptions of their hometown churches, his colleague Geoffrey Bromiley pushed them to look toward Europe. A significant number of evangelical scholars studied in Switzerland and Germany from the 1950s onward, but widespread American engagement with continental theologians depended on the translation of their works into English. Bromiley, a professor of church history and theology, worked with University of Edinburgh theo-logian T. F. Torrance to oversee the translation of Karl Barth's magnum opus, *Church Dogmatics* (all fourteen volumes). Beginning in 1956, new English volumes steadily appeared over the course of twenty years, enabling American evangelicals to read for themselves the ideas they had heretofore encountered mostly in caricature. Bromiley was not afraid to criticize Barth, but he instilled in a generation of Fuller students (and many more readers who studied his translations and critiques) respect for Barth as a brilliant theologian who attempted to recover Christianity from the attenuations of liberalism. Bromiley translated the works of several other European thinkers as well, including the German theolo-gian Wolfhart Pannenberg and the Christian anarchist Jacques Ellul. By virtue of his staggering translation output, Bromiley was probably the most important transcontinental theological mediator of his generation. He helped convince young scholars that the questions these theologians raised were more interesting than evangelicals' intramural quarrels over the details of the Flood.[34]

Barth was one of progressive evangelicals' central interlocutors, but German theologian Dietrich Bonhoeffer was their martyr and patron saint. Barth opposed the Nazis and wrote the Barmen Declaration, but while he was living in the safety of Switzerland, the Nazis imprisoned Bonhoeffer for his minor role in a plot to assassinate Hitler. They executed him in April 1945 at Flossenburg concentration camp. For idealists looking for a hero who made the ultimate sacrifice for his beliefs and rejected the corruption of politics, Bonhoeffer's life and writings, especially *The Cost of Discipleship*

(1937; English translation 1948), became the gold standard of ideological purity and Christian witness.

Bonhoeffer was an attentive reader of Barth who criticized liberal theology and desperately wanted the church to reestablish its relevance to modern life. After completing his doctorate at the University of Berlin, he studied with Reinhold Niebuhr at Union Theological Seminary and taught Sunday school at the Abyssinian Baptist Church in Harlem. Ordained by the Evangelical Church of the Old Prussian Union, Bonhoeffer helped organize the Confessing Church, the major Christian body opposing the Nazis. He denounced German Christians' cooperation with Hitler's regime and warned of the hollowness of "cheap grace," the presumption of redemption without discipleship or sacrifice. To his American admirers, fed up with evangelical churches that seemed to be always climbing into bed with the Republican Party, Bonhoeffer represented the clarity of the earliest Christians, ready martyrs and critics of power rather than docile servants.

Nearly every evangelical in the New Left movement claimed Bonhoeffer as an inspiration. Senator Mark Hatfield cited Bonhoeffer's influence on his own attitude toward Christian statesmanship. Jim Wallis gave him much of the credit for the "radical discipleship movement" in American evangelicalism: *The Cost of Discipleship* "became an early text for us, and Bonhoeffer an early teacher." Dale Brown, a radical member of the Church of the Brethren and contributing editor at *Sojourners*, called Bonhoeffer "increasingly relevant in our post-Constantinian situation." (More recently his popularity has crossed political and denominational boundaries—a 2010 biography of Bonhoeffer won praise from conservative evangelicals as well as liberals.)[35] In the late twentieth century, when traditional Christianity no longer claimed the loyalty of millions of Americans nor a monopoly on the public square, evangelicals needed a theologian who could teach them how to function as a prophetic minority. Young progressive evangelicals wanted nothing more than "authenticity". They wanted to reject the world their parents built and become first-century Christians again.

Barth, Bonhoeffer, and their academic interpreters encouraged left-leaning evangelicals to think of themselves as cosmopolitan Christians while also providing the terms on which to indict their more conservative elders. These thinkers provided a broad framework—familiar in its theological outlines, but radically challenging to fundamentalist assumptions— at the same time that young evangelicals were uncovering new resources outside the streams of the magisterial Reformation. They were hardly the first Christians to criticize the blurred line between church and state, Christian support of secular wars, or the evangelical emphasis on personal morality at the expense of social justice.

THE ANABAPTIST RENAISSANCE

Reformed evangelicals who claimed the "mainstream" as their own had always been dimly aware of the descendants of the Reformation's far left wing, but few inquired beyond the stereotypes of beards, plain coats, and pacifism. Then came a turning point when, after years of marginalization and condescension, Anabaptists became heroes and mentors: the Vietnam War. Christian pacifism had fallen widely out of favor during World War II. Reinhold Niebuhr critiqued nonresistance as naïve and morally repugnant.[36] By the late 1960s, however, some young evangelicals turned to the Anabaptists for a fully formed theology of protest with centuries of gravitas behind it.

The Christian World Liberation Front, founded at Berkeley in 1969 by a disillusioned member of Campus Crusade, sponsored church history courses aimed at rehabilitating the Anabaptists as well as ancient Christian radicals who held firm to their faith despite brutal Roman persecution. Arthur Gish and Dale Brown, contributing editors at *Sojourners* (and familiar with Anabaptist teachings through their background in the Church of the Brethren), explicitly rooted evangelical radicalism in the Anabaptist legacy. Gish called sixteenth-century Anabaptists "a group that dared to challenge the assumptions of over a thousand years of European history and its cultural synthesis called *Corpus Christianum*.... They soon learned that meaningful change was not possible within the system. Soon they, like the New Left, were forced to take the sectarian route of working outside the establishment."[37] Gish's and Brown's books would have been unremarkable had they been published by an Anabaptist church press—but both books bore the imprint of Eerdmans, one of the most esteemed Reformed evangelical presses in the country. Anabaptist radicalism had found its way to mainstream Christian bookstores.

Urban communal ministries, like Wallis's Sojourners house, Elizabeth O'Connor's Potter's House, Tom Nees's Community of Hope (all based in

Washington, DC), and Reba Place in Chicago, were more intellectually serious endeavors than the early communes of the Jesus People and drew on Anabaptist and early Wesleyan models of communal life and urban ministry. (*Sojourners* also cited the Catholic Worker movement as a key influence.)[38] Although most communities described themselves as nonsectarian, Anabaptists and Wesleyans were well represented in their leadership (Nees, for instance, was a Nazarene; Reba Place was founded by Mennonites), as they were in Evangelicals for Social Action. A small group of Anabaptists and Wesleyans made it their mission to reclaim the "evangelical" label from the *Christianity Today* crowd, and they pounced on the interest of young evangelicals with the hope of reasserting their traditions as the backbone of "true" evangelicalism. John Howard Yoder wrote to Donald Dayton at North Park Theological Seminary:

> You seem to some to be trying to "modernize" or "liberalize" evangelicalism by showing its fathers (and mothers) were socially concerned. I.e., you want to be involved because you are of the academic generation of the 60's, but you want your churches' support so you do a one-sided rewrite of Wesleyan history. The conservatism is the base line and you are the revisionist. (Same shape for me on "Anabaptists and the State.") What kind of argument, what kind of data do we need, to turn the tables and to show that the Carl Henry and Billy Graham "evangelicals" are the revisionists?[39]

This was the critical battle, the conflict that lay beneath the halting efforts of groups like Evangelicals for McGovern and the Evangelical Women's Caucus. Whose history was God's history? Most conservative Protestants could agree that, in one way or another, the passage of the centuries told a story of decline—but a decline from Calvin's Geneva, the Wesley brothers' missions, or Menno Simons' re-baptism of true believers? Dayton devoted much of his career to refuting Reformed conservatives' claims that all orthodox Protestant traditions had affirmed biblical inerrancy since their founding. He later marshaled scholars from all corners of Protestantism to articulate their ideas of the faith in a volume called, aptly, *The Variety of American Evangelicalism.*

Of the many efforts to bring "dissenting" theology to a mainstream evangelical audience, none exhilarated young progressives more than Yoder's

The Politics of Jesus, published in 1972 by Eerdmans. Through exegesis of the Gospel of Luke and Paul's Letter to the Romans, Yoder attempted to demonstrate—against Reinhold Niebuhr—that a serious consideration of Jesus Christ's life and death vindicated pacifism. Just as, in his youth, he submitted articles criticizing Christian nationalism to the NAE's *United Evangelical Action*, now he wrote not for his Mennonite brethren, but for non-Anabaptist Christians. The book was translated into ten languages and received wide and prolonged play in the Protestant media, selling more than 80,000 copies over the next 20 years—a colossal number for a volume of Anabaptist ethics. Jim Wallis's group considered it a "core book" for their "Discipleship Seminars." In 1976, Stephen Charles Mott, who taught social ethics at Gordon-Conwell Theological Seminary, called it "the most widely read political book in young evangelical circles in the United States."[40]

Another scholar with Anabaptist sympathies, Stanley Hauerwas, drew on Yoder's ideas (they were colleagues at Notre Dame) to develop his own theology of Christian pacifism and cultural critique. In 1984 Hauerwas moved to Duke Divinity School, where he taught legions of young evangelicals "how to go on after Christendom." The title of one of his well-known books, *Resident Aliens: Life in a Christian Colony* (1989), conveys the outline of his perspective on Christians' proper relationship to secular power. Along with Yoder, Hauerwas's influence radiated throughout American evangelicalism and offered many young evangelicals a powerful guide in their exodus from the ranks of the Religious Right.[41]

The new evangelical Left was radically ecumenical. Their critics would say they were carelessly so, often turning to whatever church tradition best justified their prejudices and desires rather than arriving at those prejudices from carefully considered first principles. Their theologies had origins and echoes in the peace and holiness churches, and even left-wing Roman Catholicism—all which seemed to them to be the closest approximations of the first-century church, the best strategy for counteracting the modern age's contamination of biblical religion. They were not interested in professing loyalty to any particular church tradition so much as conjuring an ideal—and therefore imaginary—image of the church as Jesus must have intended it. This, of course, was just what their fellow believers on the political Right hoped for too, but they had very different ideas about what Jesus would do.

Chapter 9

Evangelicals' Great Matter

BY THE MID-1970S, THERE WERE REASONS TO BELIEVE THAT AMERICAN evangelicals' fixation on inerrancy was fading and the happy vines of compromise had begun to grow over their internal divisions. Although several conservative scholars left Fuller Theological Seminary after the schism over inerrancy, mainstream icons Billy Graham and Harold Ockenga remained on the board of trustees. Paul Jewett, the Fuller scholar who challenged the traditional interpretation of St. Paul's teachings on gender, was not exiled to an obscure corner of academe but rather appointed dean of Young Life Institute, a national evangelistic organization aimed at high-schoolers. A handful of other scholars, such as George Ladd, Bernard Ramm, and Dewey Beegle, joined Jewett in moving away from strict inerrancy and developing more nuanced methods of biblical interpretation while still remaining in the evangelical fold. Younger evangelical academics were pursuing degrees in mainstream graduate programs, where they learned to value the latest advances in biblical scholarship. In *Confessions of a Conservative Evangelical* (1974), Fuller professor Jack Rogers admitted that his efforts to write a conservative critique of the United Presbyterians' 1967 revision of the Westminster Confession led him to realize, "to his shock and surprise," that the original Westminster doctrine of biblical authority was more subtle than the Princeton theology he had inherited.[1]

The main seminaries and church bodies of the largest American evangelical denomination, the Southern Baptist Convention, were in the hands of moderates who thought carefully about biblical authority. In 1960, participants in a meeting of the Southern Baptist Religious Education Association discussed how Sunday school teachers ought to apply the latest biblical criticism in their lessons. They complained that the worldview of church leaders did not match that of Southern Baptist laypeople. "One of the serious problems we face is the lack of understanding of what biblical criticism really is on the part of some of the people we serve," said Howard Colson of the Baptist Sunday School Board.

> This is indicated by the flurry of protest in some quarters over modern speech translations [the Revised Standard Version of the Bible]. If only these people knew the story of how the Bible came to us, they would eagerly avail themselves of the help in recent versions. But it is no easy matter to bridge the gap between the scholarly historical approach and the views of the Bible which some people hold.[2]

Colson believed that church leaders were called to enlighten their constituents. "It would be wrong for us to run roughshod over the feelings of the rank and file," he added. "They are God's people and they love his Word. We have a solemn obligation to lead them lovingly and patiently to sounder views of the sacred volume we all love." The trouble was that a nuanced hermeneutic rarely proved as persuasive as simple rules that flattered a layperson's "common sense." Baptist theologian Clark Pinnock, who was himself evolving from a staunch inerrantist position to a more moderate view, observed that "a new evangelical doctrine of biblical inspiration is emerging.... It is now a question of whether this group of evangelicals is going to be able to develop a strong and affirmative concept of biblical authority (it is not enough to be against inerrancy) such as can gain the consent and support of the evangelical constituency long used to stricter formulations."[3]

The problem was this: The doctrine of inerrancy was a comforting gauze that concealed a great deal of ugliness. It disguised the compromise and confusion that are unavoidable when moderns try to live by an ancient and often obscure text. The doctrine of inerrancy had always been, in its essence, a means of managing the Bible's vulnerability to subjective judgment. Most inerrantists were not naïve about either the necessity or the peril of submitting those "God-breathed" words to mortal interpretation. The problem was not interpretation per se, but the presuppositions that so often lay beneath. Inerrancy provided a trump card to play whenever those presuppositions became threatening—a way of asserting that the only appropriate tools for interpreting a problematic verse were other verses in the same text, and that revelation itself provided evidence of its own perfect authority. The doctrine was meant to protect the Reformers' proclamation of *sola scriptura* from the presumptions of human reason, subjective experience, or hubristic tradition. British theologian J. I. Packer dated the origins of the "evangelical 'battle for the Bible'" to the ministries of Reformation heroes Martin Luther and Huldrych Zwingli, if not to their fourteenth-century predecessor John Wycliffe. Packer was an irenic inerrantist who urged charity in the debate, but he made plain what was at stake: "As soon as you convict Scripture of making the smallest mistakes you start to abandon both the biblical understanding of biblical inspiration and also the systematic functioning of the Bible as the organ of God's authority, his rightful and effective rule over his people's faith and life."[4]

Anyone who looked around at modern life quickly observed that this rightful rule was teetering. Those evangelicals who questioned inerrancy had to come to terms with other sources of authority that could somehow help modern Christians follow the gospel into the twenty-first century. The 1970s witnessed a flood of books by evangelicals, each arguing that his particular hermeneutic and his narrative of Christian history settled the question of evangelical identity and authority: Richard Quebedeaux's *The Young Evangelicals* (1974); John Woodbridge and David Wells's *The Evangelicals: Who They Are, What They Believe, and Where They Are Changing* (1975); Donald Dayton's *Discovering an Evangelical Heritage* (1976); Carl Henry's *Evangelicals in Search of an Identity* (1976); and Harold Lindsell's incendiary 1976 book, *The Battle for the Bible*.

This tumult on Christian bookstore shelves pointed toward a riptide in evangelical culture, one that inevitably surged into politics. Commentators persist in understanding the rise of the Christian Right narrowly, in terms of conservative Christians' mobilization to fight secular liberals at the ballot box and in the courts over issues so familiar they are now cliché, ranging from the secularization of public education to women's and gay rights.[5] However, these contests unfolded alongside an intellectual awakening, and their outcome owes as much to evangelicals' internal struggles over authority as it does to their campaigns against secular liberals. The "battle for the Bible" was so brutal because something greater than the lessons taught in Sunday sermons was at stake.

Lindsell, who had succeeded Carl Henry as editor of *Christianity Today*, shattered any illusions that American evangelicals' debate over biblical authority was headed for an amicable conclusion. *The Battle for the Bible* sounded the alarm that "elites" had betrayed the average evangelical in the pew. Lindsell revealed just how far leaders in institutions ranging from the Southern Baptist Convention to Fuller Seminary and the Evangelical Theological Society had departed from biblical inerrancy. Evangelicalism's self-styled intellectuals had betrayed the authority they had vowed to defend. To argue that the inerrantist position represented the original view of the early Church Fathers and Protestant Reformers, Lindsell began with a string of quotations plucked from church history and shorn of context. He was a presuppositionalist who believed that no thinking person could escape the ultimate conclusions of his own assumptions, and warned darkly of a "domino effect." Doubting inerrancy led to the abandonment of the basic doctrines of Christianity. It was only a matter of time before these so-called Christians denied the gospel, the *evangelion*. Therefore they ought to be honest and stop claiming to be "evangelical."[6]

Conservative scholars, pleased to see their suspicions confirmed, seized the book as a mandate to act publicly. A number of Lindsell's allies resigned in disgust from the Evangelical Theological Society. A year later his friend James Montgomery Boice, a Presbyterian pastor and Harvard graduate who had followed the familiar neo-evangelical path through *Christianity Today* and graduate study at Basel, began working with other Reformed inerrantists to plan a conference that would bring more than 300 conservative evangelicals together in 1978 to sign the Chicago Statement on Biblical Inerrancy. That statement would underscore Lindsell's assertion that the inerrancy of scripture was God's eternal gift to humankind, not a man-made principle: "We affirm that the doctrine of inerrancy has been integral to the Church's faith throughout its history. We deny that inerrancy is a doctrine invented by Scholastic Protestantism, or is a reactionary position postulated in response to negative higher criticism...we further deny that inerrancy can be rejected without grave consequences, both to the individual and to the Church."[7]

Moderate evangelicals, finding themselves among Lindsell's targets, were furious. Fuller president David Hubbard accused Lindsell of imposing mortal philosophy on the Bible. He challenged the attempt to reserve the evangelical label for inerrantists: "This large and cherished word must never be given a sectarian meaning. . . . The arrogance of any one group of Christians who seek to preempt this title for themselves by robbing it of its historic breadth and richness should be more than vexing to the whole body of Christ." A range of prominent evangelicals, including the presidents of Young Life, the Evangelical Covenant Church, Eastern Baptist Theological Seminary, and the vice president of World Vision, wrote letters of support for Hubbard and Fuller faculty. Carl Henry, a fellow inerrantist and friend of Lindsell since their college days (Lindsell was best man at Henry's wedding), lamented that his colleague had "shifted the public perception of the evangelical movement from its role as a dynamic life-growing force to a cult squabbling over inerrancy."[8]

As editor of *Christianity Today*, an active member of ETS, and one-time professor at Fuller with celebrity evangelical friends, Lindsell used his place in the neo-evangelical intellectual infrastructure to mount an attack from the inside. If he alienated moderates and those who feared a return of the old fundamentalist–modernist battles, he also found a wide readership and brought evangelicalism's festering internal tensions into the national spotlight. A few months after Zondervan published *The Battle for the Bible*, it entered a third printing. The inerrancy debate attracted a readership large enough to draw attention from secular publishers. Salvos on both sides of the issue were published not by a church press or evangelical publishing house, but by Harper & Row.[9]

Between 1976—the "Year of the Evangelical," according to *Newsweek*—and 1979, *Time*, the *Wall Street Journal*, the *New York Times*, and other papers covered debates between "inerrantists" and "infallibilists," "neo-fundamentalists" and "young evangelicals." These quarrels were national news during the years that these same newspapers and magazines were reporting on evangelicals' efforts to reassert the Bible's authority through politics (the Christian Right's first national organization, the Christian Voice, was organized in 1978, and the Moral Majority appeared the following year).[10] The timing is no coincidence. Conservative evangelicals' mobilization against gay rights, the Equal Rights Amendment, abortion, and other threats to "family values" represented only the most visible, most political expression of a multidimensional panic over the Bible's authority.

A PERFECT STORM

The debate over how to reconcile the Bible with modern life had simmered for decades, but several factors—not commonly mentioned on any political platform—brought the controversy to a climax in the mid-1970s. The charismatic renewal movement, which stressed subjective experience and challenged the idea that the highest religious authority lay in a dispassionate, "scientific" reading of scripture, peaked in these years. Many evangelicals embraced charismatic worship while affirming belief in an inerrant Bible. However, the movement's exaltation of a personal, ecstatic encounter with God challenged the obsessive rationalism undergirding the doctrine of inerrancy and strained against the boundaries that Lindsell and his colleagues tried to impose on the evangelical community. The Church Growth movement, with its implicit message of cultural relativism and tendency to downplay doctrinal debates, also provoked a backlash. Conservatives viewed Church Growth—by now well established in foreign missions and in the seeker-sensitive churches sprouting throughout suburbia—as a polite excuse for flabby preaching that shied away from demanding a rational assent to biblical inerrancy. They feared that Church Growth advocates worshipped the revelations of social science at the expense of the Bible and embraced non-Christian cultures under the banner of anthropology.[11]

A more explosive controversy was also roiling evangelicals: the question of whether a woman might serve in the senior leadership of God's church. Advocates for women's right to preach had agitated American churches as early as the Great Awakening. Holiness churches and some Baptist denominations ordained women in the nineteenth century. The General Conference Mennonite Church ordained a woman in 1911, and the Assemblies of God affirmed, in a limited way, women's right to preach at the church's founding in 1914—although in practice, female pastors were exceedingly rare. Scattered Methodist and Presbyterian denominations began ordaining women in the 1940s and 1950s. Then, in the 1970s, American churches seemed to reach a tipping point. Multiple Lutheran denominations and the Episcopal Church (as well as Reform Jews) began to ordain women. Conservatives could no longer shrug off women's ordination as the outrageous error of a few liberals. By 1976—despite the failure of most evangelical feminists to win such victories in their own churches—in much of American Protestantism, female priests were mainstream.[12]

Churches that officially banned women from the highest church offices sometimes, in practice, looked the other way if a woman happened to meet the needs of a particular congregation, especially where there was a shortage of clergy (even Rome amended canon law to permit women to administer "pastoral care," but not the sacraments). Women's ordination, however, was not just a practical matter. It was a question loaded with implications for a church's view of changing gender roles, domestic and social authority, and traditional interpretations of the Bible. Sociologist Mark Chaves has argued that churches' rulings on women's ordination functioned as a signal to observers throughout the wider Christian world, a symbol of the denomination's embrace or repudiation of secular modernity and progressive politics. By the mid-1970s, a vote for female priests often implied the rejection of the conservative worldview in its entirety. The average evangelical might relax the traditional rules about husbands' duties and wives' submission in his or her own home, but it was much harder to fudge the debate over women in the pulpit. If Paul's admonitions against women's leadership in church might be relics of the first century, what were the consequences for the authority of the Bible as a whole?[13]

At the same time, the appearance of a host of new Bible translations and paraphrases during the late 1960s and early 1970s brought the problem of translation into the daily life of many evangelicals. In 1971, Kenneth Taylor—a graduate of Wheaton College and Dallas Theological Seminary and a veteran of the evangelical publishing industry—published *The Living Bible*, his groundbreaking paraphrase of scripture based on the 1901 American Standard Version of the text. The project emerged from his frustrated attempts to guide his children through old-fashioned biblical language. Despite his contacts at established publishing houses like Moody Press, the publishers that he approached found the project too controversial. Taylor decided to publish *The Living Bible* through his own company, Tyndale House, which he had founded in order to print his paraphrase of the New Testament epistles. (Many years earlier, InterVarsity Press had published his first book, a slim volume called *Is Christianity Credible?* that critiqued the "presuppositions" of an atheist: "The atheist begins with the premise that there is no God... his position is all very logical but has nothing to do with knowing the truth of his assumption.")[14]

Taylor may have picked up a knack for this line of argument in college—he was just a couple years behind Carl Henry and Harold Lindsell at Wheaton—but his real gift was his ear for modernizing God's word. *The Living Bible* was immediately popular among evangelical youth organizations like Youth for Christ and Young Life, and was the best-selling book in America in 1972 and 1973. Although more modest paraphrases had been in circulation for years, Taylor's effort irked some conservatives, who objected to his departure from the revered King James Version—and to his wild success. Commenting on *The Living Bible* four decades later, former Moody Bible Institute president Joseph Stowell wrote that Taylor caused "bucket-loads of controversy" and launched the evangelical "translation wars."15

Two years after *The Living Bible* appeared, Zondervan published a more serious challenge to the King James Version, which had reigned among American evangelicals for centuries: the New International Version. Conceived as a conservative response to the Revised Standard Version (1952), which evangelicals had widely denounced as a modernist, even "communistic" translation that succumbed to the errors of historical criticism, the NIV was prepared by a committee of evangelical scholars with impeccable credentials. Despite the translation's pedigree—scholars from institutions ranging from Dallas Theological Seminary to the Moody Bible Institute contributed—in some churches the NIV met significant resistance. Leaders in the Church of the Nazarene greeted the new translation genially, in part because they hoped the NIV would discourage Nazarenes from reading *The Living Bible*, which M. A. Lunn, the manager of the church publishing house, worried was "not pedagogically sound and of course, not theologically accurate."16

Nazarene laypeople resisted, and when church authorities finally swapped the King James for the NIV in official Nazarene educational materials a decade later, they received a flurry of protest letters. Demonstrating the extent to which Nazarenes had imbibed Reformed–fundamentalist notions of biblical literalism, they insisted that substituting any other words for the King James was sacrilege. Lunn wrote that "the people who are writing [to complain] are not speaking about the beauty of the KJV; their whole concern is that to them it is the Bible." "The KJV is our greatest authority and textbook of Armenian-Wesleyan [sic] holiness," wrote one Nazarene woman (despite the translation's origin in sixteenth- and seventeenth-century Reformed and Anglican circles in England). One irate pastor in Indiana saw a direct link between the chaos of the culture wars and this dubious new translation: "In a day of slipping standards and morals it seems our church leaders should be taking steps to tighten the rigging in our sails rather than loosen them," he wrote.[17]

This grassroots anxiety over any changes to the words of the Bible was ideological, but it was also practical. In many churches, worship, social activities, evangelism, and personal contemplation revolved around memorizing scripture. The Assemblies of God hierarchy, in a memo justifying the retention of the King James Bible, noted that if the church "should decide to use a translation other than the KJV as the basic text it would affect other programs at headquarters such as Bible Quiz, Royal Rangers and Missionettes." A Nazarene laywoman wrote that the plethora of new translations published in the past few years—the NIV joined the New American Standard Version, the *Amplified Bible*, *Good News for Modern Man* (now *Today's English Version*), and others—was a satanic maneuver to stymie her effort to learn God's word: "We feel it is a trick of the devil to fill our heads with so many translations of the Bible that when it comes down to memorizing scripture, we can't recall which one of the dozen ways we heard it is the way it should be memorized, so we end up with nothing or at least a hodge-podge in our memory to use against the devil." In an ever-expanding marketplace of Christian educational literature, denominational leaders could not force their constituents to read anything, and had to think strategically about their own publishing house's market share. One Nazarene pastor, who considered the NIV "worst [sic] than the Jehovah Witness Bible," assured his denomination's publishing house that his church would purchase its Sunday school literature elsewhere.[18]

The NIV controversy should not be exaggerated. According to Zondervan, in short order it became the most popular translation of the Bible worldwide: 300 million copies are currently in print, accounting for about one-third of all Bibles in circulation.[19] However, the NIV was a conservative evangelical endeavor from its origins, and opponents could not dismiss it as they had the Revised Standard Version. In the context of the broad assault on traditional biblical interpretation under way in the 1970s—domestic cultural upheaval, the charismatic renewal and church growth movements, and the fight over women's ordination—the sudden popularity of several new translations further unsettled the literalist view of scripture that many evangelicals took for granted. The choice of which Bible to use brought home the crucial question: What, precisely, is God's word?

THE ALLURE OF THE EVANGELICAL EXPERT

To most evangelicals, the answer to that question has always had political implications. The Lord does not desire his people to parse his revelation only to confine their conclusions to Sunday mornings. But in the mid-1970s, conservative evangelicals stormed into American political life with a new sense of mission and knack for organization that alarmed secular observers. There was more to this mobilization than clever campaign ads or get-out-the-vote efforts. Milestones such as the advent of the Moral Majority and the defeat of the Equal Rights Amendment signaled more fundamental changes in the intellectual infrastructure of American evangelicalism.

Evangelicals were fighting among themselves over the theological and historical frameworks that governed their lives. Denominational authorities competed with independent outsiders who pulled evangelicals away from their confessional heritage toward common cause with other conservatives. The late 1960s and 1970s were the age of the evangelical guru. These men (and they were mostly men) operated outside churches and established ministries, offering new wisdom and a way to Christian self-realization. The lone sage is no new phenomenon in American evangelicalism, dating back at least to Anne Hutchinson's challenges to the Puritan establishment in the early seventeenth century. This latest crop of gurus owed much to their predecessors, but they represented a new kind of leadership. With so many traditional structures of authority under attack, this generation of evangelicals needed something more than familiar proof texts. Now the most successful teachers drew on fresh sources of intellectual authority, such as the latest trends in psychology, management science, and the hidden history of Western civilization.

The Nazarene scholar Mildred Wynkoop lamented the big personalities that lured Nazarene youth away from their mother church. Too many young Nazarenes "are being drawn in to the many 'cultish' movements in our religious world, today....These include groups with a very strong Calvinistic ground, often camouflaged by social activity or flashy philosophy."[20] She noted Harold Lindsell's following, and groups that had spun off from the charismatic renewal movement—often led by an authoritarian "shepherd" who brooked no questioning of his authority—as well as Jesus People communes and parachurch organizations like Campus Crusade. Bill Gothard's ministry, Institute in Basic Youth Conflicts, deeply concerned Wynkoop. Immensely popular among a wide range of evangelicals through the 1980s, Gothard's seminars offered participants (at a significant entrance fee) several days of "training" in issues ranging from family dynamics and dating to self-confidence and anger management. Gothard based each lesson on his own exegesis of the "universal, non-optional principles" of the Bible, with an emphasis on submission to godly authority.[21]

Critics called Gothard a legalist who clothed his cult of personality in pseudo-psychology and a dangerous excess of "discipline," but he also represented the growing popularity of Christian psychological counseling. One of Wynkoop's fellow Nazarenes, James Dobson, earned a PhD in child development from the University of Southern California. Dobson founded the Focus on the Family radio program in 1977 and the Family Research Council in 1981, through which he became the most influential evangelical voice on marriage and family for the next thirty years—partly by framing flashpoints of the culture wars like gender roles and rebellious youth behavior in authoritative-sounding psychological jargon. In her memo, Wynkoop listed the dangerous common elements she saw in these figures. They offered audiences a

> Philosophically defined God rather than the God revealed in Scripture....A one-man (or woman) operation. Unable to share a place with another. Assumes all power and authority....Refuses to engage in open debate...."Divinely ordained" hierarchical structure....Fundamentalistic view of the Bible based on subjective theorizing....Proof-texting "interpretation," which rejects or ignores all Biblical scholarship...."Un-Christianizes" all those who question or reject some *theory* of Scripture...Distrust of the Church—as a hindrance to spirituality and a barrier to the "freewheeling" of the "Messiah-complexed" leader....Rationalism (by which to denounce rationalism)....Inability to distinguish central from peripheral, or supporting, truths....Over-individualism rather than social sensitivity and

responsibility.... Claiming to be a Shepherd over others (only Christ is Shepherd) rather than Servanthood, as Jesus and Paul indicated.[22]

Although they hailed from different theological perspectives, these gurus shared a common genius for using evangelicals' sense of personal and communal crisis to shut down debate. This tactic, from the secular point of view, is the very definition of anti-intellectualism. Yet the gurus turned this charge on its head, asserting expertise in systematic theology, psychological and behavioral theory, or intellectual history that their opponents ignored or elided at their own peril. Each, in his own way, claimed a kind of Gnostic familiarity with complex ideas that eluded the average American. Lindsell exposed the secret liberal conspiracies hidden from evangelicals in their very own churches, and the intellectual genealogy that vindicated the inerrantist position. Gothard impressed audiences with "more than 100 charts, many with complicated and intricate design, with arrows going different directions...with big words and Scripture verses affixed, and all described by Bill as God's unchanging 'principles.'"[23] This was something more than preaching. It was a complete intellectual system that, if it did not directly answer all modern challenges to the Bible, gave the appearance of sophistication and unassailable truth.

"A THINKING CHRISTIAN"

Francis Schaeffer had done many tours of duty in the wars over biblical authority. He was largely responsible for making sure the Lausanne Covenant affirmed inerrancy (although he worried that the statement did not go far enough).[24] International declarations on behalf of the Bible were well and good, but they rang hollow unless the average believer understood in his bones that the authority of scripture—the ballast of Western civilization—was in jeopardy. Schaeffer was a wandering preacher with a great insight: The danger of abandoning God's inerrant word could be made plain to American evangelicals through a history lesson, and that lesson would convince them to take political action.

Schaeffer was born in 1912 to a working-class, secular family in Germantown, Pennsylvania, and converted as a teenager at a local tent revival after reading the Bible to see if it provided rational answers to his questions. He met his wife, Edith, a refined Presbyterian and the child of China Inland Mission workers, in 1932 at a local church meeting when both stood up to rebut a Unitarian speaker. On one of their first dates, they passed the time by reading Machen's *Christianity and Liberalism* out loud to one another. After a bachelor's degree at Hampden-Sydney College, a Presbyterian men's school, Schaeffer studied for two years at Westminster Theological Seminary, where he absorbed the presuppositionalist apologetics that would shape his ministry. Yet he felt ill at ease with the seminary's "hyper-Calvinism," amillennialism, and moderate view of alcohol. Temperamentally, he was a fundamentalist (and leaned toward an urgent premillennialist view of the end-times). When Carl McIntire, a former student of Machen, founded Faith Theological Seminary in Wilmington, Delaware, in 1937, Schaeffer transferred. After ten years pastoring Presbyterian churches in the Northeast and in St. Louis, he sought a missionary appointment from McIntire's Independent Board for Presbyterian Foreign Missions, proposing a trip to Europe to diagnose the state of postwar Christianity. In 1948, Francis and Edith moved their young family to Switzerland.[25]

Schaeffer's primary aim was—and would remain—evangelizing the lost. It was almost by accident, when his oldest daughter Priscilla began bringing college friends home with her to talk about religion, that he founded one of the most unusual evangelical communities of the twentieth century: L'Abri, a "shelter" for all comers in the Swiss Alps. Once a staunch separatist, Schaeffer now welcomed into his home young people who dabbled in drugs and existentialism. College kids from Germany or the United Kingdom; hippies wandering their way through Europe; American evangelicals taking the summer off to see the world and seek answers: They came and stayed for days, weeks, months. They helped with the housework in the growing colony of chalets perched on the mountainside, shared meals, debated the meaning of life, and in their off-hours listened to reel-to-reel tapes of lectures and discussions that Schaeffer had led over the years. He called L'Abri "a place where we have been able to preach the Gospel to twentieth-century men." The *New York Times* called it a "combination religious community, philosophy seminar, and spiritual crash pad."[26] Most visitors were American Christians who had heard that L'Abri was a safe place to ask taboo questions—although the Schaeffers relished the opportunity to host skeptics. "There was a type of unofficial aristocracy," Schaeffer's son Frank later recalled.

> A born-again Wheaton College student...was low on the totem pole compared to, say, a British heroin addict-artist who was hanging out with Keith Richards. When former Harvard professor and LSD drug guru Timothy Leary came to [the nearby town] Villars and stayed in a hotel for several days to meet with Dad, we canceled everything and had a special day of fasting and prayer. "Just *think* of what it will mean if *he* gets saved!" Mom exalted.[27]

Surrounded by young people, Schaeffer was learning to appreciate the counterculture of long hair and rock 'n' roll—but living among the ruins and monuments of centuries of civilization also transformed his eye for art. Hans Rookmaaker, a Christian scholar who founded the art history department at the Free University in Amsterdam, tutored him in the place of high culture in Dutch Reformed theology and steered him toward the New Calvinism of Dutch theologian and politician Abraham Kuyper. Schaeffer came to view himself as an amateur art historian and cultural prophet. In 1963, he traveled to the United States and held Wheaton College students spellbound in chapel for three sessions, lecturing for a total of four hours. His long, thinning hair, white goatee, and Swiss hiking knickers cut a startling figure on campus. "Dr. Francis Schaeffer's European clothes, accent and mannerisms were alluring to many," wrote a student reporter for the *Record* (Schaeffer began referring to himself as "Doctor" after Highland College, a small Christian school in California, awarded him an honorary doctorate of divinity in 1954). "He impressed others with his erudition and sincerity....The thesis of his thought proposes that a line of desperation exists between the last generation and this. Modern man has created a massive chasm, best demonstrated in his philosophy and art."[28]

This "line of despair" represented the boundary between the happy faith of earlier Christians and the existential angst of modern man, who tried to rely on reason alone. Schaeffer drew the foreboding graphic on the blackboard at every opportunity, explaining how Thomas Aquinas triggered civilization's breakdown by suggesting that original sin had not contaminated man's intellect, thereby liberating human reason from the authority of the Bible (he mangled the poor saint's argument). Schaeffer shared what historian George Nash has called the conservative "fascination with intellectual genealogy, with tracing declension through the history of ideas." His narrative of Western decline was not all that different from the downward trajectory that Richard Weaver traced in *Ideas Have Consequences*—except that Weaver laid the blame for Western degradation at the feet of fourteenth-century theologian William of Ockham, whose nominalist philosophy denied the existence of universals and opened the way for moral relativism and drift from God.[29]

In 1965, Harold O. J. Brown, who worked with Harold Ockenga at Park Street Church in Boston, invited Schaeffer to return to America for what would become his first major speaking tour. Brown was an alumnus of Harvard and pulled strings to book a venue on campus for Schaeffer. The local InterVarsity chapter paid for it. Word spread of an evangelical minister who spoke authoritatively about Picasso, Freud, and Sartre in the heart of Ivy League unbelief. Inevitably, some whispered that Schaeffer was there at Harvard's official invitation—and he did nothing to dispel the rumor. Those who heard Schaeffer preach on "Speaking Historic Christianity into the Twentieth Century" said the effect was electric. "At that time, no one was talking about what we call today a 'thinking Christian.' It was absolutely new," said Ronald Wells, whom Schaeffer inspired to pursue an academic career in history. "Young people chose academic vocations because of that night. That was replicated in auditoriums around North America...we didn't so much listen as levitate." "Reading Schaeffer—that was my first experience of a Christian intellectual engaging those issues," recalled Lee Hardy, who went on to teach philosophy at Calvin College. "It was through Schaeffer and L'Abri that I was bitten by the philosophy bug." Harold Brown wrote that "Dr." Schaeffer was informal *doktorvater* to "a small but significantly placed number of individuals." In a 1994 study by *Christianity Today*, readers ranked him as the fifth most influential theologian, ahead of John Calvin.[30]

For the next two decades Schaeffer traveled back and forth between America and Europe. Despite his grating nasal voice and occasional speech dyslexia—he once gave a sermon on "Jews and the Genitals"—he was a brilliant demagogue who offered up all of Western history in an hour's lecture, stripped of confusing nuance. By the end of the 1970s he had published more than twenty books and booklets that sold more than two million copies in several languages. For the most part these were transcribed lectures, written for the ear in simple language and memorable slogans. "Schaeffer is pointing up the modern religious dilemma and while he is saying things that most of us have known for some time, he does it in a different and fresh way that points up the tremendous problem," Harold Lindsell wrote to a colleague.[31]

THE USES OF HISTORY

Schaeffer embraced his new calling as a conservative culture warrior. In the 1960s, his message had been a summons to general cultural engagement rather than political action. Some evangelicals on the political Left had admired his writings on the Christian obligation to fight poverty and racism. He published a book on the dangers of neglecting the environment, *Pollution and the Death of Man* (1970), long before "creation care" became a fashionable term among evangelicals. Schaeffer spent most of his time defending the rationality of the Christian faith, but he was not without appreciation for personal devotions and spiritual healing.[32]

Roe v. Wade radicalized Schaeffer's priorities—though his son, Frank, takes much of the credit for convincing Schaeffer to take a stand on what was then considered a "Catholic issue."[33] When he first took an interest in the anti-abortion cause, there was no evangelical pro-life movement to speak of. Most evangelical Protestants believed that abortion was a regrettable thing, but allowed that there were certain circumstances in which the mother's well-being required it. To Schaeffer, however, legalized abortion represented the barbaric end that he had predicted for Western civilization. In 1975, Francis and Edith met with Harold O. J. Brown and Presbyterian surgeon (and Ronald Reagan's future surgeon general) C. Everett Koop to discuss evangelical apathy toward abortion. The meeting led to the organization of the Christian Action Council, which opened hundreds of crisis pregnancy centers over the next few years.[34]

Despite receiving a diagnosis of lymphoma in 1976, Schaeffer embarked on a demanding tour to promote the multipart documentary that he had produced with his son called *How Should We Then Live?* Conceived as an evangelical response to Kenneth Clark's *Civilization*, the film dramatized Schaeffer's narrative of the West's decline, culminating in the legalization of abortion. The movie set a record for screenings for its distributor, Gospel Films. Its companion book stayed on the religious best-seller list for months and was still selling briskly years after publication. Schaeffer's gloomy message appealed to evangelicals troubled by conservative white Protestants' eroding authority in American society. And in these years of economic stagnation, rising urban crime, and what Jimmy Carter would soon call a "crisis of confidence" that "strikes at the very heart and soul of our national will," the idea that the country had crossed over a "line of despair" resonated with many Americans regardless of their theology.[35]

Schaeffer and Koop collaborated on a second documentary and book devoted more fully to the pro-life argument, *What Ever Happened to the Human Race?* (1979). Despite initially low attendance at the film's screenings—abortion was still a controversial subject among evangelicals—many pro-life activists later claimed Schaeffer as an inspiration and recommended his books. Randall Terry, who founded the pro-life protest group Operation Rescue, called Schaeffer "the greatest modern Christian philosopher."[36] Schaeffer's admirers considered him a man of ideas, not a political activist, and that was the key to his appeal. Unlike better-known figures such as Jerry Falwell, Pat Robertson, Tim LaHaye, and Cal Thomas, Schaeffer undertook Washington backroom dealings reluctantly and did not seek a national political stage. Privately, he found most of the prominent culture warriors coarse and intolerant.

Yet all these men cited Schaeffer's narrative of Western history—and its urgent conclusion—as a critical influence on their own work. LaHaye, who developed significant influence through the Moral Majority and the Council for National Policy (a secretive networking group that he founded to advance the conservative Christian cause), echoed Schaeffer's arguments in books like *Battle for the Mind* (1980), which he dedicated to Schaeffer. Historian Daniel Williams credits Schaeffer with convincing LaHaye, Falwell, and Robertson, who initially claimed an aversion to "worldly affairs" and ecumenical cooperation, to enter politics more aggressively and collaborate across doctrinal lines.[37]

Schaeffer's liminal status—known to many evangelical institutions, beholden to none—enhanced his ability to reach a variety of believers. Reformed evangelicals formed the core of his fan base, but a range of

Christians from Wesleyans to Anabaptists fell under his spell. Conservative Southern Baptist leaders—who hoped to shift their denomination toward a more Reformed perspective—warmed quickly to Schaeffer's message and sent copies of his lectures to one another. One veteran of InterVarsity Christian Fellowship wrote that by the 1970s, the organization relied "heavily on Dr. Schaeffer's apologetic." The Moody Bible Institute used his books in class, invited him to speak, and screened his films. The *Christian Standard*, a Restorationist paper far from Schaeffer's Presbyterian theology, embraced his critique of secular society and printed an excerpt from at least one of his books, *Death in the City*. Wesleyans read him. *Nazarene Preacher* magazine endorsed him, and Rob Staples, a progressive theologian in the Church of the Nazarene, was attracted to Schaeffer's early and less political writings.[38]

Schaeffer caused such a stir among Mennonites that the church leadership took notice. His Calvinist view of salvation and aggressive advocacy of Christian involvement in politics ran contrary to Anabaptist teachings, yet his critique of American culture and his emphasis on the Christian *Weltanschauung* played on old Anabaptist themes. John Howard Yoder was so worried about Schaeffer's appeal that he urged the church to produce an Anabaptist response to *How Should We Then Live?* "Francis Schaeffer has become a media power in evangelical Protestantism through a series of books of strong cultural criticism, culminating now in a massive new kind of media instrument, the Christian cultural film spectacular," he wrote to colleagues in 1982. To Yoder, the evangelist's campaign concealed the worst impulses of "old-time religion" beneath a veneer of intellectual pretense:

> Yet those who as intellectual historians criticize his intellectual history, and those who, as Christian social ethicists, criticize his social ethics, have not proceeded to encounter him on the level of his media event, which represents a kind of upper middle class apology for the moral majority. His co-star, Dr. Everett Koop, probably owes it to his partnership with Schaeffer that he is now Surgeon General in the Regan [*sic*] administration. There are leaders in both mainline and evangelical churches whose parishioners are attracted by the slick simplicity and self-confident moral superiority of the Schaeffer media message, who would be glad to have something else to compare it with. But there is nothing else of that kind.[39]

Yoder hoped that Schaeffer would provoke Mennonites to step beyond their own enclave and assert a broader Anabaptist vision. Their film should include "not simply personal narrative but cultural analysis, and with 'culture' not meaning Pennsylvania Dutch ethnicity but rather the major streams of God's work in the western world and in mission."[40] His memo, however, generated little enthusiasm. He let the idea drop.

Yoder was not the only one appalled by Schaeffer's hamfisted caricature of history. For all of his emphasis on careful argument, Schaeffer was notoriously irresponsible as a scholar. "Schaeffer didn't read books," said his son-in-law, John Sandri. "He got his material from magazines, *Newsweek*, *Time*—he'd take them to the beach. He did go to seminary too, so he had that, but when he was here [at L'Abri], he went through the summarized version. He was out to give broad strokes. It was not necessary to give you the details of Kierkegaard." Schaeffer wowed audiences by explaining 500 years of intellectual history in a paragraph and a casual chalkboard diagram—but he did so with exaggerations, oversimplifications, and misinformation that would make a specialist cry. He was a brazen editor of history. He ignored the ferment of Greco-Roman "pagan" thought that informed Christian scripture. He declared the Reformers creators of a "definite culture" pure of the "humanism" and "despair" latent in the Renaissance. (Never mind that Luther and Calvin were trained humanists. Schaeffer denied any link between their God-fearing humanism and his godless twentieth-century foe.)[41] But then, he never claimed to be a professional scholar. His books, lectures, and films offered to American evangelicals what Oswald Spengler's *The Decline of the West* offered to Germans reeling after World War I: not academic history, but a grand narrative with a big idea that explained his audience's distress. His mistakes did not matter much. He turned history into a weapon in the culture wars.

DEFENDERS OF THE WEST

Evangelicals' long-running debate over biblical authority was now a battle for civilization—and they needed to act while there was still time. Schaeffer claimed the "Christian West" and the history of ideas on behalf of evangelicals at a moment when other American conservatives were doing the same, reviving classical political philosophy, the ideals of medieval Christendom, and the ancient tradition of natural law. In contrast, many leftist intellectuals understood America's struggles over civil rights and Cold War aggression as an indictment of Western civilization. The morass of Vietnam signaled the bankruptcy of America's intellectual and political authority. The blame for the West's decline lay not on the shoulders of St. Thomas or Voltaire, but the white men who crusaded for European and American empire. Any conscientious scholar had a duty to abandon the traditional narrative taught in "Western Civ" courses in favor of history, literature, and art from the perspective of the nonwhite, non-Western, and nonwealthy. "We have in the New Left not only a rejection of American society, but a rejection of the traditions of Western Civilization," wrote one political scientist in 1969.[42]

Graduation requirements in the study of the West were shrinking. Scholars rallied to the banners of multiculturalism and secular colleges drifted away from broad liberal arts education. Evangelicals were primed to embrace the notion that they were the rightful heirs to a heritage that the American Left disdained. Their colleges stuck with the Western canon and traditional courses that offered a unified worldview rather than politically correct fragmentation. In the coming decades, private Christian academies and the burgeoning homeschool movement would flock to "classical Christian" curricula packed with Greek, Latin, and ancient philosophy. Schaeffer taught his disciples Richard Weaver's classic slogan, "ideas have consequences." By convincing evangelicals that Plato and Camus had a direct impact on their lives, that they had a stake in the history of ideas, he laid the intellectual groundwork for their political alliance with other wings of American conservatism in the 1980s.[43]

How Should We Then Live? coincided with the American bicentennial, when many churches were energetically baptizing the country's founding and promoting a messianic vision of America's role in the world. Schaeffer joined this vogue for romanticizing Protestantism's historic role in the origins of American democracy. Despite the fact that most of the sixteenth-century Reformers were more willing to grant power to princes than to the common man, Schaeffer preached that the Bible (when freed from Roman chains) always spoke for freedom, held kings accountable to the people, and shaped the Christian founding of America. He hired John Whitehead, founder of the Christian libertarian think tank the Rutherford Institute, to research his final book, *A Christian Manifesto* (1981). The book drew a direct line from the Reformers through seventeenth-century Scottish theologian Samuel

Rutherford, who advocated limited government based on the theory of covenant in Deuteronomy, to Presbyterian minister and Founding Father John Witherspoon—and called for civil disobedience if today's politicians failed to honor America's founding values. Christian lawyers who later gathered under the auspices of the Rutherford Institute to work for evangelical clients in religious liberty cases—and enjoyed high success rates in defending abortion protestors and sidewalk preachers—gave Schaeffer credit for shaping their view of faith and the law.[44]

By 1982, *A Christian Manifesto* was outselling *Jane Fonda's Workout Book*, which held first place on the *New York Times* best-seller list, by two to one (the *Times* did not include Christian books in its rankings).[45] It touched off a heated debate between Schaeffer and professional evangelical historians. George Marsden wrote him to correct factual errors in the book. Wheaton College historian Mark Noll told *Newsweek* that "the danger is that people will take [Schaeffer] for a scholar, which he is not. Evangelical historians are especially bothered by his simplified myth of America's Christian past." Chagrined by this sound bite, which excluded many kind things that he had said about Schaeffer, Noll sent a polite letter apologizing for any "unintended harm" but noting that, based on a decade of research, he found it "very difficult to see explicit biblical influence on the founding documents of the United States or in the political thinking of even the evangelical Founders like John Witherspoon."[46]

Schaeffer replied with a twelve-page screed defending his position. According to biographer Barry Hankins, over subsequent months Schaeffer's correspondence with Noll obsessed him. At L'Abri he checked the mail daily, hoping for another letter, and conscripted the whole community in his efforts to rebut the professor's case. The criticism hurt. More than that, Schaeffer was outraged at the evangelical historians' disloyalty in the midst of this battle for America's soul. "He had written *Manifesto*, not as a dispassionate historical treatise, but as a tract in the culture wars," Hankins wrote.[47]

Schaeffer wanted evangelical Americans to become soldiers of history rather than careful students. He was one of a wave of gurus who, like generations of prophets and big personalities before them, offered evangelicals an alternative authority, a rubric of certainty at a time when the consensus on the Bible's status in American culture was shakier than ever. While he inspired some young evangelicals to get to the bottom of the stories he told by pursuing graduate degrees in history and philosophy, on a larger scale Schaeffer's ministry was a grand and clever exercise in anti-intellectualism. He deployed the trappings of academic investigation—litanies of historical names and dates; an accommodating version of Enlightenment reasoning—to quash inquiry rather than encourage it, to mobilize his audiences rather than provoke them to ask questions. To Schaeffer and his admirers, there was no dishonesty in this, but only due respect for divine authority. The gospels do not offer a "neutral" historical account. What is the purpose of history if not to disclose God's intentions and displeasure?

Schaeffer's ministry revealed what the neo-evangelical campaign to build an intellectual movement around inerrancy and the "Christian worldview" had become: an adaptable ideology vague enough to welcome believers of every theological persuasion, a substrate in which political energy could flourish—and a strategy for using the authority of history to name conservative evangelicals as trustees of Christendom.

Chapter 10

God's Idea Men

Conservative evangelicals' growing power lay partly in local organization and Washington maneuvers, but also in an intellectual and rhetorical turn: the move from proof texts to presuppositions, and the decision to argue in terms of worldviews and human history rather than a string of Bible verses. Conservative Protestant opposition to certain kinds of change—to the erosion of their cultural dominance in an increasingly pluralistic society—had a long history. Yet pundits were right to perceive something novel in the Christian Right of the late 1970s and early 1980s. It was a network of new and savvy organizations, a band of activists and politicians with a plan: a new mode of reasoning, arguing, educating, and redrafting history.

THE PRESUPPOSITIONALIST PATOIS

Francis Schaeffer encouraged his audiences to speak of their culture in the lingua franca of the neo-evangelicals: presuppositionalism. To his teacher Cornelius Van Til, the chasm between Christian and non-Christian worldviews was so vast that there was little use in attempting conversation. Schaeffer, a born evangelist, argued that a prime opportunity lay in the gap between a nonbeliever's stated beliefs and his actual behavior. Without belief in a supreme power, nonbelievers had no basis on which to find meaning or order in life. Subconsciously, they lived according to "biblical presuppositions" like logic, natural order, and moral judgment. "As I look around and see all other men in their religion or in their philosophy,

I can see that they all have something that doesn't really belong to them, but it belongs to us logically," he said. "Illogical though it may be, it is there, and we can appeal to it," he said. "There is a 'neutral ground' in practice."[1]

In the public sphere, however, Schaeffer preached that there was no such thing as neutrality. True Christians, whose biblical presuppositions extended beyond Sunday worship to frame every aspect of their lives, had to fight efforts to strip religion out of public education and communal space. "Secular humanism" was not only a liberal political platform. It was an intellectual adversary, a surrogate religion. Here Schaeffer echoed the critique that nonevangelical conservatives had long levied against their ideological enemies. Whittaker Chambers, the senior *Time* editor and former communist who testified against Alger Hiss before the House Un-American Activities Committee, had called communism a false religion, worship of self, "man's second oldest faith." With Christianity banned from the classroom and the town square, secular humanist ideas would fill the vacuum, and the next generation could not help but absorb these notions from television, music, and the morass of pagan consumerism. "People have presuppositions, and they will live more consistently on the basis of these presuppositions than even they themselves may realize," Schaeffer wrote. "Most people catch their presuppositions from their family and surrounding society the way a child catches measles. But people with more understanding realize that their presuppositions should be chosen after a careful consideration of what world view is true."[2]

While Schaeffer packed lecture halls, a quieter but far more rigorous intellectual revival stirred in Reformed circles, led by scholars who would have blanched at Schaeffer's adaptation of their tradition. A handful of professional philosophers, particularly Alvin Plantinga and Nicholas Wolterstorff (who both spent many of their early teaching years at Calvin College), were compelling colleagues in their famously secular discipline to reckon with the Christian perspective. Together they built upon the insights of the ancient Church Fathers, John Calvin, and more recent Christian thinkers to develop the modern philosophical field of Reformed epistemology, which aimed to account for how a person might rationally believe in God in the skeptical twentieth century. Plantinga made his first mark on academic philosophy with his 1967 book *God and Other Minds*, in which he argued that theists' belief in an unseen God is no less warranted than every human being's working—but, technically, unproven—assumption that other people have mental faculties like his own.[3]

Over the course of their long careers Plantinga and Wolterstorff tackled nearly every intellectual threat to theism, ranging from Freud and Hegel to the modern biblical critics. They organized a supportive network for Christian philosophers trying to respond to the sometimes hostile culture of academia. Like Schaeffer, they embraced the Reformed insight that all education takes for granted some set of untested assumptions: No classroom is a perfectly neutral space. But unlike Schaeffer, they took non-Christian perspectives quite seriously and focused their efforts on a modest defense of theism rather than on proving the truth of their own Christian faith and imposing its moral strictures upon the rest of America. In so doing they transformed the study of epistemology, defended the intellectual respectability of Christianity—particularly the Reformed tradition—and inspired a generation of evangelical philosophers. Yet in the public square subtle scholarship was no match for culture-war bluster. A hodgepodge of vaguely Reformed ideas blended with an apocalyptic narrative of world history had more popular appeal than painstaking philosophical argument. American evangelicals did not hunger for a nuanced warrant for theism. They wanted a hero who would stand up for their instincts about human nature, social order, and biblical law.

Presuppositionalist language—pride in one's "Christian worldview," chants of "neutrality is a lie" and "objectivity is a myth"—already enjoyed some currency. Neo-evangelical journalists and nonevangelical conservatives had been using these slogans for years, and they echoed the mainstream media's reports on postmodernist trends in academe, art, and literature.[4] Non-Reformed evangelicals had been assimilating Reformed cultural theology, if in a softened form, for decades, and they were by now old hands at protesting the impartiality of public education. If very few were true disciples of Van Til, they were at least fluent in his students' catchphrases and had learned to pay attention to how human beings come to know things. The number of children who were homeschooled or attending Christian schools jumped in the 1970s as evangelical parents won court decisions defending their right to educate their children at home and at private Christian institutions. The Internal Revenue Service challenged the tax-exempt status of many private Christian schools, further inflaming evangelical activists and educators. By the end of the 1980s, evangelicals were second only to Catholics in the use of private education.[5]

Some years before Schaeffer became a household name in evangelical circles, their growing enthusiasm for the "Christian worldview" and distrust of secular authority had already begun to radicalize their approach to one familiar issue: the teaching of evolution in American classrooms. Traditionally, the strongholds of creationist belief—particularly "young-earth" creationism, which relies on a literal interpretation of Genesis to argue that the earth is only a few thousand years old—were not the Reformed communities most closely associated with presuppositionalist thought, but rather Seventh-day Adventist and Missouri Synod Lutheran churches. However, when it came to framing and marketing young-earth creationism in terms that resonated with a broad range of evangelicals, the method of Van Til, Gordon Clark, and their followers proved to be an asset.

John Whitcomb, a graduate of Princeton who attended and then taught at Grace Theological Seminary in Indiana, used this system of reasoning in writing the blockbuster that popularized young-earth creationism, *The Genesis Flood* (1961). Co-author Henry M. Morris, a hydraulic engineer at Virginia Polytechnic Institute, lent the book scientific clout (Whitcomb struggled unsuccessfully to find a trained geologist who would collaborate with him or even review the manuscript). But the core of *The Genesis Flood* was Whitcomb's contention that the presupposition of biblical inerrancy required the believer to affirm six-day creation and defend Noah's worldwide flood as literally true. The authors happily quoted old Princeton's Benjamin Warfield to explain inerrancy (they neglected to mention that the Princetonians generally permitted some accommodation to modern science in their reading of Genesis). "Our conclusions must unavoidably be colored by our Biblical presuppositions, and this we plainly acknowledge," Whitcomb and Morris wrote in the book's introduction. "But uniformitarian scholarship [that assumes the universal application of natural law and denies the miraculous] is no less bound by *its* own presuppositions and these are quite as dogmatic as those of our own!" Evangelical readers responded with enthusiasm. After 48 printings, *The Genesis Flood* eventually sold 300,000 copies.[6]

Davis A. Young, a young geologist, Orthodox Presbyterian, and an early supporter of Flood geology (before graduate study convinced him to abandon that view), credited none other than Cornelius Van Til with convincing him that "science must first subject itself to the authority of the Bible if it is to make any real progress."[7] Van Til originally intended his theology to discourage Christians from relying on real-world evidence. Instead, he hoped to compel them to recognize that making the case for Christ depended on persuading the skeptic to accept, on faith, the truth of the Bible and the reality of the resurrection. Yet his disciples continually found clever ways to combine presuppositionalism and empiricism, to argue that, in fact, the best scientist is a Christian scientist, for only Christians understand the universe as it truly is and rightly interpret its data.

Goaded into action by the federal government's intervention in science education in the years that followed *Sputnik* (including a push for updated science textbooks with lessons on evolution), creationists founded the Creationist Research Society in 1963 (the year of Schaeffer's first U.S. tour). By the mid-1970s advocates of creationism had used the framework of presuppositionalism to develop a campaign to force "creation science" into public schools. They dropped the biblical proof texts and instead argued that creationism—or its subsequent, more respectable form, "intelligent design"—was merely an alternative worldview, a scientific paradigm that deserved equal classroom time. Scientific creationism and evolution were conflicting "hypotheses" with different presuppositions, even if most advocates of creation science soon ceased their attempts to confirm creationism through geological research. Cheered by their discovery of philosopher Karl Popper's critiques of the scientific method and Thomas Kuhn's *The Structure of Scientific Revolutions* (1962), creationists adapted Kuhn's argument that embattled "scientific revolutionaries" who dared to challenge the prevailing orthodoxy might be prophets without honor today, but tomorrow they would force a "paradigm shift" in human knowledge and emerge as heroes.[8]

In 1970, Henry Morris collaborated with Tim LaHaye and a Southern Baptist mother and son named Nell and Kelly Segraves to found the Creation Science Research Center, affiliated with LaHaye's Christian Heritage College in San Diego (now San Diego Christian College). The center's first newsletter proclaimed a "grassroots movement" to transform public school curricula and articulate scientific creationism in terms stripped of explicitly

Christian language. John Whitcomb disapproved of this turn away from scripture, but pseudoscience masked as "intelligent design" would prove more successful than Bible verses in the expanding culture war. Later activists shifted further from any pretense of doing scientific research and explicitly linked the depravity of Darwin's disciples' principle of "survival of the fittest" to other signs of America's slide into iniquity, such as sex education and the legalization of abortion.[9] It was easier to argue that the theory of evolution was a force for social evil than to argue that evolution was scientifically false. The rhetoric of presuppositionalism—asserting that neutrality in the public school classroom was impossible and that opposing worldviews deserve equal time—gave creationists the language they needed to roll back Darwin's dominance.

An Armenian-American pastor named Rousas John Rushdoony—who, not coincidentally, was asked by Moody Press to read *The Genesis Flood* in manuscript form—served evangelical educators more quietly. Like Schaeffer, Rushdoony was a Presbyterian fundamentalist. An ordained minister who left the Presbyterian Church U.S.A. for the more conservative Orthodox Presbyterian Church, he never studied personally with Van Til but read the theologian's books during his graduate studies and while serving as a missionary among Indians in Nevada. His beliefs hardened into a conservative postmillennialism viciously opposed to the premillennial view dominant among American evangelicals. In 1953 Rushdoony became pastor of an Orthodox Presbyterian church in Santa Cruz, California, and began publishing critiques of public education. He published his first book, an exposition of Van Til's theology entitled *By What Standard?*, in 1958 and soon left his pulpit to focus on scholarship.[10]

The following year, Rushdoony began to receive support from the William Volker Fund, a shadowy foundation that also funded the *National Review* as well as conservative darlings like Richard Weaver and the libertarian Austrian economist Ludwig von Mises.[11] Rushdoony and his disciples would draw on Mises, Friedrich Hayek, and other writers in the Austrian school of economics throughout their careers. Rushdoony found much to admire in Hayek, whose provocative volume *The Road to Serfdom* (1944) protested the government's encroachment on individual liberty and stressed the need to bind the state with a fixed "Rule of Law." Rushdoony honed his blend of Reformed Christian and libertarian principles into a comprehensive indictment of twentieth-century America on biblical grounds. He prayed for a society governed by every jot and tittle of scriptural law stripped of all non-Christian accretions.[12]

At first he kept mostly to writing, occasionally for *Christianity Today*, and accepted invitations to speak at local churches and parent-teacher organizations concerned about the fate of Christian education. He preached that education ought to teach children to recognize their God-given presuppositions rather than treat them as blank slates on which the state may imprint humanistic propaganda.[13] Echoing Edmund Burke, Rushdoony warned of the hubris of *tabula rasa*, the myth that "man was able to remake man and the educator to play the role of a god." He wrote that all education was inherently religious. Bad education corrupted Christians' capacity for leadership, while good education reinforced correct presuppositions and empowered Christian "dominion" as described in the first chapter of Genesis, when God told Adam and Eve to "be fruitful, and multiply, and replenish the earth, and subdue it: and have dominion over the fish of the sea, and over the fowl of the air, and over every living thing that moveth upon the earth." In 1965 Rushdoony founded the Chalcedon Foundation, a Christian think tank in Woodland Hills, California, to promote his theology. His timing was advantageous. Lyndon Johnson's landslide victory in the 1964 presidential election had left conservatives reeling, eager for a prophet who could guide them out of exile. "Many of his early supporters were in the John Birch Society and the Goldwater movement, and they were disillusioned with the loss of Goldwater," his son Mark Rushdoony remembered. "My father was trying to turn their attention to a different focus, to a more theological view, a moral view of culture, civilization."[14]

Rushdoony did not view himself as a political activist. He harbored ambitions of turning Chalcedon into a Christian college.[15] He was deeply skeptical of Christian political involvement and believed that political victories rang hollow without deeper religious change. However, as his reading of the Bible and observations of American culture began to cohere into a consistent theology, the result was a radical proposal that had profound political implications. Van Til had demolished the validity of non-Christian worldviews but offered no guide for how Christians ought to reshape society. Rushdoony's solution, which he worked out over time and articulated most clearly in *The Institutes of Biblical Law* (1973), was Christian Reconstructionism, a plan for transforming government and culture according to Christian presuppositions. Rushdoony envisioned the gradual takeover of government by Christians who would implement Mosaic Law in all aspects of society with the aim of enacting the Kingdom of God on earth and ushering in the millennium. He observed an eccentric version of Jewish dietary laws based on his own exegesis of Leviticus and advocated capital punishment for the offenders listed in Deuteronomy, such as adulterers and rebellious sons. Some of his more zealous followers suggested a return to Old Testament execution by stoning.[16]

While these ideas have antecedents in the writings of John Calvin and the Puritans' theocratic experiments, Rushdoony recast theonomy—the rule of divine law—as the solution to twentieth-century ills. There is no way of knowing how many people in the homeschooling and Christian school movements read his books, though it is telling that the record of a large class-action suit by homeschooling parents in Texas identified him as expert witness "Dr. Rousas John Rushdoony, author of more than thirty published books in the field of education." His name also appears in dockets from cases in Georgia, Michigan, North Dakota, and Ohio. Through his writings, court testimonies, public lectures, and correspondence with parents, Rushdoony encouraged evangelicals to defend their right to nurture children in their own worldview.[17]

Christian Reconstructionism garnered a small number of influential disciples, though the theology was too radical to win a wide following. J. Howard Pew was an early fan of Rushdoony's critique of big government, but the editors at Christianity Today—perennially concerned about mainstream opinion—judged most of his ideas beyond the pale. Rushdoony spent little time in Washington, but he did occasionally address congressmen at informal gatherings and was a regular guest on Pat Robertson's 700 Club. He mentored the reclusive evangelical philanthropist Howard Ahmanson and collaborated with leading Florida megachurch minister D. James Kennedy in founding an evangelical network called the Coalition for Religious Liberty. Rushdoony was an early member of Tim LaHaye's Council for National Policy, but he frequently complained that even if some of his principles seemed to be gaining traction, mainstream evangelical activists were more willing to "steal" his ideas than to give him due credit.[18] It was a fair complaint. If Rushdoony encouraged an unknown number of political actors to ponder the Bible's implications for transforming society, Francis Schaeffer—with his larger audiences, digestible slogans, and more mainstream beliefs—deserves more credit for teaching evangelicals to reclaim culture and speak the language of presuppositionalism.

ENVOYS OF APOCALYPSE

As gloomy as Schaeffer and Rushdoony sounded when they lectured on the drift of Western culture, they were paragons of good cheer compared to those gurus who told evangelicals that there was little they could do to rescue civilization because the end was nigh. Hal Lindsey was a business school dropout and former tugboat captain who found his way to Dallas Theological Seminary, where he learned the art of biblical prophecy from the dispensationalist theologian John F. Walvoord. He plunged into youth evangelism with Campus Crusade and developed a knack for packaging the esoteric details of eschatology in terms that appealed to college students. He founded a ministry at UCLA aimed at hippies and counterculture kids who thought themselves too cool for Campus Crusade's prim approach: a blue jeans and Birkenstocks operation called the Jesus Christ Light and Power Company. In 1970, with the help of ghostwriter Carole C. Carlson, Lindsey published his breezy guide to Armageddon, *The Late Great Planet Earth*.[19]

The book found a wide audience beyond Jesus People intrigued by visions of apocalypse. The *New York Times* declared it the top nonfiction best seller of the decade (over the next quarter century it sold 28 million copies). In an era of widespread anxiety over ecological disaster, overpopulation, and Washington's faltering prestige abroad and weakening grip on upheaval at home, young people were growing more angry with each headline out of Vietnam, dabbling in escapist philosophies and substances, and crowding into movie theaters to watch dystopian films like *Planet of the Apes*, *A Clockwork Orange*, and *Soylent Green*. Lindsey's thesis—that these terrible things were no coincidence; the world was, indeed, hurtling toward ruination, and this was all in God's plan—struck a live nerve. "For many of them their hopes, ambitions, and plans are permeated with the subconscious fear that perhaps there will be no future for all mankind....People are searching for answers to basic questions," he wrote.[20]

Lindsey showed readers that amid all this chaos, the Bible alone could make sense of world events. He warned that the Kremlin was "Gog, of the land of Magog" identified by the prophet Ezekiel, and would soon attack Israel to launch World War III. The European Common Market was no innocuous economic accord. It marked the rise of the ten-nation confederacy, centered at Rome, foretold by the ten horns on the beast in Daniel's vision and in the Book of Revelation. Lindsey exploited the age-old appeal of dispensational premillennialism—its capacity to transform the Bible into a crystal ball, and a precise one at that—and he did so in a style that made stuffy theology cool. The Rapture, when all sincere Christians would vanish from earth to meet Christ in the air on the eve of his Second Coming, was better than any street drug, "the ultimate trip" when "every believer in Jesus Christ is initiated into Christ's fraternity."[21]

At first glance, Lindsey's slangy account of the end-times seemed wholly unlike—and even at cross-purposes with—Francis Schaeffer's history lessons and calls for political action. But these gurus were not so different. Lindsey wrote in a casual vernacular, but he studded his pages with footnotes and epigraphs from Hegel and Hamlet. In his argument for the Soviet Union's role in the coming apocalypse, he cited Herodotus, Josephus, and Pliny—as well as various unremembered Victorian professors—on the Russians' origins in Scythian tribes mentioned in the Bible. Arnold Toynbee, another student of civilization's inevitable decline, made a cameo. "Biblical prophecy can become a sure foundation upon which your faith can grow—and there is no need to shelve your intellect while finding this faith," Lindsey declared.[22] Like Schaeffer's offhand references to Locke and Jung, *The Late Great Planet Earth* made the reader feel smart, in the know, and personally involved in history's climax.

Lindsey preached that human history was about to end in a conflagration of world war and divine judgment. Worse, America only had a bit part in the drama (his mentor at Dallas, John Walvoord, taught that "no specific prophecy whatever is found concerning the role of the United States, indicating that its contribution will be a secondary one as the world moves on to Armageddon").[23] Such prognostications hardly seemed like a recipe for political mobilization. Yet throughout Christian history, preachers of the imminent Second Coming—ranging from the Fifth Monarchy men in Cromwell's England to Dwight Moody, the great popularizer of dispensationalism in America—preferred deeds to quietism. Lindsey and other modern prophets followed a long tradition of apocalyptic activism.

In the 1990s, Tim LaHaye's best-selling *Left Behind* novels, co-authored with Jerry B. Jenkins, would launch a cottage industry of doomsday merchandise and bring the Rapture and Great Tribulation into mainstream American consciousness. LaHaye, a godfather of the Christian Right who had fashioned himself a guru on subjects ranging from human sexuality to the creation of the Earth, saw no contradiction between predicting Armageddon and planning the Christian infiltration of Washington. The two went hand in hand. As the culture wars simmered and LaHaye perceived the growing influence of "secular humanists" in public schools, media, and government, it was only natural to organize evangelicals to roll back secularism in any way they could while accepting that all this wickedness must mean that the end was at hand. "Nobody fused eschatology, conservative politics, and antisecularism like Tim LaHaye," wrote historians Randall Stephens and Karl Giberson.[24]

For ardent premillennialists like LaHaye and Lindsey, the dictates of biblical prophecy did not dampen political zeal. Quite the opposite: Faith in prophecy bolstered their confidence in the Bible's authority to judge the modern world. If the Bible had predicted the Six-Day War (Lindsey was certain that it had), then surely it was right about abortion and homosexuality. Now conservative evangelicals ought to be all the more certain that everything they despised in modern culture was contrary to God's will. In 1970s and 1980s America—as in Savonarola's Florence, or Jan van Leiden's Munster—prophecy functioned as a political language, an idiom of cultural critique, a call for repentance. Although Schaeffer had no taste for end-times groaning, he shared the same basic eschatological beliefs as Lindsey and LaHaye. The difference, mainly, was one of style and emphasis. Schaeffer's medium was intellectual history rather than prophecy, but he would have seconded Lindsey's summons to conversion: "As history races toward this moment, are you afraid or looking with hope for deliverance? The answer should reveal to you your spiritual condition."[25]

These gurus were masters in the fusion of ideas and politics. Their attention to the power inherent in a careful telling of history, along with control of the social instruments of intellectual authority like education and media, informed the battles between conservative and progressive evangelicals in several denominations during the 1970s. By the end of the decade, conservatives were well on their way toward dominating the Southern Baptist Convention and the Lutheran Church (Missouri Synod), and progressive leaders were pessimistic about their hold on power in several Wesleyan Holiness churches.[26] Despite the efforts of progressives to advocate their own interpretation of evangelical heritage, a breed of "neofundamentalist" had emerged with potent intellectual and political savvy.

The peregrinations of gurus like Schaeffer, Rushdoony, Lindsey, and LaHaye helped stimulate a highly organized and activist strain of conservative evangelicalism very different from the militant "come-outism" of the early fundamentalists. These neofundamentalist leaders were not hayseeds in shiny suits drawling on about short skirts and lipstick. They were culturally savvy "experts" in history, psychology, and end-times theology who offered more than a string of memorized Bible verses to demonstrate their authority. They traded their ancestors' anti-intellectualism for a brand of pseudointellectualism that claimed education and ideas for their side while quashing open debate. They packaged ideology and history for popular consumption and used them to political advantage—inside Washington, and in their own churches.

THE STRATEGIC ART OF CULTURE WAR

Fundamentalism is a paradox. Its partisans—of any faith—call for the return to an imagined arcadia in which God's voice boomed plainly from scripture. Yet as a historical phenomenon, fundamentalism is wholly modern. It is a set of reactions against the aftershocks of the Enlightenment and the evolution of global capitalism: the breach between faith and reason, the rise of the secular public square, and the collapse of traditional social hierarchies and ways of life. Creatures of modernity, fundamentalists have happily availed themselves of modern technology. Fundamentalists ranging from separatist Baptist preachers to Al Qaeda propagandists have demonstrated a genius for employing the latest media and political (or military) weaponry to spread their message and accomplish their aims. To fundamentalists, history, too, is a technology: a trove of data to be strategically deployed.

Nowhere have the uses of history been clearer than in the clashes between conservative and progressive evangelicals for control of their denominations throughout the 1970s and 1980s. In the Southern Baptist Convention, many conservatives would have objected to the "fundamentalist" label as a Yankee epithet, a synonym for a barefoot bumpkin sorely lacking in southern grace. But if their self-perception was not fundamentalist, many of their goals and tactics were. The decisive battles over the meaning and role of the Bible in modern society did not, primarily, unfold in the form of dueling proof texts or Sunday pulpit ripostes, but in skirmishes for control of the machinery of intellectual authority: seminaries, missions boards, denominational presses, and authorized church history. The personal magnetism of gurus was not sufficient to stanch the secularist tide. Just as thousands of volunteers at Billy Graham's crusades worked to settle new converts into local churches before their enthusiasm could evaporate, conservative activists knew that the fervor wandering sages left in their wake would fizzle unless channeled into institutions and sustained by an infrastructure built to teach and train future generations.

Southern Baptist conservatives considered themselves the "silent majority" in their denomination. They were confident in a groundswell of support if they could mobilize laypeople for the cause. In 1969 Paul Pressler, a seventh-generation Texas Baptist, graduate of Princeton, and prominent Houston lawyer, complained to an ally, M. O. Owens: "We are in the majority but losing because we have not spent the time necessary to organize and assert ourselves. . . . With cohesive action by trained individuals who are committed to Biblical truth, we could move into influencing the Sunday School Board in the publication of their materials, in helping select editors for our state Baptist papers, and generally provide the type of sound Christian leadership which we should have in every phase of the Southern Baptist Convention and in our state and local conventions and associations." While Pressler mobilized Baptists in Houston around the cause of Christian education, Owens was organizing the Fellowship of Conservative Baptists in his home state of North Carolina.[27]

Years earlier, conservatives had begun to build an alternative system of higher education to compensate for the drift of the denomination's seminaries away from biblical inerrancy. They wanted nothing more than to reverse the policy of careful accommodation that had brought so many conservative Bible schools and seminaries into line with the expectations of secular academia, and to root out those scholars who applied the term *inerrancy* to their own pliant interpretation of the Bible, rather than to scripture's "literal" meaning. Pressler disdained accrediting agencies, which he believed were "controlled by the liberal northeastern schools." He advocated firing tenured professors so that the agencies would withdraw accreditation, seeing as "the only reason our seminaries have their accredidation [sic] with the accreditting [sic] agency is so a few liberal graduate students could attend some northeast liberal Divinity Schools."[28]

If the mainstream intelligentsia, the guardians of intellectual authority, had abandoned the faith, then the true believers in the pews must wake up and redirect the church and surrounding culture. The new conservative schools reflected a populist backlash against the perceived elitism of the denomination's main seminaries. A Jacksonville, Florida, pastor founded Luther Rice Seminary in 1962 specifically to aid local clergy who were unable to enroll in seminary full time. Conservatives seeking to build "a School of the Prophets" in the Deep South founded Mid-America Baptist Theological Seminary in Louisiana in 1971 (the school later moved to Little Rock, and eventually to the Memphis area). That same year Jerry Falwell founded Lynchburg Baptist College (now Liberty University) in Lynchburg, Virginia, and W. A. Criswell founded his eponymous Bible Institute. Criswell, a former SBC president, pastored First Baptist Church in Dallas, the largest Southern Baptist church in the country (where Billy Graham was nominally a member for fifty-five years). When he announced his "vision" for the school in 1969, Criswell emphasized the need to provide Bible training for Sunday school teachers and the "many Southern Baptist pastors who had not had the opportunity to finish college or even to begin."[29] His mission statement sounded like a noble call to democratize knowledge, but Criswell's desire to exclude was just as strong as his inclusive spirit. He wanted to reclaim Southern Baptist education from the ivory-tower elites and wave the banner of "the common man" as cover for his capture of intellectual inquiry.

A string of smaller but crucial conservative organizations appeared throughout the 1970s. In 1973, a group of Baptists incensed at the liberal sentiments evident in some of the denomination's agencies—particularly the socially concerned Christian Life Commission—organized as the Baptist Faith and Message Fellowship. They sponsored a Baptist Literature Board to offer curricula stressing biblical inerrancy as an alternative to the more moderate publications of the Sunday School Board. Despite the reports from moderate "spies" who attended these organizations' early meetings, most moderates failed to foresee the conservative grab for power at the 1979 convention. Sociologist Nancy Ammerman has suggested that moderates failed to build a coalition because in the past, fundamentalist agitation within the convention was disorganized—a few fire-breathers shooting off empty threats against the evils of Darwinism and drink. Moreover, moderates did not move to protect their control of the convention's agencies and boards because they were loath to admit that their denomination concentrated power in the hands of hierarchical leaders or bureaucrats. "They had lived for nearly 150 years with a myth of democracy.... They assumed that consensus would emerge from their common efforts to discern the will of God."[30]

The conservative leaders had no illusions about how power worked in the SBC. Their strategy was simple: elect one of their own as president of the convention for ten consecutive years, during which time all crucial denominational positions would come due for renomination, allowing conservatives to gradually populate all SBC boards, agencies, and trusteeships with their allies. They borrowed tactics from secular political parties, occupying skyboxes at the 1979 convention in Houston's Astrodome where their leaders could coordinate backroom dealings and voting procedures. That year they elected Adrian Rogers, pastor of Bellevue Baptist Church in Memphis, as president of the SBC—the first in an unbroken series of conservative presidents that continues today. The conservative plan extended beyond theology and church life to national politics. Ed McAteer, a Southern Baptist layman and wealthy sales executive who helped found the Moral Majority, used his experience as a former field director for the Conservative Caucus, a nominally secular organization founded in 1974, to ally the SBC with the emerging New Right coalition. Rogers, who prior to his election was known as a captivating preacher rather than a political activist, signaled his new ambitions in a high-profile sermon at the April 1980 "Washington for Jesus" rally on the National Mall. "The scream of the great American eagle has become but the twitter of a frightened sparrow," he warned the crowd of 200,000. "America must be born again or join the graveyard of nations."[31]

Political spectacles were not a practical way to reach the average layperson, but print media could do the job. For many evangelicals—especially Southern Baptists, who considered themselves set apart from the rest of American Protestantism and delighted in the cocoon of SBC institutions that sustained them from cradle to grave—the church newspaper remained a pillar of enlightenment and counsel. "Editors carry weight in SBC life," James Walker, who worked for the Arkansas convention, wrote to Don Harbuck, a prominent moderate in the state. "They speak to the issue before it hits the floor [at the national convention] and some people accept editorials as the 'voice of God.'" Their writers were more mission-minded now than ever before. The founding of *Christianity Today* presaged the rise of a conscious school of evangelical journalism grounded in the idea that a Christian journalist should not only report news of concern to his church, but discern the truth of all world events through an all-encompassing Christian worldview.[32] Baylor University, the oldest Southern Baptist university (and one of the few that escaped conservative control), offered a dedicated program in Christian journalism as early as the 1960s. Similar curricula sprouted at other schools. Pat Robertson, who had built his own television empire, founded Regent University in 1978 out of an express desire to boost evangelical influence in the media. From its earliest years, the university's curriculum stressed television and print journalism.

When conservatives began purging the SBC's agencies and boards of all opposition, the Baptist Press editors did their best to cover every stratagem—much to their subjects' displeasure. "SBC Journalism: Besieged!" long-time Baptist Press director Wilmer C. Fields titled his account of the "brazen, shameless attempt by fundamentalists to intimidate, bully and undermine Southern Baptist journalists and their publications." Fields argued that the campaign to co-opt church media was not merely another political tactic, but a threat to the core of Baptist identity. "Our forefathers wisely protected and cherished free access to full information," he wrote. "That structural freedom is linked to freedom of access to God, to an open Bible, to a divine right to private judgment in spiritual matters.... The state newspapers have been major channels for this ebb and flow of the Baptist mind and spirit. They are a vital part of the 'jugular' system [that Paul] Pressler and his political party set out to take over and dominate a decade ago."[33] Fields's conservative opponents would have most likely agreed. Their primary aim was, after all, to reclaim the Baptist mind and spirit for their cause, to refashion Southern Baptist identity around inerrancy and the culture wars. Obstreperous editors were only a mild inconvenience. Conservative leaders forced many—including Fields himself—to resign or retire.

HISTORY IS WRITTEN BY THE VICTORS

This battle over denominational identity and heritage was not unique to the Southern Baptist Convention. Nazarene scholar Timothy Smith, responding in the *Christian Century* to Harold Lindsell's accusations, argued that Wesleyans, Lutherans, and Calvinists who questioned inerrancy were not caving in to modern biblical scholarship but drawing "upon the writings of the Reformers themselves to affirm our conviction that the meanings, not the words, of biblical passages are authoritative, and that understanding these meanings requires close and critical study of the texts, rather than incantation of supposedly inerrant words." A young Assemblies of God scholar, observing "the tentacles of inerrancy" that strangled faculty at his church's educational institutions, noted "that the inerrancy position has never been officially adopted by the General Council and made part of the 'Statement of Fundamental Truths'"—but this had not stopped church leaders from insisting on inerrancy as a litmus test for true servants of the Assemblies of God. When Concordia Seminary faculty were forced to submit to questioning about their beliefs during the controversy in the Lutheran Church (Missouri Synod), both conservatives and their opponents described the interrogation as a chance to show "how Lutheran we really are and what it means to be Lutheran."[34] In churches riven by the debate over biblical authority in the 1970s and 1980s, both sides claimed authority through a selective reading of their shared tradition.

Historically, Southern Baptists have opposed the idea of creeds: formal statements of doctrine to which all members of a church must subscribe. Every Baptist is expected to articulate his beliefs for himself. The principle of "soul liberty" or "soul competency" means that each believer is accountable to no one but God. Few principles, however, are absolute in reality. Early Baptists approved confessions that reflected consensus and set boundaries for acceptable beliefs, although they did not recite them in worship. Southern Baptists, alarmed by Darwinism's challenge to traditional interpretations of the Bible, adopted a "Faith and Message" in 1925 declaring their belief that God created man "as recorded in Genesis." The convention elaborated on this statement in 1963 after seminary professor Ralph Elliott roiled Southern Baptists by advocating a nonliteral reading of the creation story in his book *The Message of Genesis*. The SBC emphasized the "proper balance between academic freedom and academic responsibility" in Christian education, but reiterated the fallible nature of any doctrinal statement, the possibility for future revision, and the importance of soul competency.[35]

Conservatives began to suspect that the historic Baptist resistance to creeds provided cover for heterodox interpretation of essential doctrines. They pushed for traditionalist revisions and more rigorous enforcement of statements of faith at the denomination's seminaries and colleges, and even agitated for emendation of the Baptist Faith and Message. Creeds, far from threatening the Baptist way, were the only way to preserve it. "To warn the inhabitants of the building of what is going on under the foundation is not to declare that every room in the building must be decorated exactly alike," wrote M. O. Owens. He lamented the theological promiscuity that went on in the guise of "soul competency": "Tragically, we are using that cliché ['Nobody tells a Baptist what to believe'] and concept to exalt a humanistic view of the competency of the soul, so that it would become far more definitive and important than the doctrine of the primacy and supremacy of Scripture."[36]

Moderates were furious, and accused the "creedalists" of betraying the church's founders. As early as 1969, partly in response to the publication of W. A. Criswell's inerrantist screed *Why I Preach That the Bible Is Literally True*, a small number of progressive students and professors affirmed a different strain of their heritage by founding the E. Y. Mullins Fellowship. They named the group for a turn-of-the-century theologian who helped the church grapple with modern biblical criticism and ushered in an age of relatively liberal scholarship. When reporters inquired, the fellowship named "the nature of biblical authority" as first among "the most pressing of issues facing us," along with academic freedom at the church's seminaries and publishing house, and the denomination's "minimal constructive response" to social problems like race conflict, poverty, and the Vietnam War. Samuel Hill, a progressive Southern Baptist historian who had recently published a fierce critique of Southern fundamentalism called *Southern Churches in Crisis* (1966), addressed the group's charter meeting. Members of the fellowship believed history was on their side, if only they could convince fellow believers that the "historic Baptist principle of the freedom of the individual to interpret the Bible for himself"—as well as the progressive, even mainline tilt of the SBC intelligentsia since the 1920s—was the narrative that should win out.[37]

By the late 1970s, things were not going their way. Increasingly marginalized in denominational leadership in the years that followed, moderates branded themselves as "loyalists" and the "traditional mainstream," lamenting their church's drift into the embrace of ultraconservative activists like Jerry Falwell and the Christian Reconstructionist movement. "No where in Baptist History, do I see the 'BRETHREN' our 'FOREFATHERS' ADVOCATING that Baptist churches of like faith and order sign a decree....The way I believe all Baptists believe is that the only 'CREED' that Southern Baptists could adopt, if they would adopt one 'WOULD BE THE NEW TESTAMENT,'" wrote a reader to the Baptist Press in 1977.[38]

Moderates were particularly disturbed by one enthusiasm they noticed among some conservative Southern Baptists: a zeal for Reformed theology. A small but influential cadre of conservative leaders promoted a view of biblical inerrancy that originated in Reformed scholasticism and nineteenth-century Presbyterian and Baptist scholarship, a Calvinist understanding of salvation, and a plan for engagement in politics that contravened classic Baptist conceptions of the division of church and state (not to mention the old southern doctrine of the "spirituality of the church," which had long discouraged clergy from speaking out on "worldly" matters like slavery and Jim Crow). They traced the long roots (going back at least to the Revolution-era Baptist leader Isaac Backus) of their concern that state-sponsored secularization of American public life, such as the Supreme Court's decision to ban scripture and prayer from public schools, did not reflect the Founders' intentions but rather threatened free exercise of religion. "What we demand is religious liberty, not mere toleration," wrote conservative leader Richard Land.[39] Conservatives also argued—correctly—that in the nineteenth century the dominant theology of many Baptists was far more Reformed than it later became. Therefore, they reasoned, it was the conservatives who were "traditionalist," who defended "original" Baptist identity.

Moreover, they believed that the only intellectually robust defense of inerrancy lay in the Reformed tradition's philosophical rationalism—a point that irritated conservatives in the more pietistic, revivalist wing of the SBC. Those conservative Baptists who doubted the authority of Calvin and his successors were "not aware of the basic structures of thought, rightly described as Reformed, that are necessary to protect the very gospel they insist is to be eagerly shared," said Albert Mohler, who came of age in the early days of the controversy and went on to serve as president of Southern Baptist Theological Seminary. In the 1980s and 1990s, Reformed theology began to enjoy a renaissance among conservative Southern Baptists, particularly young pastors—because, Mohler said, it was the only intellectual system that could stand up to modern American culture. "If you're a young Southern Baptist and you've been swimming against the tide of secularism . . . you're going to have to have a structure of thought that's more comprehensive than merely a deck of cards with all the right doctrines."[40] Like the neo-evangelicals who refashioned Reformed presuppositionalism and inerrancy for wide consumption decades earlier, Mohler believed his theology provided a worldview sturdy enough to withstand the perils of modern thought.

The conservatives won their crusade for a new Faith and Message in 2000. The revision added a more authoritarian preamble, calling for Baptists to accept "accountability to each other under the Word of God." In early drafts, the editors excised all mention of "soul competency" and "priesthood of believers," but after criticism from the convention, they restored these phrases in the document's preamble just before publication. The 2000 Baptist Faith and Message stressed a more Reformed theology of salvation, emphasized God-given gender roles (the justification that conservatives in 1984 used to pass a resolution against the ordination of women), and included more explicit condemnation of social "vices" like homosexuality.[41] By this time, many moderates had abandoned the SBC altogether.

The Southern Baptist conservatives won control of their church in two ways. They conquered the institutions of intellectual authority, and they used those institutions to propagate a new narrative of Southern Baptist history and identity. They portrayed their faction as a holy remnant reclaiming the God-given right to govern. Despite the denomination's long record of accommodating a range of theological opinions and forms of Baptist identity—what some Southern Baptist scholars have called the "Grand Compromise"—they insisted that only those members who shared their confidence in the inerrant Bible still belonged (leaders who favored Reformed theology could not be quite so uncompromising about that).[42]

Just as John Howard Yoder had protested Francis Schaeffer's account of history and politics, moderate Baptists flailed against the conservative juggernaut. Neither succeeded in halting the conservatives' rise to cultural and institutional power, but in their fight they made the vital point that the

Christian Right—in the unyielding and absolutist form that the movement had taken by the late 1980s—was not synonymous with American evangelicalism. Instead, the Christian Right was the product of a long struggle within evangelicalism, in which leaders with very different opinions and priorities vied to convince believers of their true duties to God and to their fellow man. In a religious tradition in which no single authority had ever reigned for long, in which *sola scriptura* had released a cascade of quarrels and no faction could resist issuing a creed, a declaration, a "call," or a list of "fundamentals" to define itself against its kin, Schaeffer, Falwell, and other self-appointed spokesmen of the Christian Right appeared, to casual observers, to reflect some kind of consensus. One must not underestimate the power in this illusion of solidarity—but one should not take it for reality, either.

Chapter 11

The Paradox of the Evangelical Imagination

IN 1994, THE EVANGELICAL HISTORIAN MARK NOLL PUBLISHED A SLIM volume called *The Scandal of the Evangelical Mind*. If anyone was in a position to assess evangelical intellectual life, it was Noll. He had become one of the most eminent scholars of American religious history, with a doctorate from Vanderbilt and a long list of books to his name (the White House would award him the National Humanities Medal in 2006). By all appearances, Noll's career seemed to prove that Carl Henry's vision for the rejuvenation of evangelical intellectual life had come true, at least in part. Yet now Noll found himself wondering whether "it is simply impossible to be, with integrity, both an evangelical and an intellectual."[1]

The Scandal of the Evangelical Mind chronicled the intellectual decay of Noll's community from the lofty heights of the Reformers, the Puritans, and Jonathan Edwards to the modern embarrassments of young-earth creationism and fundamentalist correspondence schools granting bogus PhDs. Even *Christianity Today*, once an ambitious magazine that "aspired to intellectual leadership, has been transformed into a journal of news and middle-brow religious commentary in order to simply stay in business." Noll complained that American evangelicals had lost all sense of history. The ruthless marketplace of American religion, the quest for popularity with the common man, the admixture of "Bible-onlyism," revivalism, end-times hysteria, and so-called common sense combined to sever twentieth-century evangelicals from their own tradition's resources just when they most needed help in reconciling the Bible with the modern age. Noll warned that their refusal to embrace new learning and sincerely study the world around them was not just an intellectual catastrophe, but a theological error. It placed them in league with the ancient Gnostics, Manichaeans, and other heretics who disrespected God's creation.[2]

Some reviewers wondered if Noll's own success did not belie his thesis. The *New York Times* noted that Noll was one of a number of well-regarded historians of religion who happened to be evangelical, while in other fields such as political science and philosophy, evangelical scholars were conducting innovative research and commanding mainstream respect—particularly in the areas of constitutional law and the intersection of religion and politics.[3] There was no doubt that American evangelicalism was more intellectually vibrant by the end of the millennium than it had been at any time in the past century. Many of Noll's colleagues in higher education had been working together for more than twenty years to finesse their relationships with secular academia, and to balance the tension between biblical authority and modern learning that bedeviled the evangelical classroom.

In other ways, however, the end of the century was no milestone, but a moment of frustration for reflective evangelicals. They had failed, despite growing national prominence, to solve their oldest disagreements and achieve long-standing ambitions. They had accrued political influence, built educational institutions, and expanded global ministries—yet Noll and others had good reason to fear that their community remained hostile to critical thinking and blind to the full implications of the gospel in all realms of human life. While a growing number of evangelical scholars earned secular accolades and collaborated with thinkers outside their own faith communities—particularly Roman Catholics—ordinary evangelicals seemed more inclined to listen to amateurs and demogogues with little interest in subtle theology or close attention to history. Was American evangelicalism thriving in spite of—or because of—these problems?

SCHOLARS' ANSWER TO THE "SCANDAL"

The old neo-evangelical dream of an evangelical university, first embodied in Billy Graham's plan for Crusade University in the late 1950s, never died. A generation before Noll published his manifesto, the Institute for Advanced Christian Studies—a Reformed organization that had funded earlier meetings of evangelical educators—sponsored a conference to explore the possibility of establishing a formal association of evangelical colleges that would "enable member institutions to attract the financial, professional, and social support necessary for survival as effective centers of learning" and, eventually, might culminate in a university system of affiliated colleges. Carl Henry warned attendees that "evangelical dialogue...does not engage as if the survival of civilization itself were at stake, and it is." The presidents of ten schools formally organized the Christian College Consortium in the spring of 1971.[4]

Over the next decade, these colleges transformed their approach to fundraising and drew selectively on the latest trends in professional academia. Although the consortium included non-Reformed colleges, its projects thrummed with the pulse of Reformed cultural theology, which justified all kinds of "worldly" innovations if they helped preserve the evangelical *Weltanschauung*. The CCC put on conferences to help faculty integrate their "world-and-life-views" and encouraged practical measures such as a master's program in management science for college administrators and new methods for recruiting students to consortium schools. If an applicant was rejected from Wheaton College, along with the rejection letter came a note encouraging the student to apply to less selective colleges in the consortium.[5]

The most critical advances came in the realm of funding. Passive reliance on church constituencies and alumni was no longer sufficient to finance a competitive institution. In 1973, the Lilly Endowment, an Indianapolis foundation with a special interest in education and religion, pledged $300,000 over three years to the consortium to support several cooperative endeavors, such as regular "Faith/Learning/Living Institute" conferences.[6] Over the following years, as the consortium's membership expanded and launched new projects, including foreign exchange programs and more faculty training, the funding base grew. Pew Charitable Trusts provided the bulk of the consortium's support through the 1980s. Further funds came from businesses such as ServiceMaster, a landscaping and home maintenance company founded by Marion E. Wade, a C.S. Lewis enthusiast whose family's financial gift launched Wheaton's collection. In 1978, the consortium created a National Advisory Board staffed with impressive figures from politics and business like Oregon senator Mark Hatfield and Tom Phillips, chairman of the defense technology company Raytheon, which helped impress donors.[7]

These developments ought to have provided Noll cause for optimism. He and his peers were among the main beneficiaries. In the late 1980s and 1990s, younger evangelical scholars who trained at elite secular institutions began to implement secular development schemes in Christian higher education. Perhaps the earliest evangelical academic to win considerable grant money was Timothy Smith, who used it to build his graduate program at Johns Hopkins. He mentored several notable scholars as PhD students, postdoctoral fellows, and conference participants, including Grant Wacker, Nathan Hatch, Margaret Bendroth, Darryl Hart, and Joel Carpenter. Carpenter went on to direct the religion program at the Pew Charitable Trusts, where he worked "to identify individuals and institutions who can 'make a difference' in the academic community through evangelical Christian scholarship."[8]

In 1985 Pew founded the Evangelical Scholars program, and later established a fund to support young Christians trying to make it in academia. Over the course of the 1990s, Pew spent more than $14 million funding summer seminars, lectureships, and stipends for promising evangelical academics while they finished a research project or wrote their first book. In 1990, 33 percent of Pew scholars were publishing work in secular outlets. Eleven years later that figure had risen to 80 percent.[9] Students reaped rewards from the consortium's expansion, too. Throughout the 1990s the organization's study-abroad programs multiplied (India, China, Uganda, and beyond) and a Film Studies Center opened in Los Angeles for those who wanted to dive into the trenches of culture-making. The consortium also established a sister organization, the Christian College Coalition, to represent the interests of evangelical colleges in Washington. As the CCC grew more sophisticated, the organization helped widen the distance between elite evangelical colleges—which built endowments, hired faculty trained at top universities, and attracted students from around the world—and the vast number of small, more parochial schools that continued to struggle along.[10]

In the Classroom of Catholicism

The influence of colleges in the consortium and coalition is difficult to judge. Their student enrollments remained relatively small (today the consortium's successor organization, the Council for Christian Colleges and Universities, includes 118 schools in North America and more than 50 affiliated institutions abroad).[11] Anecdotal evidence suggests that a high proportion of their graduates have gone on to serve the evangelical community in some way, and their faculty publish books read by pastors and other evangelical leaders—but these factors remain slippery and hard to trace. There was, however, another route by which evangelical scholars sought intellectual and political clout: They began working closely with Roman Catholics.

The roots of evangelicals' affinity for Catholic thinkers predate the culture wars of the 1980s and 1990s and developed on the Left as well as the Right. Fundamentalist philosopher Gordon Clark mused wistfully about Catholicism's intellectual appeal as early as the 1940s. The interconfessional charismatic revivals of the 1960s and 1970s, following on the heels of Vatican II, compelled many evangelicals to reconsider their contempt for Catholic piety and acknowledge that Catholic philosophy might, at least in part, be Christian philosophy. Evangelical scholars praised Catholic intellectuals like Jacques Maritain and Pierre Teilhard de Chardin for their ability to stir intellectual debate beyond the bounds of their own church.[12] They realized that despite many years spent trying to nurture a thriving and Christian life of the mind, evangelicals had only a shadow of the success that American Catholics enjoyed.

Their collaboration with Catholics was, in the first place, institutional. They sought accommodation in, and welcomed invitations from, the massive academic edifice that American Catholics had developed over the course of the twentieth century. In the 1970s and 1980s the University of Notre Dame began recruiting prominent evangelical academics, notably philosopher Alvin Plantinga, historians George Marsden and Nathan Hatch, as well as ethicists John Howard Yoder and Stanley Hauerwas; later on the university lured Mark Noll and sociologist Christian Smith. From the early 1990s, Notre Dame housed the headquarters of the Pew Younger Scholars Program, an influential sponsor of young evangelical academics. At Princeton University, Robert George, a Catholic legal philosopher who joined the faculty in 1985, developed a following among evangelical undergraduates. In 2000—with the help of generous donations from foundations linked to Opus Dei—he founded the James Madison Program in American Ideals and Institutions. The program has become a magnet for evangelical students and scholars. Conferences and retreats sponsored by the Intercollegiate Studies Institute, William F. Buckley's farm team for young conservatives, also attracted increasing numbers of young evangelicals. They came eager to learn from ISI's clique of libertarians, Catholics, and libertarian-inclined Catholics who modified the tenets of classical liberalism to defend capitalism as the economic system best suited for nurturing not only free individuals, but thriving Christian families.[13]

How did these conservative Catholics do it? How did they defend traditional Christian mores in a manner that the secular media seemed to grudgingly respect? Despite evangelicals' declarations of *sola scriptura* and doubts that church history had anything to teach them about Jesus, they began to envy the intellectual heft that came with two thousand years of Catholic theology and philosophy. Catholic intellectuals commanded a wider hearing by speaking in terms of natural law, a philosophical tradition that blended scholastic theology with ancient Greek and Roman ideas about the ultimate ends of humanity. The core idea was simple: God had created every human being and human relationship with a *telos*, a final goal, and he designed the universe to operate according to laws that facilitate these goals. The tradition of natural law was firmly rooted in dogma, but in a pinch—for the purposes of lobbying Congress or convincing a skeptical journalist—it could be neutered of its Christian premises and portrayed as an appeal to quasi-Kantian universals and common sense. George Marsden encouraged evangelical scholars to develop a strategy "equivalent to Catholic natural law arguments . . . their having a religious *source* does not automatically exclude one's views from acceptance in the academy so long as one argues for them on other, more widely accessible grounds." Michael Cromartie, vice president of the Ethics and Public Policy Center who has spearheaded dialogue between evangelicals and Catholics, wrote that natural law offers a "common moral grammar" that religious and secular people can both accept.[14]

Evangelicals' enthusiasm for natural law grew as they heard Catholics use it to attack abortion and gay marriage. Marriage between a man and a woman "is fundamentally *natural*," wrote Pennsylvania senator Rick Santorum, a Catholic who homeschooled his children and would soon become a darling of the evangelical Right. "The promise of natural law is that we will be the happiest, and freest, when we follow the law built into our nature as men and women. For liberals, however, *nature* is too confining, and thus is the enemy of *freedom*." Natural law enabled conservative Christians to forbid anything that they believed drew God's ire while still, they insisted, defending the Declaration of Independence and the Constitution. The Founding Fathers did not mention natural law explicitly in the nation's holiest documents because its rule was so obvious to them, implied in the immortal words "we hold these truths to be self-evident."[15]

Catholic intellectuals had realized the limits of natural law's consensus-building potential in the 1960s, when both opponents and advocates of contraception used natural law reasoning to make their case (one side emphasized the creation of life as the *telos* of sexual intercourse, while the other emphasized the fulfillment of the marriage sacrament).[16] But evangelical intellectuals were seduced by a simplistic version of natural law for the same reason that presuppositionalism and the notion of a "Christian worldview" were so attractive: It enabled them to reject the secular insistence upon a neutral public sphere in which religion had no place, and no argument could stand without basis in objective, evidence-based reasoning.

Natural law, based in God's commands, obliterates the modern distinction between values and facts. By its logic, moral judgments are not opinions based in emotional empathy or religious belief, but reflections of the way the world truly is. Alasdair MacIntyre, an ethicist at Notre Dame and late convert to Catholicism who became a hero to many evangelical intellectuals, dismissed the distinction between facts and values that has reigned over modern Western thought since the time of David Hume. Any viable moral system must be founded on the "fact" of human nature—human nature as divinely ordained.[17] Just as presuppositionalists argued that atheistic values undergirded the so-called facts of the secular public sphere, advocates of natural law reasoned that the neutrality of Enlightenment-based science and politics was an illusion. Christians had an equal right—indeed, a greater right than secular humanists—to argue about the public good from their own values-based perspective.

The Lutheran priest and commentator Richard John Neuhaus articulated this claim in his influential 1984 book *The Naked Public Square* (he would convert to Catholicism six years later). Neuhaus's biography could not have been more different from the average conservative evangelical's. In earlier years his politics were decidedly left-wing. He joined the Jesuit priest Daniel Berrigan and Rabbi Abraham Joshua Heschel to found Clergy and Laymen Concerned about Vietnam and backed Eugene McCarthy for president in 1968. But *Roe v. Wade* chastened his faith in liberalism, and by the mid-1980s he shared evangelicals' concerns about the impact of secularism on American culture. The point of *The Naked Public Square* was that the bareness of the marketplace was a bad thing. The values of American citizens—who were overwhelmingly religious—ought to frame public debate. "Christian truth, if it is true, is public truth. It is accessible to public reason. It impinges on public space. At some critical points of morality and ethics it speaks to public policy," he wrote.[18]

A few years later Neuhaus and Charles Colson founded Evangelicals and Catholics Together, a series of ecumenical conferences and declarations that signaled more than agreement on social issues like abortion and euthanasia. The organization formalized an alliance in which Roman Catholic philosophy would quietly buttress the policies of an ascendant, and outwardly Protestant, Religious Right. As Damon Linker recounts in his survey of conservative Catholics' influence on recent American politics, *The Theocons*, ECT's preliminary discussions began in 1985 among a variety of concerned pastors, politicians, and intellectuals, including the ubiquitous Carl Henry. In 1994 the organization published a formal declaration, "Evangelicals and Catholics Together: The Christian Mission for the Third Millennium." Many of the best-known signatories, such as Bill Bright and Pat Robertson, were evangelical—but most of the document's philosophical heft and moral rhetoric came straight from previous publications by Catholic intellectuals like Neuhaus, Michael Novak, George Weigel, and Pope John Paul II.[19]

ECT earned as much condemnation as praise in evangelical circles. However, the alliance presaged the prominent role that Roman Catholic intellectuals would play in the formation of national policy under George W. Bush, the darling of evangelical voters who testified to his rebirth in Christ and expanded government collaboration with religious organizations in charity and relief work. Neuhaus, Novak, and their colleagues built an infrastructure of magazines (particularly *First Things*, founded in 1990), think tanks, and relationships with sympathetic political actors—Illinois representative Henry Hyde, Rick Santorum, Supreme Court Justices Antonin Scalia and Clarence Thomas, and many others—that enabled them to influence the drafting of laws against partial-birth abortion, a proposed constitutional amendment against gay marriage, and other ideological benchmarks of the Bush administration.[20]

The Christian Right's electoral and policy successes owe much to the decades that conservative evangelicals spent quietly transforming their institutions to engage secular culture while continually repositioning themselves against that mainstream. No unified agenda drove the work of evangelical educators affiliated with the Christian College Consortium, but their minuet with secular academia and savvy cultivation of donors nurtured a prospering academic counterculture. This burgeoning evangelical intelligentsia received a boost from Catholics. Their collaboration has born political fruit because it has never been solely a political alliance, but an intellectual partnership—although the fact that evangelicals had to outsource some of their most effective political thinking to Rome hinted at the frailty of their intellectual renewal.

ANTI-INTELLECTUAL BUT THRIVING

By century's end, there was much to celebrate in American evangelicalism. Sociologist D. Michael Lindsay interviewed hundreds of evangelicals who had entered the highest ranks of business, academia, Hollywood, national politics, and the media—many of whom were nurtured by Christian colleges and thriving evangelical networks in secular academe. Surveys of the evangelical grassroots revealed a new level of curiosity and tolerance toward different cultures and beliefs.[21] The demands of the postcolonial mission field had convinced many evangelicals to scrap old prejudices and think creatively about the gospel's relationship to human culture. Christian missions abroad were booming as a result. Charismatic and liturgical renewal eroded the walls between Christian churches, and evangelicals were keen to tap the history and theology of their Anglican, Catholic, and Orthodox brethren.

"I believe we have the best intellectual networking going on anywhere," Richard Mouw, president of Fuller Theological Seminary, told *Christianity Today* in 1995. "Evangelical political scientists get together. Evangelical sociologists get together. Evangelical literati get together; evangelical philosophers, evangelical economists. We have official organizations, workshops, conferences, symposia, publications, and e-mail networks. There's nothing like it in any other part of the Christian world. I can't imagine a better place to be an intellectual right now than in evangelicalism."[22] If the evangelical mind was flourishing, was Mark Noll wrong? How could such conflicting phenomena—intellectual renaissance and anti-Enlightenment revolt; modern tolerance and antimodern dogma—coexist? How could they describe the same culture?

The divide between ivied academia and lay believers is a gap, not a chasm. It has been no barrier to legions of students who carry the lessons of the classroom into the world, not to mention the dissemination of scholars' books, sermons, and their endeavors in public policy. But if intellectuals have more influence than many believe, they have struggled to match the cultural clout of the popularizers and propagandists working in the trenches of the Christian Right. These individuals have been keenly interested in history and theology—as weapons in their campaign to align American culture with their reading of God's word.

In 1991, sociologist James Davison Hunter published *Culture Wars: The Struggle to Define America*. The book examined the recent polarization of American politics and culture: the fading of old boundaries like economic class, ethnic hatreds, and religious denominations, and Americans' realignment into blocs defined by "the impulse toward orthodoxy and the impulse toward progressivism," "different moral visions" governed by different sources of authority.[23] Hunter's anatomy of the culture wars was, in some ways, a salute to conservative evangelicals' coming of age in national politics. The leadership of the Christian Right had transformed from a disorderly mix of local organizers, rogue anticommunist crusaders, and pastor-politicians into a vanguard of canny activists who knew how to galvanize voters.

The late 1980s had been rocky. Jerry Falwell's Moral Majority lost momentum after Falwell alienated black Americans and many of his supporters with comments in favor of apartheid in South Africa. Falwell resigned in 1987, and the Moral Majority folded two years later. That same year the tongues-speaking televangelist (and, soon enough, presidential candidate) Pat Robertson tapped Georgia activist Ralph Reed to found the Christian Coalition, an organization that quickly outstripped the Moral Majority in mobilizing supporters, infiltrating local politics, and building alliances with nonevangelical conservatives. With the shrewd decision to support George Bush over the more conservative Pat Buchanan in the 1992 election, the Christian Coalition achieved unprecedented power within the Republican Party.[24] Bill Clinton won the White House, but Republicans took control of

Congress in the midterm elections two years later. Conservative Christian lobbyists thrived in the corridors of Washington.

A new generation of gurus arose to pick up where Francis Schaeffer left off, and they had little interest in the Anabaptist tradition of peace witness or Wesleyan ideas about Christ's call for social justice—or in Mark Noll's nuanced accounts of American history. They made heavy use of an ideology grounded in biblical inerrancy and the intellectual tool first popularized by the neo-evangelicals decades earlier: that all-purpose spoiler in any debate, the "Christian worldview."

In 1989 David Barton, a Texas political activist and former K-12 principal with a BA from Oral Roberts University, launched a ministry called WallBuilders. The organization, which earned a national reputation among evangelicals, offered a selective narrative of American history aimed at proving the country's foundation in a "biblical worldview" that happened to affirm the Christian Right's political platform. In Barton's telling—which he continues to broadcast as a regular guest on conservative television programs, promote in the backrooms of Washington, and peddle to schools and homeschoolers in the form of history curricula, books, DVDs, puzzles, poster sets, and other paraphernalia—the Founding Fathers were Bible-believers who never intended the separation of church and state as liberals understand it. Students ought to study the real heroes of twentieth-century social revolution, like Phyllis Schlafly and Jerry Falwell, rather than anti-American troublemakers like Cesar Chavez and Thurgood Marshall. They should learn that the "war on Islamic terrorism" is a proud American tradition that began with the Barbary Wars.[25]

Barton has won a wide following by presenting himself as an autodidact everyman who does not twist history into ivory-tower contortions. He blames academic historians for deadening Americans' interest in history and misleading them about their own heritage.[26] In 2012, the evangelical publisher Thomas Nelson sought to capitalize on Barton's self-publishing success by acquiring his book *The Jefferson Lies*, in which the famously skeptical and slave-owning president is reborn as a Bible-believer and friend of all humankind. However, when scores of critics barraged Thomas Nelson with complaints about Barton's distortions of history, the press—a Christian publishing powerhouse owned by HarperCollins, and faithful to the professional standards of the industry—recalled the book.[27]

Barton defended his work, although he has grudgingly qualified some of his more dubious evidence for the Founders' theocratic vision by acknowledging that many of his favorite quotations are "unconfirmed." He argues that he simply gives readers the facts, and they can form their own opinions through inductive reasoning—the analysis of data with one's own common sense, the learning method that long dominated fundamentalist Bible colleges and still holds sway in many evangelical circles. Yet Barton's clashes with professional historians suggest that to him, making sense of the facts is impossible outside of the "biblical worldview." His ministry epitomizes the inconsistent combination of the presuppositionalists' artful dodge (there is no use in discussion outside the Christian worldview!) with the evidence-based confidence and populist accessibility of Common Sense Realism (the Bible, as even a child knows, is a storehouse of objective facts—facts which illuminate the rest of God's history). The loyalty of Barton's fans, despite scholars' tireless exposure of his crimes against the past, confirms that truth is no obstacle to a story that people want to believe.

This strategy permits Barton—and his counterparts in the creationism business, such as Ken Ham of "Answers in Genesis"—to dismiss opposing interpretations of the evidence, be it in colonial archives or the fossil record, the latest studies on gun violence or global warming forecasts. They insist upon their own worldview as the only clear window on reality: a worldview in which the faithful Christian can revere the Enlightenment without compromising the authority of the Bible. They have joined forces with other conservative activists to discourage any talk of bipartisan compromise in favor of a vision of war between irreconcilable notions of reality. "Nothing short of a great Civil War of Values rages today throughout North America," wrote James Dobson, founder of Focus on the Family, and Gary Bauer, head of the Family Research Council, in their 1990 book *Children at Risk*. "Two sides with vastly differing and incompatible worldviews are locked in a bitter conflict that permeates every level of society...children are the prize to the winners of the second great civil war."[28]

"Our choices are shaped by what we believe is real and true, right and wrong, good and beautiful. Our choices are shaped by our worldview," wrote Charles Colson and Nancy Pearcey in their paean to Schaeffer, *How Now Shall We Live?* Colson, the Watergate-felon-turned-born-again-crusader, went on to found the Centurions Program, a series of newsletters, regular meetings, and "thought-provoking reading assignments" that promised to admit subscribers to the growing ranks of "worldview movement leaders" who run their businesses according to "biblical principles," make political decisions "from a biblical perspective," and "create God-honoring culture."[29] Colson's program is representative of the proliferation of conferences, publications, Sunday school and homeschool curricula, institutes, and summer programs that offer evangelicals "worldview training." They range from James Dobson's "Truth Project" to the Worldview Academy youth and family camps in Midland, Texas, and the "Worldview Initiative" of Bryan College in Dayton, Tennessee (named for William Jennings Bryan, and founded in the town that witnessed his Scopes Trial martyrdom). Whitefield College in Florida recruits students with a "Worldview Curriculum"; Boyce College, the Louisville school affiliated with the Southern Baptist Theological Seminary, offers a certificate in "Worldview Studies." These programs assure evangelicals that the right ideas can change the world. They have cast American politics as a battleground of good and evil, snapping in two an already stunted political spectrum.

Beyond the Christian Right

Is anti-intellectualism, then, chiefly a sin of the Christian Right? The answer is no: The confusion of authority that best accounts for the culture described in these pages is not an exclusively conservative or liberal trait. For good and for ill, it has been the defining characteristic of evangelicalism as a whole since its origins in the aftermath of the Reformation.

A vocal minority has vigorously contested the Christian Right's grip on evangelicalism's public image. Evangelicals in a variety of traditions, particularly Wesleyan Holiness Christians and Anabaptists, have decoupled Christianity from conservative politics and called for believers to sink their resources into social justice, international relief, and environmentalism. They have protested the narrow interpretation of scripture, selective notions of discipleship, and assumptions about human knowledge and religious experience that have come to dominate the Christian Right.

The same year that Mark Noll published his book, scholars at Point Loma Nazarene College (now University) presented a proposal for a "Wesleyan Center for 21st Century Studies" meant to bring Wesleyan

Holiness theology to bear on modern intellectual problems. In part, the proposal was an effort to liberate the evangelical mind from the straitjacket of Reformed, overly rationalistic theology. The center sponsors scholars and organizes conferences to enrich non-Reformed thinking about theology, culture, and politics—even as non-Reformed colleges find that they must engage more and more with Reformed ideas in order to expand student recruitment beyond denominational boundaries. They are simultaneously resisting and succumbing to what one professor at Messiah College, a school with Holiness and Anabaptist roots, called "evangelical homogenization."[30]

However, broad trends beyond the ranks of the Christian Right have hurt the evangelical mind as much as they have helped it. The Church Growth movement began as a critique of Western individualism: Donald McGavran chastised missionaries for overemphasizing individual conversions rather than plunging into indigenous culture and bringing entire "people groups" to Christ. Yet critics—especially non-Westerners—have pointed out that Church Growth morphed into a rationalistic cult of social science with an emphasis on evangelism over justice. It has encouraged Christians to think solely in terms of souls won or lost, ignoring society's larger structures and inequalities. Many megachurches—Church Growth's great success story—have fallen prey to the prosperity gospel, seeking signs of God's favor in material wealth. They endorse easy suburban existence as a way of winning seekers, and hold missions hostage "to market-driven materialism" and "Western, white culture," according to Korean-American professor of evangelism Soong-Chan Rah.[31]

Dialogue with Catholics and other nonevangelical Christians offered some correction to the Church Growth movement's fixation on cultural accommodation and baptism rates. However—save for those few who converted—evangelicals attracted to other Christian traditions have made those traditions their own. They assemble do-it-yourself liturgies from a hodgepodge of monastic prayers and mystics' visions. They lionize medieval dissenters—Celtic monks, or renegade Franciscans—but don't understand their broader Catholic context. Without quite realizing what they have done, evangelicals often use these ancient teachings and practices to confirm, rather than challenge, their own assumptions. History becomes a sidekick to one's twenty-first-century journey with Jesus.

There is no better example than a recent movement among young evangelical pastors who call themselves the "Emergent" or "Emerging" Church. Many came of age in megachurches where they resented the diet of theological pabulum sweetened with pop culture and salted with lockstep politics. In the early 1990s, they began to notice that younger members were drifting away from church. Traditional approaches to the Bible did not hold their attention. Emergent Church proponents concluded that in post-Christian America, Christians must think like missionaries in their own backyards and stop speaking of the gospel as a set of propositional truths—an obsolete language that belonged to Enlightenment philosophes rather than Christ.

These pastors, writers, and activists rhapsodize about "postmodernity," the fragmentation of narratives and truth claims, and the fluid conceptions of human identity that began to agitate Western intellectual life in the last third of the twentieth century. Emergent Church proponents view this cultural instability as a grand opportunity. Now that even atheist philosophers declare that unified, objective truth is only an illusion, Christians may assert their worldview as a valid competitor beside secular rationalism, dialectical materialism, Islam, or any other set of assumptions about reality. Postmodernism could "be a catalyst for the church to reclaim its faith not as a system of truth dictated by neutral reason but rather as a story that requires 'eyes to see and ears to hear,'" wrote James Smith, a professor at Calvin College, in a book based on lectures he gave while a visiting scholar at L'Abri.[32]

Some young evangelicals are drawn to Emergent pastors' frank acknowledgment of the Bible's inconsistencies; their confidence that Christianity can stand up to modern intellectual critique; and their call to a form of activism very different from that of the Religious Right. An evangelical activist named Shane Claiborne has become an icon of the Emergent approach to social justice. Long-haired and unkempt, a former Willow Creek intern who has worked in Calcutta alongside Mother Teresa, Claiborne founded a commune called the Simple Way devoted to feeding and ministering to its rough Philadelphia neighborhood. He lectures around the country (asking churches that invite him to "fast" from energy consumption to compensate for the impact of his travel by car or plane) and urges evangelicals to embrace their social and environmental responsibilities. In 2008 he co-authored a book, *Jesus for President*, calling on American Christians to see through the self-serving politicians who had seduced so many evangelical voters.[33] He echoes Yoder's and Hauerwas's calls for radical Christian discipleship and a return to the politics of the Sermon on the Mount.

Evangelicals who embrace the Emergent Church want to shake off their parents' politics and decide for themselves what the Bible means. They want what they call an "authentic" Christianity. Like the Jesus People movement thirty years earlier, the Emergent Church is as much a personal style as a set of beliefs. Adherents are known for their goatees, their funky glasses, their tattoos—their visible rejection of prim and uptight evangelicalism. The funny thing is that authenticity was the original aim of the megachurches against which Emergent evangelicals believe they are rebelling. Bill Hybels, founder of the Willow Creek empire, was a frustrated twenty-something once. In the early 1970s he found that even as a student at the conservative Trinity College in Deerfield, Illinois, he could not avoid "the counter-cultural emphasis on the importance of intimacy and authenticity" (after all, Jim Wallis was a classmate at Trinity's divinity school). Under the guidance of his mentor at Trinity, Gilbert Bilezikian, Hybels drifted away from his own Reformed background toward a higher view of human nature and an emphasis on the believer's intimate relationship with God. This same feel-good holiness saturates the books and articles produced by proponents of the Emergent Church. Celebrating "authenticity" glosses over the vexed dimensions of Christian theology and history, and disregards human depravity. The doctrine of original sin demands that Christians must not celebrate all that is "authentic" in their nature. "We don't talk about sin very often," admitted pastor Mike Yaconelli. "Do I believe in sin? Of course....What we're all longing for is good news."[34]

Worship is more a therapeutic means to personal fulfillment than submission to a higher authority. Many Emergent pastors seem to find the very notion of clergy slightly embarrassing. Karen Ward, who pioneered Emergent worship at a hybrid Lutheran–Episcopal church in Seattle, compared the Emergent Church to the Linux computer programming system: "Everyone's a coder; there's no fixed structure," she said. In her church's liturgy, she strives for "'godly play,' like Montessori church."[35] Emergent churches often abandon forward-facing pews for circular seating that emphasizes equality and community, and prefer a DJ mixing trance music and plainchant somewhere out of sight instead of a praise band that demands attention onstage. Worshippers may join in medieval chants and patristic prayers, but church history serves as a resource, a liturgical larder, rather than a tradition to which today's believers must conform.

The Emergent Church is the latest act in the wave of antimodernist revolt inaugurated by liturgical renewal and charismatic revival, a rebellion whose central insight is that rationalistic fundamentalism, as much as liberalism, is a mass of worldly accretions. The historical record and human feeling, not the illusion of inerrancy, are supposed to command authority in the post-Christian age. Yet American evangelicals' craving for clear authority is second only to their refusal to let any authority boss them around. Skeptics note that the Emergent Church is a movement of quintessentially evangelical individualists. "By constantly appealing to the 'capital T' Tradition, and then in effect picking and choosing from its offerings, they do not succeed in living out any of the traditions that flow from the Tradition, but create their own eclectic, ad hoc churchmanship," wrote D. A. Carson, a professor at Trinity Evangelical Divinity School. "It is controlled by what these emerging thinkers judge to be appropriate in the postmodern world—and this results, rather ironically, in one of the most self-serving appeals to tradition I have ever seen."[36]

The limitations of the Emergent Church follow the pattern apparent throughout American evangelical history: the dilemma of a community that extols individualism but ensnares every individual in a web of clashing authorities. This conflict has been sharpest in higher education, where—because of financial and cultural pressure to accommodate secular norms—evangelicals have made the greatest strides in balancing these contesting standards. They still struggle, however, to please two gods: to negotiate between the professional mainstream and their own constituents. On a recent visit to Wheaton College, political scientist Alan Wolfe proclaimed its students "as outstanding as any students in America."[37] Yet even at evangelicalism's flagship institution, the faculty, students, administrators, and watchful alumni still expect open inquiry to stop short of challenging fundamental doctrines.

Some evangelicals protest that a different orthodoxy stifles dissent in mainstream university classrooms: the tyranny of atheistic humanism. They are right, and this is exactly the point. Modern intellectual inquiry is not a free-for-all. It is a rule-bound endeavor that falls to pieces unless all parties accept—without reservation—the authority of secular reason. Several evangelical scholars, most notably George Marsden, have called for Christians in the academy to be braver in bringing their faith into their classrooms and publications. Yet Marsden's prescriptions for "the outrageous idea of Christian scholarship" shun dogmatism in favor of "arguments and evidence that are publicly accessible." Marsden, a first-rate historian, has not won the respect of his colleagues by citing scripture in his footnotes. He asks religious scholars to leave the supernatural aside and "support the rules necessary for constructive exchange of ideas in a pluralistic setting.... I am not, as some might suppose, challenging pragmatic liberalism as the modus operandi for the contemporary academy."[38]

The presuppositionalists are correct. The secular university is not neutral. Stanley Fish, in his critique of modern university culture, explains the principle that makes pathbreaking research and inquiry possible:

> Academic freedom urges the interrogation of all propositions and the privileging of none, the equal right of all voices to be heard, no matter how radical or unsettling, and the obligation to subject even one's most cherished convictions to the scrutiny of reason. What academic freedom excludes is any position that refuses that obligation—any position that rests on pronouncements such as "I am the way" or "Thou shalt have no other gods before me."[39]

The academy's worship of objectivity dissolved decades ago in the postmodern mire. Today scholars in all fields are trained to look out for their own biases and prejudices. But once we complete the ritual of scourging our assumptions, most of us strive to approach the ideal of perfect disinterest. We can never achieve it, but intellectual progress demands that we try, that we venerate the goddess we can never know.

The problem with evangelical intellectual life is not that its participants obey authority. All rational thought requires the rule of some kind of law based on irreducible assumptions. The problem is that evangelicals attempt to obey multiple authorities at the same time. They demand that presuppositions trump evidence while counting the right kind of evidence as universal fact. They insist that modern reason must buttress faith, that scripture and spiritual feeling align with scientific reality. Reflecting on his frustrations as a curious young person in a conservative Pentecostal community, Baylor University theologian Roger Olson offered some confusing advice—advice that would ring true for many evangelicals precisely because it is so muddled:

> What I am saying is that true authority, authority of this highest and most important kind, lies on the side of right and not of might. In deciding what is "right" a person ought to take into account many factors, including tradition and community consensus, but in the final analysis the person seeking truth must go with true authority against tradition and community consensus if reason in the broadest and best sense demands it. It is never right to go against reason. When rational proof is unavailable, as is often the case, a person may legitimately go with "reasons of the heart" or simply submit to tradition and community. But when these contradict themselves or prove baseless except on whims and fancies of religious leaders, the person has every right and even should break away from traditional belief and community consensus or hold belief in suspension until greater light dawns . . . in the final analysis the individual really is the only one who can and must decide what he or she believes is true—especially in matters of ultimate concern.[40]

Some version of this dilemma afflicts all thoughtful people, whether their "reasons of the heart" are based in religious experience, economic dogma, their mother's advice, emotional impulse, or some other source. However, evangelicals—in refusing to come to terms with the conflicting powers camouflaged in that thorny phrase, *sola scriptura*—have turned this torment into the hallmark of their identity.

BEYOND THE STANDARDS IN THIS WORLD

Two decades after his definitive account of the culture wars left pundits talking of little else, sociologist James Davison Hunter published a book called *To Change the World*. He took to task evangelicals of all stripes— from James Dobson to Jim Wallis, theonomists to neo-Anabaptists—for going about cultural change all wrong. To Hunter, all this talk of "world-views" is a distraction. Ideas are not nearly as important as evangelicals take them to be. While they enthuse about all the good that a Christian can do if he or she only "lives Christianly" and develops a "biblical worldview," the strongholds of cultural power in America—the mainstream media; the elite universities; the blockbuster television studios—seem to remain stridently secular. Hunter accused evangelicals of taking ideas, "hearts and minds," to be the building blocks of culture while ignoring the importance of institutions and the long-range and often subconscious influence of history and language. When evangelicals do appreciate history, Hunter observed, they warp it into self-serving myth. On both the Left and the Right, their plunge into politics has so thoroughly corrupted them that evangelicals now struggle to disentangle the gospel from the interests and assumptions of the state.[41]

In many respects, Hunter's critique is correct. Yet American evangelicals are not as naïve about the workings of culture as he suggests. The neo-evangelicals' timely adaptation of "worldview speak" caught on precisely because it did resonate with a broader cultural shift, a presuppositionalist vogue on the rise in the West. Evangelical intellectuals and activists believed that, as Carl Henry put it, "the modern ideology needs to be remade," and they understood that task to require the right infrastructure as well as the right doctrines. Those church leaders concerned about the undue influence of certain Reformed ideas know that their own theologies will wither without the protection and promotion of institutions.

In the political realm, the rise of the Christian Right demonstrates that the power of networks, organization, and media is not lost on evangelical activists. Most would agree with Hunter that cultural change unfolds gradually, over multiple generations. However, this does not nullify conservatives' legislative and political victories, such as the defunding and restriction of abortion in many states, state constitutional amendments prohibiting gay marriage, and successful campaigns to influence the content of public school history textbooks along lines that would please Francis Schaeffer and David Barton. Conservative evangelicals are not holed away in a cloistered subculture. They are embedded in and shaping the policies of mainstream institutions ranging from local school boards to Walmart. The sheer number of Americans who identity as evangelical Protestant—some 80 million, or 26.3 percent of the population, according to a recent Pew survey—makes it difficult to dismiss their cultural clout.[42]

Evangelicals are idealists, yes. They are also pragmatists. They talk so much of "the Christian worldview" because they believe in it—but also because it is a powerful rhetorical strategy. It curtails debate, justifies hardline politics, and discourages sympathetic voters from entertaining thoughts of moderation or compromise.

Neither conservative nor progressive evangelicals have achieved the influence they dream of (although sometimes they strategically exaggerate stories of their persecution). Hunter is right to note their frustrated place on the margins of the most elite institutions of American culture, such as the *New York Times* and the Ivy League. However, if evangelicals stew in their own resentments and tales of victimhood, the secular intelligentsia— supposedly ensconced in thrones of cultural power—has its own narrative of alienation and weakness. How secure or influential are the ivied battlements of Harvard when the reactionary, Bible-waving hordes are at the gate, chipping away at abortion rights, progressive taxation, and public schools? This is a hallmark of modern democracy. All parties feel equally impotent and endangered.

The phenomena that Hunter identifies spring from evangelicals' crisis of authority. The anti-intellectual inclinations in evangelical culture stem not from wholehearted and confident obedience to scripture, or the assurance that God will eventually corral all nonbelievers, but from deep disagreements over what the Bible means, a sincere desire to uphold the standards of modern reason alongside God's word—and the defensive reflexes that outsiders' skepticism provokes. The cult of the Christian worldview is one symptom of the effort by many evangelical leaders to fold competing sources of authority into one, to merge inference with assumptions. The evangelicals who adopt this soft presuppositionalism hope that it might prove to be a viable political currency, one that can buy cultural capital where proof texts and personal testimony fail.

These habits of mind have crippled evangelicals in their pursuit of what secular thinkers take to be the aims of intellectual life: the tasks of discovering new knowledge, creating original and provocative art, and puzzling out the path toward a more humane civilization. When the neo-evangelicals set out to resuscitate the evangelical mind seventy years ago they shared these goals, but they also harbored another set of ambitions. The purpose of *Christianity Today* or the Evangelical Theological Society was not to unite conservative Protestants and earn secular intellectuals' respect for the sake of that unity and respect alone. Cultural influence was a means to an end: the ultimate end of converting the world—in heart, mind, and action—to Christ.

By this measure, the ongoing battle over intellectual authority has been a good thing for American evangelicalism, a movement that "flourishes on difference, engagement, tension, conflict, and threat," as Christian Smith has written.[43] This strife spurs the diversity and energy that have enabled evangelicals to compete with the Catholic Church in evangelistic reach— not because they can match Rome's institutional organization or funding, but because their mosaic of rival dogmas, styles of piety, and pragmatic innovation has allowed evangelicals to penetrate a wide array of communities and cultures.

Conservative American evangelicals have turned their frustration with the secularization of domestic culture into an impetus to train their sights abroad—in the hope of winning converts, encouraging godly social change, and finding validation in the theological and cultural convictions of Christian communities outside the United States. Organizations like Focus on the Family lobby the United Nations to advance their defense of "Christian civilization": religious freedom, at least for Christians; rights for the unborn; and traditional "family values"—to create what one participant called "an effective pro-family movement worldwide." In the wake of the Episcopal Church's decision to ordain gay priests and a gay bishop, American evangelicals craving history, mystery, and refuge from the liberalization of Western mores joined up with their Anglican brethren in Africa. They broke from the Episcopal Church and built alliances with conservative Africans based on missionary relationships that went back decades.[44] Evangelical Anglicans did not abandon the inerrancy debate or scripture-based arguments against the ordination of women and homosexuals, but they supplemented proof texts with new authority: an appeal to history and to the global norms of the Anglican Communion.

American evangelicals have played an enormous role in the global spread of Christianity for at least two centuries, and the fading of mainline Protestant missions has accentuated that influence. By the end of the twentieth century, evangelicals accounted for 91 percent of America's Protestant missionaries abroad. Campus Crusade claimed that by the year 2007 its most popular evangelizing tool, a 1979 movie about Christ's life called the *Jesus Film*, had aired in 229 countries in more than 1,000 different languages before nearly 6 billion people (a figure equivalent to 90 percent of the earth's population at the time: If Campus Crusade's numbers may be a bit inflated or include many repeat viewings, there is little doubt that the film has enjoyed extraordinary distribution worldwide). International charities with an evangelical inclination, such as World Vision, had grown into a sprawling industry raising hundreds of millions of dollars each year. Americans watched their own entrepreneurial and conversion-oriented religious style catch on in Africa—particularly in wartorn societies where civil structures are weak—and have encouraged local Christians to take control and remodel the faith to fit their own cultures.[45] American evangelicals' recipes for do-it-yourself religious authority are well suited to the power vacuums of failed states.

If some American evangelicals find new fonts of authority in the expanding horizons of global Christendom—and take solace, despite the stagnation of churches at home, in the expanding numbers of converts worldwide—those encounters have offered challenges as well. As they began to work more closely with Christians in newly independent societies, as they witnessed the fires of revival and non-Western Christians' intimate struggles with the supernatural, many American evangelicals realized that their own assumptions about social change and religious experience fell apart outside the dominion of Enlightenment reason and the legacy of the fundamentalist–modernist battles. Evangelicalism originated as a Western phenomenon, a web of religious communities that emerged in the wake of the Reformation with a common heritage and shared concerns over the fission of faith and reason, the trustworthiness of religious experience, and the implications of secular society for the faith. Yet by the beginning of the twenty-first century, the globalization of Protestantism and Westerners' growing receptiveness to a wider range of spiritual experience and theological questions—the broadening of religious imagination—made it harder than ever to define the term "evangelical."

Christians in the Global South have forced Americans to confront unfamiliar anxieties. Many care more about warding off witches or insuring the fate of unbaptized ancestors than combating the fiends of secularism. While they affirm the authority of the Bible, Christians outside the developed West do not agonize so much over the nature of that authority or its clash with the claims of the Enlightenment. They instinctively read scripture through the lens of their own cultural contexts. The "reality of poverty, powerlessness, and oppression.... The emphasis on the content of the gospel and the teaching of the biblical text rather than on formal questions of authority and the philosophical presuppositions behind a particular doctrine of inspiration is freeing evangelical theology in the Two-Thirds World," wrote Orlando Costas, an evangelical theologian born in Puerto Rico.[46]

These jarring encounters with new worldviews are not confined to the mission field. Growing numbers of Protestants from abroad and from immigrant churches at home are joining Christian student groups on secular campuses in the United States and attending American evangelical colleges and seminaries. These schools have bolstered efforts to recruit internationally and offer scholarships to students in racial and ethnic groups outside their traditional constituencies. On some college campuses, Asian-American members—particularly those of Korean descent—outnumber Caucasians in evangelical student associations, and represent the largest nonwhite population in American evangelical seminaries. These students bring their own interpretations of Christian heritage and the implications of the gospel for public life. While self-segregation along ethnic lines remains a powerful force, they are changing the conversation in evangelical classrooms and fellowships. Particularly in Pentecostal circles—where the global scope of the movement demands a cross-cultural, multiracial perspective—nonwhite and non-American theologians are publishing some of the most adventurous and sophisticated cultural theology in evangelicalism today.[47]

The term *evangelical mind* conjures images of a creature of many faces sharing one brain, or at least a movement of people who think and act in concert. No metaphor could be further from the truth. This story of shifting and conflicting authorities, evolving alliances and feuds, and debate over the essence of Christian identity means that if we continue to speak of an evangelical mind—if we continue to use the word *evangelical* at all, and we will—we must allow room for diversity and internal contradiction, for those who love the label and those who hate it. We must recognize that American evangelicalism owes more to its fractures and clashes, its anxieties and doubts, than to any political pronouncement or point of doctrine.

It may be wiser to speak instead of an "evangelical imagination." In every individual, the imagination is the faculty of mind that absorbs ideas and sensations as fuel to conjure something new. It is a tool for stepping outside oneself or plunging into egocentric delusion. But we might also speak of the imagination that a community shares, no matter how furious its internal quarrels: a sphere of discourse and dreaming framed by abiding questions about how humans know themselves, their world, and their God. The evangelical imagination has been both an aid to intellectual life and an agent of anti-intellectual sabotage. Above all, it is a source of energy: energy that propels evangelism, institution-building, activism, care for the suffering, and a sincere passion for intellectual inquiry. It offers no clear path past the impasse of biblical authority, no firm discipline for the undecided mind, and no reconciliation with the intelligentsia of secular America. But any crisis of authority is no longer such a crisis if it has become the status quo. If the evangelical imagination harbors a potent anti-intellectual strain, it has proven, over time, to be a kind of genius.

Acknowledgments

T HE PLEASURES OF SCHOLARSHIP INCLUDE THE DEBTS THAT ONE INCURS along the way. My first thanks must go to the archivists and institutions that made my research possible: Bob Shuster, Wayne Weber, Paul Ericksen, Keith Call, and the rest of the staff at the Billy Graham Center and Wheaton College Archives, who never lost patience despite my numerous visits; Laura Schmidt at the Marion C. Wade Center; Stan Ingersol and Meri Janssen-Bond at the Church of the Nazarene Archives, who treat visiting researchers to Kansas City barbecue; Dennis Stoesz and Rich Preheim at the Mennonite Church U.S.A. Archives; Nancy Gower, who kept me piled high with files at Fuller Theological Seminary, even though the archives were only one of her many duties; David Bundy, Fuller's associate provost for Library Services, who singlehandedly reoriented my project in one fifteen-minute conversation; Joyce Lee and Darrin Rodgers at the Flower Pentecostal Heritage Center; Sue Whitehead at the Biola University Archives, who welcomed me to work in her office when there was nowhere else to sit; Bill Sumners and Taffey Hall at the Southern Baptist Historical Library and Archives; McGarvey Ice at the Disciples of Christ Historical Society; Gracia Lopez, Amy Koehler, and Andy Sherrod at Moody Bible Institute's Crowell Library Archives; Laura Mummert at the Taylor University Archives; Gary Gnidovic, who gave me free run of *Christianity Today's* fabulous photo collection; Greg Laughery at L'Abri; Martha Smalley at the Yale Divinity School Library; and the gifted and efficient staff members of Yale University's Sterling Memorial Library and the University of North Carolina library system, who must have spent hours each week handling my page requests.

My research often took me far from home, and I am grateful to those who hosted me for days and weeks at a time: Lance and Melinda Buterbaugh; Fannie Mae Hall; Paul and Julie Keim; Barbara Taylor; Penny Thieme; K. Erik and Donna Thoennes. I am indebted to the Jacob K. Javits Program, the Woodrow Wilson National Fellowship Foundation, the Ellen & Paul Gignilliat Foundation, and the Historical Society of Southern California for providing the funds necessary to see so many different corners of the sprawling world of American evangelicalism.

Many friends in New Haven were always ready to explain, listen, brainstorm, and commiserate, especially Alison Greene, Sarah Hammond, Kathryn Lofton, Kathryn Gin Lum, David Walker, and the other regulars at the American Religious History lunchtime working group. I am grateful to those who made sure I never (or almost never) personified the cliché of the monkish grad student holed away in a carrel, subsisting on granola bars and self-pity: Eric Bianchi, Gwen Bradford, Jake Dell, Charlie Edel, Andy Horowitz, Charles Keith, Laura and Randolph Miles, Aaron O'Connell, Christy and Michael Peppard, Helen Veit, Justin Zaremby, and the entire Elizabethan Club crew. Others always had time to hear about fundamentalists or the five points of Calvinism despite the distance between us: Becca Baneman, Hope DiGiusto, Anne Elliott, Kate Epstein, Deborah Friedell, Aaron Lemon-Strauss, Rachel Mackenzie, and Jordan Webster.

I first began to learn how to study religion with all my senses, how to spot theology at work in real life, during conversations with David Goa more than a decade ago. He welcomed me to Alberta, served me Norwegian pancakes and cloudberry jam, and believed in the hare-brained plan of a college sophomore to live alongside a Russian Orthodox Old Believer colony four hours northeast of Edmonton and amuse them with my terrible Russian until they agreed to let me come to their church, help butcher chickens, and ask a few questions. John Gaddis oversaw my detour into diplomatic history and my first faltering steps as a historian. Charlie Hill was the gracious guinea pig, and since then he has been just as eager to talk about Baptist–Presbyterian feuds as he was to discuss Ronald Reagan's negotiations with the Soviets. Charlie may be the only person who understood, and probably predicted, my circuitous passage from the study of Russian religion to American diplomatic history and back again to religion, this time that of evangelicals. I did not see it coming.

Carlos Eire always had time for an Americanist interloper and let me try my hand at teaching undergraduates about the Reformation. Denys Turner helped me grasp the mystery and levity in theology, and is the only person I know who can convincingly harmonize the doctrine of predestination with belief in free will (I have tried to repeat his explanation to students myself, with limited success). My dissertation committee—Skip Stout, Jon Butler, and Beverly Gage—had the faith to sign off on my project when it consisted of two or three half-baked ideas, and in the years afterward their questions, criticisms, and advice proved instrumental. Skip, who is his students' unflagging supporter from the moment they matriculate until they don their caps and gowns and beyond, nudged me toward intellectual history and encouraged my unfashionable admiration of Perry Miller. Jon, despite his day job as dean of the graduate school, always had time for lunch at Yorkside, and made me work hard to convince him of my ideas—so that when I finally did, I knew I really had something. Beverly read theology-laden drafts with a political historian's healthy skepticism and was always willing to talk about balancing academe with journalism, and career with family. She has been the mentor I did not realize I needed.

As this project neared completion, my new colleagues and students at the University of North Carolina at Chapel Hill welcomed this Yankee with open arms, thoughtful questions, and steady encouragement. Lauren Winner and Kate Bowler initiated me into the Triangle American religious history sisterhood. Lloyd Kramer and the rest of the faculty and staff of the history department had more faith in my abilities as an intellectual historian than I did myself.

This book benefited enormously from the comments of generous readers: Darren Dochuk, Stan Gaede, George Marsden, Mark Noll, Matthew Sutton, Grant Wacker, Daniel Williams, and anonymous reviewers. All read the entire manuscript and offered pages of thoughtful criticism and encouragement. Nancy Ammerman, Stan Ingersol, Randy Maddox, and Steven Nolt read chapters and saved me from many mistakes and oversights. My editor, Theo Calderara, guided this book into its final form with patience, finesse, and good humor. The confidence and enthusiasm of Theo, Sasha

Grossman, Gwen Colvin, Stacey Hamilton, and their colleagues at Oxford University Press carried me through the long slog of revision.

My family has sustained me throughout the years that this project has devoured. My parents, John and Julie Worthen, helped me maintain perspective through the highs and lows of writing and teaching. They are my unswerving supporters. I owe my curiosity and my confidence—the two essential ingredients in good scholarship—to them. My brother Dan and his wife Lilly cheered me on while also reminding me that there is more to life than archives. Barbara and Ken Morgan, my parents-in-law, never wavered in their enthusiasm and always had their eye out on my behalf— for religious news clippings, or for a fun new cookbook to get me away from my desk for a while. Tyndale and Orwell kept me company on lonely nights of writing and inspired me to follow my subjects' stories with the same passion and mental focus with which they stalk the laser pointer. Lastly, I am blessed with a husband, Michael Cotey Morgan, who is my best friend and most thoughtful critic. We are two in one flesh, instructing one another, encouraging one another, and strengthening one another, as Tertullian says. This book is dedicated to him.

Abbreviations

ASCBU Archives and Special Collections, Biola University, La Mirada, CA

BGCA Billy Graham Center Archives, Wheaton College, Wheaton, IL

CCCC Christian College Consortium Collection, Archives and Special Collections, Taylor University, Upland, IN

CLAMBI Crowell Library and Archives, Moody Bible Institute, Chicago, IL

CNA Church of the Nazarene Archives, Lenexa, KS

DAHL David Allan Hubbard Library, Fuller Theological Seminary, Pasadena, CA

DCHS Disciples of Christ Historical Society, Nashville, TN

FHL Farel House Library, L'Abri, Huemoz, Switzerland

FPHC Flower Pentecostal Heritage Center (Archives of the Assemblies of God), Springfield, MO

MCUSA Mennonite Church U.S.A. Archives, Goshen, IN

MWC Marion E. Wade Center, Wheaton College, Wheaton, IL

SBHLA Southern Baptist Historical Library and Archives, Nashville, TN

WCSC Wheaton College Special Collections, Wheaton, IL

Notes

INTRODUCTION

1. Robert Green Ingersoll, "The Christian Religion" (1881), in *The Works of Robert G. Ingersoll*, vol. 6, ed. C. P. Farrell (New York: Dresden, 1909), 93.

2. Sidney E. Mead, *The Lively Experiment: The Shaping of Christianity in America* (New York: Harper & Row, 1963), 129.

3. Alan Wolfe, personal communication with the author, September 28, 2012. Wolfe elaborated on this point in his article "The Opening of the Evangelical Mind," *Atlantic Monthly*, October 2000, 55–76.

4. David Harrington Watt, *Bible-Carrying Christians: Conservative Protestants and Social Power* (New York: Oxford University Press, 2002), 25. Here Watt is summarizing other commentators' assessments of evangelicalism. His own view is more nuanced.

5. Harold Lindsell, "Does the Term 'Evangelical' Serve a Useful Purpose Any Longer?" (paper given at the Far West Regional Conference of the Evangelical Theological Society, Escondido, CA, April 7, 1984), accessed via Theological Research Exchange Network, www.tren.com; Donald W. Dayton, "Some Doubts about the Usefulness of the Category 'Evangelical,'" in *The Variety of American Evangelicalism*, ed. Dayton and Robert K. Johnston (Knoxville: University of Tennessee Press, 1991), 245–51; D. G. Hart, *Deconstructing Evangelicalism: Conservative Protestantism in the Age of Billy Graham* (Grand Rapids, MI: Baker Academic, 2004).

6. George Rawlyk, ed., *Aspects of the Canadian Evangelical Experience* (Montreal: McGill-Queen's University Press, 1997), introduction; George Rawlyk and Mark Noll, eds., *Amazing Grace: Evangelicalism in Australia, Britain, Canada, and the United States* (Montreal: McGill-Queen's University Press, 1993), 17ff.; Mark Noll, *American Evangelical Christianity: An Introduction* (Oxford: Blackwell, 2001), introduction.

7. Noll, *American Evangelical Christianity*, chapter 1; W. R. Ward, *The Protestant Evangelical Awakening* (New York: Cambridge University Press, 1992); W. R. Ward, *Christianity under the Ancien Regime* (New York: Cambridge University Press, 1999); W. R. Ward, *Early Evangelicalism: A Global Intellectual History, 1670–1789* (New York: Cambridge University Press, 2006). The *Oxford English Dictionary* dates the first usage of "evangelicalism" to 1831, but a recognizable community of Protestants emerged much earlier.

8. For an overview of the distinctive theological and cultural priorities that distinguish most African-American Protestants from white evangelicals, see Milton G. Sernett, "Black Religion and the Question of Evangelical Identity," in *The Variety of American Evangelicalism*, 135–47.

9. The same impulses are visible in late medieval and early modern Roman Catholicism, particularly in the attention paid to private spiritual exercises by Thomas a Kempis and Ignatius of Loyola. Critics of Pietism sometimes charged that the movement steered Protestantism back toward Rome.

10. Wilfred Cantwell Smith, *Faith and Belief* (Princeton, NJ: Princeton University Press, 1979).

11. Reinhold Niebuhr, *Does Civilization Need Religion?* (New York: Macmillan, 1927), 2–3; and Richard Hofstadter, *Anti-Intellectualism in American Life* (New York: Knopf, 1962), 14, 83. Sidney Mead echoed this critique at almost the same time in *The Lively Experiment*. See also H. L. Mencken, "The Hills of Zion," in *The Vintage Mencken*, ed. Alistair Cooke (New York: Knopf, 1955), 153–61.

12. Mencken, "The Hills of Zion," 157; Hofstadter, *Anti-Intellectualism in American Life*, 27. Hofstadter granted that anti-intellectualism does not entail hostility to all ideas or to abstract thinking: "The leading anti-intellectuals are usually men deeply engaged with ideas, often obsessively engaged with this or that outworn or rejected idea" (*Anti-Intellectualism in American Life*, 21).

13. Richard Hofstadter, "The Paranoid Style in American Politics," *Harper's*, November 1964, 77–86; Lionel Trilling, *The Liberal Imagination* (New York: Viking, 1950), xv.

14. On evangelicals' above-average levels of education, see Christian Smith et al., *American Evangelicalism: Embattled and Thriving* (Chicago: University of Chicago Press, 1998), 76–77.

15. Rolin Lynde Hartt, "Deep Conflict Divides Protestantism," *New York Times*, December 16, 1923, XX5.

16. See for example Daniel K. Williams, *God's Own Party: The Making of the Christian Right* (New York: Oxford University Press, 2010); Darren Dochuk, *From Bible Belt to Sunbelt: Plain-Folk Religion, Grassroots Politics, and the Rise of Evangelical Conservatism* (New York: Norton, 2010); Barry Hankins, *Jesus and Gin: Evangelicalism, the Roaring Twenties, and Today's Culture Wars* (New York: Palgrave Macmillan, 2010); Markku Ruotsila, *The Origins of Christian Anti-Internationalism: Conservative Evangelicals and the League of Nations* (Washington, DC: Georgetown University Press, 2008); Lisa McGirr, *Suburban Warriors: The Origins of the New American Right* (Princeton, NJ: Princeton University Press, 2002); William Martin, *With God On Our Side: The Rise of the Religious Right in America* (New York: Broadway, 1996).

17. In *American Grace: How Religion Unites and Divides Us*, Robert Putnam and David Campbell marshaled data demonstrating the correlation between conservative politics and conservative religion. They suggested that political preference is the best predictor of religious affiliation and that evangelicals' primary ambition is their "desire to convert sexual morality into public policy." When survey respondents overwhelmingly ranked theology as the most important reason for switching churches—liturgy or worship style was second-most important, and political reasons were least important—the political scientists concluded that theology had become merely a mask for politics (Robert D. Putnam and David E. Campbell, *American Grace: How Religion Unites and Divides Us* [New York: Simon & Schuster, 2010], 131, 170–72).

18. Sociologist Christian Smith offers a thorough account of the strengths and limitations of survey data in analyzing American evangelical culture in *Christian America? What Evangelicals Really Want* (Berkeley: University of California Press, 2000), introduction and appendix. His book emphasizes the diversity and ambivalence of evangelical political opinion, but the reader is left wondering how the respondents' rhetoric aligns with their actual behavior and how their religious communities' history and theology inform their views.

19. Edward Gibbon, *The History of the Decline and Fall of the Roman Empire*, vol. 4 (London: Bonn, 1854 [1788]), 351.

CHAPTER 1: ERRAND FROM THE WILDERNESS

1. Henry recounts this anecdote in detail in his autobiography. Carl F. H. Henry, *Confessions of a Theologian: An Autobiography* (Waco, TX: Word Books, 1986), 211. Barth's earlier lectures were at the University of Chicago Divinity School and Princeton Theological Seminary.

2. Qtd. in George Dugan, "Dr. Barth Defines Evangelical Way," *New York Times*, April 30, 1962, 21. When conservatives critiqued Barth's work thoughtfully, he responded with equal grace, as in his correspondence with G. C. Berkouwer regarding Berkouwer's 1956 volume *The Triumph of Grace in the Theology of Karl Barth*. See Gregory C. Bolich, *Karl Barth and Evangelicalism* (Downers Grove, IL: InterVarsity Press, 1980), 76.

3. Barth, January 2, 1968, in *Karl Barth: Letters, 1961–1968*, ed. Geoffrey Bromiley (Grand Rapids, MI: Eerdmans, 1981), 284.

4. Henry, qtd. in "Standing on the Promises," *Christianity Today*, September 16, 1996, 28; Henry, *Confessions*, 26, 36; qtd. in Laurie Goodstein, "Rev. Dr. Carl F. H. Henry, 90, Brain of Evangelical Movement," *New York Times*, December 13, 2003.

5. Henry, *Confessions*, chapter 5, "God and Newspaperman at Wheaton," 60ff.

6. Paul Bechtel, *Wheaton College: A Heritage Remembered, 1860–1984* (Wheaton, IL: Shaw, 1984), 146–50, 116; Michael Hamilton, "The Fundamentalist Harvard: Wheaton College and the Continuing Vitality of American Evangelicalism, 1919–1965" (PhD diss., University of Notre Dame, 1994), 96ff.; Henry, *Confessions*, 68.

7. 2 Timothy 3:16; Clement, *Letter to the Corinthians*, chapter 45, in *Ante-Nicene Fathers*, trans. John Keith and ed. Allan Menzies, vol. 9 (Buffalo, NY: Christian Literature Publishing, 1896), revised and edited for *New Advent* website by Kevin Knight: http://www.newadvent.org/fathers/1010.htm, Irenaeus, *Against Heresies*, trans. John Keble (London: James Parker, 1872), 174-78.

8. Martin Luther, "Preface to the Old Testament" and "The Meaning of Large Numbers in the Bible," in *Luther's Works*, vol. 35, ed. E. Theodore Bachmann and trans. Bachmann and Charles M. Jacobs (Philadelphia: Muhlenberg, 1960); John Calvin, *Commentaries of the First Book of Moses Called Genesis*, 35:7, vol. 2., Latin ed. 1554, first English ed. 1578, ed. and trans. John King (Grand Rapids, MI: Eerdmans, 1948). In his argument for "divine accommodation," Calvin wrote that "when God descends to us, he, in a certain sense, abases himself, and stammers with us, so he allows us to stammer with him. And this is to be truly wise, when we embrace God in the manner in which he accommodates himself to our capacity."

9. Turretin wrote that Christ "could not bear to use corrupted books" and believed that even the vowel points of the Hebrew scriptures were inerrant (the ninth-century Masoretic text of the Hebrew scriptures contains diacritical signs used to represent vowel sounds, but ancient Hebrew did not). See Francis Turretin, *Institutes of Elenctic Theology*, vol. 1, trans. George Musgrave Giger and ed. James T. Dennison, Jr. (Phillipsburg, NJ: Presbyterian and Reformed, 1992 [1679]), 107. It is worth noting that Irenaeus, too, taught that "the Scriptures were translated by inspiration of God." (*Against Heresies*, 288.)

10. Charles Hodge, *Systematic Theology*, vol. 1 (Peabody, MA: Hendrickson, 1999 [1873]), 10–12, 170.

11. Archibald Alexander Hodge and Benjamin Breckenridge Warfield, "Inspiration," Presbyterian Review 2 (April 1881): 225–60, reprinted in *The Princeton Theology 1812–1921*, ed. Mark A. Noll (Grand Rapids, MI: Baker Academic, 2001 [1983]), 232.

12. Benjamin Warfield, "The Biblical Idea of Revelation" (1915), in *The Inspiration and Authority of the Bible*, ed. Samuel A. Craig (Philadelphia: Presbyterian and Reformed, 1948), 92. Elsewhere, Warfield elaborates: "Inspiration is thus brought before us as, in the minds of the writers of the New Testament, that particular operation of God in the production of Scripture which takes

effect at the very point of the writing of Scripture—understanding the term 'writing' here as inclusive of all the processes of the actual composition of Scripture, the investigation of documents, the collection of facts, the excogitation of conclusions, the adaptation of exhortations as means to ends and the like—with the effect of giving to the resultant Scripture a specifically supernatural character, and constituting it a Divine, as well as human, book" ("The Biblical Idea of Inspiration" [1915], in Craig, *Inspiration and Authority of the Bible*, 160). For an extended treatment of Warfield's thoughtful encounter with Darwin's theory of evolution, see David N. Livingstone and Mark A. Noll, "B. B. Warfield (1851–1921): Inerrantist as Evolutionist," *Isis* 91, no. 2 (June 2000): 283–304.

13. Mark Noll, *Between Faith and Criticism: Evangelicals, Scholarship, and the Bible in America* (Grand Rapids, MI: Baker, 1991 [1986]), 22–25.

14. Warfield, "The Real Problem of Inspiration" (1893), in Craig, *Inspiration and Authority of the Bible*, 180. Despite the inductive spirit that characterized the Common Sense Realism of Warfield's day, he charged modernist scholars with applying the inductive method too freely, tossing aside the crucial presupposition of plenary inspiration: "If we start from the Scripture doctrine of inspiration, we approach the phenomena with the question whether they will negative this doctrine, and we find none able to stand against it, commended to us as true, as it is, by the vast mass of evidence available to prove the trustworthiness of the Scriptural writers as teachers of doctrine. But if we start simply with a collection of the phenomena, classifying and reasoning from them, whether alone or in conjunction with the Scriptural statements, it may easily happen with us, as it happened with certain of old, that meeting with some things hard to be understood, we may be ignorant and unstable enough to wrest them to our own intellectual destruction, and so approach the Biblical doctrine of inspiration set upon explaining it away" ("The Real Problem of Inspiration," 225).

15. Hodge and Warfield, "Inspiration," 232. On the nuances of James Orr's analysis of biblical authority, see Gary Dorrien, *The Remaking of Evangelical Theology* (Louisville, KY: Westminster John Knox, 1998), 43ff.

16. Noll, *Between Faith and Criticism*, 41; William Jennings Bryan, "The Fundamentals," *The Forum* 70 (July 1923), in *Controversy in the Twenties: Fundamentalism, Modernism, and Evolution*, ed. Willard B. Gatewood, Jr. (Nashville, TN: Vanderbilt University Press, 1969), 137.

17. Henry, *Confessions*, 65.

18. Ibid., 106; Garth M. Rosell, *Surprising Work of God: Harold John Ockenga, Billy Graham, and the Rebirth of Evangelicalism* (Grand Rapids, MI: Baker Academic, 2008), 101ff.

19. James DeForest Murch, *Cooperation Without Compromise: A History of the National Association of Evangelicals* (Grand Rapids, MI: Eerdmans, 1956), 19.

20. Harold J. Ockenga, "Christ for America," Presidential Address, May 4, 1943, in National Association of Evangelicals, *United … We Stand: A Report of the Constitutional Convention of the National Association of Evangelicals, May 3–6, 1943* (Boston: NAE, 1943), 11. He would reprise many of the same themes in his convocation address at Fuller Theological Seminary in October 1947, "The Challenge to the Christian Culture of the West." See George Marsden, *Reforming Fundamentalism: Fuller Seminary and the New Evangelicalism* (Grand Rapids, MI: Eerdmans, 1987), 13, 61ff.

21. For a useful overview, see David K. Naugle, *Worldview: The History of a Concept* (Grand Rapids, MI: Eerdmans, 2002), 6ff.; for Henry's recollection, see Henry, *Confessions*, 75.

22. "Hitler as an Orator: Full Translation of an Electioneering Speech, 'Vision of the Future Germany,'" *Manchester Guardian*, March 16, 1933, 12.

23. Sigrid Schultz, "Pagan Rituals for Weddings Issued by Nazis," *Chicago Daily Tribune*, April 2, 1938, 1.

24. Paul Winkler, "Nazism vs. Religion," *Washington Post*, May 14, 1944, B4; Guido Enderis, "F.D.R. and 'Weltanschauung,'" *New York Times*, September 26, 1937, 67.

25. Norman Thomas, "The Dissenter's Role in a Totalitarian Age," *New York Times*, November 20, 1949, 78.

26. George F. Kennan, "The Charge in the Soviet Union (Kennan) to the Secretary of State," February 22, 1946, 861.00/2-2246 (telegram, National Security Archive, George Washington University), available at http://www.gwu.edu/~nsarchiv/coldwar/documents/episode-1/kennan.htm.

27. Qtd. in Philip Gleason, *Contending With Modernity: Catholic Education in the Twentieth Century* (New York: Oxford University Press, 1995), 119.

28. L. Brent Bozell, "The Strange Drift of Liberal Catholicism," *National Review*, August 12, 1961, 83. See also W. F. Buckley, "Ecce Ike," *National Review*, December 12, 1963, 487; Buckley, "The Ivory Tower," *National Review*, September 24, 1960, 172. John Hallowell, an Anglican political scientist at Duke and conservative essayist, also chastised liberalism for its "individualistic *Weltanschauung*." Understanding any human being required knowledge of "the conceptual scheme in terms of which he observes 'facts,' the things which he presupposes and tends to regard as self-evident," Hallowell wrote in 1942 (John H. Hallowell, "The Decline of Liberalism," *Ethics* 52, no. 3 [April 1942]: 323).

29. Mont Pelerin Society, "Statement of Aims," April 10, 1947, available at https://www.montpelerin.org/montpelerin/mpsGoals.html.

30. For an overview of these authors' views and their role in the rise of the American conservative movement, see George H. Nash, *The Conservative Intellectual Movement in America* (Wilmington, DE: Intercollegiate Studies Institute, 1996 [1976]), 30–73.

31. Marsden, *Reforming Fundamentalism*, 78; Gordon H. Clark, *A Christian Philosophy of Education* (Grand Rapids, MI: Eerdmans, 1946), 62.

32. J. Gresham Machen, *Christianity and Liberalism* (Grand Rapids, MI: Eerdmans, 2009 [1923]), 2.

33. J. Gresham Machen, "Lusk Laws Repeal," *New York Times*, February 27, 1923, 18; Machen, "The Beauty of the Forest," *New York Times*, February 18, 1925, 18; Machen, "Compulsory Fingerprinting," *New York Times*, February 12, 1935, 12.

34. J. Gresham Machen, "What Fundamentalism Stands for Now," *New York Times*, June 21, 1925, XX1.

35. D. G. Hart, *Defending the Faith: J. Gresham Machen and the Crisis of Conservative Protestantism in America* (Baltimore, MD: Johns Hopkins University Press, 1994), 63.

36. Hofstadter, *Anti-Intellectualism in American Life*, 132; H. L. Mencken, "Dr. Fundamentalist," *Baltimore Evening Sun*, January 18, 1937, section 2, 15.

37. "Text of Truman Speech on Religious Faith," *New York Times*, October 31, 1949, 26; Margaret Lamberts Bendroth, *Growing Up Protestant: Parents, Children, and Mainline Churches* (New Brunswick, NJ: Rutgers University Press, 2002), 99.

38. "Churches Given Warning on Overoptimism," *Los Angeles Times*, May 8, 1957, 23; Andrew S. Finstuen, *Original Sin and Everyday Protestants: Reinhold Niebuhr, Billy Graham, and Paul Tillich in an Age of Anxiety* (Chapel Hill: University of North Carolina Press, 2009); Alan Petigny, *The Permissive Society: America, 1941–1965* (New York: Cambridge University Press, 2009).

39. Ockenga, "Christ for America," 13.

40. Gordon H. Clark, foreword, in Carl Henry, *Remaking the Modern Mind* (Grand Rapids, MI: Eerdmans, 1946), 12.

41. Ibid., 13.

42. Ibid., 38–40, 63, 289–90.

43. Ibid., 292, 300–301. On American fundamentalists' dual identity as alienated outsiders and the holy remnant of authentic America, see George M. Marsden, *Fundamentalism and American Culture: The Shaping of Twentieth-Century Evangelicalism, 1870–1925* (New York: Oxford University Press, 1980).

Chapter 2: The Authority Problem

1. J. Narver Gortner to Stanley H. Frodsham, March 9, 1943, 1. NAE Correspondence, Fldr 1, FPHC.

2. Ibid., 1, 2.

3. D. Shelby Corlett to General Superintendents, May 12, 1943, 1. 790-1, Board of Gen. Superintendents, CNA.

4. By 1956, the NAE boasted the membership of forty-one denominations and more than two million members (Murch, *Cooperation Without Compromise*, 202–3). The Southern Baptist Convention, in its 1950 census, counted more than seven million members (Chuck Lawless and Adam Greenway, eds., *The Great Commission Resurgence: Fulfilling God's Mandate in Our Time* [Nashville, TN: B & H, 2010], 8). Some prominent Southern Baptists joined the NAE as individuals.

5. The question of whether or not Southern Baptists are evangelicals has emerged as a source of persistent anxiety for Southern Baptist scholars in the past thirty years. Those who embrace the term cite American Baptists' origins in Puritanism and the Great Awakenings, as well as the conservative social and theological beliefs that they share with many evangelicals. Southern Baptists who reject the label emphasize their free church heritage (as opposed to those evangelicals who trace their roots to the magisterial Reformed and Lutheran churches of Europe); distinctive Baptist doctrines such as "soul liberty," believer's baptism, and anti-creedalism; their rejection of evangelical ecumenical projects like the NAE; and the influence of cultural and theological questions unique to the southern context. See James Leo Garrett, Jr., et al., *Are Southern Baptists "Evangelicals"?* (Macon, GA: Mercer University Press, 1983), and David S. Dockery, ed., *Southern Baptists & American Evangelicals: The Conversation Continues* (Nashville, TN: Broadman & Holman, 1993).

6. J. Matthew Price, *We Teach Holiness: The Life and Work of H. Orton Wiley* (Holiness Data Ministry, 2006, online edition), 15. The following biographical details are from Price's account.

7. Price, *We Teach Holiness*, 128, 206.

8. H. Orton Wiley, "Christian Education," address delivered at the Third Educational Conference, Church of the Nazarene, Pasadena College, Pasadena, CA, October 17–19, 1951 (qtd. in Price, *We Teach Holiness*, 173); Rob Staples to William Arnett, October 23, 1973, 2. 3433-5, Rob Staples Collection, CNA.

9. Paul Merritt Bassett, "The Theological Identity of the North American Holiness Movement," in Dayton and Johnston, *The Variety of American Evangelicalism*, 93.

10. H. Orton Wiley, "The Morning Watch," *Nazarene Messenger*, October 1922 (qtd. in Price, *We Teach Holiness*, 146); on Wesley's theological prudence, see Frederick Dreyer, "Evangelical Thought: John Wesley and Jonathan Edwards," *Albion* 19, no. 2 (Summer 1987): 177–92.

11. Timothy L. Smith, *Called Unto Holiness: The Story of the Nazarenes: The Formative Years* (Kansas City, MO: Nazarene Publishing House, 1962), 294ff. Smith cites the example of B. F. Haynes, the editor of the Nazarene church's largest newspaper, the *Herald of Holiness*, who wrote sympathetically about labor unions prior to World War I—yet after the war (and a decade of reading fundamentalist literature) he changed his mind, writing in 1919 that the federal government had spoiled the unions, and now they would stop at nothing less than socialist revolution (317–18); Paul Merritt Bassett, "Fundamentalist Leavening of the Holiness Movement, 1914–1940: Church of the Nazarene: A Case Study," *Wesleyan Theological Journal* 13 (Spring 1978): 69–72.

12. The Higher Life movement originated in a series of conferences that began in 1875 in Keswick, England. In 1910 Charles G. Trumbull, editor of the *Sunday School Times*, introduced an American version of Keswick teachings at a conference in New Jersey. Any Christian could emerge "victorious" in the battle against sin if he or she gave up the struggle to play "some part in overcoming the power of their sin"—the mistaken belief that "for sanctification, we must paddle our own

canoe"—and instead surrendered to Christ. See Douglas W. Frank, *Less Than Conquerors: How Evangelicals Entered the Twentieth Century* (Grand Rapids, MI: Eerdmans, 1986), 114ff.; Charles G. Trumbull, *Victory in Christ* (Whiting, NJ: America's Keswick, 2011 [1959]), 14.

13. Smith, *Called Unto Holiness*, 319–21. The Church of the Nazarene still adheres to the statement of faith adopted in 1928: "Preamble and Articles of Faith," available at http://nazarene.org/ministries/administration/visitorcenter/articles/display.html (accessed January 14, 2013).

14. By the mid-twentieth century a wide variety of Mennonite groups flourished in the United States. I have chosen to focus on the largest body, the so-called (Old) Mennonite Church, also known as the Mennonite Church (MC), whose members were concentrated in a band from Pennsylvania and Virginia across the Great Lakes states and into Iowa and Kansas. This church's members were, by this time, largely English-speaking and more likely to be engaged with their evangelical contemporaries than more cloistered Amish communities. Yet they retained a stronger sense of distinctive Mennonite theology and cultural identity than more revivalist, "Americanized" denominations such as the Brethren in Christ. In 2002 the Mennonite Church merged with the General Conference Mennonite Church to form the Mennonite Church U.S.A. On Mennonites' engagement with evangelical and secular influences, see Theron F. Schlabach, "Mennonites, Revivalism, Modernity, 1683–1850," *Church History*, December 1979, 298–415.

15. C. Norman Kraus, "Evangelicalism: A Mennonite Critique," in Dayton and Johnston, *Variety of American Evangelicalism*, 190.

16. Steven M. Nolt, "Activist Impulses across Time: North American Evangelicalism and Anabaptism as Conversation Partners," in *The Activist Impulse: Essays on the Intersection of Evangelicalism and Anabaptism*, ed. Jared S. Burkholder and David C. Cramer (Eugene, OR: Pickwick, 2012), 25.

17. Paul Toews, *Mennonites in American Society, 1930–1970: Modernity and the Persistence of Religious Community* (Scottsdale, PA: Herald Press, 1996), 66, 68–81; Nathan E. Yoder, "'I Submit:' Daniel Kauffman and the Legacy of a Yielded Life," in Burkholder and Cramer, *The Activist Impulse*, 144. The institutional upheaval that resulted in the closure of Goshen originated partly in theological and cultural conflicts connected to the fundamentalist movement, but also in a generational divide between young leaders and the "old-boy network" long in charge of Mennonite Church institutions, as well as skirmishes over church discipline in the church's Indiana-Michigan conference (Albert N. Keim, *Harold S. Bender, 1897–1962* [Scottsdale, PA: Herald Press, 1998], 138–43).

18. Keim, *Harold S. Bender*, 123, 162, 205. See also chapters 5 and 8–9.

19. Ibid., 119ff., 123, 174ff.

20. Qtd. in Guy F. Hershberger, "Harold S. Bender and His Time," *Mennonite Quarterly Review* 38 (April 1964): 87.

21. Harold S. Bender, *The Anabaptist Vision* (Scottsdale, PA: Heritage Press, 1944). Available at http://www.mcusa-archives.org/library/anabaptistvision/anabaptistvision.html.

22. Keim, *Harold S. Bender*, 300.

23. Harold S. Bender, "Outside Influences on Mennonite Thought," *Mennonite Life* 10, no. 1 (January 1955): 46, 48.

24. "Rev. C. L. Fuller, Famed Radio Evangelist, Will Hold Services at Garden Tomorrow," *Daily Boston Globe*, October 11, 1941, 14; Daniel Fuller, *Give the Winds a Mighty Voice: The Story of Charles E. Fuller* (Waco, TX: Word Press, 1972), 149–52; Marsden, *Reforming Fundamentalism*, 18, 38–41. Fuller's middle name was Edward; the *Globe* headline mistakes his middle initial.

25. "Rev. C. L. Fuller," 14; Marsden, *Reforming Fundamentalism*, chapters 2, 7.

26. Marsden, *Reforming Fundamentalism*, 54, 107ff. By 1977, the total enrollment in the seminary's various schools and extension ministries was nearly two thousand (ibid., 263), and today tops three thousand. Friedrich Hayek, Peter Viereck, Leo Strauss, Stefan Possony, and Robert

Strausz-Hupe—to name a few—were all born in Germany or Austria and played important roles in the resurgence of American conservative intellectual life.

27. Marsden, *Reforming Fundamentalism*, 174-75. Carl Henry writes that Woodbridge studied with Machen and Harnack in *Confessions*, 140.

28. Edward John Carnell, *The Case for Orthodox Theology* (Philadelphia: Westminster, 1959), 113.

29. Wilbur M. Smith, letter to Harold Lindsell, April 24, 1961, p. 1. Fldr 18, Box 3, Coll 192, Harold Lindsell Papers; C. D. Weyerhaeuser, letter to Edward L. Johnson, December 10, 1962, pp. 1, 3. Fldr 12, Box 1, Lindsell Papers, BGCA.

30. Roger Finke, "The Quiet Transformation: Changes in Size and Leadership in Southern Baptist Churches," *Review of Religious Research* 36, no. 1 (September 1994): 5; E. P. Ellyson, quoted in Smith, *Called Unto Holiness*, vol. 1, 261; W. T. Purkiser, *Called Unto Holiness: Volume 2, the Second Twenty-five Years, 1933–58* (Kansas City, MO: Nazarene Publishing House, 1983), 204.

31. Marsden, *Reforming Fundamentalism*, 46.

32. Paul Bauman to Sam Sutherland, August 31, 1943, 1–2. Samuel Sutherland Papers, B Corresp., File 1, Section C, ASCBU. The National Fellowship of Brethren Churches changed its name to the Fellowship of Grace Brethren Churches in 1987. R. T. Williams, qtd. in Purkiser, *Called Unto Holiness*, 205; Nazarene Theological Seminary in Kansas City, MO, opened in the fall of 1945.

33. Keim, *Harold S. Bender*, 332ff., qtd. on 341. The seminary modeled its curriculum on that of the Biblical Seminary in New York City, a nondenominational school that had hosted many Mennonite students before their church opened a seminary of its own. See Steven M. Nolt, "Activist Impulses Across Time," in Burkholder and Cramer, *The Activist Impulse*, 28.

34. Ockenga, letter to Carl McIntire, September 24, 1945. Qtd. in Garth Rosell, *Surprising Work of God*, 197; Clarence Bouma, "Orthodox Theological Scholarship" (reprint of keynote address delivered at the Cincinnati YMCA, December 27, 1949), *Calvin Forum*, January 1950, 134, 132. Scholars from fundamentalist Bob Jones University, for example, attended the conferences of the Evangelical Theological Society in its early years and took on a significant leadership role in the first meeting of the society's southern section in 1953 (program, Southern Section of the Evangelical Theological Society, first annual meeting, March 20–21, 1953. Fldr 13, Box 1, Coll 243, Records of the Evangelical Theological Society, BGCA; ETS Constitution, as adopted December 28, 1949, Fldr 2, Box 1, ETS, BGCA). Gleason discusses analogous Catholic endeavors in *Contending With Modernity*, 150.

35. See for example "Abstracts of Papers of the Southern Section of the Evangelical Theological Society," 1954. Representative examples include J. Barton Payne's paper, "Arise, And Go To The South," which warned his colleagues of "a threat, as a carefully disguised liberalism is using evangelical vocabulary to infiltrate with an apostasy from Scripture, which should give the Bible believer a concern for the south." Daniel Krusich's "Paul and the Practical Problems in Corinthians" was a pastoral paper concerned with how to best apply I Corinthians to daily Christian life. Alfred Cierpke's "Communism of Christianity? Karl Marx or Jesus Christ?" comprised a standard fundamentalist screed against the "octopuslike" spread of communism. Fldr 13, Box 1, ETS, BGCA.

36. Richard H. Bube, "A Perspective on Biblical Inerrancy," *Journal of the American Scientific Affiliation* 15, no. 86 (September 1963): 86.

37. Vernon Grounds, letter to ETS officers, June 16, 1965; anonymous, letter to Grounds, March 29, 1965, p. 1. Fldr 4, Box 1, ETS, BGCA.

38. Marsden, *Reforming Fundamentalism*, 228.

39. Kenneth Kantzer, the inerrantist dean of Trinity Evangelical Divinity School, assured readers of *His* magazine that "apparent discrepancies" did not mean the Bible contained error: "If the Bible is verbally inspired and inerrantly true, yet expresses its truths from different viewpoints and from various cultural backgrounds, this type of problem should be common" (Kantzer, "Christ and Scripture," *His*, January 1966, 16–20, qtd. in Marsden, *Reforming Fundamentalism*, 229).

40. Christian Smith has observed that the neo-evangelicals developed "a distinct, publicly recognizable collective identity, in relation to which individuals, congregations, denominations, and para-church organizations were thereafter able to recognize and form their own faith identities and action-commitments" (*American Evangelicalism*, 15).

CHAPTER 3: FUNDAMENTALIST DEMONS

1. Henry, *Confessions*, 145; John Pollock, *A Foreign Devil in China: The Story of Dr. L. Nelson Bell* (Minneapolis, MN: World Wide Publications, 1988 [1971]), 306. The Presbyterian Church in the United States originated in the merger of the southern wing of Old School Presbyterianism with a small southern branch of revivalistic New School Presbyterians after the southern Old Schoolers separated from their northern brethren in 1861. After World War II, debates over ecumenism (in the form of a possible merger with the northern United Presbyterian Church in the United States of America), and later the civil rights movement, polarized the PCUS. In 1973, a conservative faction broke away to form the Presbyterian Church in America. In 1983, the moderates who remained in the PCUS merged with the UPCUSA to form the Presbyterian Church (U.S.A.), now the largest Presbyterian denomination in the country.

2. Qtd. in Pollock, A Foreign Devil in China, 306.

3. Qtd. in "Churches in Politics," *Chicago Daily Tribune*, February 7, 1956, 16.

4. Qtd. in ibid.

5. "Bible 'Airlift' Lauded," *New York Times*, September 5, 1953, 18.

6. L. Nelson Bell, letter to Andrew Blackwood, November 25, 1955. Fldr 1, Box 19, Coll 318, L. Nelson Bell Papers, BGCA; Board of Directors, minutes, June 18, 1958, p. 1. Fldr 10, Box 1; Board of Directors, minutes, February 7, 1957, p. 2. Fldr 3, Box 1; Scrapbook, Fldr 1, Box 9; Carl Henry, editor's report, May 28, 1957, p. 1. Fldr 3, Box 1, Coll 008, Records of Christianity Today International (CTI), BGCA.

7. Kenneth Dole, "News of the Churches," *Washington Post and Times Herald*, September 14, 1957, B5; Ad #4, *U.S. News & World Report*, in memo from Clair Burcaw to Nelson Bell, October 20, 1960. Fldr 16, Box 1, CTI, BGCA.

8. Carl Henry, editor's report, November 3, 1960, p. 3. Fldr 16, Box 1, CTI, BGCA. The London office opened in 1961 (Henry, *Confessions*, 207).

9. On Henry's careerism see for example Bell, letter to Harold Ockenga, January 7, 1958. Fldr 28, Box 5, CTI; Henry, editor's report, January 12, 1967, p. 4. Fldr 4, Box 4, Lindsell Papers, BGCA.

10. "A Letter from the Publisher," *Time*, May 2, 1960. Available at http://www.time.com/time/magazine/article/0,9171,826342,00.html; "Conservatism Today," *Time*, July 13, 1962; Donald T. Critchlow, *The Conservative Ascendancy: How the GOP Right Made Political History* (Cambridge, MA: Harvard University Press, 2007), 22; Henry, *Confessions*, 179. By the end of his tenure as editor in chief in 1968, the magazine would claim a circulation of 160,000 ("Evangelical Protestants Must Unite, Editor Says," *Los Angeles Times*, July 13, 1968, B10).

11. "Conservatism Today," *Time*, July 13, 1962. Available at http://www.time.com/time/magazine/article/0,9171,827412,00.html; Kenneth A. Briggs, "Evangelical Shift to Pluralism," *New York Times*, February 24, 1978, A13; "Evangelical Protestants Must Unite"; "Clergy: A Gentle Fundamentalist," *Time*, December 11, 1964, available at http://www.time.com/time/magazine/article/0,9171,897417,00.html; Finstuen, *Original Sin and Everyday Protestants*, 38.

12. William S. Schlamm, "Arts and Manners," *National Review*, July 27, 1957, 114; D. B. Lockerbie, review, *National Review*, April 23, 1963, 330.

13. On Carl McIntire's collaboration with Catholics, see Markku Ruotsila, "Carl McIntire and the Fundamentalist Origins of the Christian Right," *Church History* 81, no. 2 (June 2012): 388;

"Editorial Announcement," *America*, April 17, 1909, 5. *Commonweal* asserted Catholics' commitment to religious liberty and hoped to convert the reader not to Roman doctrine, but to "the Catholic outlook on life and the Catholic philosophy of living," in Martin Marty's phrase (Martin E. Marty, *Righteous Empire: The Protestant Experience in America* [New York: Dial Press, 1970], 211).

14. Drew Pearson, "Tax Men Eye Church 'Politicians,'" *Washington Post and Times Herald*, November 13, 1960, E5; J. Howard Pew to Bell, March 31, 1958, 1. Fldr 57, Box 1, CTI, BGCA.

15. Emil Brunner, "The Cleveland Report on Red China," *Christianity Today*, April 25, 1960, 3–5; Karl Barth, "When Spirit Forsakes Theology," *Christianity Today*, January 4, 1963, 3. Reprinted from his *Evangelical Theology: An Introduction*, trans. Grover Foley (New York: Holt, Rinehart, and Winston, 1963).

16. J. F. Balzer, letter to Bell, March 12, 1960. Fldr 7, Box 2, CTI, BGCA.

17. Hofstadter, "Paranoid Style in American Politics"; Nash, *Conservative Intellectual Movement in America*, 125.

18. Qtd. in Nash, *Conservative Intellectual Movement in America*, 139; Peter Braestrup, "Now Birch Society Polarizes the Right," *New York Times*, April 9, 1961, E10.

19. Brian Doherty, *Radicals for Capitalism: A Freewheeling History of the Modern American Libertarian Movement* (New York: PublicAffairs, 2007), 61, 93, 170; Ralph Chapman, "New Group Formed to 'Expose and Correct' John Birch Society," *Boston Globe*, September 23, 1964, 9.

20. "The Sharon Statement," available at http://www.yaf.org/InnerPageTemplate.aspx?id=6877&terms=%22sharon+statement%22.

21. Chesly Manly, "Shift to Conservatism Found on Campuses," *Chicago Daily Tribune*, May 21, 1961, 1, 2.

22. William F. Buckley, Jr., "The Young Americans for Freedom" (reprinted from the *National Review*, 1960), in Gregory L. Schneider, ed., *Conservatism in America Since 1930: A Reader* (New York: New York University Press, 2003), 226–27; "Sharon Statement."

23. Bell, letter to Gordon Clark, February 17, 1955. Fldr 19, Box 19, Bell Papers. When Marcellus Kik resigned from the associate editorship, Bell strongly urged Carl Henry to select a "Reformed or Presbyterian" successor (Bell, letter to Henry, December 3, 1959. Fldr 13, Box 1); Henry, letter to Timothy L. Smith, September 24, 1958, p. 1. Fldr 92, Box 17, CTI, BGCA. One instance of the editors' theological neutrality, which earned them much praise from readers, was their even-handed coverage of the burgeoning charismatic revival: Frank Farrell, "Outburst of Tongues: The New Penetration," *Christianity Today*, September 13, 1963, 3ff.

24. Claude H. Thompson, letter to Bell, April 2, 1955. Fldr 29, Box 18, Bell Papers, BGCA.

25. Pew was active in the magazine's administration, fancied himself a lay theologian and historian, and had an opinion on every doctrinal and social question. He insisted throughout his years of involvement with *Christianity Today* that the magazine criticize all political activism by denominational bodies and show no sympathy for the ecumenical movement, which he viewed as a socialistic and heterodox prelude to one-world government. See for example these representative letters from Pew to Bell: January 28, 1957, Fldr 57, and June 30, 1960, Fldr 58, Box 1, CTI; "Conservatism Today," *Time*; Bell to Paul Rees, November 8, 1962. Fldr 1, Box 2; Bell to Ockenga, January 7, 1958, Fldr 28, Box 5, CTI; Henry, *Confessions,* 350ff.; Henry, letter to Lindsell, February 8, 1968, p. 2. Fldr 4, Box 4, Lindsell Papers, BGCA.

26. J. Marcellus Kik, letter to J. Lewis McLean, May 21, 1956, p. 1. Fldr 23, Box 1; Henry, editor's report, September 11, 1962, p. 1. Fldr 19, Box 1, CTI, BGCA.

27. Bell, letter to Art Anderson, March 8, 1957, p. 1. Fldr 4, Box 2, CTI, BGCA.

28. Bell, letter to Wayne Freeman, May 10, 1957. Fldr 10, Box 11, Bell Papers, BGCA. To another correspondent, he wrote: "Much that I see in modern day 'Fundamentalism' smacks strongly of Phariseeism. This does not mean that I am not a Fundamentalist, for I am. But I am certainly not

the kind that is represented by Dr. Jones, Dr. Rice, and others" (Bell, letter to Dean Blough, June 22, 1957. Fldr 27, Box 11, Bell Papers, BGCA).

29. Daniel L. Turner, *Standing Without Apology: The History of Bob Jones University* (Greenville, SC: Bob Jones University Press, 1997), 38, 138. Today Bob Jones University has a combined undergraduate and graduate enrollment of 4,228 ("School Snapshot: Bob Jones University," *New York Times*, available at http://topics.nytimes.com/topics/reference/timestopics/organizations/b/bob_jones_university/index.html [accessed May 29, 2012]); Bob Jones, Sr., *The Perils of America*, delivered at the Chicago Gospel Tabernacle, March 5, 1934 (Cleveland, TN: Bob Jones College, 1934), 23.

30. Bob Jones, Sr., letter to L. Nelson Bell, May 11, 1957, p. 2. Fldr 19, Box 11, Bell Papers, BGCA.

31. James Kilgore, letter to Bell, April 22, 1957, Fldr 32, Box 1, CTI; Lew Miller, letter to Bell, June 12, 1957, Fldr 19, Box 11; David Michael, letter to Bell, May 19, 1957, Fldr 9, Box 12; Bell, letter to James Price, May 25, 1957, Fldr 19, Box 11, Bell Papers, BGCA.

32. Anonymous, n.d., Fldr 27, Box 11, Coll 318, Bell Papers, BGCA.

33. Qtd. in Mark Taylor Dalhouse, *An Island in a Lake of Fire: Bob Jones University, Fundamentalism, and the Separatist Movement* (Athens: University of Georgia Press, 1996), 44.

34. Robert G. Sherrill, "Bob Jones University: New Curricula for Bigotry," *Nation*, March 29, 1965, 327.

35. Bell, letter to Bob Jones, Sr., May 7, 1957, p. 3. Fldr 19, Box 11, Bell Papers, BGCA.

36. Charles Finney, *Reflections on Revival*, ed. Donald Dayton (Minneapolis, MN: Bethany Fellowship, 1979 [1845]), 93–94; Robert F. Martin, *Hero of the Heartland: Billy Sunday and the Transformation of American Society, 1862–1935* (Bloomington: Indiana University Press, 2002), 118.

37. Joel Carpenter, "Contending for the Faith Once Delivered: Primitivist Impulses in American Fundamentalism," in *The American Quest for the Primitive Church*, ed. Richard T. Hughes (Urbana: University of Illinois, 1988), 101; Harold Lindsell, "Who Are the Evangelicals?," *Christianity Today*, June 18, 1964, 3, 5.

38. Kik to Henry, June 25, 1956, 1. Fldr 6, Box 4, Lindsell Papers; Pew to Bell, January 28, 1957. Fldr 57, Box 1, CTI, BGCA.

39. Jones to Bell, June 1, 1957, 1. Fldr 19, Box 11, Bell Papers, BGCA.

40. Geoffrey Kabaservice, *Rule and Ruin: The Downfall of Moderation and the Destruction of the Republican Party from Eisenhower to the Tea Party* (New York: Oxford University Press, 2012), 49; C. Stacey Woods, letter to Frederick Bronkema, June 23, 1948, p. 1. Fldr 1, Box 1, Coll 300, InterVarsity Christian Fellowship Records, BGCA.

41. John Bolten, quoted in Rosell, *Surprising Work of God*, 210. See the 1959 brochure: *A Time for Decision in Higher Education: Billy Graham Presents Crusade University*, Fldr 22, Box 23, Bell Papers, BGCA.

42. Mark Noll has noted "the diffused structure of evangelical culture, which promotes a rich breadth, but also an appalling thinness, in educational institutions." He also lamented the presumption of evangelists like Oral Roberts and Jerry Falwell in founding their own universities despite their lack of academic credentials (Noll, *The Scandal of the Evangelical Mind* [Grand Rapids, MI: Eerdmans, 1994], 16–17).

43. "An Evangelical Protestant Strategy for the Late 1960s," Fldr 4, Box 4, Lindsell Papers; Carl Henry, editor's report, January 12, 1967, p. 2. Fldr 4, Box 4, Lindsell Papers, BGCA.

CHAPTER 4: REFORM AND ITS DISCONTENTS

1. John Howard Yoder to Henry, June 16, 1955, 3. Fldr 15, Box 83, Hist. Mss 1-48, John Howard Yoder Collection, MCUSA. It is worth noting, however, that Yoder did admire Machen, whom he

took to represent the "truly evangelical movement" uncorrupted by fundamentalist obscurantism (Yoder to Henry, March 4, 1955, 2. In ibid.).

2. Yoder to Henry, August 29, 1955, 1, 2, Fldr 15; Henry to Yoder, September 8, 1955. Fldr 15, Box 83, Yoder Collection, MCUSA.

3. Hannah Arendt, *The Origins of Totalitarianism* (New York: Harcourt, 1979 [1951]), 468. On Marx's disciples' innovations: Lenin, for example, had no qualms about manipulating Marx's theories in order to defeat his enemies. Where Marx considered imperialism a phase in the prehistory of capitalism, Lenin adapted Marx's ideas to fit reality in Russia. He defined imperialism as the final stage of capitalism in which finance-capital uses the machinery of the state to exploit raw resources on the periphery, leading to the creation of an elite aristocracy, a stratum of well-paid workers loyal to the bourgeoisie, and temporarily deflecting class struggle into nationalist sentiments as states vie for global resources (see Vladimir Ilyich Lenin, *Imperialism: The Highest Stage of Capitalism* [1917], in *Essential Works of Lenin: "What Is To Be Done?" and Other Writings*, ed. Henry M. Christman (New York: Bantam Books, 1966), 177–265). Lenin's theory is curiously like the innovation that John Nelson Darby, the father of modern dispensational premillennialism, added to prior schemas of the end-times. Darby posited that when the angel Gabriel revealed the epochs of history to Daniel, he could not have known that the Jews would reject Christ; therefore God had to insert a "Great Parenthesis," the "Church Age" in which we live today, in between the penultimate and final "weeks" (seven-year periods) in Gabriel's prophecy. Successful dogmatists understand that doctrines are malleable.

4. Arendt, *The Origins of Totalitarianism*, 470.

5. Mark Thiessen Nation, *John Howard Yoder: Mennonite Patience, Evangelical Witness, Catholic Convictions* (Grand Rapids, MI: Eerdmans, 2006), 18. The anecdote regarding Yoder's encounters with Barth comes from Paul Keim, professor at Goshen College, June 2009, interview with the author.

6. Yoder to Paul Minear, August 8, 1955. Fldr 15, Box 83, Yoder Collection, MCUSA. Kenneth Kantzer brought some Lutheran influence to bear on the debates within neo-evangelicalism and at *Christianity Today*. He grew up in a Lutheran home and was ordained in the Evangelical Free Church of America, a denomination created through the merger of several Lutheran churches. The EFCA operates Trinity Evangelical Divinity School.

7. Yoder to C. N. Hostetter, April 14, 1955. Fldr 15, Box 83, Yoder Collection. From 1959 to 1967, Hostetter would chair both the World Relief Commission and the Mennonite Central Committee (Hostetter, Christian N., Jr., *Global Anabaptist Mennonite Encyclopedia Online*, available at http://www.gameo.org/encyclopedia/contents/H6831.html). For another example of Yoder's identification with the evangelical movement, see Yoder to Henry, March 4, 1955. Fldr 15, Box 83, Yoder Collection, MCUSA.

8. Daniel Payton Fuller to Robert Meye, March 28, 1963, 2. Fldr 14, Box 14, Daniel Payton Fuller Papers, DAHL. Fuller names five such students in this letter alone, and his correspondence, which I did not examine exhaustively, includes letters to and from at least a dozen additional students and colleagues who studied at Basel.

9. Fuller to Paul Jewett, February 27, 1960, 1. Fldr 9, Box 34, Fuller Papers, DAHL. At the time Hans Conzelmann was on faculty at the University of Zurich. Perhaps he visited Basel or Fuller traveled to Zurich, since less than 100 kilometers separate the two cities.

10. Bernard Ramm, "Helps from Karl Barth," in *How Karl Barth Changed My Mind*, ed. Donald McKim (Grand Rapids, MI: Eerdmans, 1986), 121. See also Gary Dorrien, *The Remaking of Evangelical Theology*, 123–29.

11. Brevard S. Childs, *Biblical Theology in Crisis* (Philadelphia: Westminster, 1976 [1970]), 18–30, 53. The movement was influential in mainline seminaries and encouraged many pastors to shift from topical preaching to expository preaching that moved carefully through the biblical text. The ecumenical movement took biblical theology to heart: After its 1948

organizational meeting in Amsterdam, the World Council of Churches commissioned a study on "The Bible and the Church's Message to the World." Arthur F. Glasser, "Non-Conciliar Protestants and the World Council of Churches," May 1, 1974, 3. Fldr 10, Box 65, Arthur F. Glasser Papers, DAHL.

12. James M. Gray, qtd. in Virginia Brereton, *Training God's Army: The American Bible School, 1880–1940* (Bloomington: Indiana University Press, 1990), 88. Brereton notes that fundamentalists often referred to their biblical hermeneutic as the "inductive method," by which they meant that students would approach scripture with no preconceived assumptions, evaluate the evidence, and arrive at objective conclusions. This reflected the general affection for Common Sense Realism that saturated America in the nineteenth century and continued to frame fundamentalists' thinking well into the twentieth century—in many quarters, up until the present day. The implications of the "inductive method" changed in the hands of evangelicals who embraced biblical theology. Dan Fuller used this term to describe his own philosophy and recommended Mortimer Adler's *How To Read a Book* (1940) as a guide to careful analysis and comprehension of a biblical author's argument (Fuller to Joseph H. Brady, March 8, 1971. Fldr 2, Box 14, Fuller Papers, DAHL). For Fuller, the inductive method convinced him to abandon dispensationalism and seriously revise his view of biblical inerrancy.

13. William Greathouse to Mildred Bangs Wynkoop, February 20, 1971, 1. 2223-6, Mildred Bangs Wynkoop Papers, CNA; Willard Taylor, "Report On Sabbatical," Fall 1969. 2054-26, Willard Taylor Material, CNA; James D. Strauss, "The Bible and Politics," *Christian Standard*, October 22, 1960, 4. DCHS; Stephen Dintaman, memo, December 11, 1967, 1. Fldr "Biblical Theology," Box 215, Yoder Collection, MCUSA.

14. Roger Forster and V. Paul Marston, with foreword by F. F. Bruce, *God's Strategy in Human History* (Bromley, UK: Send the Light Trust, 1973), foreword.

15. Rudolph Nelson, *The Making and Unmaking of an Evangelical Mind: The Case of Edward Carnell* (New York: Cambridge University Press, 1987), 55–56; Catalog of the Bible Institute of Los Angeles, 1953–1954, 29–30. ASCBU; *Theology News & Notes* 5, no. 3 (March 1958), and 6, no. 1 (October 1958). When Fuller's School of Psychology was founded, it hired a faculty equipped with PhDs from New York University, the University of Minnesota, and the University of London (Fuller Theological Seminary Course Catalog, 1966–1967, 8. DAHL). At the popular Winona Lake School of Theology summer program in Indiana, eight of the fifteen faculty members teaching in the early 1960s had PhDs; five had neither a PhD nor a ThD (Winona Lake School of Theology Catalog, Summer 1963. Fldr 2, Box 101, Hubbard Papers, DAHL; Noll, *Scandal of the Evangelical Mind*, 22).

16. John Goldingay, interview with the author, March 29, 2009.

17. S. A. Yoder, memo to members of the Seminar on Christianity and Culture, June 11, 1958. Fldr 2, Box 65, Hist. Mss. 1-278, Harold S. Bender Collection, MCUSA. William Greathouse wrote that he drew "heavily on Niebuhr's *Nature and Destiny of Man* (while trying to avoid his pessimism)" (Greathouse to Wynkoop, February 20, 1971, 2. 2223-6, Wynkoop Collection, CNA).

18. Earl E. Grice, "The Realignment of Faith and Our Witness," *Christian Standard*, August 5, 1950, 11; "From the Book Shelf," *Christian Standard*, February 25, 1950; "From the Book Shelf," *Christian Standard*, September 9, 1950, 13; Charles Gresham, "The Minister's Library," *Christian Standard*, November 12, 1955, 8. *Seminary Review*, the journal of the Cincinnati Bible Seminary (a Restorationist institution), also published frequent reviews of books from Eerdmans, Baker, Zondervan, and other mainstream Reformed/evangelical presses from the 1950s onward. See for example *Seminary Review* 3, no. 1 (Fall 1956) (Cincinnati Bible Seminary, Cincinnati, Ohio, DCHS). The *Restoration Herald*, while generally more conservative than the *Christian Standard*, followed a similar pattern of cautious engagement with mainstream evangelicalism and current theological debates (see R. C. Foster, "The New Testament and the Unity of the Church," *Restoration Herald*, January 1, 1965, 5. DCHS).

19. See for example Jack Cottrell, "Sovereignty and Free Will," *Seminary Review* 9, no. 3 (Spring 1963): 39–51; W. Charles Gillespie, "The Need For Christian Schools," *Restoration Herald*, March 1967 (vol. 41, nos. 5, 7, 10, DCHS). The Mennonite Church also granted that when it came to thinking through the relationship between the church and secular culture, Anabaptists had something to learn from the Reformed tradition. In a 1968 memo entitled "Philosophy of Mennonite Education: Progress Report," the author noted that Mennonite statements on education show a "lack of a position on the influence of culture on the person and his development. In contrast, C. Ellis Nelson in a recent book devotes a chapter to 'The Formative Power of Culture.' Nelson, a Presbyterian, writes from the standpoint of the nurture-within-covenant as the infant-baptism tradition would view this. The cultural focus of the slogans is outward rather than inward, seeing the Christian as a cultural refugee, a member of a radical innovative minority, separated from yet participating in cultural development where his Christian commitment calls for this" (Daniel Hertzler, "Philosophy of Mennonite Education: Progress Report," October 7, 1968, 4. Fldr 12, Box 22, Yoder Collection, MCUSA).

20. J. Roswell Flower to J. Elwin Wright, July 3, 1947, 2. Fldr 4, NAE Correspondence; Thomas F. Zimmerman to V. Raymond Edman, May 1, 1958, 1. Exec. Files—Central Bible College, 8-2-10-61. FPHC.

21. "Constitution and By-Laws of the Society for Pentecostal Studies," 1970, 1. Fldr 16, Box 1, Society for Pentecostal Studies Papers, DAHL.

22. J. Lawrence Burkholder, "Revelation and Reason," 19. Fldr 1, Box 65, Bender Collection, MCUSA.

23. Ronald B. Mayers, *Both/And: A Balanced Apologetic* (Chicago: Moody Press, 1984), 198. Another striking example of effective theological fusion was fundamentalist Carl McIntire's combination of Reformed cultural theology with urgent dispensational premillennialism. The covenant theology of the Reformed tradition, which holds that the Christian church inherited God's covenant with Israel, is, on its face, mutually exclusive with dispensationalists' belief in successive and distinct covenants between God and his people. See Ruotsila, "Carl McIntire," 404.

24. John H. Yoder wrote to the neo-evangelical colleagues that he met at the University of Basel: "We can't go further into Scripture's authority, what inspiration means, what is the nature of its implicit claim to reliability, except with people who agree already with us on at least this much. This would explain why it is impossible to discuss with certain classes of people; not only with unbelievers, but also with people who insist on certain philosophical presuppositions, with mystics, and with people who don't care about disagreement since they don't believe truth is one. This would mean that we come to grips seriously with the fact that, with people who don't accept Scripture as a court of appeal, conversation is impossible; with such people we will not speak either in apologetics (i.e., taking their unbelief consciously into account) or in terms of comparative religion" (Yoder to Kenneth Kantzer and David Wallace, September 25, 1955, 3. Fldr 15, Box 83, Yoder Collection, MCUSA). However, Yoder stopped short of the unforgiving view of Van Til, suggesting "a new way of understanding apologetics" that communicates with the unbeliever by showing him where his own presuppositions lead (5). Indeed, on this point if on no others, he had something in common with Francis Schaeffer (see chapter 9).

25. A. James Reimer, "Mennonites, Christ, and Culture: The Yoder Legacy," *Conrad Grebel Review* 16, no. 2 (Spring 1998): 6.

26. Yoder, "Relationship to Holiness Denominations," August 12, 1966, 4-5. Fldr 10, Box 23, Yoder Collection, MCUSA.

27. Betty Medsger, "Mennonites Plan N. Vietnam Relief," *Washington Post, Times Herald*, February 28, 1970, B7; "Sect Raps War 'Evil' In Vietnam," *Washington Post, Times Herald*, August 26, 1967, B5.

28. Ed Metzler, "Peace Section concerns," March 3, 1967, 1, 2-3. Fldr 12, Box 83, Yoder Collection, MCUSA.

29. Guy F. Hershberger to Elmer Neufeld, September 10, 1959. Fldr 13, Box 45, Bender Collection; Yoder to Hershberger, May 2, 1960. Fldr 9, Box 83; Hershberger to Yoder, November 14, 1960. Fldr 9, Box 83; Arthur F. Glasser to Yoder, September 15, 1964. Fldr 9, Box 83; Yoder to Myron Augsburger, March 31, 1967, 1. Fldr 9, Box 83; Paul N. Kraybill, "Notes of Breakfast Meeting with Billy Graham," August 31, 1961, 6. Fldr 9, Box 83, Yoder Collection, MCUSA. The Mennonites were also engaging a broad array of Protestants beyond American evangelical circles, sending delegates—including Bender and Yoder—to discuss "The Lordship of Christ Over Church and State" with Lutheran and Reformed scholars at a series of conferences in Puidoux, Switzerland, between 1955 and 1962.

30. Kraybill, "Notes of Breakfast Meeting," 1, 2. The early Anabaptist martyrs probably numbered around 2,000, rather than 5,000 (Sigrun Haude, "Anabaptism," in *The Reformation World*, ed. Andrew Pettegree [London: Routledge, 2000], 248).

31. Kraybill, "Notes of Breakfast Meeting," 7, 8.

32. Virgil A. Mitchell, "Wesleyan Methodists Chart a New Course, 1935–1968," in *Reformers and Revivalists: The History of the Wesleyan Church*, ed. Wayne E. Caldwell (Indianapolis, IN: Wesley Press, 1992), 330; Stephen W. Paine, "Maintaining the Witness to Inerrancy," first published in *Bulletin of the Evangelical Theological Society*, Winter 1966. Reprinted in the *Nazarene Preacher*, December 1966, 7.

33. Donald W. Dayton, "Holiness and Pentecostal Churches: Emerging from Cultural Isolation," *Christian Century*, August 15, 1979, 789; Rob L. Staples to A. Elwood Sanner, March 21, 1968, 1, 2. 3433-4, Rob Staples Collection, CNA.

34. Sanner to Staples, March 28, 1968. 3433-4, Staples Collection, CNA.

35. Paul Bassett, remarks in honor of Mildred Wynkoop to the "Breakfast Club," February 27, 1992, 3, 1561-32, NTS [Nazarene Theological Seminary] Breakfast Club, CNA. Bassett notes that Western Evangelical Seminary was an unusual institution, the only Holiness graduate school west of the Rockies and "at some remove from the geographical center of the Holiness Movement." During Wynkoop's time there, the seminary was awash in an individualistic, biblicist, Baptist style of piety as well as a mounting "defender of the faith" mentality as Paul Petticord, the school's first president, battled with his own denomination, the Evangelical United Brethren Church. This tense, theologically charged environment was at odds with Wynkoop's background in Nazarene circles (and also quite different from the more "churchly" Baptist tradition that she encountered at Northern Baptist Theological Seminary), but may have prepared her for the fundamentalist and Calvinistic influences that she battled later in her career. On the role of female ministers in the Nazarenes' early years, see Rebecca Laird, *Ordained Women in the Church of the Nazarene: The First Generation* (Kansas City, MO: Nazarene Publishing House, 1993).

36. H. Orton Wiley to Mildred Bangs Wynkoop, February 8, 1960. 1427-12; Ross E. Price to Wynkoop, September 6, 1967, 2. 1427-12; Wynkoop to Stephen Nease, May 7, 1979. 1427-15, Wynkoop Collection, CNA.

37. Wynkoop to Westlake Purkiser, October 30, 1969, 1. 1427-12, Wynkoop Collection, CNA.

38. William Greathouse to Wynkoop, June 5, 1973, 1. 2223-6; Paul N. Ellis to Wynkoop, November 22, 1974. 2223-4; Howard A. Snyder and Donald W. Dayton to Wynkoop, February 14, 1977. 1427-7; Dayton to Wynkoop, March 9, 1974, 1. 1427-10, Wynkoop Collection, CNA. Dayton went on to make a career out of challenging Reformed historians' definitions of evangelicalism, publishing accounts that emphasized the Holiness and pietistic strains of American Protestantism and disputing the emphasis that historians like George Marsden have placed on Princeton theology and the fundamentalist-modernist controversy. See Donald W. Dayton, " 'The Search for the Historical Evangelicalism': George Marsden's History of Fuller Seminary as a Case Study," symposium, *Christian Scholar's Review* 23 (September 1993): 34–40. See also Dayton, *Discovering an Evangelical Heritage* (New York: Harper & Row, 1976).

39. Cathy Stonehouse to Wynkoop, August 4, 1975. 2223-4, Wynkoop Collection, CNA.

40. David Duffie to Wynkoop, August 29, 1978. 1427-16, Wynkoop Collection, CNA.

Chapter 5: The Marks of Campus Conversion

1. Hugh Andrews to Samuel Sutherland, March 14, 1962, 2. Sutherland Papers, "A," File 1, Section C, ASCBU.

2. Sutherland to John Pais, Jr., May 19, 1965. Sutherland Papers, B Corresp., File 1, Section C. In another letter to friends of the college, he dismissed *Christianity Today* as "neo-orthodox" (Sutherland to Mr. and Mrs. Walter L. Coats, November 14, 1966. Sutherland Papers, B Corresp., File 1, Section C, ASCBU).

3. Burton J. Bledstein, *The Culture of Professionalism: The Middle Class and the Development of Higher Education in America* (New York: Norton, 1976), 52, 85–86. Bledstein explains this social function of professionalism in chapter 3, "The Culture of Professionalism," 80–128.

4. William K. Selden, *Accreditation: A Struggle Over Standards in Higher Education* (New York: Harper & Brothers, 1960), 30ff.

5. Other exceptions to the generally belated pattern of evangelical and fundamentalist college accreditation include the following: The Western Association of Schools and Colleges accredited the Southern Baptist institution Baylor University in 1914. Emmanuel Missionary College (now Andrews University), a Seventh-day Adventist school in Berrien Springs, Michigan, gained accreditation from the North Central Association in 1922, and Calvin College followed in 1930. The Southern Association of Colleges and Schools accredited Samford University in 1920, Erskine College (Associate Reformed Presbyterian) in 1925, Lynchburg College (Christian Churches/Churches of Christ) in 1927, and Asbury College (Methodist) in 1940. Date of accreditation varied somewhat by region and depended on when the local accrediting association formed (per listings of affiliated institutions, available at www.ncahlc.org; www.sacscoc.org; www.neasc.org; www.wascweb.org). By way of further comparison, Yeshiva University, a Jewish research university founded in 1886 in New York, was accredited in 1948 (http://www.msche.org/institutions_view.asp?idinstitution=553).

6. On conservative Protestants' understanding of the decline of American higher education, see George Marsden, *The Soul of the American University: From Protestant Establishment to Established Nonbelief* (New York: Oxford University Press, 1994). David Riesman and Christopher Jencks describe the professional ethos as "relatively colleague-oriented rather than client-oriented." Riesman and Jencks, *The Academic Revolution* (New York: Anchor, 1969 [1968]), 251. Sam Sutherland to Robert McQuilkin, December 16, 1948, 1. Accrediting Association of Bible Colleges [AABC], Misc., Section A, Sutherland Papers, ASCBU.

7. *Sixty-Second Annual Catalog, Sessions of 1949–50*, Moody Bible Institute, Chicago, IL, 26–30, 11. Moody Bible Institute Catalog, CLAMBI. For a comprehensive overview of North American Bible college curricula as they stood in 1960, see S. A. Witmer, *The Bible College Story: Education With Dimension* (Manhasset, NY: Channel Press, 1962). The best scholarly history of the Bible college movement is Brereton, *Training God's Army*, but her history includes only scant coverage of the years under consideration here.

8. An undated manuscript from the early days of the Accrediting Association of Bible Colleges, probably from the late 1940s, estimated that between 100 and 120 fundamentalist Bible colleges were operating in the United States and Canada, representing a total enrollment of only 25,000 at any given time ("What Does Bible School Accreditation Mean?," 1. AABC, Misc., Section A, Sutherland Papers, ASCBU).

9. Joel A. Carpenter, *Revive Us Again: The Reawakening of American Fundamentalism* (New York: Oxford University Press, 1997), 16ff.

10. Sutherland to Louis S. Bauman, November 10, 1943, p1. B Corresp., File 1, Section C, Sutherland Papers, ASCBU.

11. "Born of Controversy: the G.I. Bill of Rights," U.S. Department of Veterans Affairs, available at http://www.gibill.va.gov/GI_Bill_Info/history.htm. Edward Humes writes that the GI Bill made possible the educations of "fourteen future Nobel Prize winners, three Supreme Court justices, three presidents, a dozen senators, two dozen Pulitzer Prize winners, 238,000 teachers, 91,000 scientists, 67,000 doctors, 450,000 engineers, 240,000 accountants, 17,000 journalists, 22,000 dentists—along with a million lawyers, nurses, businessmen, artists, actors, writers, pilots, and others" (Humes, *Over Here: How the G.I. Bill Transformed the American Dream* [New York: Harcourt, 2006], 6).

12. Committee on the Objectives of General Education in a Free Society, *General Education in a Free Society: Report of the Harvard Committee* (Cambridge, MA: Harvard University Press, 1945), v; Thomas A. Askew, "The Shaping of Evangelical Higher Education Since World War II," in *Making Higher Education Christian*, ed. Joel A. Carpenter and Kenneth W. Shipps (Grand Rapids, MI: Eerdmans, 1987), 144–45; "Ivy Roots of Harvard and Yale Feel Sharp Prods of Curriculum Shuffles," *Christian Science Monitor*, August 31, 1945, 9.

13. Luella Smith to Sutherland, August 4, 1943, and Sutherland to Smith, December 31, 1943. B Corresp., File 1, Section C, Sutherland Papers. Shortly thereafter, even Wheaton turned its back on Biola: "I have contacted Wheaton and other colleges in behalf of our own students and, although they are very sympathetic, yet they say their hands are tied because we are not accredited. I am sure you have had the same experiences," Sutherland wrote to Robert McQuilkin, president of Columbia Bible College, in 1946 (Sutherland to McQuilkin, October 31, 1946, 1. AABC, Old Files, Section A, Sutherland Papers). Bethel College (now Bethel University, in St. Paul, Minnesota) rejected Biola credits despite not obtaining regional accreditation itself until 1959 (Witmer to Sutherland, November 30, 1942. AABC, Old Files, Section A, Sutherland Papers, ASCBU). The war also inspired many young Christians to become military chaplains—a boon to the Bible colleges, at first—but after the war ended, the U.S. military tightened its requirements for chaplains, insisting on an accredited seminary degree. In 1953, the president of Nazarene Theological Seminary cited this as a central reason for the school's pursuit of accreditation from the American Association of Theological Schools, assuring trustees that accreditation "will in nowise affect or influence the fundamental purpose of the seminary" ("President's Report to Board of Trustees," January 8, 1953, 6. 1128-14, Seminary correspondence, CNA). The Assemblies of God Committee on Graduate School also took military chaplaincy requirements into account when considering the addition of graduate programs to Central Bible Institute in 1957 ("Report of Committee on Graduate School Program," March 1, 1957, 1. Exec. Files—Central Bible College, 8-2-10-61, FPHC).

14. Sutherland to Ray Myers, October 11, 1948, 2. "Significant Papers," Sutherland Papers, ASCBU; Milton T. Wells to Ralph Riggs, October 5, 1956, 3. Education Department, 13-50, FPHC.

15. Ralph Riggs, "Glad Tidings Bible Institute Seminar" (stenographically recorded), May 9–13, 1949, 17. Bible Institute Seminars, FPHC.

16. "Eleventh Annual Meeting: Minutes," Accrediting Association of Bible Institutes and Bible Colleges, October 24–25, 1957, 2. AABC, Annual Rept, Section A, Sutherland Papers, ASCBU.

17. Wells to Riggs, October 5, 1956, 2.

18. Robert Maynard Hutchins, *The Higher Learning in America* (New Haven, CT: Yale University Press, 1936), 31; John Henry Newman, *The Idea of a University Defined and Illustrated* (London: Longmans, Green, and Co., 1901 [1852]), Discourse 7, 153.

19. Sutherland to Howard W. Ferrin, January 15, 1947. AABC, Old Files, Section A, Sutherland Papers. Dallas Theological Seminary president Lewis Sperry Chafer advised a student considering matriculation at Moody Bible Institute: "Any recognition of a Bible institute is a liability rather than an asset when you come to move among thoroughly trained men, as you must do. The

prejudice which is abroad against Bible institutes is somewhat justified in view of the fact that the students have been encouraged to assume that they are prepared for the ministry, and educated men have resented this, and always will" (qtd. in John D. Hannah, *An Uncommon Union: Dallas Theological Seminary and American Evangelicalism* [Grand Rapids, MI: Zondervan, 2009], 82). "The Role of the AABC as a Professional Accrediting Agency," September 1967. AABC, Annual Mtgs, Section A; Terrelle Crum to the Association, December 15, 1947, 1. AABC, Misc., Section A, Sutherland Papers. Like the NAE, the AABC organized partly with the intention of gaining "something of a voice" among politicians and Department of Education regulators in Washington. After World War II, the federal government began pouring funds into student loans and scientific research—subsidies that were flooding mainstream universities' coffers at the rate of $150 million a year by 1952. This bonanza largely excluded Bible colleges. Washington's new role in higher education was an especially hard blow for Baptist institutions, which often interpreted their tradition's objection to government interference in religion to mean that Baptist students could not apply for federal loans, and that Baptist colleges could not seek federal aid, thereby also losing out on matching funds from private donors ("The Role of the AABC," 3; "Higher Education and National Affairs," Bulletin No. 193 (American Council on Education), November 12, 1952, 1. Fldr 4, Box 93, Bender Collection, MCUSA; "Baptist Education Study Task," sponsored by Education Commission of the Southern Baptist Convention, September 15, 1967, 28–30 (Fldr 1, Box 6, Wilmer C. Fields Collection, SBHLA; Crum to the Association, December 15, 1947, 1. AABC, Misc., Section A, Sutherland Papers, ASCBU).

20. Sutherland to Crum, March 23, 1950, 1. AABC, Misc., Section A, Sutherland Papers, ASCBU. Many faculty at Pasadena College, the Nazarene institution now called Point Loma University, had PhDs from the University of Southern California in the 1950s (see Pasadena College Bulletins, 369-3, Pasadena College, CNA).

21. Leland Keys to Riggs, September 21, 1956, 2. Education Department, 13-50, FPHC.

22. Robert McQuilkin to Sutherland, January 10, 1947, 2. AABC, Old Files, Section A, Sutherland Papers; Philip Goff, "Fighting Like the Devil in the City of Angels: The Rise of Fundamentalist Charles E. Fuller," in *Metropolis in the Making: Los Angeles in the 1920s*, ed. Tom Sitton and William Deverell (Berkeley: University of California, 2001), 220–52; Charles Mayes to Sutherland, July 13, 1951, 1. Mayes, Charles, Corresp., Section C, Sutherland Papers, ASCBU.

23. McQuilkin to Sutherland, November 29, 1946, 3, 1. AABC, Old Files, Section A, Sutherland Papers, ASCBU. The Bible college movement's close association with premillennialist eschatology alienated some evangelical denominations that historically rejected this view of the end-times and associated Bible colleges with "legalism and fanaticism." When the Church of the Nazarene finally moved to found a Bible college in the mid-1960s, the decision was controversial. See G. B. Williamson, n.d., "Plea for Nazarene Bible College," 2. 1234-1, Educational Addresses, CNA. McQuilkin was a passionate disciple of a spiritual movement that pervaded many Bible colleges in the early twentieth century: the Victorious Life, an American offshoot of holiness teachings that ignited evangelicals in the late nineteenth century at the Keswick conferences in England. Disciples of the Victorious Life, who played a large role in the Bible college movement, stressed complete surrender to Christ and abandonment of worldly ambition. See Douglas W. Frank, *Less Than Conquerors*, 114ff.; Charles G. Trumbull, *Victory in Christ*, 14.

24. Sutherland to Ray Myers, October 11, 1948, 1. "Significant Papers," Sutherland Papers, Brereton, *Training God's Army*, 85. In 1952, Biola added an art department and offered twenty-six art courses by 1958 (offerings in the sciences remained weakest). *Catalog of Biola Bible College* (1952–1954), 38; *Catalog of Biola Bible College* (1958), ASCBU; Robert P. Lightner, *Neoevangelicalism Today* (Schaumburg, IL: Regular Baptist Press, 1978 [1965]), 41.

25. Ernest Sandeen likened the World Christian Fundamentals Association's plan, initiated by Moody Bible Institute president James Gray, to an "agency of Christian accreditation" (Sandeen, *The Roots of Fundamentalism* [Grand Rapids, MI: Baker, 1978], 244).

26. Malone College and Messiah Bible College were two other schools that followed the same trajectory as Azusa; see the minutes of the twelfth annual AABC meeting, October 29, 1958, 1. AABC, Annual Rept, Section A, Sutherland Papers; John Mostert to G. Allen Fleece, April 5, 1965; also Fleece to Mostert, October 12, 1965, 2. AABC, Annual Mtgs, Section A, Sutherland Papers, ASCBU.

27. Fleece to Mostert, October 12, 1965, 2; John Mostert to Sutherland, December 3, 1965, 1. AABC, Annual Mtgs, Section A, Sutherland Papers, ASCBU. Today the AABC is called the Association for Biblical Higher Education and includes about two hundred institutions in its membership. Christian Smith remarked on evangelicals' skillful ambivalence toward mainstream culture in his survey of evangelical laypeople in the late twentieth century: "The American evangelical movement…has been relatively successful because it has managed to formulate and sustain a religious strategy that maintains both high tension with and high integration into mainstream American society simultaneously" (*American Evangelicalism*, 150). See also his critique of secular sociologists' shallow theories of cultural accommodation by traditional religious groups (96–99).

28. Riggs, "Glad Tidings Bible Institute Seminar," 5, 6.

29. Ibid., 39.

30. "Faculty Handbook," Central Bible Institute, 1963, 6, 7. Exec. Files—Central Bible College, 8-2-10-61, FPHC. For much of its history, Point Loma Nazarene College (now University) issued no statement of academic freedom in its faculty handbook; instead, "faculty were trusted to have differing opinions so long as they were circumspect in their presentations" (Ronald B. Kirkemo, "Point Loma Nazarene College: Modernization in Christian Higher Education," in *Models for Christian Higher Education: Strategies for Success in the Twenty-First Century*, ed. Richard T. Hughes and William B. Adrian [Grand Rapids, MI: Eerdmans, 1997], 357). Pepperdine University, which is affiliated with the Churches of Christ but has always exercised an unusual degree of independence because George Pepperdine's large bequest freed the school from complete dependence on religious giving, has never required faculty to sign a statement of faith. However, it asks applicants to provide a statement explaining how they will "support the Christian mission of the University" and reserves the right to prefer members of the Churches of Christ in hiring (Richard T. Hughes, "Faith and Learning at Pepperdine University," in ibid., 414; see also Darren Dochuk, *From Bible Belt to Sunbelt*, 71ff., and http://seaver.pepperdine.edu/dean/faculty/).

31. Purkiser, "Teaching in a Nazarene College" and "Report to the Board," October 12, 1948, qtd. in Ronald B. Kirkemo, *For Zion's Sake: A History of Pasadena/Point Loma* College (San Diego, CA: Point Loma Press, 1992), 206–7. In 1987 the American Association of University Professors moved to censure Southern Nazarene University in Oklahoma City for failing to prove that "financial exigency" required the firing of several professors ("Committee A Update," *Oklahoma Conference American Association of University Professors Newsletter*, May 1987, 2. 2890-42, SNU correspondence, CNA). The American Scientific Affiliation, founded in 1941 by evangelical scientists, organized fifteen years before the first major wave of evangelical academic societies. The Conference on Christianity and Literature and the Christian Association for Psychological Studies both organized in 1956, the Christian Legal Society in 1961, and the Conference on Faith and History in 1967. The Christian Sociological Society, the Society of Christian Philosophers, the Society for Pentecostal Studies, and Christian anthropologists all organized—the anthropologists only informally—in the 1970s, though networking between evangelical academics was already under way in the previous decade. "Who is there who is doing a respectable job as a Christian sociologist?" William H. Anderson, a Presbyterian minister-turned-sociology professor, wrote to Carl Henry in 1964. "I am interested in something more than a sociologist who goes to church. Many Christian colleges according to the directory of the American Sociological Association seem to have a sociologist caged somewhere in the institution, but I never hear from them" (Anderson to Henry, December 22, 1964. Fldr 7, Box 17, CTI, BGCA).

32. The 1953 Biola catalog's faculty listing includes individuals with PhDs from Northwestern University, Johns Hopkins University, the University of Edinburgh, and the California Institute of Technology (*Catalog of Biola Bible College*, 1953–1954, 29–30, ASCBU). Mark Noll has noted that in the years after World War II, most prominent evangelical scholars taught at liberal arts colleges, which "have a different goal from the research universities. Most important, they function under entirely different reward structures" (*Scandal of the Evangelical Mind*, 16ff).

33. "Report to Evangel College," January 13–14, 1965, 1. Exec. Files—Evangel College, 8-2-10-59, FPHC.

34. Chris R. Vanden Bossche, "Moving Out: Adolescence," in *A Companion to Victorian Literature and Culture*, ed. Herbert F. Tucker (Malden, MA: Blackwell, 1999), 82. The psychologist and educator G. Stanley Hall deserves much of the credit for inventing our modern notion of adolescence. See Hall, *Adolescence: Its Psychology and Its Relations to Physiology, Anthropology, Sociology, Sex, Crime, Religion and Education* (1904). See the entry for "teenager," *Oxford English Dictionary* (1989 ed.), available at http://dictionary.oed.com/cgi/entry/50248209?single=1&query_type=word &queryword=teenager&first=1&max_to_show=10; Thomas Doherty, *Teenagers and Teenpics: The Juvenilization of American Movies in the 1950s* (Boston: Unwin Hyman, 1988); James Gilbert, *Cycle of Outrage: America's Reaction to the Juvenile Delinquent in the 1950s* (New York: Oxford University Press, 1986); David L. Angus and Jeffrey Mirel, *The Failed Promise of the American High School, 1890–1995* (New York: Teachers College Press, 1999).

35. Ockenga, "Can Fundamentalism Win America?," *Moody Student*, June 27, 1947, 2. Personal Fldr, Box 1, William Culbertson Papers, CLAMBI.

36. David [last name missing due to torn page], University of Rhode Island, "What Is Man?," *Moody Student*, October 25, 1963. 2; Leith Anderson, "Immune Christians?," *Moody Student*, May 15, 1964, 2; "Civil Rights Controversy," *Moody Student*, May 1, 1964, 2. This editorial is cautiously egalitarian: "Let us not forget that Jesus Christ died on the cross for the salvation of men from every race. When torn by prejudice or difficult questions, consider the work of the cross.... We must not make decisions quickly. Since most students of the Institute will serve in positions of church leadership, the responsibility is great."

37. Dennis Shippy, "Reaction to 'buffoonery' in skits," *Moody Student*, March 1, 1968, 2.

38. Student survey, June 1964, 2. "Alumni," Section D, Sutherland Papers; "Alumni Information," June 1963, 1. "Alumni," Section D, Sutherland Papers, ASCBU.

39. "MOODY STUDENT under fire," *Moody Student*, February 14, 1969, 2. CLAMBI; Sutherland, memo, January 27, 1969. *Chimes*, Section A, Sutherland Papers, ASCBU.

40. Sutherland to Todd Lewis, January 21, 1969. *Chimes*, Section A, Sutherland Papers; Sutherland to Bill Siemens, May 21, 1968. Student Problems, Section A, Sutherland Papers; interview transcript, Sutherland and Bob Guernsey (1968), 3. Sutherland Papers, *Chimes*, Section A, ASCBU.

41. William B. Adrian, Jr., "The Christian University: Maintaining Distinctions in a Pluralistic Culture," in Hughes and Adrian, *Models for Christian Higher Education*, 447. For examples of how some sectarian schools have embraced a self-consciously nondenominational evangelical identity, see Paul Toews, "Religious Idealism and Academic Vocation at Fresno Pacific College," Steven Moore and William Woodward, "Clarity Through Ambiguity: Transforming Tensions at Seattle Pacific University," and Douglas Jacobsen, "The History and Character of Messiah College, 1909–1995," all in Hughes and Adrian, *Models for Christian Higher Education*.

42. Dalhouse, *Island in a Lake of Fire*, 42. Bob Jones College (later Bob Jones University) eventually moved to Cleveland, Tennessee, and then to Greenville, South Carolina.

43. John Stam, "Fundamentalist Formalism," *Kodon*, December 1949, 7, 18. WCSC. Stam's intellectual independence would mature into full-fledged rebellion from the evangelical establishment. In the 1980s, the local church association in Costa Rica stripped him of his ministerial credentials for criticizing Ronald Reagan and expressing support for the Sandinista rebels

in Nicaragua. See David Stoll, *Is Latin America Turning Protestant? The Politics of Evangelical Growth* (Berkeley: University of California Press, 1990), 171.

44. Art Kinsler, "Windows for the Cloister," *Kodon*, April 1955, 9ff.; Jim Gustafson, "Le Grande Chartreuse," *Kodon*, October 1953, 12ff.; Don Remnick(?), "How Right Is Capitalism?," *Kodon*, April 1956, 18; Letter to the Editor, *Record*, December 8, 1960, 2; "If Man Created Life...," *Record*, October 19, 1962, 2. WCSC. *Kodon* also reviewed Fuller professors' books, such as Wilbur M. Smith's *Therefore Stand* (1945), interestingly paired with reviews of G. K. Chesterton's autobiography and Theodore Dreiser's *The Bulwark*; *Kodon*, October 1946, 10–12; Hans Burki, "Scholars for God's Research," *Kodon*, March 1948, 5ff. WCSC. Wheaton's students included some of the brightest evangelical youth. By 1965, the annual college report boasted that 10 percent of the newly admitted class were high school valedictorians and 65 percent came from the highest tenth of their class (Bechtel, *Wheaton College*, 287). By the 1960s, it was generally acknowledged that Wheaton's poor faculty salaries often failed to attract professors who could intellectually match the student body (Hamilton, "Fundamentalist Harvard," 161).

45. Wesley Earl Craven, "A Warning from the Editor," *Kodon*, September 1962, 3. WCSC.

46. Craven, "Kodon Answers Its Self-Styled Critics," *Wheaton Record*, November 29, 1962, 3. WCSC.

47. *Kodon*, October 1963. WCSC.

48. Dale E. Soden and Arlin Migliazzo, "Whitworth College: Evangelical in the Reformed Tradition," in Hughes and Adrian, *Models for Christian Higher Education*, 175; James D. Bratt and Ronald A. Wells, "Piety and Progress: A History of Calvin College," in Hughes and Adrian, *Models for Christian Higher Education*, 152-153.

49. David R. Swartz, *Moral Minority: The Evangelical Left in an Age of Conservatism* (Philadelphia: University of Pennsylvania Press, 2012), 31ff.; "'Civilization On Trial' This Semester," *Wheaton Record*, January 31, 1963, 1; "Historian Arnold Toynbee to Lecture Next Semester," *Wheaton Record*, October 19, 1962, 4. WCSC.

50. "Modern Art for Christians?," *Wheaton Record*, October 13, 1961, 2; "Objectives of the Art Major," memo, February 27, 1969. J. Richard Chase Papers, Curriculum Committee, ASCBU. Smaller networks, such as the Institute for Christian Art and the Fellowship of Christians in the Arts, Media, and Entertainment (founded in 1967 in the United States, 1970 in Europe), also appeared (1970–1971 Bulletin, Institute for Christian Art, Fall 1970. Box IX F 2, Coll SC-18, Hans Rookmaaker Papers, WCSC); "Introducing...The Fellowship of Christians in the Arts, Media, and Entertainment," newsletter, January 1970. Box IX F 1, Rookmaaker Papers. The International Arts Movement, another influential evangelical network of artists, began in 1991 and hosts an annual conference in New York City. This interest in fine art has extended beyond classrooms and studios. In recent decades, churches across a range of denominations have begun to invite artists to hang shows in their buildings, make more room in their budgets for artistic programming, and expand the role of lay creativity in worship and prayer, performing parables and painting the Beatitudes (Robert Wuthnow, *All in Sync: How Music and Art Are Revitalizing American Religion* [Berkeley: University of California Press, 2003]).

51. Miriam Hunter to Board of Trustees, April 19, 1979, 1–2; April 30, 1975, 2. Fldr 30, Box 9, Lindsell Papers, BGCA. Hunter, a colleague, observed: "The vulval theme is carried out to a large extent in Mr. Steffler's sculpture—in semi-abstract form for the most part, although the subject is easily recognized by the untrained eye. One lady, in coming upon the sculpture series unexpectedly in the Art Department exclaimed, 'Is that what I think it is!' to which her husband replied, 'Yes, I think it is.' He remarked at a later point that 'Someone ought to tell Alva that there are parts above certain parts and parts below certain parts.' Mr. Steffler's response, when approached, was to suggest renaming one of his pieces 'Peach Halves'...In speaking to my sculpture class about his sculpture, using slides, he said, 'I know it's a taboo subject among Christians, but I think it's beautiful and ought to be celebrated.'" See also "Report of

a Visit to the Wheaton College Art Department," April 21–22, 1980. Fldr 32, Box 9, Lindsell Papers, BGCA.

52. Paul M. Bechtel, "Clyde Kilby: A Sketch," in *Imagination and the Spirit: Essays in Literature and the Christian Faith*, ed. Charles A. Huttar (Grand Rapids, MI: Eerdmans, 1971), 467–70; Bechtel, *Wheaton College*, 208.

53. Clive Staples Lewis, in *The Letters of C.S. Lewis to Arthur Greeves*, ed. Walter Hooper (New York: Collier Books, 1986), 427; Calvin D. Linton, "C. S. Lewis Ten Years Later," *Christianity Today*, November 9, 1973, 5; qtd. in Virginia Ramey Mollencott, "Fiction, Fact, and Truth," *Christianity Today*, September 24, 1965, 10. Toward the end of his life, A. W. Tozer lamented the state of evangelical literature and complained that "we have developed a 'fiction mind,' that is a mind unable to think abstractly. We must be told a story like a child" (qtd. in Priscilla Parce, "Tozer Asks for Original Christian Fiction; Believes in Christian Higher Education," *Wheaton Record*, October 2, 1952, 1; Clyde S. Kilby, "C. S. Lewis: Everyman's Theologian," *Christianity Today*, January 3, 1964, 11–13; Gilbert Meilaender, Jr., "The New Paganism," *Christianity Today*, September 24, 1971, 4–5; Jud Olsen, "Collegiate Christian," *Moody Student*, September 24, 1965, 2; Nigel John Sandor, "Lewis Shows Reality in Fantasy," *Moody Student*, December 16, 1966, 2; Fred W. Smith, "Is the Bible a Textbook on Science?," *Restoration Herald*, April 1, 1969, 5; qtd. in Mark Noll, "Opening a Wardrobe: Clyde S. Kilby (1902–1986)," *Reformed Journal*, December 1986, 7.

54. Stan Shank, "Books For Young Evangelicals," *Christian Bookseller Magazine*, January 1975, 25; Clyde Kilby, "History of the Marion E. Wade Collection at Wheaton College From Its Beginning to the End of 1979," 1980, 2. Clyde S. Kilby Papers, MWC; "The Region of the Pit," *Kodon*, November 1946, 19; Ileen Sebby, "Dear Wormwood," *Kodon*, October 1948, 6 (later a regular feature, "The Gallwood Letters"); "Warning, Wormwood!" *Wheaton Record*, February 21, 1946, 2; "Dear Wormwood," *Wheaton Record*, December 19, 1963, 2; WCSC; "How to Beat the Beaten Path" (interview with Clyde Kilby), *Christianity Today*, September 9, 1977, 31.

55. Kilby, "How to Beat the Beaten Path," 16.

56. Kilby, "The Decline and Fall of the Christian Imagination," *Eternity*, March 1965, 15, 16, 17, 46; Kilby, "The Aesthetic Poverty of Evangelicalism," *Wheaton Alumni Magazine*, November 1967, 5. The Wheaton College administration finally came around to the collection's potential in the mid-1970s when friends and family of a prominent alumnus, Marion E. Wade, made a large bequest to Kilby's project. Lectures, festivals, and conferences associated with the collection proliferated.

57. Kilby to Dorothy Alford, May 23, 1980, 2. Fldr 12, Kilby Correspondence, MWC "Some Comments From Students Taking the Course 'Modern Mythological Literature' at Wheaton College," May 1975, 3. Series 1, Fldr 37, Wade History Collection, MWC.

58. "Narnia Wardrobe at Westmont," *Inside*, November 1976, 1. Fldr 19, Kilby Correspondence. American evangelicals' Anglophilia was somewhat hampered by their abstinence from favored British refreshments. Kilby related an anecdote from a campus visit by Christopher Derrick, a Roman Catholic disciple of Lewis: "Christopher was flabbergasted that Wheaton had no beer, not even the Kilbys. We took him to a saloon on the edge of town, the Righteous waiting while he went inside for a six-pack. We brought him back…and we promptly drank two cans all the time talking about people like these funny ones at Wheaton who don't know that the Bible requires one to drink beer and its cousins" (Kilby to Thomas Howard, October 24, 1978. Fldr 243.5[2], Kilby Correspondence). On another occasion, Kilby apologized to Warren Lewis: "Sorry I embarrassed you in tea-houses by drinking Coca-Cola and promise to do better next time" (Kilby to Warren Lewis, August 28, 1969, Fldr 305, Kilby Correspondence, MWC). I have personally toured Taylor's shrine to C. S. Lewis.

59. Robert E. Webber, "Are Evangelicals Becoming Sacramental?," *Ecumenical Trends*, March 1985, 37.

60. John A. Schmalzbauer and C. Gray Wheeler, "Between Fundamentalism and Secularization: Secularizing and Sacralizing Currents in the Evangelical Debate on Campus Lifestyle Codes," *Sociology of Religion* 57, no. 3 (Autumn 1996): 254. See also Christian Smith et al., *American Evangelicalism*, 97–101.

61. R. Wayne Wever, letter to members, August 1971. Box 13, Fldr 2, Glasser Papers, DAHL; "Faculty Witness in Campus and Community: Opportunities and Objectives" (IVCF memo), June 1976, 3. Fldr 5, Box 21, Records of InterVarsity Christian Fellowship, BGCA.

62. Kilby, "How to Beat the Beaten Path," 30.

CHAPTER 6: MISSIONS BEYOND THE WEST

1. "Billy in India," *Time*, February 13, 1956; Billy Graham, *Just As I Am: The Autobiography of Billy Graham* (New York: HarperCollins, 1997), 264–69.

2. P. Lal, "Billy Graham in India," *The Nation*, April 7, 1956, 276; "Reconversion in India," *Time*, July 30, 1956.

3. As of the year 2000, American evangelicals spent $12 on missions and international relief for every single dollar they donated to political organizations; they spent twice that on Christian higher education (Michael S. Hamilton, "More Money, More Ministry: The Financing of American Evangelicalism Since 1945," in *More Money, More Ministry: Money and Evangelicals in Recent North American History*, ed. Larry Eskridge and Mark A. Noll [Grand Rapids, MI: Eerdmans, 2000], 130–31).

4. William Clarkson, *Christ and Missions: Facts and Principles of Evangelism* (London: John Snow, 1858), 256.

5. Chester L. Schneider, *Whaddya Mean By That?* (Maitland, FL: Xulon Press, 2004), 142–43; Gordon Hedderly Smith, *The Missionary and Anthropology: An Introduction to the Study of Primitive Man for Missionaries* (Chicago: Moody Press, 1945), 5, 18, 26, 15. Bethel University in St. Paul began a strong anthropology program in the 1960s. In his study of Fuller Theological Seminary, *Reforming Fundamentalism*, George Marsden writes that the Church Growth proponents at Fuller in the 1960s were among the first evangelicals to discover the social sciences and the idea of cultural conditioning. Until then, "such sensitivities had been almost exclusively the property of the liberal side of the American Protestant tradition" (Marsden, *Reforming Fundamentalism*, 239). While evangelicals' earlier forays into sociology and anthropology may have been less sophisticated than those of their liberal peers, conservative evangelicals were sincerely interested in the social sciences much earlier than Marsden suggests.

6. Darrell Whiteman, "Anthropology and Mission: An Uneasy Journey toward Mutual Understanding," in *Paradigm Shifts in Christian Witness: Insights from Anthropology, Communication, and Spiritual Power*, ed. Charles Van Engen, Darrell Whiteman, and J. Dudley Woodberry (Maryknoll, NY: Orbis, 1993), 8; Graham, *Just As I Am*, 65; Whiteman, "Anthropology and Mission," in Van Engen, Whiteman, and Woodberry, *Paradigm Shifts in Christian Witness*, 9; Eugene A. Nida, *Customs and Cultures: Anthropology for Christian Missions* (New York: Harper & Brothers, 1954), 52.

7. Arthur Glasser, "A Roman Witness to Christ" (review of Joseph A. Grassi, M.M., *A World To Win: The Missionary Methods of Paul the Apostle* [Maryknoll, NY: Maryknoll, 1965]), in *Christianity Today*, November 19, 1965, 35. Fuller Theological Seminary's School of World Mission also used Catholic anthropologist Louis Lutzebak's textbook in class, and some of its faculty published with the Catholic press Maryknoll; Paul Witte, "Can Catholics Learn Anything from Evangelical Protestants?," *Christianity Today*, December 18, 1970, 12–13. Witte was a Roman Catholic missionary who enrolled in SIL in the summer of 1966; Robert J. Priest, "Anthropology

and Missiology: reflections on the Relationship," in Van Engen, Whiteman, and Woodberry, *Paradigm Shifts in Christian Witness*, 25.

8. Edmund P. Clowney, "The Theology of Evangelism," *Christianity Today*, April 29, 1966, 5.

9. Donald A. McGavran, *The Bridges of God: A Study in the Strategy of Missions* (London: World Dominion Press, 1955), 8, 19, 21. J. Waskom Pickett's 1933 study, *Christian Mass Movements in India: A Study with Recommendations* (Nashville, TN: Abingdon Press, 1933), offered a similar critique. McGavran considered Pickett a mentor and called his book "the most significant missionary publication of the twentieth century." McGavran's book, however, reached a wider audience among American evangelicals (qtd. in Charles H. Kraft, *SWM/SIS at Forty: A Participant/Observer's View of Our History* [Pasadena, CA: William Carey Library, 2005], 7).

10. 1 Corinthians 9:22; *The Heliand: The Saxon Gospel*, trans. G. Ronald Murphy, S.J. (New York: Oxford University Press, 1992); Timothy Yates, *Christian Mission in the Twentieth Century* (New York: Cambridge University Press, 1994), 36–41. The rise of Nazi ideology exalting the *Volk* tainted the nineteenth-century German missiologists' analysis of tribal communities and rendered their work somewhat inadmissible for Anglo-American missionaries and scholars. One Buddha crucifix used by the Jesuits is in the possession of the Paris Foreign Missions Society.

11. For a detailed account of McGavran's philosophy and Church Growth at Fuller Theological Seminary, see Marsden, *Reforming Fundamentalism*, chapter 11.

12. Marsden, *Reforming Fundamentalism*, 239; Priest, "Anthropology and Missiology," in Van Engen, Whiteman, and Woodberry, *Paradigm Shifts in Christian Witness*, 28–29. Evangelicals' highly scientific view of anthropology is at odds with Clifford Geertz's characterization of anthropology as a discipline belonging to the humanities, in which mechanistic laws do not fairly apply.

13. Edward Dayton to Arthur Glasser, April 1, 1975. Fldr 20, Box 3, Glasser Papers, DAHL.

14. McGavran, "Why Neglect the Gospel-Ready Masses?," *Christianity Today*, April 29, 1966, 19.

15. Brochure for Church Growth International's "Natural Church Growth Seminar," April 29, 1981, co-hosted by Fridley Assembly of God and North Heights Lutheran Church, Minneapolis, MN. Fldr 19, Box 71, David du Plessis Papers, DAHL; "Advanced Degree Program," presentation to the Board of Directors, Assemblies of God Graduate School, November 12–13, 1973, 10. Exec. Files—AGTS, 8-2-10-60, FPHC; McGavran, "The God Who Finds and His Mission (first of three parts)," *Christian Standard*, June 12, 1965, 3–4 (the *Christian Standard* editors applauded McGavran because he was a disillusioned ex-member of the Disciples of Christ); Tim Stafford, "The Father of Church Growth," *Missions Frontiers*, January 1, 1986, 8.

16. W. E. Lyons to Glasser, February 18, 1975. Fldr 8, Box 13, Glasser Papers. DAHL; *Christian Beacon*, January 25, 1973, 1. The Reformed Presbyterian Church, Evangelical Synod, merged with the Presbyterian Church in America in 1982.

17. Rob Staples, "Wesleyan Theology and the HUP," February 9, 1979, 4. 3431-31, Staples Collection, CNA; Lesslie Newbigin to Glasser, September 28, 1973. Fldr 5, Box 12, Glasser Papers, DAHL.

18. Yoder, "The Homogeneous Unit Concept in Ethical Perspective," delivered at Pasadena consultation, May 31–June 2, 1977, 1. Fldr 7, Box 5, Glasser Papers, DAHL. Charles Kraft, interview with the author, March 27, 2009. Kraft's view is that "the mission leaders felt threatened by me because they couldn't trust me to wholeheartedly support certain mission rules. We sponsored Christian 'dances' (actually more like games), advocated the baptism of believing polygamists and did not support the mission's disciplinary practices. I also spoke Hausa better than any of the other missionaries. Furthermore, we were well-liked by the Nigerians who elected me, a first termer, over the Field Secretary of the mission to the body that was in charge of church polity and life."

19. Yoder, "Homogeneous Unit Concept," 6.

20. David Howard, Elisabeth Elliot's brother, served with the Latin American Mission in Colombia and Costa Rica from 1953 to 1968 before becoming director of missions for InterVarsity,

then general secretary of the World Evangelical Fellowship. Tim Stafford was a missionary in Kenya before becoming a prominent staff writer for *Christianity Today*. A third-generation missionary born in Hong Kong, Clyde Cook, served in the Philippines before becoming president of Biola College.

21. For discussion of the intersection of modern psychoanalysis and pastoral care, see Alan Petigny, *Permissive Society*.

22. Abraham Kuyper, in speech delivered October 20, 1880, at New Church, Amsterdam. Qtd. in James Bratt, ed., *Abraham Kuyper: A Centennial Reader* (Grand Rapids, MI: Eerdmans, 1998), 488.

23. Nida, *Customs and Cultures*, 66, 70, 255.

24. Harold Lindsell, *Missionary Principles and Practice* (Westwood, NJ: Revell, 1955), 281, 196; Richard V. Pierard, "*Pax Americana* and the Evangelical Missionary Advance," in *Earthen Vessels: American Evangelicals and Foreign Missions, 1880–1980*, ed. Joel A. Carpenter and Wilbert R. Shenk (Grand Rapids, MI: Eerdmans, 1990), 161.

25. Glenda Elizabeth Gilmore, *Defying Dixie: The Radical Roots of Civil Rights, 1919–1950* (New York: Norton, 2008), chapter 1; Mary L. Dudziak, *Cold War Civil Rights: Race and the Image of American Democracy* (Princeton, NJ: Princeton University Press, 2000); Thomas Borstelmann, *The Cold War and the Color Line: American Race Relations in the Global Arena* (Cambridge, MA: Harvard University Press, 2001).

26. Qtd. in Alan Scot Willis, *All According to God's Plan: Southern Baptist Missions and Race, 1945–1970* (Lexington: University Press of Kentucky, 2005), 51, 70.

27. Herschel Hobbs to Wayne Dehoney, October 15, 1965, 1. Fldr 72, Box 20, William Wayne Dehoney Collection, SBHLA.

28. Qtd. in David L. Chappell, *A Stone of Hope: Prophetic Religion and the Death of Jim Crow* (Chapel Hill: University of North Carolina Press, 2004), 117; Steven P. Miller, *Billy Graham and the Rise of the Republican South* (Philadelphia: University of Pennsylvania Press, 2009), 32.

29. Press release, Bob Jones University, December 9, 1970. Rice Fldr, Box 1, William Culbertson Papers, CLAMBI; William Culbertson to John R. Rice, December 8, 1970; Culbertson to Menno Harms, January 25, 1971. John Rice Fldr, Box 1, Culbertson Papers. Earlier that same year, a black Moody student had ripped up his diploma in front of the school in protest, challenging an emeritus dean "to defend publicly over [Moody radio station] WMBI...a statement he made in May, 1969, to the effect that 'the Bible teaches that interracial marriage is inherently wrong'" ("Ex-Students protest 'Moody white racism,'" *Moody Student*, February 13, 1970, 1.). At least one black pastor took Rice's side: William Dinkins, former president of Selma University, wrote to Culbertson: "We Negroes often try to inject Civil rights into every circumstance, without sensing the effect of what we are doing. It makes us little...if Moody is going to yield to pressures like this, I just do not know where to put my feet on solid ground in reference to Moody. Yes, I stand with Dr. Rice for fundamentalism and the old-time religion all that goes with it" (William H. Dinkins to Culbertson, January 21, 1971. Rice Fldr, Box 1, Culbertson Papers, CLAMBI).

30. In 1963 the *Christianity Today* editors wrote of interracial marriage: "There may be nothing per se immoral about intermarriage. But the fact that despite the race's [*sic*] unity in Adam, God has preserved distinct nations whose social components are often racial (Acts 17:26) raises a question whether even spiritual redemption is intended in this life wholly to cancel racial distinctions" ("What of Racial Intermarriage?," *Christianity Today*, October 11, 1963, 27); Lois M. Ottoway, "Read, Baby, Read: A First Step to Action," *Christianity Today*, December 19, 1969, 7; Meeting Agenda, School of Theology, Daniel Fuller to Glenn Barker, October 26, 1972. Fldr 3, Box 24, Fuller Papers, DAHL; "Course Offerings, Gordon-Conwell Theological Seminary, Christianity and Society and Black Studies," 1974, Fldr 11, Box 1, Coll 37, Records of Evangelicals for Social Action (ESA), BGCA.

31. James S. Tinney, "Black Origins of the Pentecostal Movement," *Christianity Today*, October 8, 1971, 4–6; Margaret M. Poloma, *The Charismatic Movement: Is There A New Pentecost?*

(Boston: Twayne, 1982), 18. This section heading is the title of C. Peter Wagner's *Look Out! The Pentecostals Are Coming* (Carol Stream, IL: Creation House, 1973).

32. Margaret Poloma, *Charismatic Movement*, 13; Allan Heaton Anderson, *To the Ends of the Earth: Pentecostalism and the Transformation of World Christianity* (New York: Oxford University Press, 2013), 205; "Study Commission on Glossolalia, Preliminary Report" (Diocese of California, Division of Pastoral Services), 1962, 3. Fldr 2, Box 43, du Plessis Papers; Dennis J. Bennett, *Nine O'Clock in the Morning* (Plainfield, NJ: Logos, 1970), 61; Walter H. Steele, memo to the Reverend Clergy of Baton Rouge, March 5, 1962. Fldr 20, Box 30, du Plessis Papers, DAHL; R. E. Armstrong to du Plessis, October 30, 1963. Fldr 71, Box 7, du Plessis Papers; Frank Farrell, "Outburst of Tongues: The New Penetration," *Christianity Today*, September 13, 1963, 3; Brick Bradford, *Charismatic Communion* newsletter, March 1967. Fldr 89, Box 8, du Plessis Papers, DAHL.

33. Scott Billingsley, *It's A New Day: Race and Gender in the Modern Charismatic Movement* (Tuscaloosa: University of Alabama Press, 2008), 26, 29.

34. Ibid., 32–33, 38–41; David Wilkerson with John Sherrill and Elizabeth Sherrill, *The Cross and the Switchblade* (Grand Rapids, MI: Chosen Books, 2008 [1962]); see also "The Cross and the Switchblade," World Challenge, Inc., available at http://www.worldchallenge.org/en/about_david_wilkerson/cross_and_the_switchblade (accessed May 28, 2012). Kathryn Kuhlman followed in the footsteps of the pioneering female Pentecostal evangelist Aimee Semple McPherson.

35. Stephen Hunt, *A History of the Charismatic Movement in Britain and the United States of America: The Pentecostal Transformation of Christianity*, vol. 2 (Lewiston, NY: Mellen, 2009), 678.

36. H. A. Maxwell Whyte, *Charismatic Gifts* [pamphlet], 1972, 3. Fldr 4, Box 8, Hist. Mss. 1–105, Nelson and Ada Litwiller Collection, MCUSA.

37. "Oxford Begins Work on Revised Edition of Scofield Reference Bible," press release, January 10, 1954, 1. Fldr "Revision of Scofield," Box 1, Culbertson Papers, CLAMBI; Herbert W. Bateman IV, "Dispensationalism Yesterday and Today," in *Three Central Issues in Contemporary Dispensationalism: A Comparison of Traditional and Progressive Views*, ed. Bateman et al. (Grand Rapids, MI: Kregel, 1999), 27–31; Robert Saucy, interview with the author, April 9, 2009. See also Saucy, *The Case for Progressive Dispensationalism: The Interface Between Dispensational & Non-Dispensational Theology* (Grand Rapids, MI: Zondervan, 1993), 8–10; Robert L. Thomas, "The Hermeneutics of Progressive Dispensationalism," in *The Master's Perspective on Contemporary Issues*, ed. Thomas (Grand Rapids, MI: Kregel, 1998), 187ff.

38. Bennett, *Nine O'Clock*, 3–4, 20; Richard Ostling, "Ministering to the Middle Class," *Christianity Today*, October 11, 1963, 38; Donald E. Miller, *Reinventing American Protestantism: Christianity in the New Millennium* (Berkeley: University of California Press, 1997), 92ff. Chuck Smith, originally a Foursquare Gospel pastor and founder of the charismatic Calvary Chapel, made a habit of wearing a suit when he led worship and encouraged a culture of spiritual decorum. Smith kept such a tight rein that he barred young children from services—so one can imagine his attitude toward outbursts of the Spirit (Miller, *Reinventing American Protestantism*, 31).

39. Hunt, *History of the Charismatic Movement*, vol. 1, 316.

40. John J. Thompson, "Larry Norman: A Tribute," *Today's Christian Music*, March 31, 2008, http://www.todayschristianmusic.com/artists/larry-norman/features/larry-norman-a-tribute/; Sherwood Lingenfelter, interview with the author, March 25, 2009. See Miller, *Reinventing American Protestantism*, 8off.

41. Arlene M. Sánchez Walsh, *Latino Pentecostal Identity: Evangelical Faith, Self, and Society* (New York: Columbia University Press, 2003), 16off.

42. Minutes of the September 19–20, 1971, meeting of the Consultation on Evangelistic Strategy, 5. Fldr 17, Box 3, Glasser Papers, DAHL; Donald Williams, "Close-up of the Jesus People," *Christianity Today*, August 27, 1971, 6.

43. Billy Graham, *The Jesus Generation* (Grand Rapids, MI: Zondervan, 1971), 16, 22.

44. John Wimber, "Power Evangelism: Definitions and Directions," in *Wrestling with Dark Angels: Toward a Deeper Understanding of the Supernatural Forces in Spiritual Warfare*, ed. C. Peter Wagner and F. Douglas Pennoyer (Ventura, CA: Regal Books, 1990), 29–30; Wimber with Kevin Springer, *Power Evangelism* (Ventura, CA: Regal Books, 1986), 83ff.

45. Charles Kraft, in *Signs and Wonders Today*, ed. C. Peter Wagner (Wheaton, IL: *Christian Life Magazine*, 1982), 62, 37; Wagner, "Some Missiological Reasons for Considering the Issue of the Miraculous Works of the Holy Spirit at Fuller Seminary," April 4, 1986, 1. Fldr 13, Box 95, David A. Hubbard Papers, DAHL.

46. On Christians' oscillation between the extremes of rationalism and enthusiasm, especially since the sixteenth century, see Ronald A. Knox, *Enthusiasm: A Chapter in the History of Religion* (New York: Oxford University Press, 1950.)

47. T. M. Luhrmann, *When God Talks Back: Understanding the American Evangelical Relationship with God* (New York: Knopf, 2012), xxi.

CHAPTER 7: RENEWING THE CHURCH UNIVERSAL

1. Fr. Paul to du Plessis, December 25, 1969, 1–2. Fldr 2, Box 69, du Plessis Papers, DAHL.

2. Robert Wuthnow, *The Restructuring of American Religion: Society and Faith Since World War II* (Princeton, NJ: Princeton University Press, 1988).

3. *Unitatis Reintegratio*, promulgated November 21, 1964; *Dei Verbum*, promulgated November 18, 1965.

4. Glasser, "Bangkok: An Evangelical Evaluation," June 8, 1973, 2. Fldr 3, Box 19, Glasser Papers, DAHL; Jim Byrne to du Plessis, October 25, 1972. Fldr 16, Box 10, du Plessis Papers; C. B. Hastings to W. C. Fields, November 13, 1970. Fldr 39, Box 21, Fields Papers. The seeds of evangelical–Catholic collaboration in the "Moral Majority" vein are clear in a letter from Jim Walsh, the director of the Office of Lay Affairs for the Diocese of Nashville, to W. C. Fields, director of Public Relations for the Southern Baptist Convention. After complaining about the prevalence of sex and violence on television, he wrote, "There are two philosophies abroad in the land today. One might be said to reflect the Judeo-Christian heritage which asserts that human acts are good or bad, moral or immoral, in accordance with their conformity or nonconformity to the will of our Creator. The other philosophy might be described as more or less secularistic reflecting the concept that whatever one does, or says, is his own business and has no relationship to any kind of moral, or theological, code" (Jim Walsh, Jr., to Fields, Fldr 41, Box 21, Fields Papers, SBHLA).

5. Ray Bringham to du Plessis, October 7, 1969. Fldr 33, Box 9, du Plessis Papers; Carlton Spencer to Kilian McDonnell, July 12, 1976, 1. Fldr 1, Box 30, du Plessis Papers, DAHL. The Claretians are a Catholic community of priests and lay brothers founded by St. Anthony Claret in Spain in 1849. They are formally known as Missionaries, Sons of the Immaculate Heart of Mary.

6. Qtd. in Edward Plowman, "Catholics Get the Spirit," *Christianity Today*, July 16, 1971, 31; Plowman, "Memo from Notre Dame: The Spirit is Moving," *Christianity Today*, June 22, 1973, 36–37.

7. Roman Catholic–Pentecostal Commission, "Final Report: Roman Catholic—Pentecostal Dialogue" (Eldoret, Kenya: GABA Publications, 1977), 1. Fldr 14, Box 66, Glasser Papers; John Cardinal Willebrands to du Plessis, June 25, 1970. Fldr 6, Box 59, du Plessis Papers; "Final Report," 1; Hamer to du Plessis, August 6, 1971, 1. Fldr 16, Box 17, du Plessis Papers; G. Raymond Carlson to Cecil M. Robeck, February 11, 1993, 1. Robeck, Cecil M., Jr., Correspondence, FPHC.

8. Miller, *Reinventing American Protestantism*, 69; Nick Cavnar, "Why Are Catholic Charismatics Getting So Catholic?," *New Covenant*, unpublished ms., 1970, 3, 5. Fldr 9, Box 42, du Plessis Papers, DAHL.

9. George Devine, *Liturgical Renewal: An Agonizing Reappraisal* (New York: Alba House, 1973), 19, 27–28; Keith Pecklers and Gilbert Ostdiek, "The History of Vernaculars and Role of Translation," in *A Commentary on the Order of Mass of the Roman Missal*, ed. Order of St. Benedict (Collegeville, MN: Liturgical Press, 2011); *Sacrosanctum concilium*, "Constitution on the Sacred Liturgy," promulgated by Paul VI, December 4, 1963. Online Vatican Archives, available at http://www.vatican.va/archive/hist_councils/ii_vatican_council/documents/vat-ii_const_19631204_sacrosanctum-concilium_en.html.

10. Frank C. Senn, *Christian Liturgy: Catholic and Evangelical* (Minneapolis: Fortress Press, 1997), 626, 639.

11. Ibid., 614.

12. Ibid., 627, 634.

13. On the growth of large institutions, see Richard M. Abrams, *America Transformed: Sixty Years of Revolutionary Change, 1941–2001* (New York: Cambridge University Press, 2006), 28–38.

14. Robert H. Schuller, *My Journey: From an Iowa Farm to a Cathedral of Dreams* (New York: HarperCollins, 2001), 207. Schuller liked to say that, thanks to his Reformed background, he had the advantage of Calvin's "logical" thinking that Peale never had. Gregory A. Pritchard, *Willow Creek Seeker Services: Evaluating A New Way of Doing Church* (Grand Rapids, MI: Baker, 1996), 53, fn. 54.

15. Unpublished Willow Creek paper, qtd. in Martin Robinson, *A World Apart: Creating a Church for the Unchurched* (Oxford, UK: Monarch, 1992), 57; George Barna, *Marketing the Church* (Colorado Springs, CO: Navpress, 1988), 32.

16. "Our Story," available at https://www.willowcreek.com/about/.

17. Lee E. Dirks, *Religion in Action: How America's Faiths Are Meeting New Challenges* (Silver Spring, MD: Newsbook, 1965), 41; L. R. Barnard, "Not Our Sort of Art," *Watchman-Examiner*, January 4, 1960, 34; John R. Claypool, "The Lost Chord of Worship," *Proceedings of the Eighth Annual Meeting of the Southern Baptist Religious Education Association*, Kansas City, MO, May 6–7, 1963, 1. Fldr 4, Box 5, Baptist Association of Christian Educators Records, SBHLA.

18. Natalie Strombeck, "Students See Renewal in Christian Church," *Wheaton Record*, January 21, 1965, 4. WCSC; Louise Stoltenberg, "What's Wrong with Church Renewal?," *Christianity Today*, April 23, 1965, 3–6.

19. "Evangelicals and Ecclesiastical Tradition," *Christianity Today*, October 23, 1964, 27.

20. Donald G. Bloesch, *Centers of Christian Renewal* (Cleveland, OH: United Church Press, 1964); Stephen C. Neill, *Brothers of the Faith* (New York: Abingdon, 1960); Patrick C. Rodger, ed., *Ecumenical Dialogue in Europe* (Richmond, VA: John Knox Press, 1966). Evangelical presses have continued to publish books on Taizé; see Jason Brian Santos, *A Community Called Taize: A Story of Prayer, Worship, and Reconciliation* (Downers Grove, IL: IVP Books, 2008).

21. Roger Schutz, *Living Today for God*, trans. Stephen McNierney and Louis Evrard (Baltimore, MD: Helicon, 1962 [1961]), 7, 57.

22. "Protestant monk visits MBI," *Moody Student*, December 1, 1967, 3. CLAMBI; David C. George to Don B. Harbuck, July 22, 1972, 2. Fldr 40, Box 8, Don B. Harbuck Papers, SBHLA.

23. Martin Luther, "Of the Antichrist," Parts 481 and 483, in *Table Talk*, trans. William Hazlitt (Philadelphia, PA: Lutheran Publication Society, 1824 [1566]); "The Lord's Prayer," in *Larger Catechism*, trans. Adolph Spaeth, L. D. Reed, and Henry Eyster Jacobs (Philadelphia, PA: A. J. Holman, 1915 [1529]), available at the Christian Classics Ethereal Library, http://www.ccel.org.

24. Kilian McDonnell to Dan Fuller, March 13, 1968. Fldr 14, Box 14, Fuller Papers, DAHL; "Thomas Merton: A Spiritual Biography" [cover story], Conrad C. Hoover, "The Pilgrimage of Prayer," and "The Contemplative Life: A Dialogue," all in *The Post-American* 4, no. 7 (August/September 1975); "Book Catalog," *Sojourners*, 1982. Box IV 1, SC-23, Records of *Sojourners*, WCSC; Kevin Bean, "A Transfigured Monasticism," *Sojourners* 8, no. 4 (April 1979): 29–30; James H. Forest, "Small as a Mustard Seed," *Sojourners* 9, no. 5 (August/September 1975): 20–22;

Sherwood E. Wirt, "Let's Lengthen Lent," *Christianity Today*, February 15, 1974, 5–6. Wirt is another example of the American evangelical enthusiasm for graduate study in Europe. He completed doctorates in theology and psychology at the University of Edinburgh in Scotland.

25. Greg Adkins (creative arts pastor at West Towne Christian Church in Knoxville), August 23, 2008, interview with the author.

26. Archer Torrey to "Prayer Partners," June 8, 1972. Fldr 62, Box 31, du Plessis Papers, DAHL. Reuben A. Torrey, Sr., had a charismatic streak himself and was not a strict cessationist; Julia Duin, "Charismatic Catholics: Why Christians Are Joining Communities," *Wall Street Journal*, February 10, 1978, B1, B6. On Protestant monks in Europe, see Donald Bloesch, *Centers of Christian Renewal*, and Francois Biot, O.P., *The Rise of Protestant Monasticism*, trans. W. J. Kerrigan (Baltimore, MD: Helicon, 1963). Evangelicals acknowledged and admired Anglican monasticism, which arose in the wake of the Oxford Movement in the mid-nineteenth century, but—perhaps because those Anglican nuns and monks did not have to bridge nearly the same theological and cultural chasm in order to embrace monasticism—evangelicals do not seem to have studied them with the same enthusiasm.

27. Yoder to Father John Michael, February 18, 1966, 1; Fr. John Michael to Yoder, February 25, 1966, 1. Fldr 8. Box 9, Yoder Collection, MCUSA.

28. Robertson McQuilkin, *Understanding the Bible* (East Peoria, IL: Versa, 1983), chapter 2. Robertson McQuilkin was, as his name suggests, the son of the Accrediting Association of Bible Colleges' co-founder Robert McQuilkin and served as president of Columbia Bible College from 1968 to 1990.

29. Robert E. Webber, *Evangelicals on the Canterbury Trail: Why Evangelicals Are Attracted to the Liturgical Church* (Harrisburg, PA: Morehouse, 1985), 24–29, 81.

30. Ibid., 11.

31. Bob Dahlstrom, "This In Remembrance," *Kodon*, December 1957, 10, 12. WCSC; Webber, *Evangelicals on the Canterbury Trail*, 34.

32. Kenneth L. Woodward, "Roots for Evangelicals," *Newsweek*, May 23, 1977, 76.

33. Thomas Howard to Clyde Kilby, November 14, 1962. Fldr 243.5(2), Kilby Correspondence, MWC.

34. Howard to Kilby, October 26, 1976. Fldr 243.5(2); Howard to Kilby, August 10, no year [ca. 1967], 1. Fldr 243.5(2), Kilby Correspondence, MWC.

35. Howard to Kilby, March 30, 1973. Fldr 243.5, Kilby Correspondence, MWC. For a similar conversion story, see Howard to Kilby, September 2, 1978, in ibid.

36. Donald R. Mitchell to Howard, November 29, 1973. Fldr 243.5(2); Howard to Kilby, January 25, 1968. Fldr 243.5(2); Howard to Kilby, September 2, 1975. Fldr 243.5(2); Howard to Kilby, April 19, 1975, 1–2. Fldr 243.5(2), Kilby Correspondence, MWC.

37. Christmas letter, November 1985, 1. Fldr 243.5(2), Kilby Correspondence, MWC. See for example David B. Currie, *Born Fundamentalist, Born Again Catholic* (San Francisco, CA: Ignatius Press, 1996); Scott Hahn and Kimberly Hahn, *Rome Sweet Home: Our Journey to Catholicism* (San Francisco, CA: Ignatius Press, 1993); Mark P. Shea, *By What Authority? An Evangelical Discovers Catholic Tradition* (Huntington, IN: Our Sunday Visitor, 1996); Stephen K. Ray, *Crossing the Tiber: Evangelical Protestants Discover the Historic Church* (San Francisco, CA: Ignatius Press, 1997), among others. Elizabeth Altham, "Protestant Pastors on the Road to Rome," *Sursum Corda!*, Special Promotional Edition (1996), 2–13.

38. Howard to Kilby, April 26, 1971. Fldr 243.5, Kilby Correspondence, MWC; Peter Gillquist recounts his conversion in *Becoming Orthodox: A Journey to the Ancient Christian Faith* (Ben Lomond, CA: Conciliar Press, 1992 [1989]); Dellas Oliver Herbel, "Orthodoxy in North America," in *The Orthodox Christian World*, ed. Augustine Casiday (New York: Routledge, 2012), 173.

39. Glasser to Philip Potter, August 7, 1973, 1. Fldr 2, Box 19; Glasser, "Non-Conciliar Protestants and the World Council of Churches," 1974, 2. Fldr 10, Box 65, Glasser Papers, DAHL. "U.S.

Evangelicals: Moving Again," *Time*, September 19, 1969, available at http://www.time.com/time/ magazine/article/0,9171,901470-1,00.html. Parachurch organizations are Christian groups that operate independent of church oversight, usually in the fields of social welfare or evangelism.

40. Carl Henry, "A Door Swings Open," 1. Circulated as an advance draft of an editorial that would appear in the June 18, 1966, issue of *Christianity Today*. Fldr 1, Box 1, Coll 37, ESA, BGCA; Lindsell, "The Frankfurt Declaration," *United Evangelical Action*, December 1970, 16.

41. See the official reference volume of the congress, J. D. Douglas, ed., *Let the Earth Hear His Voice: International Congress on World Evangelization, Lausanne, Switzerland* (Minneapolis, MN: World Wide Publications, 1975), 94ff., 213ff.; C. Peter Wagner to Paul Little, September 13, 1973, Records of the Lausanne Committee for World Evangelization (LCWE), Fldr 11, Box 1. Coll 46, BGCA.

42. Billy Graham, "Why Lausanne?," in Douglas, *Let the Earth Hear His Voice*, 26; John Stott, "The Biblical Basis for Evangelism," in ibid., 65; "Lausanne Covenant," in ibid., 4–5.

43. Billy Graham, "Our Mandate from Lausanne '74," *Christianity Today*, July 4, 1975, 5.

44. One participant declared that "the reasoning of natural man works and is based on its own pre-suppositions, and this reasoning is diametrically opposed to Christian presuppositions.... Under such circumstances, in an effort to seek contact with unbelievers for the purpose of winning them for the Lord, if we allow any compromise with the natural man, this amounts to digging the grave of the evangelist" (Susumu Ida, "Biblical Authority and Evangelism," in Douglas, *Let the Earth Hear His Voice*, 89); Peter Beyerhaus, "World Evangelization and the Kingdom of God," in ibid., 289. The Lausanne Covenant itself laments the "constant spiritual warfare" of life on earth (7).

45. Graham to A. J. Dain, August 8, 1972. Fldr 2, Box 1, LCWE Papers, BGCA.

46. Gerhard Hoffmann, "A Response to Lausanne," *A Monthly Letter About Evangelism*, no. 8, August 1974, 2. Fldr 16, Box 1, LCWE. Catholics also had some interest in the proceedings at Lausanne. Members of the Vatican's Secretariat for Promoting Christian Unity attended, presaging the Evangelical Roman Catholic Dialogue on Mission that began in 1977 (David Hubbard, "Evangelical/Roman Catholic Dialogue on Mission," lecture manuscript, March 14, 1987, 4. Fldr 7, Box 11, Hubbard Papers, DAHL; Stott to Graham, May 30, 1972, 1–2. Fldr 1, Box 1, LCWE, BGCA).

47. Wagner, "Lausanne Twelve Months Later," *Christianity Today*, July 4, 1975, 7–8; Bent Reidar Eriksen to A. J. Dain, August 20, 1975, 1. Fldr 19, Box 16, LCWE, BGCA.

48. "The Spirit of Lausanne," *Theological News* 6, no. 3 (July–September 1974): 3. Fldr 4, Box 19, Glasser Papers, DAHL; Henry to Dain, April 26, 1972, 1. Fldr 22, Box 32, LCWE, BGCA.

CHAPTER 8: THE GOSPEL OF LIBERATION

1. Porter Warren Carr, "On Politicized Christianity's False Prophets," manuscript of sermon delivered November 4, 1979, at Wake Forest Baptist Church, Winston-Salem, NC, 7. Fldr 6, Box 6, Fields Collection, SBHLA. "My kingship is not of this world" is the Revised Standard Version translation of John 18:36, more commonly translated as "my kingdom is not of this world."

2. David O. Moberg, *The Great Reversal: Evangelicalism Versus Social Concern* (Philadelphia, PA: Lippincott, 1972).

3. Minutes, Commission on Evangelical Action, September 29, 1960, 2. Fldr "NAE—Evangelical Social Action Commission," FPHC.

4. Robert D. Linder, *Resurgent Evangelical Social Concern in America: An Historical Analysis* (Abingdon, 1986), 16–21 [manuscript in the Carl Bangs Papers, CNA].

5. *Study Papers: Congress on the Church's Worldwide Mission, April 9–16, 1966, Wheaton, Illinois* (Glen Ellyn, IL: Scripture Press Foundation, 1966), 7; Victor B. Nelson to members of the

National Committee on the U.S. Congress on Evangelism, memo, May 1, 1969. Fldr 3, Box 1, ESA, BGCA.

6. Sherwood Eliot Wirt, *The Social Conscience of the Evangelical* (New York: Harper & Row, 1968), 53.

7. Richard Quebedeaux, *The Young Evangelicals: Revolution in Orthodoxy* (New York: Harper & Row, 1974), 60; Swartz, *Moral Minority*, 27. This book offers an insightful overview of the history of the evangelical Left since the 1960s.

8. Joyce Hollyday, "A Little History...," *Sojourners*, September 1981, 24; Swartz, *Moral Minority*, 50ff.; Marlin J. Van Elderen, "Won't You Please Come to Chicago?," *Reformed Journal*, January 1975, 21. One of the People's Christian Coalition's early supporters was Baptist scholar Clark Pinnock, a regular contributor to *Christianity Today* and, incongruously, mentor to Southern Baptist conservative mastermind Paige Patterson at New Orleans Baptist Theological Seminary. In the early 1970s, Pinnock was on faculty at Trinity, sympathized with Wallis, and was a contributing editor at *Sojourners*, but disassociated himself from the magazine in 1983 because he felt it had become "rigidly one-sided" ("A Sojourner Returns," n.d., Critiques, Box IV 1, SC-23, Records of *Sojourners*, WCSC).

9. David Kucharsky to James Wallis, September 17, 1973, 1. Fldr 120, Box 17, CTI , BGCA; Wallis, "The Sojourners Community—A Case Study in Committed Journalism," March 1, 1978, 1. Critiques, Box IV 1, *Sojourners* Records; *Sojourners* staff to John Alexander, Phil Harnden, Mark Olson, and Eunice Amarantides Smith, May 20, 1983. Correspondence, Box V 1, *Sojourners* Records, WCSC.

10. *Sojourners* published 58,545 single-issue copies in 1985 (see "Statement of Ownership, Management & Circulation,"1985, Circulation Repts, Box IV 1, *Sojourners* Records, WCSC). On Catholic subscribers, see Swartz, *Moral Minority*, 249.

11. Carolyn Gifford to *Sojourners* staff member, April 16, 1977. Correspondence, Box V 1, *Sojourners* Records, WCSC; "Special Section," *Time*, August 6, 1979, 48; "Comment: The IRS and the Nonprofit Press," *Columbia Journalism Review*, May 1987, 20; Joe Roos, "The IRS: On Our Case," *Sojourners*, May 1987, 6.

12. "Relocating," *Sojourners*, September 1977; Bob Sabath, "A Community of Communities," *Sojourners*, January 1980; David McKenna, "Memo to Consortium Presidents," December 28, 1971, 4. Fldr 6, Box 1, CCCC.

13. Qtd. in Margaret Lamberts Bendroth, *Fundamentalism and Gender: 1875 to the Present* (New Haven, CT: Yale University Press, 1993), 99.

14. Prudence Allen, *The Concept of Woman: The Aristotelian Revolution, 750 B.C.–1250 A.D.* (Grand Rapids, MI: Eerdmans, 1993 [1985]), 97ff.; Catherine A. Brekus, *Strangers and Pilgrims: Female Preaching in America, 1740-1845* (Chapel Hill: University of North Carolina Press, 1998), 14; Karen Offen, "Defining Feminism: A Comparative Historical Approach," *Signs* 14, no. 1 (Autumn 1988): 134ff. Recent sociological studies of American evangelical home life have revealed that even couples who say they believe in wifely submission and male headship make decisions jointly and view marriage as an equal partnership. See Sarah Sumner, *Men and Women in the Church: Building Consensus on Christian Leadership* (Downers Grove, IL: InterVarsity, 2003), 202ff.; Sally Gallagher and Christian Smith, "Symbolic Traditionalism and Practical Egalitarianism: Contemporary Evangelicals, Family, and Gender," *Gender & Society* 13, no. 2 (April 1999): 211–33.

15. Mary Bouma, "Liberated Mothers," *Christianity Today*, May 7, 1971, 4–6.

16. Letha Scanzoni, "The Feminists and the Bible," *Christianity Today*, February 2, 1973, 10–15; Letha Scanzoni and Nancy Hardesty, *All We're Meant to Be: A Biblical Approach to Women's Liberation* (Waco, TX: Word Books, 1974), 152, 154; Randall Balmer, *Encyclopedia of Evangelicalism* (Louisville, KY: Westminster John Knox, 2002), 391.

17. "Women, Awake!," *Wheaton Record*, January 4, 1963, 2; Verla Thruman, "Have Modern Women Lost Their Identity?," *Wheaton Record*, October 1, 1964, 5. WCSC; Shank, "Books for Young Evangelicals," 59; Swartz, *Moral Minority*, 199.

18. Lucille Sider Dayton, "Our Foremothers," *Daughters of Sarah* (Chicago, IL) 1, no. 1 (November 1974): 1; Donald W. Dayton and Lucille Sider Dayton, "Women as Preachers: Evangelical Precedents," *Christianity Today*, May 23, 1975, 4–7. *Christianity Today* adopted a cautiously moderate line toward sexuality in the late 1960s, publishing evenhanded assessments of birth control and youth sex education (see John Warwick Montgomery, "How To Decide The Birth Control Question," *Christianity Today*, March 4, 1966, 8–12; Lewis Penhall Bird and Christopher T. Reilly, "Sex Education and the Church," *Christianity Today*, June 5, 1970, 10–13). In 1971 the editors published an article that took the evangelical church to task for its subjugation of women: Ruth A. Schmidt, "Second-Class Citizenship in the Kingdom of God," *Christianity Today*, January 1, 1971, 13–15.

19. Bendroth, *Fundamentalism and Gender*, 7, 15, 36. See also Susie C. Stanley, *Holy Boldness: Women Preachers' Autobiographies* (Knoxville: University of Tennessee Press, 2004).

20. Nancy Hewitt, *Women's Activism and Social Change: Rochester, New York, 1822–1872* (Lanham, MD: Lexington, 2001); Ruth Bordin, *Frances Willard: A Biography* (Chapel Hill: University of North Carolina Press, 1986); Mary Taylor Huber and Nancy C. Lutkehaus, eds., *Gendered Missions: Women and Men in Missionary Discourse and Practice* (Ann Arbor: University of Michigan Press, 1999), 41ff.; Dana Lee Robert, *American Women in Mission: A Social History of Their Thought and Practice* (Atlanta: Mercer University Press, 1997), 55; Joel Carpenter, *Revive Us Again*, 68ff.

21. Marsden, *Reforming Fundamentalism*, 280.

22. "About Eerdmans," http://www.eerdmans.com/Pages/About.aspx.

23. Agenda, Academic Affairs Committee, February 20, 1975, 1. Fldr 1, Box 24, Dan Fuller Papers, DAHL; Thomas Howard to Clyde Kilby, January 26, 1976, 2. Fldr 243.5(2), Kilby Correspondence, MWC.

24. Walden Howard, September 1972, 1. Fldr 4, Box 1, Coll 37, ESA, BGCA.

25. Ronald Sider to Stephen Charles Mott, November 14, 1972. Fldr 4, Box 1, Coll 37, ESA, BGCA. Swartz, *Moral Minority*, 176, 173; Richard J. Mouw, "Evangelicals and Political Activism," *Christian Century*, December 27, 1972, 1316; Michael McIntyre, "Religionists on the Campaign Trail," *Christian Century*, December 27, 1972, 1320.

26. "A Declaration of Evangelical Social Concern," reprinted in *Christianity Today*, December 21, 1973, 38. A few participants, such as John Howard Yoder, refused to sign the declaration on the grounds that it didn't go far enough.

27. Ronald J. Sider, "News Release," November 27, 1973, 1. Fldr 17, Box 1; "Action Proposals," November 23, 1973. Fldr 8, Box 1, ESA, BGCA.

28. James M. Dunn to Ronald Sider, January 17, 1974. Fldr 11, Box 88, John Howard Yoder Collection, MCUSA; Donald Dayton, "The Holiness and Pentecostal Churches: Emerging From Cultural Isolation," *Christian Century*, August 15, 1979, 786; Ronald Sider, memo, December 19, 1974. Fldr 1, Box 4, ESA; Lester DeKoster, "Evangelical Awakening...To What?," *Banner*, January 11, 1974, 4; Paul Jewett, "Why I Won't Sign," *Reformed Journal*, May 1974, 8–10.

29. Sider, news release, December 3, 1974, 1. Fldr 3, Box 3, ESA, BGCA; Richard V. Pierard, "Floundering in the Rain," *Reformed Journal*, October 1975, 7; qtd. in Thomas G. Nees, "The Holiness Social Ethic and Nazarene Urban Ministry" (D.Min. thesis, Wesley Theological Seminary, 1976), 112, 738–14, Thomas Nees Collection, CNA. See also Swartz, *Moral Minority*, chapter 10.

30. Swartz, *Moral Minority*, chapters 10–12.

31. Qtd. in Swartz, *Moral Minority*, 233, 246. The latter insult was Jerry Falwell's assessment of Jim Wallis and *Sojourners*. Swartz does not attach importance to the Christian Right's grand narrative

but instead blames the collapse of the evangelical Left on the movement's internal quarrels as well as shifts in the strategies and agendas of both Republicans and Democrats in Washington.

32. Quebedeaux, *Young Evangelicals,* 71. Quebedeaux notes Ladd's influence in moving young evangelicals away from dispensationalism (*Young Evangelicals,* 74–75). Plenty of historic premillennialists, such as Francis Schaeffer, retained conservative political views (though Schaeffer's moderate eschatology partly explains his discomfort with many of his more prominent colleagues in the Christian Right). See also Timothy P. Weber, "Premillennialism and the Branches of Evangelicalism," in Dayton and Johnston, *Variety of American Evangelicalism,* 15–16. Ladd's emphasis on Christians' duty to manifest the Kingdom of God on earth also helped John Wimber develop his ideas regarding power evangelism. See Wimber, "Power Evangelism: Definitions and Directions," 14–15.

33. Stanley Grenz, *The Millennial Maze: Sorting Out Evangelical Options* (Downers Grove, IL: InterVarsity, 1992), 93–94; Henry A. Virkler and Karelynne Gerber Ayayo, *Hermeneutics: Principles and Processes of Biblical Interpretation* (Grand Rapids, MI: Baker, 1981), 128–29.

34. T&T Clark published one earlier English translation of the first volume of Barth's *Church Dogmatics,* a 1936 edition translated by G. T. Thompson. Donald Dayton to Ronald Sider, October 8, 1974, 1. Fldr 10, Box 1, Lindsell Papers, BGCA. Even the editors of the *Christian Standard,* a Restorationist Christian publication oblivious to many currents and controversies in mainstream Protestantism, recognized Bromiley's translation as one of the most important publications of the 1960s (James G. Van Buren, "Some Books of Significance," *Christian Standard,* January 13, 1970, 7).

35. Jim Wallis, "Counting the Cost: A Sermon on Discipleship," in *The Rise of Christian Conscience: The Emergence of a Dramatic Renewal Movement in the Church Today,* ed. Jim Wallis (San Francisco: Harper & Row, 1987), 147; Dale W. Brown, *The Christian Revolutionary* (Grand Rapids, MI: Eerdmans, 1971), 46. Another contributing editor, Arthur G. Gish, agreed in a similar book: *The New Left and Christian Rationalism* (Grand Rapids, MI: Eerdmans, 1970), 109. See also Eric Metaxas, *Bonhoeffer: Pastor, Martyr, Prophet, Spy* (Nashville, TN: Thomas Nelson, 2010).

36. Reinhold Niebuhr, *Why the Christian Church Is Not Pacifist* (London: Student Christian Movement Press, 1940).

37. Gish, *The New Left,* 51, 55.

38. "Friday Night Community Forum," July 7, 1978. Community Forums, Box VI 8, *Sojourners* Records; "editorial staff retreat notes," October 27, 1981, 1. Editorial Retreat Repts, Box IV 2, *Sojourners* Records, WCSC.

39. Yoder to Dayton, September 16, 1974, 1. Fldr "Dayton/Evangelicals," Box 194, Yoder Collection, MCUSA.

40. See for example David Claydon, "On Being A Christian Radical," *Christianity Today,* November 8, 1974, 6–7; Nation, *John Howard Yoder,* 110; "The Quest for Discipleship," June 1973, 4. Post-American Discipleship Seminar, Box IV 3, *Sojourners* Records, WCSC; Stephen Charles Mott, "'The Politics of Jesus' and Our Responsibilities," *Reformed Journal* vol. 26, no. 2 (February 1976): 7.

41. Stanley Hauerwas, *Hannah's Child: A Theologian's Memoir* (Grand Rapids, MI: Eerdmans, 2010), 146, 194. Samuel Escobar praised Yoder's scholarship in his address at the Lausanne Congress in 1974 (Escobar, "Evangelism and Man's Search for Freedom, Justice and Fulfillment," in Douglas, *Let the Earth Hear His Voice,* 320). On Yoder's more recent influence, see Paul Alexander, *Peace to War: Shifting Allegiances in the Assemblies of God* (Telford, PA: Cascadia, 2009), 24; James Bradley, Fuller Theological Seminary professor of church history, interview with the author, March 24, 2009; Joe Boyd, pastor of Vineyard Community Church in Cincinnati, OH, interview with the author, July 22, 2008.

Chapter 9: Evangelicals' Great Matter

1. Donald Dayton, "'Battle for the Bible,'" *Christian Century*, November 10, 1976, 979; Jack B. Rogers, *Confessions of a Conservative Evangelical* (Philadelphia, PA: Westminster, 1974), 98.

2. Howard Colson, in "Proceedings of the Fifth Annual Meeting of the Southern Baptist Religious Education Association," May 16–17, 1960, 32. Fldr 1, Box 5, Baptist Association of Christian Educators Records, SBHLA.

3. Ibid.; Pinnock, "Evangelicals and Inerrancy: The Current Debate," *Theology Today* 35, no. 1 (April 1978): 67.

4. J. I. Packer, *Beyond the Battle for the Bible* (Westchester, IL: Cornerstone Books, 1980), 38, 46.

5. See most recently Williams, *God's Own Party*.

6. Harold Lindsell, *The Battle for the Bible* (Grand Rapids, MI: Zondervan, 1976), 45ff., 139. Lindsell recapitulated this argument in a sequel, *The Bible in the Balance* (Grand Rapids, MI: Zondervan, 1979), 15ff.

7. "Chicago Statement on Biblical Inerrancy," articles XVI and XIX. Available at http://library.dts.edu/Pages/TL/Special/ICBI.shtml.

8. Donald M. Lake to Vernon Grounds, December 16, 1976, and Gene L. Jeffries to Vernon Grounds, May 10, 1976, Fldr 1, Box 2, Coll 243, ETS, BGCA; David Hubbard, "Reflections on Fuller's Theological Position and Role in the Church," April 8, 1976, 4–5. Fldr 8, Box 103, Hubbard Papers; Hubbard to Jay Kesler, April 19, 1976; Hubbard to Milton Engrebretson, April 19, 1976; Daniel E. Weiss to Glenn W. Barker, April 5, 1976; Ted W. Engstrom to Hubbard, June 11, 1976, Fldr 1, Box 105, Hubbard Papers, DAHL; Lindsell, *Bible in the Balance*, 31; Carl Henry, *Evangelical Newsletter*, December 16, 1977.

9. Donald Dayton, "'The Battle for the Bible:' Renewing the Inerrancy Debate," *Christian Century*, November 10, 1976, 976. On the rich and complex history of Harper & Row's religion department, see Matthew S. Hedstrom, *The Rise of Liberal Religion: Book Culture and American Spirituality in the Twentieth Century* (New York: Oxford University Press, 2012), chapter 3.

10. "Religion: Bible Battles," *Time*, May 10, 1976, 57; Douglas R. Sease, "The Battle Over Inerrancy," *Wall Street Journal*, November 18, 1977; "Interpretations of the Bible Divide Protestant Denominations," *New York Times*, September 16, 1979, 60; Williams, *God's Own Party*, 164.

11. Priest, "Anthropology and Missiology: reflections on the Relationship," in Van Engen, Whiteman, and Woodberry, *Paradigm Shifts in Christian Witness*, 29.

12. Catherine Brekus, *Strangers and Pilgrims: Female Preaching in America, 1740–1845* (Chapel Hill: University of North Carolina, 1998), chapters 1 and 2; Susan Hill Lindley and Eleanor J. Stebnor, eds., *The Westminster Handbook to Women in American Religious History* (Louisville, KY: Westminster John Knox, 2008), 4; Lisa P. Stephenson, *Dismantling the Dualisms for American Pentecostal Women in Ministry: A Feminist Pneumatological Approach* (Leiden: Brill, 2012), 41ff.; Grant Wacker, *Heaven Below: Early Pentecostals and American Culture* (Cambridge, MA: Harvard University Press, 2001), 166ff.

13. Ann Braude, *Sisters and Saints: Women in American Religion* (New York: Oxford University Press, 2001), 105; Mark Chaves, *Ordaining Women: Culture and Conflict in Religious Organizations* (Cambridge, MA: Harvard University Press, 1997).

14. Kenneth N. Taylor with Virginia J. Muir, *My Life: A Guided Tour* (Carol Stream, IL: Tyndale House, 1991), 123, 203ff.

15. Ibid., 237–40, 259; Joseph Stowell, "Foreword," in *Which Bible Translation Should I Use?*, ed. Andreas Köstenburger and David Croteau (Nashville, TN: B&H, 2012), ix.

16. M. A. Lunn to Orville Jenkins, November 15, 1973, 1. 1008–30, Publishing Interests, CNA.

17. Lunn to Board of General Superintendents, November 28, 1984, 1. 1328–2, Charles Strickland Collection; Mrs. Joseph Reed to Gene Van Note, June 26, 1984. 868–17, General Board Collection; Dallas L. Robinson to Van Note, June 24, 1984. 868–17, General Board Collection,

CNA. Some Restorationist pastors also rallied to the King James Version's defense even before the NIV controversy, despite their forefather's desire "to relegate the King James Version to the museum...and to put the Word of God before the common people in their own modern speech or vernacular, based upon the latest textual evidence for what the original manuscripts actually contained, and without the theologically orientated (Calvinistic) vocabulary which was so far from the meaning of the original" (J. W. Roberts, "The New Bibles—Versions or Perversions," *Firm Foundation*, June 8, 1965, Firm Foundation Publishing House, Austin, TX, 355. DCHS).

18. "Bible Translations in Headquarters Literature," July 29, 1977, 1. Biblical Inerrancy Congress, FPHC. The Assemblies of God decided to retain the KJV in its official literature, finally approving the NIV in 1990 (Thomas Zimmerman, "Bible Translations in Headquarters Literature," August 29, 1977. Fldr "Bible Inerrancy Congress," FPHC; Mrs. Glendon Stroud to whom it may concern, June 20, 1984, 868–17, General Board Collection; Dennis E. King to M. A. Lunn, June 25, 1984. 868–17, General Board Collection, CNA).

19. Christian Booksellers Association, "CBA Bestsellers: Bible Translations," January 2011, http://www.cbaonline.org/nm/documents/BSLs/Bible_Translations.pdf; "World's Most Popular Bible to Be Revised," MSNBC.com, September 1, 2009 (available at http://www.msnbc.msn.com/id/32644719/ns/us_news-faith/). For the purposes of comparison, 150 million copies of J. R. R. Tolkien's *Lord of the Rings* and more than 100 million copies of *The Hobbit*, two books popular with American evangelicals, have sold to date (Vit Wagner, "Tolkien Proves He's Still King," *Toronto Star*, April 16, 2007, available at http://www.thestar.com/entertainment/article/203389; "Tolkien's *Hobbit* Fetches £60,000," BBC News, March 18, 2008, available at http://news.bbc.co.uk/2/hi/uk_news/england/dorset/7302101.stm).

20. Wynkoop to colleagues, May 5, 1978, 1. 2227–21, Wynkoop Collection, CNA.

21. "Institute in Basic Youth Conflicts: Seminar Report," 1972. Fldr "Gothard/Youth Conflicts," Box 182, Yoder Collection, MCUSA. Gothard's organization is now called the Institute in Basic Life Principles.

22. Wynkoop to colleagues, 2–3.

23. Paul M. Miller, "Basic Youth Conflicts Seminar—An Evaluation," *Gospel Herald* [Mennonite Church USA], August 28, 1973, 653. Fldr "Gothard/Youth Conflicts," Box 182, Yoder Collection, MCUSA.

24. Francis Schaeffer, *The Great Evangelical Disaster* (Wheaton, IL: Crossway, 1984), 56; Barry Hankins, *Francis Schaeffer and the Shaping of Evangelical America* (Grand Rapids, MI: Eerdmans, 2008), 146.

25. Hankins, *Francis Schaeffer*, 3, 7, 13.

26. Francis Schaeffer, "Apologetics," Farel House lecture, 1964, 20. FHL; Edward B. Fiske, "Fundamentalist Conducts A Spiritual Haven in Alps," *New York Times*, September 10, 1973, 7. Although the Schaeffers held strictly to traditional social mores and eschewed drinking and dancing, Frank Schaeffer noted in his memoir that his father and mother were unusually accepting of gay young people who came to L'Abri. They believed homosexual sex was sinful but counseled gay people against marrying a member of the opposite sex in the hope of changing themselves, and defended them to other conservative Christians. Schaeffer also assured his children that he would support them if they chose to marry a black person—a progressive position for a conservative Presbyterian in the 1950s and 1960s (Frank Schaeffer, *Crazy for God: How I Grew Up as One of the Elect, Helped Found the Religious Right, and Lived to Take All (or Almost All) of It Back* [New York: Carroll & Graf, 2007], 77–78).

27. Frank Schaeffer, *Crazy for God*, 211.

28. Claude Cookman, "Schaeffer Communicates; Explains Pessimistic View," *Wheaton Record*, November 29, 1963, 1. WCSC. To my knowledge, every other historical account of Schaeffer's career in America dates his first stateside lecture trip to 1965. While the 1965 trip was longer and reached a wider audience, it was not his first.

29. Francis Schaeffer, *Escape from Reason* (Downers Grove, IL: InterVarsity, 1968), 10; Nash, *Conservative Intellectual Movement in America*, 42; Richard Weaver, *Ideas Have Consequences* (Chicago: University of Chicago Press, 1948), 3.

30. Ronald Wells, September 14, 2007, interview with the author; Lee Hardy, September 26, 2007, interview with the author; Harold O. J. Brown, "Standing Against the World," in *Francis A. Schaeffer: Portraits of a Man and His Work*, ed. Lane Dennis (Westchester, IL: Crossway, 1986), 15; *Christianity Today*, April 4, 1994, 40. In D. Michael Lindsay's sociological study of evangelicals who occupy elite positions in politics, business, the arts, and the academy, many of his interview subjects cited Schaeffer as a primary influence (*Faith in the Halls of Power: How Evangelicals Joined the American Elite* [New York: Oxford University Press, 2007], 39).

31. Hankins, *Francis Schaeffer*, 8; Philip Yancey, "Francis Schaeffer: A Prophet for Our Time?," *Christianity Today*, March 23, 1979, 16; Lindsell to David W. Baker, March 21, 1969, Fldr 13, Box 18, CTI, BGCA.

32. Francis Schaeffer, "Race and Economics," *Christianity Today*, January 4, 1974, 18–19; Francis Schaeffer, *True Spirituality: How to Live for Jesus Moment by Moment* (Carol Stream, IL: Tyndale House, 1971). Schaeffer's wife, Edith, who published irenic books on the community at L'Abri and the challenges and joys of raising a Christian family, had a following of her own. Harold Lindsell gave her a regular column in *Christianity Today*. While the culture wars yielded combative female activists like Phyllis Schlafly and Anita Bryant, Edith Schaeffer had no interest in leading rallies against the Equal Rights Amendment. But if her method was maternal and restrained, she staunchly supported her husband's activism.

33. Frank Schaeffer, *Crazy for God*, 266.

34. Daymon Johnson, "Reformed Fundamentalism in America: The Lordship of Christ, the Transformation of Culture, and Other Calvinist Components of the Christian Right" (PhD diss., Florida State University, 1994), 169. Sherwood Wirt, a friend of Billy Graham and founder of *Decision* magazine, articulated a typical Protestant evangelical view in 1968: "In religious circles the Roman Catholic Church has taken a strong position against liberalizing the abortion laws....Evangelical opinion may differ from the official Roman view in placing more emphasis on the health and well-being of the mother than on the survival of the fetus. However, evangelicals who take the sinfulness of man seriously would hold it an extremely dangerous practice to give any man, medically trained or not, the power over life and death" (Wirt, *Social Conscience of the Evangelical*, 141). In 1973, W. A. Criswell famously commented on *Roe v. Wade*: "I have always felt that it was only after a child was born and had life separate from the mother that it became an individual person, and it always has, therefore, seemed to me that what is best for the mother and for the future should be allowed" (qtd. in "What Price Abortion?," *Christianity Today*, March 2, 1975, 39 [565]). Criswell later changed his mind and became a firm opponent of abortion.

35. Yancey, "Francis Schaeffer," 17. Billy Zeoli, the president of Gospel Films, was the son of Anthony Zeoli, the Italian-American evangelist at whose tent revival Schaeffer was born again at age eighteen. Frank Schaeffer suggests that this "special connection" encouraged his father to overcome his doubts about making the film and "capitalize on his growing fame" (Frank Schaeffer, *Crazy for God*, 257–58); Jimmy Carter, "Crisis of Confidence Speech," July 15, 1979, available at http://www.pbs.org/wgbh/americanexperience/features/primary-resources/carter-crisis/.

36. Johnson, "Reformed Fundamentalism in America," 171–72; Randall Terry, qtd. in Garry Wills, *Under God: Religion and American Politics* (New York: Simon & Schuster, 1990), 324. Wills was possibly the first prominent outside observer to note Schaeffer's influence on the Christian Right.

37. Frank Schaeffer, *Crazy for God*, 315; Williams, *God's Own Party*, 155ff.; Cal Thomas, vice president of the Moral Majority, called Schaeffer's *Christian Manifesto* his organization's "battle plan for the rest of the century" (qtd. in Johnson, "Reformed Fundamentalism in America," 161).

Pat Robertson also admired Schaeffer and relied heavily on *A Christian Manifesto* in his book *The Secret Kingdom: A Promise of Hope and Freedom in a World of Turmoil* (Nashville, TN: Thomas Nelson, 1982). The mainstream secular media's refusal to treat Schaeffer as a serious intellectual helped motivate Robertson to embark on his political career (John Donovan, *Pat Robertson: The Authorized Biography* [New York: Macmillan, 1988], 177).

38. Joe T. Odle to M. O. Owens, Jr., August 30, 1974. Fldr 21, Box 2, M. O. Owens Papers, SBHLA; Thomas V. Morris, *Francis Schaeffer's Apologetics: A Critique* (Chicago: Moody Press, 1976), back copy; Schaeffer, "Twofold Restoration," *Christian Standard*, January 24, 1970, 20; Rob Staples to Richard S. Taylor, September 10, 1971. 3433–5, Staples Collection, CNA.

39. Yoder to Whom It May Concern, "A Communications Ministry," May 10, 1982, 1. Fr. "Alternative Schaeffer," Box 185, Yoder Collection, MCUSA.

40. Ibid., 2.

41. John Sandri, August 24, 2007, interview with the author; qtd. in Worthen, "Not Your Father's L'Abri," *Christianity Today*, March 2008; Schaeffer, *The God Who Is There: Speaking Historic Christianity into the Twentieth Century* (Downers Grove, IL: InterVarsity, 1968), 59; Schaeffer, *Escape from Reason*, 74–84; Schaeffer, *The Church at the End of the Twentieth Century* (Downers Grove, IL: InterVarsity, 1968), 33–34.

42. Nash, *Conservative Intellectual Movement in America*, 50ff.; Paul Eidelberg, "The Temptation of Herbert Marcuse," *Review of Politics* 31, no. 4 (October 1969): 442.

43. Elizabeth Fox-Genovese, "The Crisis of Our Culture and the Teaching of History," *History Teacher* 13, no. 1 (November 1979): 89; see Dennis, *Francis Schaeffer*. On the vogue among conservative evangelicals for classical Christian education, see Michael Farris, "Classics a solid ingredient in education," *Washington Times*, September 23, 1997, E6. Conservative Presbyterian Doug Wilson established an influential hub of classical Christian education in Moscow, Idaho in the 1980s through a K-12 institution, Logos School, and later a college called New St. Andrews College. See Doug Wilson, *Recovering the Lost Tools of Learning: An Approach to a Distinctively Christian Education* (Wheaton, IL: Crossway, 1991).

44. Schaeffer, *How Should We Then Live? The Rise and Decline of Western Thought and Culture* (New York: Fleming Revell, 1976), 108; Johnson, "Reformed Fundamentalism in America," 156–58.

45. Carol Flake, *Redemptorama: Culture, Politics, and the New Evangelicalism* (Garden City, NY: Anchor Press, 1984), 165.

46. Noll, qtd. in Kenneth Woodward, "Guru of Fundamentalism," *Newsweek*, November 1, 1982, 88; Barry Hankins, "I Was Only Making a Point: Francis Schaeffer and the Irony of Faithful Christian Scholarship," *Fides et Historia*, 39, no. 1 (Spring 2007): 19–21, Noll qtd. in 22.

47. Hankins, "I Was Only Making a Point," 23ff., 26.

Chapter 10: God's Idea Men

1. Schaeffer, "Apologetics," transcript of Farel House Lecture, 1964, 12–13. FHL. John H. Hallowell made this same charge against modern liberalism (Hallowell, "Modern Liberalism: An Invitation to Suicide," *South Atlantic Quarterly* 46 [October 1947]: 453–66).

2. Whittaker Chambers, *Witness* (Washington, DC: Regnery, 1980 [1952]), 9; Schaeffer, *How Should We Then Live?*, 19–20.

3. Alvin Plantinga, *God and Other Minds* (Ithaca, NY: Cornell University Press, 1967).

4. By the mid-1970s, presuppositionalist language already saturated the materials of the InterVarsity Christian Fellowship, a mainstream evangelical organization: "One of the lingering myths of the academic world is the assumed objectivity of the scholar, especially the scientist. So this Christian professor surprises his students by teaching them that everyone has his own set of presuppositions" ("Faculty Christian Witness," IVCF, June 1976, 1. Fldr 5, Box 21, Records

of InterVarsity Christian Fellowship, BGCA). The editors of *Time* showed a continuing interest in postmodern intellectual and artistic trends: "To Be Catholic and American," *Time*, December 12, 1960, available at http://www.time.com/time/magazine/article/0,9171,871923,00.html; Robert Hughes, "Art: The Scions and Portents of Dada," *Time*, February 6, 1978, available at http://www.time.com/time/magazine/article/0,9171,945962,00.html.

5. Martin, *With God On Our Side*, 173. Ronald Reagan accused Carter of an IRS-backed "vendetta" against independent schools. From the 1970s through the 1990s, pastors' magazines featured regular articles explaining the nuances of U.S. tax code as it applied to churches and lamenting the IRS's treatment of clergy. James Guinn, "What Is A Minister Worth?, *Ministries Today*, November 1, 1990, 70–74 (*Ministries Today*, 20–00, FPHC); Susan D. Rose, *Keeping Them Out of the Hands of Satan: Evangelical Schooling in America* (New York: Routledge, 1988), 35.

6. John C. Whitcomb, Jr. and Henry M. Morris, *The Genesis Flood* (Phillipsburg, NJ: Presbyterian and Reformed, 1964 [1961]), xx, xxi. Later the authors write: "After all, any real *knowledge* of origins or of earth history antecedent to human historical records can only be obtained through divine revelation. Since historical geology, unlike other sciences, cannot deal with currently observable and reproducible events, it is *manifestly impossible* ever to really *prove*, by the scientific method, any hypothesis relating to pre-human history." (213); Paul Scharf, "The Genesis Flood, Tidal Wave of Change," *Baptist Bulletin* (July 9, 2010), available at http://baptistbulletin.org/?p=9502. The best history of Whitcomb's and Morris's contribution to the young-earth creationist movement is in Ronald L. Numbers, *The Creationists: From Scientific Creationism to Intelligent Design* (Cambridge, MA: Harvard University Press, 2006 [1992]), chapter 10.

7. Qtd. in Numbers, *The Creationists*, 304. Davis Young's father, the Old Testament scholar E. J. Young, taught with Van Til at Westminster Theological Seminary.

8. Ibid., 238ff., 246–47.

9. Ibid., 313, 273.

10. Ibid., 224; Mark Rushdoony, November 1, 2006, interview with the author.

11. Mark Rushdoony, interview with the author; Michael J. McVicar, *Reconstructing America: Religion, American Conservatism, and the Political Theology of Rousas John Rushdoony* (PhD diss., Ohio State University, 2010), 119; Herbert C. Cornuelle, *"Mr. Anonymous": The Story of William Volker* (Caldwell, ID: Caxton Printers, 1951), 208–12; Nash, *Conservative Intellectual Movement in America*, 169. In 1962, William Volker's nephew Harold Luhnow dissolved the fund and reorganized it as the Center for American Studies (McVicar, *Reconstructing America*, 113ff.).

12. See for example Rousas John Rushdoony, "Hard Money and Society in the Bible," in *Gold Is Money*, ed. Hans F. Sennholz (Westport, CT: Greenwood Press, 1975); Rousas John Rushdoony, *Roots of Reconstruction* (Vallecito, CA: Ross House Books, 1991), 539, 590–593; see also Gary North, "Isaiah's Critique of Inflation," *Journal of Christian Reconstruction* 7, nos. 10–30 (1980): 31–39; Gary North, *The Dominion Covenant: Genesis. An Economic Commentary on the Bible*, vol. 1 (Tyler, TX: Institute for Christian Economics, 1987 [1982]), 92, 93; and an appendix by Gary North in Rousas John Rushdoony, *The Institutes of Biblical Law* (Philadelphia, PA: Presbyterian and Reformed, 1973), 799–824; Friedrich A. Hayek, *The Road to Serfdom* (Chicago: University of Chicago Press, 1976 [1944]), 72.

13. Marcellus Kik to Carl Henry and L. Nelson Bell, March 2, 1956. Fldr 6, Box 4, Lindsell Papers, BGCA; Rousas John Rushdoony, *Intellectual Schizophrenia: Culture, Crisis and Education* (Philadelphia, PA: Presbyterian and Reformed, 1961). The book emerged from a set of lectures that Rushdoony delivered in Washington State to the Christian Teachers' Association of the Northwest in October 1959. Rushdoony's theory of pedagogy is oddly reminiscent of Plato's anamnesis.

14. Rushdoony, *Intellectual Schizophrenia*, 2; Mark Rushdoony, interview with the author. The Chalcedon Foundation later moved to Vallecito (McVicar, *Reconstructing America*, 141).

15. McVicar, *Reconstructing America*, 141.

16. Rushdoony wrote that to believe that life must be preserved at all times—even in violation of God's law—is to make a golden calf out of human life and commit idolatry: "If man is his own god, then man and man's life are the highest value. The greatest sin then becomes the taking of life" (*Institutes of Biblical Law*, 225). In this line of reasoning, capital punishment ought to be associated with the first commandment—"Thou shalt have no other gods before me"—rather than the sixth, "Thou shalt not kill," which is better translated as "Thou shalt not murder." On the merits of stoning, see Gary North, *Tools of Dominion: The Case Laws of Exodus* (Tyler, TX: Institute for Christian Economics, 1990), 44–45.

17. *Texas Educ. Agency v. Leeper*, No. 2-87-216-CV, Court of Appeals of Texas, Second District, Fort Worth, 843 S.W. 2nd 41, decided November 27, 1991. Accessed at LexisNexis Academic, available at http://web.lexis-nexis.com/universe/document?_m=9b32f25b86cc1b9164a8a898fa52d1a6&_docnum=1&wchp=dGLbVzW-zSkVb&_md5=06f072562f8fede4668e50dc4f9824c5. The theocratic visions of John Calvin and the New England Puritans assumed the validity of natural law, which Rushdoony doubted as unbiblical.

18. McVicar, *Reconstructing America*, 375,ff., 349, 306, 345ff.; D. James Kennedy to Harold Lindsell, June 14, 1982. Fldr 4, Box 12, Lindsell Papers, BGCA; Mark Rushdoony, interview with the author. John Whitehead suggested that Rushdoony was a major influence on Herb Titus, a colleague of Pat Robertson who helped Robertson establish Regent University. Titus, along with Schaeffer, may have helped push Robertson to abandon his early resistance to political involvement and assume a leading role in the Religious Right (Whitehead, October 27, 2006, interview with the author).

19. Randall J. Stephens and Karl W. Giberson, *The Anointed: Evangelical Truth in a Secular Age* (Cambridge, MA: Belknap Press of Harvard University Press, 2011), 152–58.

20. Hal Lindsey (with C. C. Carlson), *The Late Great Planet Earth* (Grand Rapids, MI: Zondervan, 1970), 17.

21. Ibid., chapter 5, 94, 135, 139.

22. Ibid., 65, 103, 18.

23. John F. Walvoord, *Armageddon, Oil and the Middle East Crisis: What the Bible Says about the Future of the Middle East and the End of Western Civilization* (Grand Rapids, MI: Zondervan, 1990 [1974]), 62.

24. Stephens and Giberson, *The Anointed*, 169.

25. Lindsey, *Late Great Planet Earth*, 168.

26. Wynkoop to Nease, May 7, 1979. 1427–15, Wynkoop Collection, CNA.

27. Ray Sadler, "Come Home," October 16, 1972, 2. Fldr 1, Box 2, M. O. Owens Papers; Paul Pressler to M. O. Owens, Jr., November 12, 1969. Fldr 5, Box 6, Owens Papers; Owens to Randall Jones, November 21, 1969. Fldr 10, Box 8, Owens Papers, SBHLA. For personal details on Pressler, see Jan Jarboe, "The War For Thee University," *Texas Monthly*, November 1991, 159.

28. Official Minutes, Association of Baptist Professors of Religion, 43rd Annual Session, February 20–21, 1970, 2. Fldr 14, Box 2, Records of the Education Commission; Pressler, qtd. in Kyle Johnson to Roy Honeycutt, April 14, 1982, 2. Fldr 22, Box 4, Don B. Harbuck Papers, SBHLA. The purification of Southern Baptist belief in "inerrancy" was easier said than done: in 1985, six years after the conservative takeover began, Nancy Ammerman's survey of SBC pastors revealed that while 85 percent agreed that the Bible is the "inerrant Word of God," more than half of these inerrantists also agreed with a nonliteral reading of Genesis (Nancy Tatom Ammerman, *Baptist Battles: Social Change and Religious Conflict in the Southern Baptist Convention* [New Brunswick, NJ: Rutgers University Press, 1990], 74).

29. "History," Mid-America Baptist Theological Seminary. Available at http://www.mabts.edu/templates/System/details.asp?id=23267&PID=69046. Originally affiliated with Baptist Bible Fellowship International, Falwell's church, Thomas Road Baptist Church, later affiliated with the Southern Baptist Convention. Falwell's role in the SBC grew more prominent as the denomination

moved right in the 1980s. "History," Criswell College. Available at http://www.criswell.edu/about/history/.

30. Certificate of incorporation for the Baptist Faith and Message Fellowship, September 5, 1973, DeKalb, Georgia. Fldr 6, Box 6, Fields Collection; "Verbal Inspiration Literature for SBC Churches," January 24, 1976. Fldr 6, Box 6, Fields Collection; Charles Ashcraft to W. C. Fields, March 15, 1978, 1. Fldr 6, Box 6, Fields Collection, SBHLA; Ammerman, *Baptist Battles*, 204.

31. H. Leon McBeth, "Fundamentalism in the Southern Baptist Convention in Recent Years," in "Fundamentalism and the Southern Baptist Convention," *Review and Expositor* 79, no. 1 (Winter 1982, Louisville: Southern Baptist Theological Seminary): 99; Stan Hastey, "McAteer Key Figure in SBC Swing to Right," *Baptist Public Affairs*, July 8, 1982. Fldr 22, Box 4, Harbuck Papers, SBHLA; Adrian Rogers, qtd. in Penny Girard and Sean Dunnahoo, "Christian Rally Draws 200,000," *Los Angeles Times*, April 30, 1980, A17.

32. James A. Walker to Don Harbuck, April 13, 1981. Fldr 67, Box 4, Harbuck Papers, SBHLA. Marvin Olasky, a son of Russian Jewish immigrants and former communist who is best known as the "father of compassionate conservatism," one of the rhetorical cornerstones of George W. Bush's presidency, reinvigorated Christian journalism in *Telling the Truth: How to Revitalize Christian Journalism* (Eugene, OR: Wipf & Stock, 1996). Editor of the evangelical *World* magazine, Olasky roused Christian journalists to join the culture wars of the 1990s by urging them to think through the Bible's bearing on all news events. Olasky argued that if they wrote with a coherent Christian worldview, they could "fight a limited war against secular liberal culture" (21). Though Olasky was writing in the politically charged atmosphere of the 1990s, his observations reflect the broader school of conservative Christian journalism that had begun to develop thirty years earlier.

33. Fields, "SBC Journalism: Besieged!," July 14, 1989, 1, 3. Fldr 58, Box 15, Fields Collection, SBHLA. The fundamentalist takeover in the Lutheran Church (Missouri Synod) offers another case study in the influence of denominational newspapers and how fundamentalists used them. Liberals credited editors of the *Christian News*, one of the denomination's newspapers, with "programming the unseating" of moderate synod president Oliver Harms in favor of more conservative Jacob Preus in 1969. Preus promptly signed a disclaimer in order to assert his independence, though he encouraged the *News* to take aim at the denominational seminary's liberal president, John Tietjen (Frederick W. Danker, assisted by Jan Schambach, *No Room in the Brotherhood: The Preus-Otten Purge of Missouri* [St. Louis, MO: Clayton, 1977], 42).

34. Timothy L. Smith, "Reader's Response," *Christian Century*, March 2, 1977, 198. Lindsell quoted this in his rebuttal, "Reactions of the Critics," in *The Bible in the Balance*, and repeated his claim that prior to the Civil War all Protestants (except Unitarians) believed in plenary inspiration and inerrancy. Murray Dempster, "Errant Ethics and Inerrant Church Politics: A Scenario of Irony," *Agora*, Summer 1978, 3. FPHC; John Tietjen, qtd. in Danker, *No Room in the Brotherhood*, 48.

35. Baptist Faith and Message, 1963. Available at http://www.sbc.net/bfm/bfmcomparison.asp.

36. M. O. Owens, Jr., "Creedalism is Not a Danger to Baptists," n.d., 1–2. Fldr 22, Box 2, Owens Papers, SBHLA.

37. Robison B. James, "The Beginnings of the E. Y. Mullins Fellowship," June 9, 1969, 1–4. Fldr 93, Box 4, Harbuck Papers, SBHLA; Official Minutes, E. Y. Mullins Fellowship Charter Meeting, June 9–10, 1969, 2, 4, in ibid.

38. Cecil Sherman to "Friends," July 1, 1982, 1. Fldr 22, Box 4, Harbuck Papers; *Baptist Bedrock Beliefs: The Traditional Mainstream Southern Baptist Family* [newsletter], San Antonio, TX, October 15, 1994. Fldr 2, Box 16, Fields Collection; John Baugh, August 18, 1989, 2. Fldr 51, Box 15, Fields Collection; G. Lloyd Denham to Editor, January 1, 1977, 1. Fldr 6, Box 6, Fields Collection, SBHLA. (interestingly, Denham identified himself as a student at New Orleans

Baptist Theological Seminary, the most conservative of the denomination's four largest seminaries and the only one that fundamentalists refrained from purging).

39. Barry Hankins, *Uneasy in Babylon: Southern Baptist Conservatives and American Culture* (Tuscaloosa: University of Alabama Press, 2002), 115ff.; Land, qtd. in Hankins, *Uneasy in Babylon*, 124. Southern Baptists in the Calvinistic camp often point to James Boyce, who studied at Princeton Theological Seminary in its inerrantist heyday and helped found the Southern Baptist Theological Seminary, as one of the founding fathers of the Reformed stream of Southern Baptist theology. See Thomas Nettles, *James Petigru Boyce: A Southern Baptist Statesman* (Phillipsburg, NJ: P&R, 2009).

40. Albert Mohler, April 15, 2010, interview with the author. Qtd. in Worthen, "The Reformer," *Christianity Today*, October 2010.

41. "What's All the Fuss About?," Cooperative Baptist Fellowship, June 14, 2000, 3. Fldr 9, Box 6, Fields Collection, SBHLA; "Baptist Faith and Message," 2000, available at http://www.sbc.net/bfm/bfmcomparison.asp.

42. Bill J. Leonard, *God's Last and Only Hope: The Fragmentation of the Southern Baptist Convention* (Grand Rapids, MI: Eerdmans, 1990), 9.

CHAPTER 11: THE PARADOX OF THE EVANGELICAL IMAGINATION

1. Noll, *Scandal of the Evangelical Mind*, preface.
2. Ibid., 15, and part 2, "How the Scandal Has Come to Pass."
3. Peter Steinfels, "Beliefs: An evangelical intellectual finds a kind of heresy in evangelicalism's neglect of the life of the mind," *New York Times*, September 10, 1994.
4. Carl Lundquist, "From Beginnings to Futures," March 19, 1986, 1–2. Fldr 2, Box 1; Earl McGrath, qtd. in ibid.; Carl Henry, "A Rationale for the Christian College," in "Cooperation—A Response to Crisis in Christian Colleges: Report of a Planning Conference in Phoenix, AZ," December 2-4, 1970, 10. Fldr 3, Box 1, CCCC. Bethel, Eastern Mennonite, Gordon, Greenville, Malone, Messiah, Seattle Pacific, Taylor, Wheaton, and Westmont Colleges were the founding members of the consortium (ibid., 3–4).
5. At the 1970 organizational meeting in Arizona, Harold Ockenga spoke on the consortium's "Philosophy and Purpose," stressing that a Christian college "is committed to the Christian world- and life-view and integrates every discipline of learning in this *Weltanschauung*" ("Cooperation," 36). "Graduate Program in Christian Management," August 12, 1975, Fldr 2, Box 23; Edward Neteland to Ronald L. Keller, March 21, 1973, Fldr 8, Box 1; Gordon R. Werkema, Spring 1975. Fldr 17, Box 1, CCCC.
6. "Cooperation," 3; Clyde F. Johnson to Gordon Werkema, June 1975. Fldr 30, Box 3; "News Release," October 1, 1973. Fldr 2, Box 23. In 1979, Lilly put up $200,000 to establish the Institute for the Study of American Evangelicals at Wheaton College (Lindsay, *Faith in the Halls of Power*, 81). Lindsay notes other Lilly projects from which evangelicals have benefited, including the Theological Exploration of Vocation initiative, which supports the study of how professionals in various sectors link their faith and work. "Evangelical Colleges Gain," *Chronicle of Higher Education*, January 27, 1975.
7. David L. McKenna, "Consortium of Christian Colleges: Support," November 2, 1990. Fldr 2, Box 1; Carl Lundquist to Laura A. Bornholdt, January 20, 1986, 2. Fldr 2, Box 23; Gordon R. Werkema to McKenna, August 12, 1974, Fldr 5, Box 3; Werkema to Christian College Task Force on Development, May 25, 1977, 2. Fldr 3 Box 23; John R. Dellenback to CCC [Christian College Consortium] Presidents, July 21, 1982, Fldr 5, Box 18. A National Endowment for the Humanities grant supported a series of "inter-disciplinary workshops" focused on helping faculty

integrate their Christian faith with their academic discipline. "National Advisory Board," n.d., Fldr 1, Box 18, CCCC.

8. McKenna, "Consortium," 6. Before leaving Pew to serve as provost of Calvin College in 1996, Joel Carpenter encouraged grant programs and "Centers of Excellence" to support evangelical scholarship in various fields, yielding institutes devoted to the study of religion and culture at elite schools like Yale, Emory, and the University of Virginia.

9. Michael Paulson, "Evangelicals Find Place at Mainstream Colleges," *Boston Globe*, February 20, 2000, A1; James Bradley, interview with the author, March 24, 2009. Around the same time, Dennis Bakke, former CEO of the energy company AES Corporation, founded the Harvey Fellows Program to support evangelical graduate students. Lindsay, *Faith in the Halls of Power*, 80–83.

10. McKenna, "Consortium," 1 (McKenna also served as president of Seattle Pacific University and vice president of the National Association of Evangelicals); Lundquist to C. David Weyerhaeuser, April 2, 1982, 1. Fldr 38, Box 1; "Christian College Consortium," memo, 1975. Fldr 2, Box 1; John R. Dellenback, March 1979, 1. Fldr 1, Box 18; Werkema to Chester Nolte, March 13, 1975. Fldr 7, Box 3; Dellenback to Richard Halverson, August 29, 1979, Fldr 39, Box 1, CCCC.

11. "Profile," Council for Christian Colleges and Universities, available at http://www.cccu.org/about/profile.

12. See for example Clyde S. Kilby, "The Aesthetic Poverty of Evangelicalism," *Wheaton Alumni Magazine*, November 1967, 6.

13. Lindsay, *Faith in the Halls of Power*, 98; Neir Eschel, "Spotted history aside, Opus Dei forges close campus links," *Daily Princetonian*, March 22, 2005; Evan Baehr, November 2006, interview with the author; Ryan Anderson, November 2006, interview with the author; Patrick Allitt, *Catholic Intellectuals and Conservative Politics in America, 1950–1985* (Ithaca, NY: Cornell University Press, 1993), 2.

14. George M. Marsden, *The Outrageous Idea of Christian Scholarship* (New York: Oxford University Press, 1997), 48; Michael Cromartie, ed., *A Preserving Grace: Protestants, Catholics, and Natural Law* (Washington, DC: Ethics and Public Policy Center, 1997), vii.

15. Rick Santorum, *It Takes a Family: Conservatism and the Common Good* (Wilmington, DE: Intercollegiate Studies Institute, 2005), 28; J. Budziszewski, *The Line Through the Heart: Natural Law as Fact, Theory, and Sign of Contradiction* (Wilmington, DE: ISI Books, 2011 [2009]), 149; Hadley Arkes, *Constitutional Illusions & Anchoring Truths: The Touchstone of Natural Law* (Cambridge: Cambridge University Press, 2010), 24ff.

16. Allitt, *Catholic Intellectuals and Conservative Politics in America*, 8.

17. Alasdair MacIntyre, *After Virtue: A Study in Moral Theory* (London: Gerald Duckworth, 1981), chapter 5.

18. Richard John Neuhaus, *The Naked Public Square: Religion and Democracy in America* (Grand Rapids, MI: Eerdmans, 1997 [1984]), 19.

19. Damon Linker, *The Theocons: Secular America Under Siege* (New York: Doubleday, 2006), 81ff.

20. See ibid., chapters 4 and 5. Government collaboration with "faith-based organizations" was not an innovation of the George W. Bush administration. For the longer history of how evangelical organizations deftly made use of government funding and dovetailed their own work in evangelism and social work with Washington's expanding military-industrial complex during the Cold War—despite their rhetoric in favor of small government and the separation of church and state—see Axel R. Schäfer, *Piety and Public Funding: Evangelicals and the State in Modern America* (Philadelphia: University of Pennsylvania Press, 2012).

21. Lindsay, *Faith in the Halls of Power*; Putnam and Campbell, *American Grace*. See especially chapters 9 and 13.

22. Richard Mouw, qtd. in "A Forum on the Evangelical Mind," *Christianity Today*, August 14, 1995.

23. James Davison Hunter, *Culture Wars: The Struggle to Define America* (New York: Basic Books, 1991), 43, 48.

24. Williams, *God's Own Party*, 229ff.

25. See for example David Barton, *Developing a Biblical Worldview* (audio CD, Wallbuilders, Inc., 2006). Stephens and Giberson, *The Anointed*, 89. For a full account of Barton's career and influence, see Stephens and Giberson, chapter 2. The authors note that Barton had sold more than 100,000 videotapes by 1994 (85).

26. Stephens and Giberson, *The Anointed*, 86.

27. David Barton, "Unconfirmed Quotations," available at http://www.wallbuilders.com/libissuesarticles.asp?id=126 (accessed April 28, 2012). Molly Driscoll, "'The Jefferson Lies' is Recalled by publisher Thomas Nelson," *Christian Science Monitor*, August 13, 2012, available at http://www.csmonitor.com/Books/chapter-and-verse/2012/0813/The-Jefferson-Lies-is-recalled-by-publisher-Thomas-Nelson (accessed August 13, 2012).

28. James Dobson and Gary L. Bauer, *Children at Risk: What You Need to Know to Protect Your Family* (Waco, TX: Word Books, 1990), 19, 21.

29. Charles Colson and Nancy Pearcey, *How Now Shall We Live?* (Wheaton, IL: Tyndale House, 1999), 13; "You Are Not Alone: Centurions Program," *Breakpoint*, available at http://www.breakpoint.org/resources/centurions.

30. Wesleyan Study Center Committee, "Proposal to President Jim Bond regarding the establishment of a Wesleyan Center for 21st Century Studies," February 24, 1994, 4–5. 2067-13, Proposal for Wesleyan Center, CNA; Douglas Jacobsen, "The History and Character of Messiah College, 1909–1995," in Hughes and Adrian, *Models for Christian Higher Education*, 329.

31. Soong-Chan Rah, *The Next Evangelicalism: Releasing the Church from Western Cultural Captivity* (Downers Grove, IL: IVP Books, 2009), 98.

32. James K. A. Smith, *Who's Afraid of Postmodernism? Taking Derrida, Lyotard, and Foucault to Church* (Grand Rapids, MI: Baker Academic, 2006), 28.

33. Shane Claiborne and Chris Haw, *Jesus For President: Politics for Ordinary Radicals* (Grand Rapids, MI: Zondervan, 2008).

34. Pritchard, *Willow Creek Seeker Services*, 46–48; Mike Yaconelli, "The Illegitimate Church," in *Stories of Emergence: Moving from Absolute to Authentic*, ed. Mike Yoconelli (Grand Rapids, MI: Zondervan, 2003), 18.

35. Qtd. in ibid., 162, 165. DJs are particularly popular in Emergent churches in the United Kingdom, where evangelicals have mimicked urban club culture.

36. D. A. Carson, *Becoming Conversant with the Emerging Church: Understanding a Movement and Its Implications* (Grand Rapids, MI: Zondervan, 2005), 141.

37. Wolfe, "Opening of the Evangelical Mind."

38. Marsden, *Outrageous Idea of Christian Scholarship*, 48, 45–46.

39. Stanley Fish, "What's Sauce for One Goose: The Logic of Academic Freedom," in *Academic Freedom and the Inclusive University*, ed. Sharon E. Kahn and Dennis J. Pavlich (Vancouver: University of British Columbia Press, 2000), 6. Fish goes on to lament the deterioration of academia into a circus of political correctness that asks participants to "inhabit your moral convictions loosely" and tolerate even the most intolerable viewpoints, but there is a rather long leap between the premise that one must subject all opinions to the same standards of evidence and the conclusion of moral paralysis.

40. Roger E. Olson, "On Loving the Truth More than Religion: Confessions of a Rebellious Christian Mind," in *By What Authority: The Vital Question of Religious Authority in Christianity*, ed. Robert L. Millet (Macon, GA: Mercer University Press, 2010), 190–91.

41. James Davison Hunter, *To Change the World: The Irony, Tragedy, and Possibility of Christianity in the Late Modern World* (New York: Oxford University Press, 2010), 25, essay II.

42. As of this writing, numerous states have passed laws restricting the circumstances of legal abortion and defunding Planned Parenthood, while thirty-six states have adopted laws or constitutional amendments banning the legal recognition of gay marriage. In 2010, the Texas Board of Education—which dictates requirements for one of the country's largest markets for history textbooks—approved a social studies curriculum that emphasizes the role of Christianity in America's founding and the superiority of the capitalist system and presents "Republican political philosophies in a more positive light" (James C. McKinley, Jr., "Texas Conservatives Win Curriculum Change," *New York Times*, March 10, 2010, A10). On evangelicals' strength in local community organizations—as well as in Hollywood, education, and other spheres—see Monique El-Faizy, *God and Country: How Evangelicals Have Become America's New Mainstream* (New York: Bloomsbury, 2006); also Bethany Moreton, *For God and Wal-Mart: The Making of Christian Free Enterprise* (Cambridge, MA: Harvard University Press, 2009). Pew Forum on Religion & Public Life, "U.S. Religious Landscape Survey" (2007), available at http://religions.pewforum.org/affiliations.

43. Smith et al., *American Evangelicalism*, 121.

44. Qtd. in Doris Buss and Didi Herman, *Globalizing Family Values: The Christian Right in International Politics* (Minneapolis: University of Minnesota Press, 2003), xiv; Miranda K. Hassett, *Anglican Communion in Crisis: How Episcopal Dissidents and Their African Allies Are Reshaping Anglicanism* (Princeton, NJ: Princeton University Press, 2007), 49.

45. Mark A. Noll, *The New Shape of World Christianity: How American Experience Reflects Global Faith* (Downers Grove, IL: IVP Academic, 2009), 84–87, 116.

46. Orlando E. Costas, "Evangelical Theology in the Two-Thirds World," in Carpenter and Shenk, *Earthen Vessels*, 241, 247.

47. Fuller Theological Seminary offers scholarship opportunities for African-American, Latino, and Native American students, as well as students from the Global South (http://www.fuller.edu/admissions/financial-aid/scholarships/all-seminary-scholarships.aspx); Dallas Theological Seminary's "International Leaders Scholarship" (http://www.dts.edu/foundation/ilsp/). Moody Bible Institute offers scholarships for African, African-American, and other minority students (http://mmm.moody.edu/genmoody/default.asp?SectionID=46B18AB5CE7048C59F7DB99E9 A3A17C2). Rebecca Y. Kim, *God's New Whiz Kids? Korean American Evangelicals on Campus* (New York: New York University Press, 2006). Kim notes that many Korean American students opt to join Asian-majority groups rather than majority-white or mixed groups (6). Elaine Howard Ecklund, *Korean American Evangelicals: New Models for Civic Life* (New York: Oxford University Press, 2006), 6. One influential Pentecostal theologian challenging white and Western assumptions is Amos Yong, an Assemblies of God minister who directs Regent University's PhD program and has written widely on religious pluralism, faith and reason, and Pentecostal cultural theology.

Selected Bibliography

Archival Collections

Billy Graham Center Archives (Wheaton, IL)

L. Nelson Bell Papers
Records of the Billy Graham Evangelistic Association
Records of Christianity Today International
Records of Evangelicals for Social Action
Records of the Evangelical Theological Society
Records of InterVarsity Christian Fellowship
Records of the Lausanne Committee for World Evangelization
Harold Lindsell Papers

Biola University Archives and Special Collections (La Mirada, CA)

Samuel Sutherland Papers
Bible Institute of Los Angeles Course Catalogs
Periodical Collection

Taylor University Archives and Special Collections (Upland, IN)

Christian College Consortium Collection

Crowell Library and Archives (Moody Bible Institute, Chicago, IL)

William Culbertson Papers
Moody Bible Institute Course Catalogs
Periodical Collection

David Allan Hubbard Library (Fuller Theological Seminary, Pasadena, CA)

Daniel Payton Fuller Papers
Arthur F. Glasser Papers

David Allan Hubbard Papers
David du Plessis Papers
Fuller Theological Seminary Course Catalogs
Society for Pentecostal Studies Papers

Disciples of Christ Historical Society (Nashville, TN)

Periodical Collection

Farel House Library (L'Abri, Huemoz, Switzerland)

Francis Schaeffer Lecture Files

Flower Pentecostal Heritage Center (Archives of the Assemblies of God, Springfield, MO)

Bible Institute Seminars
Biblical Inerrancy Congress
Education Department Files
Executive Files
NAE Correspondence
Robeck, Cecil M., Jr., Correspondence

Marion E. Wade Center (Wheaton, IL)

Clyde S. Kilby Papers
Wade History Collection

Mennonite Church USA Archives (Goshen, IN)

Harold S. Bender Collection
Nelson and Ada Litwiller Collection
John Howard Yoder Collection

Church of the Nazarene Archives (Lenexa, KS)

Carl Bangs Papers
Educational Addresses
Papers of the Board of General Superintendents
General Board Collection
Thomas Nees Collection
Pasadena College Files
Publishing Interests Files
Seminary Correspondence
Southern Nazarene University Correspondence
Rob Staples Papers
Willard Taylor Papers
Mildred Bangs Wynkoop Papers

Southern Baptist Historical Library and Archives (Nashville, TN)

Baptist Association of Christian Educators Records
William Wayne Dehoney Collection

Records of the Education Commission
Wilmer C. Fields Collection
Don B. Harbuck Papers
M. O. Owens Papers

Wheaton College Special Collections (Wheaton, IL)

Periodical Collection
Hans Rookmaaker Papers
Records of *Sojourners*

Periodicals

America (Society of Jesus)
Baltimore Evening Sun
Biola Chimes
Boston Globe
Bulletin of the Evangelical Theological Society
Chicago Daily Tribune
Christian Beacon
Christian Century
Christian Science Monitor
Christian Standard
Christianity Today
Eternity
Firm Foundation
Journal of Christian Reconstruction
Kodon (Wheaton College)
Los Angeles Times
Manchester Guardian
Missions Frontiers
Moody Student
Nation
National Review
Nazarene Preacher
New York Times
Newsweek
Post-American
Restoration Herald
Reformed Journal
Seminary Review (Cincinnati Bible Seminary)
Sojourners
Theology News & Notes (Fuller Theological Seminary)
Time
United Evangelical Action
Wall Street Journal
Washington Post
Wheaton Record

SELECTED BIBLIOGRAPHY

BOOKS, ARTICLES, AND DISSERTATIONS

Abrams, Richard M. *America Transformed: Sixty Years of Revolutionary Change, 1941–2001*. New York: Cambridge University Press, 2006.

Alexander, Paul. *Peace to War: Shifting Allegiances in the Assemblies of God*. Telford, PA: Cascadia, 2009.

Allen, Prudence. *The Concept of Woman: The Aristotelian Revolution, 750 B.C.–1250 A.D.* Grand Rapids, MI: Eerdmans, 1993 [1985].

Allitt, Patrick. *Catholic Intellectuals and Conservative Politics in America, 1950–1985*. Ithaca, NY: Cornell University Press, 1993.

Ammerman, Nancy Tatom. *Baptist Battles: Social Change and Religious Conflict in the Southern Baptist Convention*. New Brunswick, NJ: Rutgers University Press, 1990.

Anderson, Allan Heaton. *To the Ends of the Earth: Pentecostalism and the Transformation of World Christianity*. New York: Oxford University Press, 2013.

Angus, David L. and Jeffrey Mirel. *The Failed Promise of the American High School, 1890–1995*. New York: Teachers College Press, 1999.

Arendt, Hannah. *The Origins of Totalitarianism*. New York: Harcourt, 1979 [1951].

Arkes, Hadley. *Constitutional Illusions & Anchoring Truths: The Touchstone of Natural Law*. Cambridge: Cambridge University Press, 2010.

Balmer, Randall. *Encyclopedia of Evangelicalism*. Louisville, KY: Westminster John Knox, 2002.

Barna, George. *Marketing the Church*. Colorado Springs, CO: Navpress, 1988.

Barth, Karl. *Evangelical Theology: An Introduction*. Trans. Grover Foley. New York: Holt, Rinehart, and Winston, 1963.

Bassett, Paul Merritt. "Fundamentalist Leavening of the Holiness Movement, 1914–1940: Church of the Nazarene: A Case Study." *Wesleyan Theological Journal* 13 (Spring 1978): 65–91.

Bateman, Herbert W., et al., eds. *Three Central Issues in Contemporary Dispensationalism: A Comparison of Traditional and Progressive Views*. Grand Rapids, MI: Kregel, 1999.

Bechtel, Paul. *Wheaton College: A Heritage Remembered, 1860–1984*. Wheaton, IL: Shaw, 1984.

Bender, Harold S. *The Anabaptist Vision*. Scottsdale, PA: Heritage Press, 1944.

———. "Outside Influences on Mennonite Thought." *Mennonite Life* 10, no. 1 (January 1955): 45–58.

Bendroth, Margaret Lamberts. *Fundamentalism and Gender: 1875 to the Present*. New Haven, CT: Yale University Press, 1993.

———. *Growing Up Protestant: Parents, Children, and Mainline Churches*. New Brunswick, NJ: Rutgers University Press, 2002.

Bennett, Dennis J. *Nine O'Clock in the Morning*. Plainfield, NJ: Logos, 1970.

Billingsley, Scott. *It's A New Day: Race and Gender in the Modern Charismatic Movement*. Tuscaloosa: University of Alabama Press, 2008.

Biot, Francois, O.P. *The Rise of Protestant Monasticism*. Trans. W. J. Kerrigan. Baltimore, MD: Helicon, 1963.

Bledstein, Burton J. *The Culture of Professionalism: The Middle Class and the Development of Higher Education in America*. New York: Norton, 1976.

Bloesch, Donald G. *Centers of Christian Renewal*. Cleveland, OH: United Church Press, 1964.

Bolich, Gregory C. *Karl Barth & Evangelicalism*. Downers Grove, IL: InterVarsity Press, 1980.

Bordin, Ruth. *Frances Willard: A Biography*. Chapel Hill: University of North Carolina Press, 1986.

Borstelmann, Thomas. *The Cold War and the Color Line: American Race Relations in the Global Arena*. Cambridge, MA: Harvard University Press, 2001.

Bratt, James, ed. *Abraham Kuyper: A Centennial Reader*. Grand Rapids, MI: Eerdmans, 1998.

Braude, Ann. *Sisters and Saints: Women in American Religion*. New York: Oxford University Press, 2001.

Brekus, Catherine. *Strangers and Pilgrims: Female Preaching in America, 1740–1845*. Chapel Hill, NC: University of North Carolina, 1998.

Brereton, Virginia. *Training God's Army: The American Bible School, 1880–1940*. Bloomington: Indiana University Press, 1990.

Bromiley, Geoffrey, ed. *Karl Barth: Letters, 1961–1968*. Grand Rapids, MI: Eerdmans, 1981.

Brown, Dale W. *The Christian Revolutionary*. Grand Rapids, MI: Eerdmans, 1971.

Budziszewski, J. *The Line Through the Heart: Natural Law as Fact, Theory, and Sign of Contradiction*. Wilmington, DE: ISI Books, 2011 [2009].

Burkholder, Jared S., and David C. Cramer, eds. *The Activist Impulse: Essays on the Intersection of Evangelicalism and Anabaptism*. Eugene, OR: Pickwick, 2012.

Buss, Doris, and Didi Herman. *Globalizing Family Values: The Christian Right in International Politics*. Minneapolis: University of Minnesota Press, 2003.

Caldwell, Wayne E., ed. *Reformers and Revivalists: The History of the Wesleyan Church*. Indianapolis, IN: Wesley Press, 1992.

Calvin, John. *Commentaries of the First Book of Moses Called Genesis*. 2 vols. Ed. and trans. John King. Grand Rapids, MI: Eerdmans, 1948.

Carnell, Edward John. *The Case for Orthodox Theology*. Philadelphia: Westminster, 1959.

Carpenter, Joel A. *Revive Us Again: The Reawakening of American Fundamentalism*. New York: Oxford University Press, 1997.

Carpenter, Joel A., and Wilbert R. Shenk, eds. *Earthen Vessels: American Evangelicals and Foreign Missions, 1880–1980*. Grand Rapids, MI: Eerdmans, 1990.

Carpenter, Joel A., and Kenneth W. Shipps, eds. *Making Higher Education Christian*. Grand Rapids, MI: Eerdmans, 1987.

Carson, D. A. *Becoming Conversant with the Emerging Church: Understanding a Movement and Its Implications*. Grand Rapids, MI: Zondervan, 2005.

Casiday, Augustine, ed. *The Orthodox Christian World*. New York: Routledge, 2012.

Chambers, Whittaker. *Witness*. Washington, DC: Regnery, 1980 [1952].

Chappell, David L. *A Stone of Hope: Prophetic Religion and the Death of Jim Crow*. Chapel Hill: University of North Carolina Press, 2004.

Chaves, Mark. *Ordaining Women: Culture and Conflict in Religious Organizations*. Cambridge, MA: Harvard University Press, 1997.

Childs, Brevard S. *Biblical Theology in Crisis*. Philadelphia: Westminster, 1976 [1970].

Claiborne, Shane, and Chris Haw. *Jesus For President: politics for ordinary radicals*. Grand Rapids, MI: Zondervan, 2008.

Clark, Gordon H. *A Christian Philosophy of Education*. Grand Rapids, MI: Eerdmans, 1946.

Clarkson, William. *Christ and Missions: Facts and Principles of Evangelism*. London: John Snow, 1858.

Colson, Charles, and Nancy Pearcey. *How Now Shall We Live?* Wheaton, IL: Tyndale House, 1999.

Committee on the Objectives of General Education in a Free Society. *General Education in a Free Society: Report of the Harvard Committee*. Cambridge, MA: Harvard University Press, 1945.

Cooke, Alistair, ed. *The Vintage Mencken*. New York: Knopf, 1955.

Cornuelle, Herbert C. *"Mr. Anonymous": The Story of William Volker*. Caldwell, ID: Caxton Printers, 1951.

Craig, Samuel L., ed. *The Inspiration and Authority of the Bible*. Philadelphia: Presbyterian and Reformed, 1948.

Critchlow, Donald T. *The Conservative Ascendancy: How the GOP Right Made Political History*. Cambridge, MA: Harvard University Press, 2007.

Cromartie, Michael, ed. *A Preserving Grace: Protestants, Catholics, and Natural Law*. Washington, DC: Ethics and Public Policy Center, 1997.

Currie, David B. *Born Fundamentalist, Born Again Catholic*. San Francisco, CA: Ignatius Press, 1996.

Dalhouse, Mark Taylor. *An Island in a Lake of Fire: Bob Jones University, Fundamentalism, and the Separatist Movement*. Athens: University of Georgia Press, 1996.

Danker, Frederick W., assisted by Jan Schambach. *No Room in the Brotherhood: The Preus-Otten Purge of Missouri*. St. Louis, MO: Clayton, 1977.

Dayton, Donald W. *Discovering an Evangelical Heritage*. New York: Harper & Row, 1976.

———. "'The Search for the Historical Evangelicalism': George Marsden's History of Fuller Seminary as a Case Study." *Christian Scholar's Review* 23 (September 1993): 34–40.

Dayton, Donald W., and Robert K. Johnston, eds. *The Variety of American Evangelicalism*. Knoxville: University of Tennessee Press, 1991.

Dennis, Lane, ed. *Francis A. Schaeffer: Portraits of a Man and His Work*. Westchester, IL: Crossway, 1986.

Devine, George. *Liturgical Renewal: An Agonizing Reappraisal*. New York: Alba House, 1973.

Dirks, Lee E. *Religion in Action: How America's Faiths Are Meeting New Challenges*. Silver Spring, MD: Newsbook, 1965.

Dobson, James, and Gary L. Bauer. *Children at Risk: What You Need to Know to Protect Your Family*. Waco, TX: Word Books, 1990.

Dochuk, Darren. *From Bible Belt to Sunbelt: Plain-Folk Religion, Grassroots Politics, and the Rise of Evangelical Conservatism*. New York: Norton, 2010.

Dockery, David S., ed. *Southern Baptists & American Evangelicals: The Conversation Continues*. Nashville: Broadman & Holman, 1993.

Doherty, Brian. *Radicals for Capitalism: A Freewheeling History of the Modern American Libertarian Movement*. New York: Public Affairs, 2007.

Doherty, Thomas. *Teenagers and Teenpics: The Juvenilization of American Movies in the 1950s*. Boston: Unwin Hyman, 1988.

Donovan, John. *Pat Robertson: The Authorized Biography*. New York: Macmillan, 1988.

Dorrien, Gary. *The Remaking of Evangelical Theology*. Louisville, KY: Westminster John Knox, 1998.

Douglas, J. D., ed. *Let the Earth Hear His Voice: International Congress on World Evangelization, Lausanne, Switzerland*. Minneapolis, MN: World Wide Publications, 1975.

Dreyer, Frederick. "Evangelical Thought: John Wesley and Jonathan Edwards." *Albion* 19, no. 2 (Summer 1987). 177–92.

Dudziak, Mary L. *Cold War Civil Rights: Race and the Image of American Democracy*. Princeton, NJ: Princeton University Press, 2000.

Ecklund, Elaine Howard. *Korean American Evangelicals: New Models for Civic Life*. New York: Oxford University Press, 2006.

Eidelberg, Paul. "The Temptation of Herbert Marcuse." *Review of Politics* 31, no. 4 (October 1969): 442–58.

El-Faizy, Monique. *God and Country: How Evangelicals Have Become America's New Mainstream*. New York: Bloomsbury, 2006.

Eskridge, Larry, and Mark A. Noll, eds. *More Money, More Ministry: Money and Evangelicals in Recent North American History*. Grand Rapids, MI: Eerdmans, 2000.

Finke, Roger. "The Quiet Transformation: Changes in Size and Leadership in Southern Baptist Churches." *Review of Religious Research* 36, no. 1 (September 1994): 3–22.

Finney, Charles. *Reflections on Revival*. Ed. Donald Dayton. Minneapolis, MN: Bethany Fellowship, 1979 [1845].

Finstuen, Andrew S. *Original Sin and Everyday Protestants: Reinhold Niebuhr, Billy Graham, and Paul Tillich in an Age of Anxiety*. Chapel Hill: University of North Carolina Press, 2009.

Flake, Carol. *Redemptorama: Culture, Politics, and the New Evangelicalism*. Garden City, NY: Anchor Press, 1984.

Forster, Roger and V. Paul Marston, with foreword by F. F. Bruce. *God's Strategy in Human History*. Bromley, UK: Send the Light Trust, 1973.

Fox-Genovese, Elizabeth. "The Crisis of Our Culture and the Teaching of History." *History Teacher* 13, no. 1 (November 1979): 89–101.

Frank, Douglas W. *Less Than Conquerors: How Evangelicals Entered the Twentieth Century*. Grand Rapids, MI: Eerdmans, 1986.

Fuller, Daniel. *Give the Winds a Mighty Voice: The Story of Charles E. Fuller*. Waco, TX: Word Press, 1972.

Gallagher, Sally, and Christian Smith. "Symbolic Traditionalism and Practical Egalitarianism: Contemporary Evangelicals, Family, and Gender." Gender & Society 13, no. 2 (April 1999): 211–33.

Garrett, James Leo, Jr., et al. *Are Southern Baptists "Evangelicals"?* Macon, GA: Mercer University Press, 1983.

Gatewood, Willard B., Jr., ed. *Controversy in the Twenties: Fundamentalism, Modernism, and Evolution*. Nashville, TN: Vanderbilt University Press, 1969.

Gibbon, Edward. *The History of the Decline and Fall of the Roman Empire*. 8 vols. London: Bonn, 1854 [1788].

Gilbert, James. *Cycle of Outrage: America's Reaction to the Juvenile Delinquent in the 1950s*. New York: Oxford University Press, 1986.

Gillquist, Peter E. *Becoming Orthodox: A Journey to the Ancient Christian Faith*. Ben Lomond, CA: Conciliar Press, 1992 [1989].

Gilmore, Glenda Elizabeth. *Defying Dixie: The Radical Roots of Civil Rights, 1919–1950*. New York: Norton, 2008.

Gish, Arthur G. *The New Left and Christian Rationalism*. Grand Rapids, MI: Eerdmans, 1970.

Gleason, Philip. *Contending With Modernity: Catholic Education in the Twentieth Century*. New York: Oxford University Press, 1995.

Graham, Billy. *The Jesus Generation*. Grand Rapids, MI: Zondervan, 1971.

———. *Just As I Am: The Autobiography of Billy Graham*. New York: HarperCollins, 1997.

Grenz, Stanley. *The Millennial Maze: Sorting Out Evangelical Options*. Downers Grove, IL: InterVarsity, 1992.

Hahn, Scott, and Kimberly Hahn. *Rome Sweet Home: Our Journey to Catholicism*. San Francisco, CA: Ignatius Press, 1993.

Hallowell, John H. "The Decline of Liberalism." *Ethics* 52, no. 3 (April 1942): 323–49.

———. "Modern Liberalism: An Invitation to Suicide." *South Atlantic Quarterly* 46 (October 1947): 453–66.

Hamilton, Michael. "The Fundamentalist Harvard: Wheaton College and the Continuing Vitality of American Evangelicalism, 1919–1965." PhD diss., University of Notre Dame, 1994.

Hankins, Barry. *Francis Schaeffer and the Shaping of Evangelical America*. Grand Rapids, MI: Eerdmans, 2008.

———. "I was Only Making a Point: Francis Schaeffer and the Irony of Faithful Christian Scholarship." *Fides et Historia* 39, no. 1 (Spring 2007).

————. *Jesus and Gin: Evangelicalism, the Roaring Twenties, and Today's Culture Wars.* New York: Palgrave Macmillan, 2010.

————. *Uneasy in Babylon: Southern Baptist Conservatives and American Culture.* Tuscaloosa: University of Alabama Press, 2002.

Hannah, John D. *An Uncommon Union: Dallas Theological Seminary and American Evangelicalism.* Grand Rapids, MI: Zondervan, 2009.

Hart, D. G. *Deconstructing Evangelicalism: Conservative Protestantism in the Age of Billy Graham.* Grand Rapids, MI: Baker Academic, 2004.

————. *Defending the Faith: J. Gresham Machen and the Crisis of Conservative Protestantism in America.* Baltimore, MD: Johns Hopkins University Press, 1994.

Hassett, Miranda K. *Anglican Communion in Crisis: How Episcopal Dissidents and Their African Allies Are Reshaping Anglicanism.* Princeton, NJ: Princeton University Press, 2007.

Hauerwas, Stanley. *Hannah's Child: A Theologian's Memoir.* Grand Rapids, MI: Eerdmans, 2010.

Hayek, Friedrich A. *The Road to Serfdom.* Chicago: University of Chicago Press, 1976 [1944].

Hedstrom, Matthew S. *The Rise of Liberal Religion: Book Culture and American Spirituality in the Twentieth Century.* New York: Oxford University Press, 2012.

The Heliand: The Saxon Gospel. Trans. G. Ronald Murphy, S.J. New York: Oxford University Press, 1992.

Henry, Carl F. H. *Confessions of a Theologian: An Autobiography.* Waco, TX: Word Books, 1986.

————. *Remaking the Modern Mind.* Grand Rapids, MI: Eerdmans, 1946.

————. *The Uneasy Conscience of Modern Fundamentalism.* Grand Rapids, MI: Eerdmans, 1947.

Hershberger, Guy F. "Harold S. Bender and His Time." *Mennonite Quarterly Review* 38 (April 1964): 83–112.

Hewitt, Nancy. *Women's Activism and Social Change: Rochester, New York, 1822–1872.* Lanham, MD: Lexington, 2001.

Hodge, Charles. *Systematic Theology.* 3 vols. Peabody, MA: Hendrickson, 1999 [1873].

Hofstadter, Richard. *Anti-Intellectualism in American Life.* New York: Knopf, 1962.

————. "The Paranoid Style in American Politics," *Harper's*, November 1964, 77–86.

Huber, Mary Taylor, and Nancy C. Lutkehaus, eds., *Gendered Missions: Women and Men in Missionary Discourse and Practice.* Ann Arbor: University of Michigan Press, 1999.

Hughes, Richard T., ed. *The American Quest for the Primitive Church.* Urbana: University of Illinois, 1988.

Hughes, Richard T., and William B. Adrian, eds. *Models for Christian Higher Education: Strategies for Success in the Twenty-First Century.* Grand Rapids, MI: Eerdmans, 1997.

Humes, Edward. *Over Here: How the G.I. Bill Transformed the American Dream.* New York: Harcourt, 2006.

Hunt, Stephen. *A History of the Charismatic Movement in Britain and the United States of America: The Pentecostal Transformation of Christianity.* 2 vols. Lewiston, NY: Mellen, 2009.

Hunter, James Davison. *Culture Wars: The Struggle to Define America.* New York: Basic Books, 1991.

————. *To Change the World: The Irony, Tragedy, and Possibility of Christianity in the Late Modern World.* New York: Oxford University Press, 2010.

Hutchins, Robert Maynard. *The Higher Learning in America.* New Haven, CT: Yale University Press, 1936.

Huttar, Charles A., ed. *Imagination and the Spirit: Essays in Literature and the Christian Faith.* Grand Rapids, MI: Eerdmans, 1971.

Johnson, Daymon. "Reformed Fundamentalism in America: The Lordship of Christ, the Transformation of Culture, and Other Calvinist Components of the Christian Right." PhD diss., Florida State University, 1994.

Jones, Bob, Sr. *The Perils of America.* Cleveland, TN: Bob Jones College, 1934.

Kabaservice, Geoffrey. *Rule and Ruin: The Downfall of Moderation and the Destruction of the Republican Party from Eisenhower to the Tea Party*. New York: Oxford University Press, 2012.

Kahn, Sharon E., and Dennis J. Pavlich, eds. *Academic Freedom and the Inclusive University*. Vancouver: University of British Columbia Press, 2000.

Keim, Albert N. *Harold S. Bender, 1897–1962*. Scottsdale, PA: Herald Press, 1998.

Kim, Rebecca Y. *God's New Whiz Kids? Korean American Evangelicals on Campus*. New York: New York University Press, 2006.

Kirkemo, Ronald B. *For Zion's Sake: A History of Pasadena/Point Loma* College. San Diego, CA: Point Loma Press, 1992.

Knox, Ronald A. *Enthusiasm: A Chapter in the History of Religion*. New York: Oxford University Press, 1950.

Köstenburger, Andreas, and David Croteau, eds. *Which Bible Translation Should I Use?* Nashville, TN: B&H, 2012.

Kraft, Charles H. *SWM/SIS at Forty: A Participant/Observer's View of Our History*. Pasadena, CA: William Carey Library, 2005.

Laird, Rebecca. *Ordained Women in the Church of the Nazarene: The First Generation*. Kansas City, MO: Nazarene Publishing House, 1993.

Lawless, Chuck and Adam Greenway, eds. *The Great Commission Resurgence: Fulfilling God's Mandate in Our Time*. Nashville, TN: Broadman & Holman, 2010.

Lenin, Vladimir Ilyich. *Essential Works of Lenin: "What Is To Be Done?" and Other Writings*. Ed. Henry M. Christman. New York: Bantam Books, 1966.

Leonard, Bill J. *God's Last and Only Hope: The Fragmentation of the Southern Baptist Convention*. Grand Rapids, MI: Eerdmans, 1990.

Lewis, Clive Staples. *The Letters of C. S. Lewis to Arthur Greeves*. Ed. Walter Hooper New York: Collier Books, 1986.

Lightner, Robert P. *Neoevangelicalism Today*. Schaumburg, IL: Regular Baptist Press, 1978 [1965].

Lindley, Susan Hill, and Eleanor J. Stebnor, eds. *The Westminster Handbook to Women in American Religious History*. Louisville, KY: Westminster John Knox, 2008.

Lindsay, D. Michael. *Faith in the Halls of Power: How Evangelicals Joined the American Elite*. New York: Oxford University Press, 2007.

Lindsell, Harold. *The Battle for the Bible*. Grand Rapids, MI: Zondervan, 1976.

———. *The Bible in the Balance*. Grand Rapids, MI: Zondervan, 1979.

———. *Missionary Principles and Practice*. Westwood, NJ: Revell, 1955.

Lindsey, Hal, with C. C. Carlson. *The Late Great Planet Earth*. Grand Rapids, MI: Zondervan, 1970.

Linker, Damon. *The Theocons: Secular America Under Siege*. New York: Doubleday, 2006.

Livingstone, David N., and Mark A. Noll. "B. B. Warfield (1851–1921): Inerrantist as Evolutionist." *Isis* 91, no. 2 (June 2000): 283–304.

Luhrmann, T. M. *When God Talks Back: Understanding the American Evangelical Relationship with God*. New York: Knopf, 2012.

Luther, Martin. *Larger Catechism*. Trans. Adolph Spaeth, L. D. Reed, and Henry Eyster Jacobs. Philadelphia, PA: A. J. Holman, 1915 [1529].

———. *Luther's Works*. 55 vols. Trans. E. Theodore Bachmann and Charles M Jacobs. Ed. E. Theodore Bachmann. Philadelphia: Muhlenberg Press, 1960.

———. *Table Talk*. Trans. William Hazlitt. Philadelphia, PA: Lutheran Publication Society, 1824 [1566].

Machen, J. Gresham. *Christianity and Liberalism*. Grand Rapids, MI: Eerdmans, 2009 [1923].

MacIntyre, Alasdair. *After Virtue: A Study in Moral Theory*. London: Gerald Duckworth, 1981.

Marsden, George M. *Fundamentalism and American Culture: The Shaping of Twentieth-Century Evangelicalism, 1870–1925*. New York: Oxford University Press, 1980.

———. *The Outrageous Idea of Christian Scholarship*. New York: Oxford University Press, 1997.

———. *Reforming Fundamentalism: Fuller Seminary and the New Evangelicalism*. Grand Rapids, MI: Eerdmans, 1987.

———. *The Soul of the American University: From Protestant Establishment to Established Nonbelief*. New York: Oxford University Press, 1994.

Martin, Robert F. *Hero of the Heartland: Billy Sunday and the Transformation of American Society, 1862–1935*. Bloomington: Indiana University Press, 2002.

Martin, William. *With God On Our Side: The Rise of the Religious Right in America*. New York: Broadway, 1996.

Marty, Martin E. *Righteous Empire: The Protestant Experience in America*. New York: Dial Press, 1970.

Mayers, Ronald B. *Both/And: A Balanced Apologetic*. Chicago: Moody Press, 1984.

McGavran, Donald A. *The Bridges of God: A Study in the Strategy of Missions*. London: World Dominion Press, 1955.

McGirr, Lisa. *Suburban Warriors: The Origins of the New American Right*. Princeton, NJ: Princeton University Press, 2002.

McKim, Donald, ed. *How Karl Barth Changed My Mind*. Grand Rapids, MI: Eerdmans, 1986.

McQuilkin, Robertson. *Understanding the Bible*. East Peoria, IL: Versa, 1983.

McVicar, Michael J. *Reconstructing America: Religion, American Conservatism, and the Political Theology of Rousas John Rushdoony*. PhD diss., Ohio State University, 2010.

Mead, Sidney E. *The Lively Experiment: The Shaping of Christianity in America*. New York: Harper & Row, 1963.

Menzies, Allan, ed. *Ante-Nicene Fathers*. Vol. 9. Buffalo, NY: Christian Literature Publishing, 1896.

Metaxas, Eric. *Bonhoeffer: Pastor, Martyr, Prophet, Spy*. Nashville, TN: Thomas Nelson, 2010.

Miller, Donald E. *Reinventing American Protestantism: Christianity in the New Millennium*. Berkeley: University of California Press, 1997.

Miller, Steven P. *Billy Graham and the Rise of the Republican South*. Philadelphia: University of Pennsylvania Press, 2009.

Millet, Robert L., ed. *By What Authority: The Vital Question of Religious Authority in Christianity*. Macon, GA: Mercer University Press, 2010.

Moberg, David O. *The Great Reversal: Evangelicalism Versus Social Concern*. Philadelphia, PA: Lippincott, 1972.

Moreton, Bethany. *For God and Wal-Mart: The Making of Christian Free Enterprise*. Cambridge, MA: Harvard University Press, 2009.

Morris, Thomas V. *Francis Schaeffer's Apologetics: A Critique*. Chicago: Moody Press, 1976.

Murch, James DeForest. *Cooperation Without Compromise: A History of the National Association of Evangelicals*. Grand Rapids, MI: Eerdmans, 1956.

Nash, George H. *The Conservative Intellectual Movement in America*. Wilmington, DE: Intercollegiate Studies Institute, 1996 [1976].

Nation, Mark Thiessen. *John Howard Yoder: Mennonite Patience, Evangelical Witness, Catholic Convictions*. Grand Rapids, MI: Eerdmans, 2006.

National Association of Evangelicals. *United…We Stand: A Report of the Constitutional Convention of the National Association of Evangelicals, May 3–6, 1943*. Boston: NAE, 1943.

Naugle, David K. *Worldview: The History of a Concept*. Grand Rapids, MI: Eerdmans, 2002.

Nees, Thomas G. "The Holiness Social Ethic and Nazarene Urban Ministry." D. Min. thesis, Wesley Theological Seminary, March 1976.

Neill, Stephen C. *Brothers of the Faith*. New York: Abingdon, 1960.

Nelson, Rudolph. *The Making and Unmaking of an Evangelical Mind: The Case of Edward Carnell*. New York: Cambridge University Press, 1987.

Nettles, Thomas. *James Petigru Boyce: A Southern Baptist Statesman*. Phillipsburg, NJ: P&R, 2009.

Neuhaus, Richard John. *The Naked Public Square: Religion and Democracy in America*. Grand Rapids, MI: Eerdmans, 1997 [1984].

Newman, John Henry. *The Idea of the University Defined and Illustrated*. London: Longmans, Green, and Co., 1901 [1852].

Nida, Eugene A. *Customs and Cultures: Anthropology for Christian Missions*. New York: Harper & Brothers, 1954.

Niebuhr, Reinhold. *Does Civilization Need Religion?* New York: Macmillan, 1927.

———. *Why the Christian Church Is Not Pacifist*. London: Student Christian Movement Press, 1940.

Noll, Mark A. *American Evangelical Christianity: An Introduction*. Oxford: Blackwell, 2001.

———. *Between Faith and Criticism: Evangelicals, Scholarship, and the Bible in America*. Grand Rapids, MI: Baker, 1991 [1986].

———. *The New Shape of World Christianity: How American Experience Reflects Global Faith*. Downers Grove, IL: IVP Academic, 2009.

———. "Opening a Wardrobe: Clyde S. Kilby (1902–1986)." *Reformed Journal*, December 1986.

———, ed. *The Princeton Theology 1812–1921*. Grand Rapids, MI: Baker Academic, 2001 [1983].

———. *The Scandal of the Evangelical Mind*. Grand Rapids, MI: Eerdmans, 1994.

North, Gary. *The Dominion Covenant: Genesis. An Economic Commentary on the Bible*. Tyler, TX: Institute for Christian Economics, 1987 [1982].

———. *Tools of Dominion: The Case Laws of Exodus*. Tyler, TX: Institute for Christian Economics, 1990.

Numbers, Ronald L. *The Creationists: From Scientific Creationism to Intelligent Design*. Cambridge, MA: Harvard University Press, 2006 [1992].

Offen, Karen. "Defining Feminism: A Comparative Historical Approach." *Signs* 14, no. 1 (Autumn 1988): 119–57.

Olasky, Marvin. *Telling the Truth: How to Revitalize Christian Journalism*. Eugene, OR: Wipf & Stock, 1996.

Order of St. Benedict, ed. *A Commentary on the Order of Mass of the Roman Missal*. Collegeville, MN: Liturgical Press, 2011.

Packer, J. I. *Beyond the Battle for the Bible*. Westchester, IL: Cornerstone Books, 1980.

Petigny, Alan. *The Permissive Society: America, 1941–1965*. New York: Cambridge University Press, 2009.

Pettegree, Andrew. ed. *The Reformation World*. London: Routledge, 2000.

Pickett, J. Waskom. *Christian Mass Movements in India: A Study with Recommendations*. Nashville, TN: Abingdon Press, 1933.

Plantinga, Alvin. *God and Other Minds*. Ithaca, NY: Cornell University Press, 1967.

Pinnock, Clark. "Evangelicals and Inerrancy: The Current Debate." *Theology Today* 35, no. 1 (April 1978): 65–69.

Pollock, John. *A Foreign Devil in China: The Story of Dr. L. Nelson Bell*. Minneapolis, MN: World Wide Publications, 1988 [1971].

Poloma, Margaret M. *The Charismatic Movement: Is There A New Pentecost?* Boston: Twayne, 1982.

Price, J. Matthew. *We Teach Holiness: The Life and Work of H. Orton Wiley*. Holiness Data Ministry, 2006 [online edition].

Pritchard, Gregory A. *Willow Creek Seeker Services: Evaluating A New Way of Doing Church*. Grand Rapids, MI: Baker, 1996.

Purkiser, W. T. *Called Unto Holiness: Volume 2, the Second Twenty-five Years, 1933–58*. Kansas City, MO: Nazarene Publishing House, 1983.

Putnam, Robert D. and David E. Campbell. *American Grace: How Religion Unites and Divides Us*. New York: Simon & Schuster, 2010.

Quebedeaux, Richard. *The Young Evangelicals: Revolution in Orthodoxy*. New York: Harper & Row, 1974.

Rah, Soong-Chan. *The Next Evangelicalism: Releasing the Church from Western Cultural Captivity*. Downers Grove, IL: IVP Books, 2009.

Rawlyk, George, ed. *Aspects of the Canadian Evangelical Experience*. Montreal: McGill-Queen's University Press, 1997.

Rawlyk, George, and Mark A. Noll, eds. *Amazing Grace: Evangelicalism in Australia, Britain, Canada, and the United States*. Montreal: McGill-Queen's University Press, 1993.

Ray, Stephen K. *Crossing the Tiber: Evangelical Protestants Discover the Historic Church*. San Francisco, CA: Ignatius Press, 1997.

Reimer, A. James. "Mennonites, Christ, and Culture: The Yoder Legacy." *Conrad Grebel Review* 16, no. 2 (Spring 1998): 5–14.

Riesman, David, and Christopher Jencks. *The Academic Revolution*. New York: Anchor, 1969 [1968].

Robert, Dana Lee. *American Women in Mission: A Social History of Their Thought and Practice*. Atlanta: Mercer University Press, 1997.

Robertson, Pat. *The Secret Kingdom: A Promise of Hope and Freedom in a World of Turmoil*. Nashville, TN: Thomas Nelson, 1982.

Robinson, Martin. *A World Apart: Creating a Church for the Unchurched*. Oxford, UK: Monarch, 1992.

Rodger, Patrick C., ed. *Ecumenical Dialogue in Europe*. Richmond, VA: John Knox Press, 1966.

Rogers, Jack B. *Confessions of a Conservative Evangelical*. Philadelphia, PA: Westminster, 1974.

Rose, Susan D. *Keeping Them Out of the Hands of Satan: Evangelical Schooling in America*. New York: Routledge, 1988.

Rosell, Garth M. *Surprising Work of God: Harold John Ockenga, Billy Graham, and the Rebirth of Evangelicalism*. Grand Rapids, MI: Baker Academic, 2008.

Ruotsila, Markku. "Carl McIntire and the Fundamentalist Origins of the Christian Right." *Church History* 81, no. 2 (June 2012): 378–407.

———. *The Origins of Christian Anti-Internationalism: Conservative Evangelicals and the League of Nations*. Washington, DC: Georgetown University Press, 2008.

Rushdoony, Rousas John. *The Institutes of Biblical Law*. Philadelphia, PA: Presbyterian and Reformed, 1973.

———. *Intellectual Schizophrenia: Culture, Crisis and Education*. Philadelphia, PA: Presbyterian and Reformed, 1961.

———. *Roots of Reconstruction* Vallecito, CA: Ross House Books, 1991.

Sánchez Walsh, Arlene M. *Latino Pentecostal Identity: Evangelical Faith, Self, and Society*. New York: Columbia University Press, 2003.

Sandeen, Ernest. *The Roots of Fundamentalism*. Grand Rapids, MI: Baker, 1978.

Santorum, Rick. *It Takes a Family: Conservatism and the Common Good*. Wilmington, DE: Intercollegiate Studies Institute, 2005.

Santos, Jason Brian. *A Community Called Taizé: A Story of Prayer, Worship, and Reconciliation*. Downers Grove, IL: IVP Books, 2008.

Saucy, Robert L. *The Case for Progressive Dispensationalism: The Interface Between Dispensational & Non-Dispensational Theology*. Grand Rapids, MI: Zondervan, 1993.

Scanzoni, Letha, and Nancy Hardesty. *All We're Meant To Be: A Biblical Approach to Women's Liberation*. Waco, TX: Word Books, 1974.

Schaeffer, Francis. *The Church at the End of the Twentieth Century*. Downers Grove, IL: InterVarsity, 1968.

———. *Escape from Reason*. Downers Grove, IL: InterVarsity, 1968.

———. *The God Who Is There: Speaking Historic Christianity into the Twentieth Century*. Downers Grove, IL: InterVarsity, 1968.

———. *The Great Evangelical Disaster*. Wheaton, IL: Crossway, 1984.

———. *How Should We Then Live? The Rise and Decline of Western Thought and Culture*. New York: Fleming Revell, 1976.

———. *True Spirituality: How to Live for Jesus Moment by Moment*. Carol Stream, IL: Tyndale House, 1971.

Schaeffer, Frank. *Crazy for God: How I Grew Up as One of the Elect, Helped Found the Religious Right, and Lived to Take All (or Almost All) of It Back*. New York: Carroll & Graf, 2007.

Schäfer, Axel R. *Piety and Public Funding: Evangelicals and the State in Modern America*. Philadelphia: University of Pennsylvania Press, 2012.

Schlabach, Theron F. "Mennonites, Revivalism, Modernity, 1683–1850." *Church History* 48, no. 4 (December 1979), 298–415.

Schmalzbauer, John A., and C. Gray Wheeler. "Between Fundamentalism and Secularization: Secularizing and Sacralizing Currents in the Evangelical Debate on Campus Lifestyle Codes." *Sociology of Religion* 57, no. 3 (Autumn 1996): 241–57.

Schneider, Chester L. *Whaddya Mean By That?* Maitland, FL: Xulon Press, 2004.

Schneider, Gregory L., ed. *Conservatism in America Since 1930: A Reader*. New York: New York University Press, 2003.

Schuller, Robert H. *My Journey: From an Iowa Farm to a Cathedral of Dreams*. New York: HarperCollins, 2001.

Schutz, Roger. *Living Today for God*. Trans. Stephen McNierney and Louis Evrard. Baltimore, MD: Helicon, 1962 [1961].

Selden, William K. *Accreditation: A Struggle Over Standards in Higher Education*. New York: Harper & Brothers, 1960.

Senn, Frank C. *Christian Liturgy: Catholic and Evangelical*. Minneapolis: Fortress Press, 1997.

Sennholz, Hans F., ed. *Gold Is Money*. Westport, CT: Greenwood Press, 1975.

Shea, Mark P. *By What Authority? An Evangelical Discovers Catholic Tradition*. Huntington, IN: Our Sunday Visitor, 1996.

Sitton, Tom, and William Deverell, eds. *Metropolis in the Making: Los Angeles in the 1920s*. Berkeley: University of California, 2001.

Smith, Christian, et al. *American Evangelicalism: Embattled and Thriving*. Chicago: University of Chicago Press, 1998.

———. *Christian America? What Evangelicals Really Want*. Berkeley: University of California Press, 2000.

Smith, Gordon Hedderly. *The Missionary and Anthropology: An introduction to the study of primitive man for missionaries*. Chicago: Moody Press, 1945.

Smith, James K. A. *Who's Afraid of Postmodernism? Taking Derrida, Lyotard, and Foucault to Church*. Grand Rapids, MI: Baker Academic, 2006.

Smith, Timothy L. *Called Unto Holiness: The Story of the Nazarenes: The Formative Years*. Kansas City, MO: Nazarene Publishing House, 1962.

Smith, Wilfred Cantwell. *Faith and Belief*. Princeton, NJ: Princeton University, 1979.

Stanley, Susie C. *Holy Boldness: Women Preachers' Autobiographies*, Knoxville: University of Tennessee Press, 2004.

Stephens, Randall J., and Karl W. Giberson. *The Anointed: Evangelical Truth in a Secular Age*. Cambridge, MA: Belknap Press of Harvard University Press, 2011.

Stephenson, Lisa P. *Dismantling the Dualisms for American Pentecostal Women in Ministry: A Feminist Pneumatological Approach*. Leiden: Brill, 2012.

Stoll, David. *Is Latin America Turning Protestant? The Politics of Evangelical Growth*. Berkeley: University of California Press, 1990.

Sumner, Sarah. *Men and Women in the Church: Building Consensus on Christian Leadership*. Downers Grove, IL: InterVarsity, 2003.

Swartz, David R. *Moral Minority: The Evangelical Left in an Age of Conservatism*. Philadelphia: University of Pennsylvania Press, 2012.

Taylor, Kenneth Nathaniel, with Virginia J. Muir. *My Life: A Guided Tour*. Carol Stream, IL: Tyndale House, 1991.

Thomas, Robert L., ed. *The Master's Perspective on Contemporary Issues*. Grand Rapids, MI: Kregel, 1998.

Toews, Paul. *Mennonites in American Society, 1930–1970: Modernity and the Persistence of Religious Community*. Scottsdale, PA: Herald Press, 1996.

Trilling, Lionel. *The Liberal Imagination*. New York: Viking, 1950.

Trumbull, Charles G. *Victory in Christ*. Whiting, NJ: America's Keswick, 2011 [1959].

Tucker, Herbert F. ed. *A Companion to Victorian Literature and Culture*. Malden, MA: Blackwell, 1999.

Turner, Daniel L. *Standing Without Apology: The History of Bob Jones University*. Greenville, SC: Bob Jones University Press, 1997.

Turretin, Francis. *Institutes of Elenctic Theology*. 3 vols. Trans. George Musgrave Giger. Ed. James T. Dennison, Jr. Phillipsburg, NJ: Presbyterian and Reformed, 1992 [1679].

Van Engen, Charles, Darrell Whiteman, and J. Dudley Woodberry, eds. *Paradigm Shifts in Christian Witness: Insights from Anthropology, Communication, and Spiritual Power*. Maryknoll, NY: Orbis, 1993.

Virkler, Henry A., and Karelynne Gerber Ayayo. *Hermeneutics: Principles and Processes of Biblical Interpretation*. Grand Rapids, MI: Baker, 1981.

Wacker, Grant. *Heaven Below: Early Pentecostals and American Culture*. Cambridge, MA: Harvard University Press, 2001.

Wagner, C. Peter. *Look Out! The Pentecostals Are Coming*. Carol Stream, IL: Creation House, 1973.

———, ed. *Signs and Wonders Today*. Wheaton, IL: Christian Life Magazine, 1982.

Wagner, C. Peter, and F. Douglas Pennoyer, eds. *Wrestling with Dark Angels: Toward a Deeper Understanding of the Supernatural Forces in Spiritual Warfare*. Ventura, CA: Regal Books, 1990.

Wallis, Jim, ed. *The Rise of Christian Conscience: The Emergence of a Dramatic Renewal Movement in the Church Today*. San Francisco: Harper & Row, 1987.

Walvoord, John F. *Armageddon, Oil and the Middle East Crisis: What the Bible says about the future of the Middle East and the end of Western civilization*. Grand Rapids, MI: Zondervan, 1990 [1974].

Ward, W. R. *Christianity Under the Ancien Regime*. New York: Cambridge University Press, 1999.

———. *Early Evangelicalism: A Global Intellectual History, 1670–1789*. New York: Cambridge University Press, 2006.

———. *The Protestant Evangelical Awakening*. New York: Cambridge University Press, 1992.

Watt, David Harrington. *Bible-Carrying Christians: Conservative Protestants and Social Power*. New York: Oxford University Press, 2002.

Weaver, Richard. *Ideas Have Consequences*. Chicago: University of Chicago Press, 1948.

Webber, Robert E. *Evangelicals on the Canterbury Trail: Why Evangelicals Are Attracted to the Liturgical Church*. Harrisburg, PA: Morehouse, 1985.

Whitcomb, John C., Jr. and Henry M. Morris. *The Genesis Flood*. Phillipsburg, NJ: Presbyterian and Reformed, 1964 [1961].

Wilkerson, David, with John Sherrill and Elizabeth Sherrill. *The Cross and the Switchblade*. Grand Rapids, MI: Chosen Books, 2008 [1962].

Williams, Daniel K. *God's Own Party: The Making of the Christian Right*. New York: Oxford University Press, 2010.

Willis, Alan Scot. *All According to God's Plan: Southern Baptist Missions and Race, 1945–1970*. Lexington: University Press of Kentucky, 2005.

Wills, Garry. *Under God: Religion and American Politics*. New York: Simon & Schuster, 1990.

Wilson, Doug. *Recovering the Lost Tools of Learning: An Approach to a Distinctively Christian Education* Wheaton, IL: Crossway, 1991.

Wimber, John, with Kevin Springer. *Power Evangelism*. Ventura, CA: Regal Books, 1986.

Wirt, Sherwood Eliot. *The Social Conscience of the Evangelical*. New York: Harper & Row, 1968.

Witmer, S. A. *The Bible College Story: Education With Dimension*. Manhasset, NY: Channel Press, 1962.

Wolfe, Alan. "The Opening of the Evangelical Mind." *Atlantic Monthly*, October 2000, 55–76.

Wuthnow, Robert. *All in Sync: How Music and Art Are Revitalizing American Religion*. Berkeley: University of California Press, 2003.

———. *The Restructuring of American Religion: Society and Faith Since World War II*. Princeton, NJ: Princeton University Press, 1988.

Wynkoop, Mildred Bangs. *John Wesley: Christian Revolutionary*. Kansas City, MO: Beacon Hill, 1970.

———. *A Theology of Love: The Dynamic of Wesleyanism*. Kansas City, MO: Beacon Hill, 1972.

Yaconelli, Mike, ed. *Stories of Emergence: Moving from Absolute to Authentic*. Grand Rapids, MI: Zondervan, 2003.

Yates, Timothy. *Christian Mission in the Twentieth Century*. New York: Cambridge University Press, 1994.

Index

colleges. *See also specific colleges*
   accreditation, 18, 101–2, 106–9, 111, 114,
     288n5, 289n13
   Bible, 99–115, 232–33
   evangelical, 18–19, 24–25, 30, 39–40, 51,
     68–69, 115–19, 121, 179, 212, 243–44,
     253–54
   politics and, 103–4, 114–15, 217, 224
   secular, Christian student groups at,
     122–23, 264
Colson, Charles, 248, 252–53
Columbia Bible College, 107–9, 301n28
Commission on Evangelical Action, of NAE,
   178
Committee on Overseas Evangelistic Strategy,
   145
Common Sense Realism, 21–22, 76, 87, 252,
   276n14, 285n12
communism, 28, 34, 57, 62, 65, 66, 77, 135,
   137, 178, 180, 182, 191, 221, 280n35,
   284n3
Community of Hope, of Nees, 195
complementarian theology, 183–84
Conant, James, 104
consensus historians. *See also* Hoftadter,
   Richard and Louis, Hartz, 63
Concerned Women for America, of LaHaye,
   Beverly, 184
Concordia Seminary, 179, 236
Conference of Catholic Bishops, U.S., 151
Conferences for the Advancement of
   Evangelical Scholarship, 51
Confessing Church, 194
Confessions of a Conservative Evangelical
   (Rogers), 198
Congress on Evangelism, U.S. (1969), 180
The Conscience of a Conservative (Goldwater),
   64–65
The Conservative Mind (Kirk), 29
conservative revival, postwar, 63–67
conservatives, 63–67, 201, 213–21, 223–31,
   250–53, 262,
   on women's roles, 184–85, 187, 203
   on evangelical Left, 191
   nonevangelical, 28–29, 63–65, 226, 246–47
   Southern Baptist, 231–40
Constitution on the Sacred Liturgy, 153
Contemporary Christian Music (CCM), 144
conversion, 4, 6, 18, 41, 128–31, 135, 138, 143,
   145–46, 230, 254, 262

from evangelicalism to other traditions,
   162–67
cooperative evangelism, 167
Corlett, D. Shelby, 37
Costas, Orlando, 264
The Cost of Discipleship (Bonhoeffer), 193–94
Cottrell, Jack, 85
Council for Christian Colleges and
   Universities. *See* Christian College
   Consortium
Council for National Policy, 214, 227
Counter-Reformation, 20, 274n9
Craven, Wesley Earl, 116–17
Creasman, Myrtle Robinson, 136
creationism, 22, 223–25, 241, 252, 310n6
Creationist Research Society, 224
Creation Science Research Center, 224
creeds, 38, 143, 236–40, 278n5
Criswell, W. A., 233, 237, 308n34
Cromartie, Michael, 246
The Cross and the Switchblade (Wilkerson),
   140
crusade evangelism, 128–29
Crusade University, 72–74, 242–43
C. S. Lewis Collection, 120, 294n56
CT. See Christianity Today
Culbertson, William, 137, 141, 297n29
Cullmann, Oscar, 78, 81, 82
cultural relativism, 131, 203, 212
culture war, 106, 149, 177, 184, 205–6, 208,
   213–19, 222–23, 230–35, 245, 250–53,
   299n4
Culture Wars: The Struggle to Define America
   (Hunter), 250
curriculum
   Bible school, 102, 107
   worldview, 253
Curriculum Ministries, at Free Methodist
   Publishing house, 94–95
Customs and Cultures (Nida), 127, 135

Dain, A. J., 171
Dallas Theological Seminary, 165, 204, 205,
   228, 289n19, 316n47
Darby, John Nelson, 107, 284n3
Darwin, Charles, 9, 17, 19, 21, 22, 34, 110, 225,
   234, 236, 275n12
Day, Dorothy, 160
Dayton, Donald, 94, 186, 196, 200, 287n38
Dayton, Lucille Sider, 186